Segregation

Segregation: The Rising Costs for America documents how discriminatory practices in the housing markets through most of the past century, practices that continue today, have produced extreme levels of residential segregation that result in significant disparities in access to good jobs, quality education, homeownership attainment and asset accumulation between minority and nonminority households.

The book also demonstrates how problems facing minority communities are increasingly important to the nation's long-term economic vitality and global competitiveness as a whole. Solutions to the challenges facing the nation in creating a more equitable society are not beyond our ability to design or implement, and it is in the interest of all Americans to support programs aimed at creating a more just society.

The book is uniquely valuable to students in the social sciences and public policy, as well as to policy makers and city planners.

Segregation

The Rising Costs for America

Edited by
James H. Carr
Nandinee K. Kutty

Routledge
Taylor & Francis Group

NEW YORK AND LONDON

First published 2008
by Routledge
270 Madison Ave, New York, NY 10016

Simultaneously published in the UK
by Routledge
2 Park Square, Milton Park, Abingdon, Oxon OX14 4RN

Routledge is an imprint of the Taylor & Francis Group, an informa business

Typeset in Minion by Keystroke, 28 High Street, Tettenhall, Wolverhampton
Printed and bound in the United States of America on acid-free paper by
Edwards Brothers, Inc.

Library of Congress Cataloging in Publication Data
Segregation : the rising costs for America / edited by James H. Carr,
Nandinee Kutty
p. cm.
ISBN-13: 978-0-415-96534-7 (cloth)
ISBN-13: 978-0-415-96533-0 (pbk.)
1. Discrimination in housing—United States. 2. Housing policy—United States. 3. United
States—Race relations. 4. African Americans—Housing. I. Carr, James H. II. Kutty, Nandinee.
HD7288.76.U5S38 2008
363.5'1—dc22
2007030238

ISBN10: 0–415–96534–9 (hbk)
ISBN10: 0–415–96533–0 (pbk)
ISBN10: 0–203–89502–9 (ebk)

ISBN13: 978–0–415–96534–7 (hbk)
ISBN13: 978–0–415–96533–0 (pbk)
ISBN13: 978–0–203–89502–3 (ebk)

Contents

JAMES H. CARR and NANDINEE K. KUTTY
Introduces the issue of residential segregation in America;
provides an overview of the book, and argues that the issue
of segregation is not solely about social justice; in fact, it is
increasingly impacting the future competitiveness of the
nation and the well-being of all Americans.

DOUGLAS S. MASSEY
Reviews the history of residential segregation in the U.S. and
shows that the black ghetto and the hyper-segregated cities
of the U.S. are twentieth century phenomena. Reviews the
discriminatory practices in U.S. housing markets since the
turn of the twentieth century; documents the role played by
individuals, private institutions and government institutions

in the creation of segregated communities and the resulting
stark economic disparities across racial groups.

Figures

Tables

Preface

This publication was initially conceived by Shanna Smith, president and CEO of the National Fair Housing Alliance (NFHA). Her goal was to publish a series of papers that examined the relationship between housing and access to economic and social opportunities such as quality education, good jobs, safe streets, positive health outcomes, and valuable social networks. Her goal was to build support for greater enforcement of fair housing and fair lending laws by helping policy makers and the public better understand the multi-faceted harm caused to individuals and families that experience housing discrimination. The driving force behind her commitment to fair housing and fair lending enforcement is her knowledge and awareness of the continuing practice of housing discrimination that, each day, denies thousands of households access to the housing of their choice, and that, each year, is documented by NFHA, an organization she helped found and leads. The result of decades of unfair housing market practices has been severe levels of hypersegregation of communities of color that often are completely isolated from the opportunities most Americans take for granted.

My reason for participating in this effort is that much of my work in recent years has focused on the role housing plays in building household and family wealth. I have also examined and documented the manner in which housing discrimination undermines the effective functioning of the markets in lower-income and minority communities. My work has focused on the severe and growing wealth disparities between non-Hispanic white households and people of color, and the increasing importance of that reality as today's minorities rapidly approach becoming half of the U.S. population. This publication presented the chance to combine the issues of access to opportunities and asset accumulation into a single volume. My co-editor, Nandinee

Kutty, was invited to join this project because of her broad-based knowledge and awareness of fair housing issues and the multifaceted and negative impacts of housing discrimination on families and communities. A debt of gratitude is also due to Emily Rosenbaum, who reviewed and contributed to the original outline of the book and provided comments on the initial chapter submissions. We are also indebted to Gregory Squires, who both contributed a chapter to this effort and offered valuable insights and suggestions concerning many other aspects of the book.

The book begins with an overview of the ways in which housing discrimination harms communities and why, given demographic trends, this issue is of increasing importance to America. It then traces the historic roots of housing discrimination in the United States and examines its continued existence today, and links those practices to the severe disparities in economic and social mobility between minorities and nonminorities. The book focuses on the reality that problems caused by housing discrimination are actually growing at an alarming rate. Also we document the importance of purging bias from the housing markets as a way to improve access to education, jobs, better health outcomes, social networks, and wealth accumulation. The book concludes with a series of articles that focus more deeply on current levels of segregation in the United States, the increasing role minorities will play in the U.S. economy in coming years, specific recommendations to better enforce fair housing laws, and why success in enforcing fair lending laws would benefit all Americans.

In the end, however, we recognize that no single publication can capture in totality the extent to which housing discrimination occurs each day, or the seriously detrimental impacts it has on households and communities. No book, regardless of how thoughtful it may be, can answer every question pertaining to the negative influences of the legacy of discrimination in further perpetuating the negative economic and social outcomes for residents of heavily segregated minority communities. And no series of articles, regardless of how thorough, can respond to every argument pertaining to why these issues are important to the nation as a whole. Rather, with this manuscript we seek a more modest, but nevertheless important, goal, namely an enhanced public policy dialogue on the issues and arguments presented in this book. Acknowledging and discussing the reality of past and continued housing discrimination, and its negative impacts on families and communities, is the first step toward changing positively the environment for fair housing enforcement. Purging discriminatory housing practices is essential to ensuring that all Americans are allowed to achieve their full human potential and value as contributing members of U.S. society.

James H. Carr

Abbreviations

ADA	average daily attendance
ARM	adjustable-rate mortgage
BEST	Building Educational Success Together
BLS	Bureau of Labor Statistics
BMI	body mass index
BtW	Bridges-to-Work
CBD	central business district
CBO	community-based organization
CD	certificate of deposit
CFED	Corporation for Enterprise Development
CHA	Chicago Housing Authority
CMS	Centers for Medicare and Medicaid Services
CPI	consumer price index
DOJ	Department of Justice
ECOA	Equal Credit Opportunity Act 1974
EU	European Union
FFIEC	Federal Financial Institutions Examination Council
FHA	Federal Housing Administration; Fair Housing Act 1968
FHAP	Fair Housing Assistance Program
FHIP	Fair Housing Initiatives Program
GDR	gross domestic revenue
HMDA	Home Mortgage Disclosure Act
HOLC	Home Owners Loan Corporation

HUD	U.S. Department of Housing and Urban Development
IDA	Individual Development Account
IRA	individual retirement account
JPA	Joint Powers Authority
MTO	Moving to Opportunity
NAEP	National Assessment of Educational Progress
NCLB	No Child Left Behind
NFHA	National Fair Housing Alliance
OCC	Office of the Comptroller of the Currency
OECD	Organisation for Economic Co-operation and Development
PPP	purchasing power parity
PRBC	PayRentBuildCredit
SEM	shared equity mortgage
SES	socioeconomic status
VA	Veterans Administration

CHAPTER 1

The New Imperative for Equality

JAMES H. CARR & NANDINEE K. KUTTY

> The grave problem facing us is the problem of economic depriva-
> tion, with the syndrome of bad housing and poor education and
> improper health facilities all surrounding this basic problem.
> (The Reverend Dr. Martin Luther King, Jr.
> in an interview one week before his death in 1968)

The link between access to decent housing and the attainment of economic
and social mobility has been known for decades. Access to quality schools,
good jobs, healthy and safe environments, supportive social networks, and
accumulation of housing wealth are all influenced by the ability to secure
housing in neighborhoods of opportunity and choice (Katz, 2004). Denial
of access to housing is arguably the single most powerful tool to undermine
and marginalize the upward mobility of people. A series of mechanisms
directly intended to restrict the housing choice of minority households,
beginning in the late 1800s and continuing throughout most of the twentieth
century, largely explain the severe wealth disparities in America by race/
ethnicity. They also largely explain the seemingly intractable concentrated
poverty faced by a disproportionate share of African American, Latino, and
Native American populations. Failure to honestly acknowledge and address
this unfortunate, but nevertheless real, past, and its consequences, will
increasingly present major economic and social challenges for the nation's
future.

Unequal treatment of minorities in the housing markets includes providing them with incomplete or misleading information about available housing units on the market, providing them with inaccurate information about the quality of neighborhoods and local schools, giving them inferior and unnecessarily costly access to mortgage credit, and other unequal costs or terms. These biased practices directly limit housing options for home-seekers, in direct contravention of the law. Moreover, it relegates them, unnecessarily, to severely disadvantaged housing conditions with the attendant problems of poor schools, unsafe streets, limited access to jobs, stifled housing equity accumulation, and concentrated poverty. In the end, housing discrimination artificially limits individuals from achieving their full potential as contributing members of society, stifles human achievement, creates unnecessary social program dependencies, and breeds dysfunctional behavior. It promotes an unproductive and divisive political environment along race, ethnic, and class lines. In short, housing discrimination is counterproductive to the national interest.

As the share of America's minority populations grows relative to the total U.S. population, failure to address lingering and significant roadblocks to economic mobility for minority households presents increasing challenges for the nation as a whole. Issues ranging from the United States' economic status in an increasingly competitive global economy to the solvency of Social Security and Medicare are affected as the nation's population of financially disadvantaged households.

By the middle of this century, today's minorities will constitute half of the U.S. population—and that fast-growing population is disproportionately impoverished, ill-housed, poorly educated, and tenuously linked to labor markets. The first major step toward seriously addressing the substantial barriers to economic and social mobility for minority households is to eliminate disparate treatment from the housing markets. By taking that single step, hundreds of thousands, if not millions, of households who are ready and prepared to succeed in the competitive marketplace will not be stymied by the continued artificial barrier of illegal discrimination.

This chapter addresses the many challenges and obstacles faced by minority households in achieving economic and social mobility. Five key points are discussed:

- America's wealth disparities along race and ethnic lines, as well as the disproportionate concentrated poverty among minority households, are largely the result of decades of public policies intended to economically marginalize minority households.
- The severe levels of concentrated poverty, segregation, and isolation resulting from those policies have created a complex web of socio-

economic challenges that defy piecemeal and uncoordinated intervention. The problems are growing. As these problems grow, they increasingly take on grave significance for the nation beyond the sole issue of social justice.

• Housing is the centerpiece of opportunity. Successful housing-based strategies will help overcome barriers to economic mobility, and will thus create positive outcomes that go well beyond just providing affordable shelter.

• The millions of members of minority groups who today find themselves outside the mainstream of opportunities in America are a valuable human resource that is increasingly costly to neglect.

• Successful interventions are not beyond our ability to understand, design, and implement.

At the outset, it is important to point out that this book focuses most significantly on the experiences of African Americans. This focus is not intended to suggest that African Americans are the only or the most important group to experience significant denial of opportunity in America. To the contrary, the book recognizes that every racial and ethnic minority group in the United States has experienced its unique history of prejudice, discrimination, and denial of opportunities. Documenting injustices to each group would justify a book in itself (Lui *et al.*, 2006). Focusing on each group's experiences and histories is a useful way to understand the problems and propose successful public policy interventions. While it is true that many antidiscrimination policies have great applicability across minority groups, focusing on each group's unique challenges is also essential. Finally, to the extent that many contemporary opportunity gaps for Latinos in the United States mirror those of African Americans, several challenges applicable to that population are also addressed.

The Role of Public Policies in the Creation of Inequality

Policies and Programs Impacting Housing Choice and Access to Finance

The hypersegregation and isolation that characterize a majority of African American communities in the United States are a *twentieth century pheno-menon*—not the direct extension of slavery. In the late 1800s and early 1900s, African Americans and whites lived in close physical proximity to one another in both the North and the South; middle-class and upper-class African Americans in northern cities often lived as neighbors to whites of similar economic class and professional status. As neighbors and within professional classes, blacks and whites maintained easy interactions with each other.

In fact, only a short period after the Emancipation Proclamation of 1863, African Americans had achieved a measure of success in resettling their lives. They were farming land, acquiring property, establishing trades and businesses, building or buying houses, getting educated, working in jobs for wages, and raising their families. They were on their way to acquiring economic and political power. They had the right to vote, and they became involved in the political process not only as voters but also as governmental representatives at the local, state, and national levels. It may be surprising to some readers to know that in the 1870s the newly enfranchised voters of South Carolina voted for enough African American representatives to provide African Americans with a majority in the state assembly (Library of Congress, 2002).

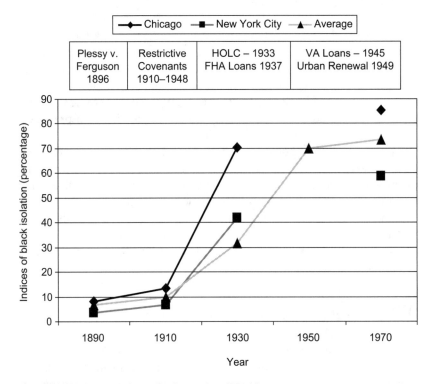

Figure 1.1 Black segregation on the rise: northern U.S. cities

Source: Data points are from Douglas S. Massey, "Origins of Economic Disparities: The Historical Role of Housing Segregation," Chapter 2 of this book.

Notes: "Indices of black isolation" refers to the percentage of blacks in the ward of the average black citizen. The isolation index measures the extent to which blacks live within neighborhoods that are predominantly black. A value of 100 percent indicates complete ghettoization and means that all blacks live in totally black areas; a value under 50 percent means that blacks are more likely to have whites than blacks as neighbors.

Values have not been estimated where exact figures were not found.

African Americans were becoming educated at a rapid rate at the end of the nineteenth century. While only a small proportion of African Americans had been literate at the end of the Civil War (state laws had forbidden literacy for the enslaved), by the turn of the twentieth century the majority of all African Americans were literate (Library of Congress, 2002). But this remarkable progress was stalled and tragically reversed with a series of private actions, reinforced and institutionalized by public laws, judicial mandates, and regulatory guidelines.

Programs and practices that systematically harmed minority households and communities included the use of restrictive housing covenants that limited housing location for minorities; a wide range of discriminatory practices by real estate professionals that further marginalized housing choice for African Americans; lack of government redress against violence to minorities who sought to move out of their segregated communities; biased underwriting policies of the Home Owners Loan Corporation (HOLC), the

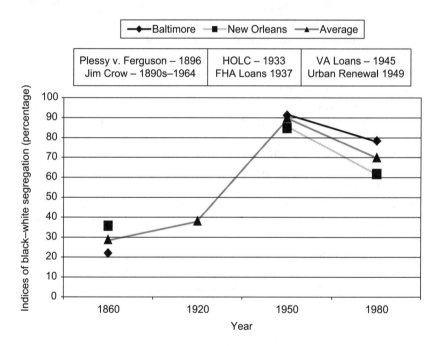

Figure 1.2 Black segregation on the rise: southern U.S. cities

Source: Data points are from Douglas S. Massey, "Origins of Economic Disparities: The Historical Role of Housing Segregation," Chapter 2 of this book.

Notes: The index of dissimilarity represented here as "Indices of black–white segregation" gives the percentage of blacks who would have to move to achieve an "even" residential pattern—one where every neighborhood replicates the racial composition of the city.

Values have not been estimated where exact figures were not found.

Federal Housing Administration (FHA), and Veterans Administration (VA) that further limited minority locational choice, as well as undermined the value of properties in minority communities; urban renewal programs that targeted the destruction of minority communities in several U.S. cities; forced relocation of African American families to isolated, unsafe, and poorly constructed high-rise public housing projects; and inferior treatment of minorities in the GI Bill, New Deal programs, and other public housing assistance efforts.

These policies and practices related to housing and other economic areas, as well as the general national climate in which these policies and practices thrived, explain much of the present state of disadvantage faced by millions of American families.

One of the earliest and most important blows to the civil rights of African Americans after the abolishment of slavery came in the form of the 1896 *Plessy v. Ferguson* U.S. Supreme Court decision, which upheld the right of states to require segregation and ruled that segregation did not violate the Thirteenth Amendment of the U.S. Constitution. This decision upheld and established the doctrine of "separate but equal" and viewed the segregation of races as merely a matter of social policy; it asserted that segregation did not imply inequality. In reality, however, segregated facilities such as public schools, parks, swimming pools and other recreation facilities, cafés and restaurants, public facilities, and seating in transportation were systematically and significantly unequal in quality; minority facilities were rarely if ever even close to the same level of quality. The 1896 *Plessy* decision marked a significant turning point after which all levels of government passed further segregation laws and expanded segregation practices.

By 1900, all Deep South states had passed legislation and enforced social behaviors instituting segregation and the subordination of African Americans by whites (Jaynes, forthcoming). Under these laws, which came to be known as "Jim Crow" laws, African Americans were denied the right to vote through poll taxes, unfair literacy tests, and physical and economic intimidation. Their employment mobility was curtailed by anti-enticement laws that made it a crime for any employer to attempt to hire a worker under contract with another employer. Many agricultural laborers and sharecropper families who had borrowed money from their employer (in order to subsist during the year) were placed in debt peonage for several years. States passed vagrancy laws aimed at restricting the occupational mobility and general free movement of African Americans. One response of some African Americans in the South was to migrate to other parts of the nation (Jaynes, forthcoming). But the discriminatory practices employed in the South followed African Americans to northern cities, in different guises, and continued to expand and proliferate throughout most of the century.

Chapter 2 of this book, by Douglas Massey ("Origins of Economic Disparities: The Historical Role of Housing Segregation"), discusses the evolution of the black ghetto in America. Among his other insights, Massey shows that no ethnic or racial group in the history of the United States, other than African Americans, has ever experienced ghettoization, even briefly; while for urban African Americans the ghetto has constituted the typical residential experience for nearly a century. Massey points out that the immigrant ethnic enclaves that have existed in the United States are different from the black ghetto in three important respects. Immigrant enclaves were never homogeneous; they contained a variety of ethnicities, even when they were identified with one particular group. European ethnic groups did not experience the same high degree of isolation from American society as have African Americans living in hypersegregated communities. And third, most members of other racial, religious, or ethnic groups did not live within the confines of the enclaves named after them. In fact, living in European ethnic enclaves was not the permanent condition for immigrant families; those neighborhoods served as springboards for moving on to a better life. In contrast, African Americans living in black ghettos remained permanently trapped in those surroundings. According to Massey, the American black ghetto has endured now for about a hundred years.

Massey highlights that restrictive covenants were a critical tool in the creation of the ghetto. Restrictive covenants were contractual agreements among property owners to prohibit African Americans from owning or occupying homes in white neighborhoods. After 1910, restrictive covenants were being used widely throughout the United States; indeed, they were found to be very effective in maintaining the color line. Other mechanisms to bring about racial segregation included blockbusting, violence and intimidation, a variety of discriminatory practices by real estate agents, and predatory lending to minorities. African Americans who faced violence to their property and person seldom found any redress from the authorities who chose to look the other way.

The federal government, in the twentieth century, became an instrument of widespread and systematic discrimination in housing through the formal underwriting policies of the HOLC, FHA, and VA. The HOLC, established in 1933 as the first government-sponsored program to introduce long-term, self-amortizing mortgages on a mass scale, institutionalized the practice of redlining. Under its system of rating loan risks, loans for homes located in older central city neighborhoods, with racially or ethnically mixed populations, were rated as too risky; and therefore such loans were seldom approved. Under HOLC criteria, African American neighborhoods were inevitably redlined and not served. The HOLC had not invented these racial standards of evaluating risks; these practices were already widespread in the real estate industry by the 1920s. But the HOLC took the lead in formally institutionalizing them. HOLC practices became models for other lending institutions, both private and public. According to Douglas Massey and Nancy Denton, the authors of the book *American Apartheid,* "It [the HOLC] lent the power, prestige, and support of the federal government to the systematic practice of racial discrimination in housing" (1993, p. 52).

The FHA and VA (established in 1937 and 1944, respectively) followed the HOLC's precedent; they applied similar racially discriminatory standards on a massive scale in housing markets all across the nation. The FHA's 1939 Underwriting Manual stated that "if a neighborhood is to retain stability, it is necessary that properties shall continue to be occupied by the same social and racial classes" (Jackson, 1985, p. 208; see Figure 1.3). The FHA recommended the use of racially restrictive covenants in order to maintain the

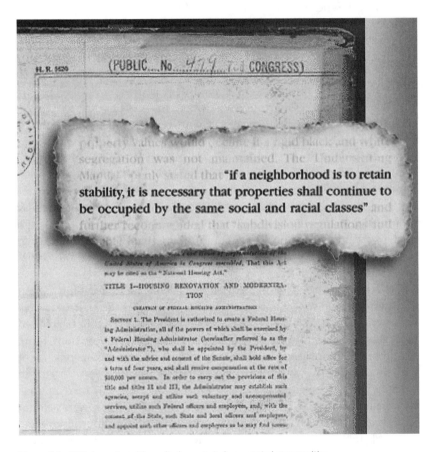

Figure 1.3 F.H.A. underwriting criteria promoted segregated communities

homogeneity of neighborhoods. The result was that the vast majority of FHA and VA loans were for homes in white middle-class suburbs. The federal transportation policy of this period focused on highway construction on a massive scale. Highways helped the growth of suburban housing markets and accelerated the process of suburbanization. Thus, by the late 1950s many cities fell into a spiral of decline induced by federal housing and transportation policies that encouraged middle-class whites to abandon inner cities for the suburbs. During this period, poor and lower-income African Americans from the South continued to migrate into northern cities, which further induced many middle-class whites to flee these cities (Massey and Denton, 1993).

Seeking a better life, many blacks began to migrate to northern and midwestern cities. As their populations grew, many white households who remained in the cities became concerned for their communities as well as major institutions that could not relocate, such as universities, theaters and other cultural institutions, parks, and other amenities. Viewing blacks as a threat, they appealed to the federal government for help to remove what they viewed to be urban slums that were spoiling the physical and social environment of their cities. The federal government responded by making funds available for local authorities to remove or "redevelop" slums. In many cities, slum removal translated directly into massive destruction of struggling but vibrant lower-income African American communities and the construction of large-scale public housing (Massey and Denton, 1993).

These programs were collectively called urban renewal. Public housing, intended for African Americans in conjunction with urban renewal, was built largely at the most undesirable locations, and frequently at very high densities. Poor and lower-income African Americans were displaced from the more dispersed slums and adjacent black neighborhoods and put into the far more segregated and crowded public housing (Massey and Denton, 1993). There they lived in overcrowded conditions, removed from the rest of society, in unaesthetic concrete spaces. Living conditions were not only physically undesirable but damaging to the human spirit. Residents of public housing projects had few interactions with the rest of society. According to historian Arnold Hirsch, public housing was a federally sponsored "second ghetto" which was "solidly institutionalized and frozen in concrete," where "government took an active hand not merely in reinforcing prevailing patterns of segregation, but in lending them a permanence never seen before" (1983, pp. 252–254).

Collectively, these programs had the impact of denying African Americans access to quality housing in growing and vibrant communities with good access to quality public educational institutions and jobs. This reality greatly undermined the accumulation of black wealth, in the form of housing assets, as well as denying blacks access to broader societal opportunities. Further, within black communities, African Americans were denied equal access to housing finance options available to white families. This further eroded housing wealth within African American communities since homes sales were stifled by inadequate access for blacks to mortgage credit. Furthermore, unequal access to finance to renovate and repair the housing stock all but guaranteed its diminished quality.

Contemporary Housing Discrimination and Segregation

Although some progress has been made in purging some of the most blatant and obvious forms of discrimination from the housing markets, significant levels of discrimination continue, much of which builds directly on the infrastructure created by decades of discrimination. This perpetuating nature of discrimination ensures that the legacy of past discriminatory practices will not easily fade as mere relics of the past. In part, this lack of success in purging discrimination from the markets is directly attributable to the fact that enforcement of fair housing and lending laws is woefully underfunded and low on the public policy priority agenda. For example, although the Fair Housing Act was passed in 1968, the U.S. Department of Justice did not prosecute a major case against a mortgage lending institution until the early 1990s—the case against Decatur Federal S&L.

The Fair Housing Amendments Act of 1988 provided enormous enforcement powers to the U.S. Department of Housing and Urban Development (HUD), including the power to the HUD Secretary to initiate fair housing cases even if not connected with a complaint. However, HUD's enforcement powers have for various reasons largely remained underutilized. In 2003 HUD brought only four racial discrimination cases, although it had received more than 2,700 complaints that year. Nearly forty years after the passage of the federal Fair Housing Act, at least 3.7 million fair housing violations still occur each year (National Fair Housing Alliance, 2004).

Fair lending enforcement has remained mired in ambiguity and inaction. There have been virtually no court decisions in cases related to home mortgage lending discrimination. According to Professor John Yinger of Syracuse University, "because courts have rendered almost no decisions concerning lending discrimination, it is not clear exactly what type of evidence courts would require to prove that lending discrimination exists" (1995, p. 194). Ross and Yinger further point out that federal enforcement agencies such as the Office of the Comptroller of the Currency (OCC) and the Federal Reserve Board have been reluctant to investigate cases of disparate impact discrimination, despite clear guidance from the Federal Financial Institutions Examination Council (FFIEC) that establishing disparate impact discrimination is a method of proving lending discrimination (Ross and Yinger, 2002).

Although fair housing and fair lending laws were passed in the 1960s and early 1970s, the tools for their enforcement, such as data on loan features, characteristics of borrowers and lenders, outcome of loan applications, and the race and ethnicity of applicants, did not become available until the early 1990s, in the form of enhanced borrower characteristics in the Home Mortgage Disclosure Act (HMDA) data. And information on mortgage pricing did not become available until late 2005. Yet HMDA data even today are plagued with limitations related to their ability to identify and estimate illegal or predatory lending practices (LaCour-Little, 2006). Needless to say, without reliable and dependable data to detect misbehavior in the markets, enforcement of the law is not achievable.

The most recent national Housing Discrimination Study (HDS 2000) found that while discrimination in sales and rental markets had decreased since the previous HDS of 1989, significant levels of discriminatory behavior against minority groups nevertheless remain. Phase I of the study found that African Americans and Hispanics who visit rental or real estate offices to inquire about the availability of advertised apartments and homes face a significant risk of less favorable treatment than comparable white customers. African American renters receive unfavorable treatment more than one out of five times, and Hispanic renters receive unfavorable treatment more than one out of four times. More than one in six African American and Hispanic homebuyers receives unfavorable treatment compared to equally qualified whites (Turner *et al.*, 2002). Since the HDS methodology covers only some types of searches and observes only certain phases of housing market transactions, these results provide a very conservative estimate of the true extent of discrimination in housing markets. The HDS 2000 found that steering of African Americans has actually increased since 1989. Steering directly reinforces existing segregation, and prevents integration that might naturally occur as African Americans seek new neighborhoods of their choice.

A Closer Examination of Subprime Lending

Subprime home loans constitute a significant form of the high-cost lending to minority and lower-income households. Subprime lending has grown rapidly since the early 1990s. In 2005, annual subprime loan originations were worth $625 billion, *a fivefold increase* since 2001 and *a thirteen-fold increase* since 1994 (*Inside B&C Lending*, 2006). By 2006 the subprime share of total mortgage originations had reached 23 percent (*Inside B&C Lending*, 2006). The proliferation of subprime lending was accompanied by greatly increased predatory practices in lending. Predatory lending generally refers to subprime lending practices that are considered to be so detrimental to borrowers as to be abusive (Quercia *et al.*, 2004). Predatory practices include the steering of borrowers to high-cost subprime loans when they may qualify for lower-cost prime-rate mortgages, inappropriate loans products, irre-sponsible underwriting practices, bloated home value appraisals, abusive prepayment penalties, excessive broker fees, and restricted legal rights to appeal under lender misconduct.

The easier availability of mortgage credit boosted homeownership rates among historically underserved communities. The excessive reliance on high-cost lending, however, is having serious negative effects on low-income and minority families.

Excessive mortgage costs and fees are one driving force behind the growth of severe housing cost burdens among minority homeowners (National Community Reinvestment Coalition, 2006, 2007b). The good news of rising homeownership rates among minority families in the 1990s was dampened by the burgeoning in the share of minority homeowners who pay more than half their income for housing. In the nation's largest twenty-five cities, over the 1990s the number of African American homeowners increased by 16 percent, but the number of African American homeowners who paid more than half their income for housing grew by 39 percent. Similarly, while the number of Latino homeowners increased by an impressive 54 percent, Latino owners with severe affordability problems grew by a full 98 percent (Simmons, 2004).

Many individual cities experienced growth in severe affordability problems for minority homeowners that far outpaced their minority homeownership growth. In Memphis, African American homeownership increased by 40 percent, but this was overshadowed by a 71 percent increase in the number of African American homeowners paying at least half their incomes for housing. In Philadelphia, the number of Latino homeowners increased by 60 percent; again, this was overshadowed by a 167 percent jump in the number of Latino homeowners with severe affordability problems (Simmons, 2004). This rapidly rising level of excessive housing cost burdens is clearly a cause for concern.

The net result of the excessive use of high-cost lending in minority com-munities is clear: the nation is in the middle of one of the most significant foreclosure crises in history. Moreover, this crisis is occurring when the general economy is relatively strong. There is no way of knowing the full potential disaster waiting in the wings should the economy soften signifi-cantly. Already, the proportion of home mortgages entering foreclosure has grown steadily since 2000. In 2006, in the third quarter alone, 318,000 new foreclosures were filed—43 percent higher than in the same quarter in 2005 (Eakes, 2007). By the third quarter of 2007, mortgage foreclosures had ballooned. According to RealtyTrac data, there were just under 450,000 foreclosures in the U.S., up a full 100 percent from the same period in 2006. And foreclosures were up in 45 out of 50 states. It is projected that about one out of five subprime loans made in the last two years will fail. This rate is nearly double the expected failure rate for subprime loans made in 2002 (Center for Responsible Lending, 2006).

The Center for Responsible Lending (2006) estimates that 2 million American families with subprime mortgages are currently at risk of losing their homes to foreclosure, at a cost of as much as $164 billion. The losses from subprime foreclosures will fall hardest on families in communities of color. Although white families received more subprime loans, higher proportions of African Americans and Latinos received high-cost loans than any other group. More than half of African American families and 40 percent of Latino families who obtain home loans get them in the subprime market (Center for Responsible Lending, 2006; Eakes, 2007). The disproportionate impact of predatory lending on African American households is already clear; black homeownership is falling rapidly. Since its high point in the second quarter of 2004, the homeownership rate for African Americans has fallen a full 2.6 percentage points, from 49.7 to 47.1 percent in the second quarter of 2007. During this period, the non-Hispanic white homeowner-ship rate fell by only 0.8 percentage points, from 76.2 to 75.4 percent. Assuming the homeownership rate had remained at its 2004 high point, there would be between 298,000 to 382,000 additional African American homeowners.

Foreclosures not only add to the economic distress of the household but also impose heavy economic costs on the communities in which the foreclosed properties are located, as local governments incur significant costs related to home foreclosures (Apgar et al., 2005). And because excessive subprime lending has been heavily concentrated in African American and Latino communities for the past decade, those communities are already beginning to feel the disproportionate loss of aggregate community wealth. Thus, many minority households and communities have actually been made worse off as a result of increased access to mortgage credit because of deceptive outreach and marketing practices, abusive loan products and underwriting criteria, and inadequate consumer financial protections that have allowed fraudulent practices to flourish. In their contribution to this book, Kathleen Engel and Patricia McCoy (Chapter 3, "From Credit Denial to Predatory Lending: The Challenge of Sustaining Minority Homeownership") discuss these issues related to the proliferation of subprime lending and predatory practices.

In some important respects, this most recent round of predatory market behavior can be viewed in the continuum of history as not a new phenomenon but only the most recent form of market abuse. Excessive subprime lending in minority communities has been described as the "new redlining" (Squires and Kubrin, 2006). Some studies conclude that as a result of multiple actions to take land from blacks over the past century, African

Americans own less property today than they held nearly one hundred years ago. In 1920, African American farmers owned about 15 million acres of land; but by 1999, their ownership of land had fallen to less than 1 million acres (Gilbert and Eli, 2000; Mittal and Powell, 2000).

Finally, another effect of disproportionately high housing costs has been that lower-income homeowners who are not in official poverty find themselves facing poverty standards of living after paying for their housing. There are about 2 million lower-income homeowners in the United States who, although not in official poverty, can afford only a poverty standard of living after paying their housing costs. Thus, they are in housing-induced poverty (Kutty, 2005).

The Complex Economic and Social Impacts of Segregation

Years of abusive policies and practices of denial of opportunity have led to severe wealth disparities, including significant levels of poverty and concentrated poverty, in both black and Latino communities in cities across the nation. Over 18 percent of poor African Americans and almost 14 percent of poor Latinos live in poverty neighborhoods; in contrast, less than 6 percent of poor whites live in such neighborhoods (Jargowsky, 2003). In fact, it is not only poor African Americans but *most* African Americans who face a significant likelihood of living in poor neighborhoods. Sociologist Lincoln Quillian (2003) has estimated that most African Americans, in contrast with only 10 percent of whites, will live in a poor neighborhood at some point in a decade.

Poor black neighborhoods in U.S. cities underwent a transformation during the late 1970s and the 1980s: the black ghetto increasingly became the jobless ghetto and a place of concentrated poverty (Wilson, 1996). Previously, heavily segregated black neighborhoods contained both workers and jobless people. But in the 1970s and 1980s, structural changes in the economy caused cutbacks in certain types of jobs. Low-skilled and less educated workers who lived in such neighborhoods, and who were precluded by discriminatory housing market practices from relocating to areas of new job growth, were severely impacted by the job cuts. Increasingly, ghettos became dominated by jobless adults and families. High levels of crime, violence, and drug trafficking created extreme social disorder in America's jobless ghettos. Joblessness contributed to a decline in marriage and the growth of out-of-wedlock births (Wilson, 1996).

A complex web of problems began to grow in the segregated, impoverished neighborhoods of America. Hardworking, law-abiding families were not able to find avenues for upward mobility within the desperate conditions of the ghettos. There was a dearth of positive role models in such neighborhoods. Residents here were condemned to the worst poverty of all—a poverty of hope.

Income and Wealth Disparities

Against the backdrop of a history of slavery, racial prejudice and discrimination, and Jim Crow laws, modern-day public programs and policies (including an increasingly less progressive federal tax system) have reinforced and enhanced large disparities in wealth between minority and white households. In 1999, the typical African American household had 59 cents of income and only 16 cents of wealth for every corresponding dollar in the typical white American household; and the typical Latino American household had 59 cents of income and less than 10 cents of wealth for every corresponding dollar in the typical white American household (Lui *et al.*, 2006). And in 2004, the typical African American household had only 15 cents for every dollar of wealth held by a white American household; a typical Latino household had about 11 cents (Roblés, 2007). Interestingly, public perceptions do not always match this reality. A 2001 national survey found that four in ten white Americans believe that the typical African American earns as much as or more than the typical white (Morin, 2001).

Housing is the foremost source of wealth creation for the typical American family. Substantially lower homeownership rates for African American and Latino households, due directly to discriminatory actions of the past that continue today, translate into severe wealth disparities by race/ethnicity in America. While more than 75 percent of non-Hispanic whites own homes, less than 50 percent of African Americans and Latinos are homeowners. Furthermore, households in these leading minority groups typically own homes of lower value than non-Hispanic white households. And yet, home equity for these groups makes up a larger share of all assets. For African Americans, housing makes up as much as two-thirds of all assets; for white households, housing accounts for much less than half (two-fifths) of all assets (Oliver and Shapiro, 1995). For minority households who are homeowners, an owned home remains the principal asset, and housing price appreciation remains the chief source of wealth accumulation. Segregation directly reduces the wealth of African Americans. Wealth-accumulation opportunities that are generally available to homeowners across the nation are not available in distressed, segregated neighborhoods. A study by David Rusk (2001) found that African American homeowners receive lower returns on the investment in their homes compared to white homeowners, and that residential segregation is responsible for the lower return.

In addition to segregation and housing discrimination, discrimination in education and employment has also contributed to income disparities across ethnic groups. Wealth disparities have become cumulative over time through inheritance. Public programs, including tax policies, continue to shelter large wealth holdings and encourage asset accumulation for the already wealthy.

Rise and Complexity of Concentrated Poverty

Living in poverty in America today reflects a relatively worse situation than being poor some fifty years ago; being poor today means living farther below the economic midpoint than it did in the middle of the twentieth century (Rant, 2005). Poverty has increased over the past five years, despite declines in the 1990s; moreover, the share of people living in poverty, whose income is at or below one-half of the poverty line is at an all-time high at more than 40 percent. The nation appears to be headed in a wrong direction, with 5.4 million more Americans in poverty today than in 2000 (The Opportunity Agenda, 2006).

In some important ways the economic growth experienced in the 1990s was a rising tide that lifted all boats. Reports from the Brookings Institution (*Stunning Progress, Hidden Problems*; Jargowsky, 2003) and the Urban Institute (Kingsley and Pettit, 2002, 2003) highlight the finding that, at the national level, the population living in concentrated poverty declined steeply over the 1990s—by a stunning 24 percent. But as those studies and others caution, a careful examination of the data reveals cause for concern, because in some parts of the nation the problem of concentrated poverty became much worse over the 1990s. For example, during this period the West region saw a *27 percent increase* in people living in high-poverty areas (Joint Center for Housing Studies, 2006a).

The reductions in concentrated poverty over the 1990s occurred in the Midwest and South regions, with the Northeast registering no change. Also, much of the reductions in concentrated poverty occurred in rural areas rather than in urban areas (Joint Center for Housing Studies, 2006a). Drilling down into specific cities also reveals some dramatic findings: during that same period of the 1990s, Washington, DC saw a more than 200 percent increase in the population living in high-poverty neighborhoods (Joint Center for Housing Studies, 2006b). And taking a longer view of the trend in concentrated poverty reveals that over the thirty-year period 1970 to 2000, the population in high-poverty neighborhoods almost doubled nationwide (Squires and Kubrin, 2006).

Even in the ninety-one largest metropolitan areas of the nation, where concentrated poverty declined near the central business district (CBD), it increased at distances 10 miles or more from the central business districts (Joint Center for Housing Studies, 2006a). Hence, even the extraordinary economic growth of the 1990s was insufficient to overcome the more intractable and complex problems facing many impoverished U.S. communities, particularly impoverished African American and Latino enclaves.

Residents of neighborhoods of concentrated poverty suffer from a variety of social and economic problems that are not experienced at the same level by impoverished households living in more income-diverse neighborhoods. Families living in high-poverty communities are more likely to face poorly funded schools, inadequate access to jobs, inadequate access to jobs and transportation, racial profiling, address discrimination by employers, environmental hazards, high crime rates, lack of personal safety, inadequate health care, lack of representation in government, absence of good role models, low self-esteem, and a culture of the poverty of hope (The Opportunity Agenda, 2006; Squires and Kubrin, 2006). High rates of unemployment, drug activity, teen pregnancies, and school dropouts are also characteristics of high-poverty areas. The physical landscape of such neighborhoods often consists of abandoned buildings, poor-quality housing stock, unclean streets, and a low quality of municipal services—particularly schools and recreational facilities. A lack of access to mainstream financial services is also a consistent characteristic of concentrated impoverished communities.

In communities of concentrated poverty, problems interact with each other and create a complex pathology far more challenging than the individual problems. While certain piecemeal interventions to address individual problems could have worked some fifty years ago, they are unlikely to change significantly today's neighborhoods of concentrated poverty because an accumulation of layers of problems has resulted in whole new dimensions to the problems that defy piecemeal solutions. Turning these neighborhoods around and providing their residents with hope and a constructive way of engaging in the mainstream economic life of the nation will require holistic, comprehensive approaches. We demonstrate the complexity of the problems facing families in disadvantaged communities by means of two examples: access to quality education and to mainstream financial services.

Complexity of the Problems Related to Education

Frustration over the poor educational performance of children in inner-city schools often focuses on single issues at a time, such as the perceived inferior quality of individual schools or school administrations, lack of certified teachers, insufficient funding, lax parental engagement, and other individual causes. But in severely impoverished communities the entire socioeconomic context of the children impacts their performance at school. And the entire socioeconomic context of the community influences the performance of the school system. As is shown in Figure 1.4, there are at least three sets of influences that undermine the educational attainment of children living in disadvantaged communities. These influences are widely prevalent in neighborhoods of concentrated poverty and segregation.

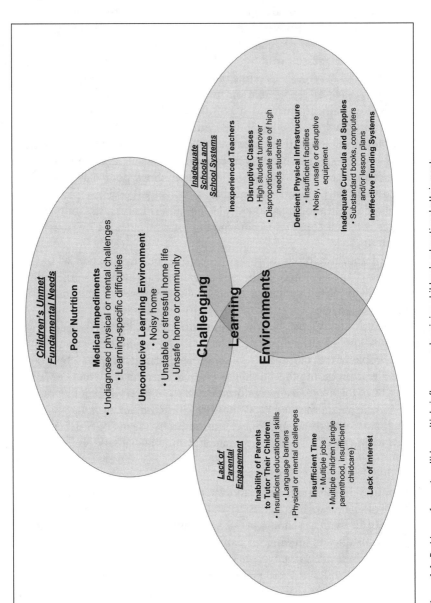

Figure 1.4 Problems of poverty collide: multiple influences undermining children's educational attainment.

First, schoolchildren have unmet fundamental needs. Children living in disadvantaged neighborhoods are likely to suffer from poor nutrition, undiagnosed physical and mental challenges, learning difficulties, and a home or neighborhood environment that is not conducive to learning (this includes a noisy home, an unstable or stressful home life, and an unsafe home or community). In 2004 about 31 percent of African American children, 30 percent of Latino children, and 43 percent of all low-income children lived in homes that experienced periods of food insecurity (The Opportunity Agenda, 2006).

A second set of influences relate to the parents of the child. Parents in distressed communities may be unable to tutor their children because of their own lack of education, language barriers, and physical or mental challenges. Parents with multiple jobs and with inadequate child care may not have sufficient time to be engaged in the educational activities of their school-going children. Some parents may simply lack the interest as a result of their own negative school experiences (Shipler, 2004). Recent studies show that children in poor or low-income families are raised differently from children in middle-class families (Laureau, 2003). Differences in upbringing affect the values and skills of children. Researchers including Annette Laureau (author of the book *Unequal Childhoods*), Jeanne Brooks-Gunn (of Teachers College), and Martha Farah (of the University of Pennsylvania) have found that children from lower-income backgrounds are at a disadvantage for educational attainment as well as economic success in life because they are less likely to learn from parents the values, negotiating skills, and language usage that are important for success.

The third set of influences relate to inadequate schools and school systems. Inexperienced teachers, high student turnover, a high share of special needs students, deficient physical infrastructure, lead paint in school buildings, threats to the physical safety of students, substandard books, lesson plans, computers and other equipment, as well as insufficient funding and ineffective funding systems, all undermine the educational attainment of children. Even within the context of the school system, community socioeconomic characteristics can influence school outcomes. Highly skilled teachers or principals, for example, may avoid inner-city schools because of the many challenges those institutions face. Or they may avoid accepting jobs in heavily impoverished communities owing to an inability to secure decent, affordable housing, or out of concern for their own physical safety. These intersecting challenges are explained in some detail by Deborah McKoy and Jeffrey Vincent in their chapter "Housing and Education: The Inextricable Link" (Chapter 4).

Moreover, many researchers have argued that in neighborhoods with concentrated poverty, local revenues are never high enough to make effective investments in school quality. Goodwin Liu, a law professor at the University of California at Berkeley, reports that in states with a greater number of poor children, spending per pupil is lower. In Mississippi, for instance, spending per pupil is $5,391 per year; in Connecticut it is $9,588. According to Liu, the federal supplement for poor children in school, Title 1, is regressive because it is tied to the amount each state spends. As a result, it gives Arkansas only $964 per poor student, while it gives Massachusetts $2,048 (Tough, 2006).

These three sets of influences intersect with each other to create extremely challenging learning environments. Each of these sets of influences represents complex and lingering impacts of the history of discrimination against minorities, and an evolution of a system of school funding which is pro-privilege and not designed to address the unique and demanding needs of poor communities.

Recognizing the complexity of the problems related to education, Richard Rothstein, author of the book *Class and Schools*, concludes that the problems of poor minority students are simply too great to be overcome by any school, no matter how effective. He argues that the achievement gap can be reduced only by correcting, or at least addressing, the deep socioeconomic inequities that divide the races and the classes (Tough, 2006).

Complexity of the Problems Related to Financial Services

Years of discrimination and denial of access to formal avenues of credit have created a bifurcated financial system in the United States where access to mainstream sources of credit varies greatly, depending on the income and race/ethnicity of the residents of communities. As is shown in Figure 1.5, mainstream financial services (such as prime mortgages, savings and checking accounts, home equity loans, loans to buy consumer durables such as autos, individual retirement accounts (IRAs), and certificates of deposits (CDs)) are available mainly to middle- and upper-income and nonminority communities. Alternative financial services (such as those provided by pawnshops, check cashers, payday lenders, rent-to-own shops, title lenders, and predatory subprime lenders) tend to dominate lower-income and minority communities.

Check cashers, pawn shops, title lenders, rent-to-own, and similar financial service providers experienced explosive growth over the past fifteen years. The number of payday lenders, for example, increased from 300 outlets in 1993 to more than 10,000 in 2001, and to about 22,000 in 2005 (Carr, 2002; Bair, 2005). Fees on payday loans translate into an annualized interest rate of 400 percent to 1,000 percent (Snarr, 2002). The lack of access to mainstream financial services and, hence, reliance on fringe providers extracts a huge price from the residents of distressed and disproportionately

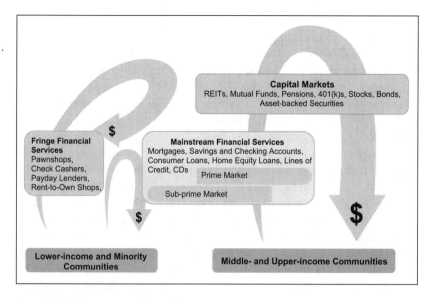

Figure 1.5 Bifurcated nature of the U.S. financial system.

minority neighborhoods. The Center for Responsible Lending conservatively estimates that payday lending fees cost U.S. families more than $3 billion annually (Ernst *et al.*, 2004). Alternative financial services are far more costly than the same services from a conventional bank.

The Federal Reserve Bank of Kansas City, for example, estimates that a family with $24,000 annual income would spend $400 on services at a check casher that would cost only $110 at a bank (Lunt, 1993). Another study estimates that a family without a bank account pays alternative providers as much as $15,000 in fees over a lifetime for basic financial services (Stegman *et al.*, 2004). A study by the Brookings Institution (2006) further found that lower-income families are more likely to obtain tax refund anticipation loans which, on average, charge interest rates of between 70 percent and over 1,800 percent. Minority groups are disproportionately composed of lower-income or impoverished households; therefore, it is the family budgets of America's minorities that are disproportionately impacted by these fees.

Alternative financial service providers have strategically located themselves in minority neighborhoods. A study in North Carolina found that African American neighborhoods had three times as many payday lending outlets per capita as white neighborhoods; and these disparities persisted even after controlling for various socioeconomic characteristics (King *et al.*, 2005). This pattern is seen in other parts of the country as well.

Texas payday lenders are also more concentrated in counties that have high proportions of minority and poor residents (Mahon, 2005). A study of low-income families in Charlotte, North Carolina, estimated that African Americans are about twice as likely as whites to have taken out a payday loan in a two-year period; and after controlling for relevant socioeconomic characteristics it was found that African Americans were five times more likely than whites to take out multiple payday loans (Stegman and Farris, 2001, 2005).

As was mentioned previously, subprime and predatory loans are heavily concentrated in minority neighborhoods. A study published by HUD showed that subprime loans are five times more likely in African American neighborhoods than in white neighborhoods (U.S. Department of Housing and Urban Development, 2000). A report by ACORN, *Separate and Unequal: Subprime Lending in America*, estimated that, in 2002, African Americans were four times more likely, and Latinos were two and a half times more likely, than whites to receive a refinance loan from a subprime lender (ACORN, 2004). Even upper-income African Americans seem to be targeted by subprime lenders (National Community Reinvestment Coalition, 2007a). The Center for Responsible Lending (2005) has estimated that, in 2002, upper-income African Americans in predominantly African American neighborhoods were three times more likely to have a subprime purchase loan than low-income white borrowers.

The reasons for the disproportionate reliance of America's most economically vulnerable groups on high-cost lending and services are complex. First, mainstream financial institutions are underrepresented in minority and lower-income communities, leaving these neighborhoods as prime targets for high-cost and predatory financial services. The result is that financial services that are offered to such neighborhoods tend to be not competitively priced. Distressed neighborhoods become captive markets for a host of high-cost financial service providers; and highly segregated minority communities appear to be the most heavily targeted sites.

Second, most residents of lower-income and minority neighborhoods are not financially savvy. Poverty and segregation contribute to their limited financial acumen. Many do not own a checking account or have any formal and stable relationship with a bank. Those who have grown up in such neighborhoods have often not seen a parent or relative have a sustained relationship with a bank. Some of them feel that they are not welcome at mainstream banks or feel too intimidated to approach mainstream institutions. As a result of inadequate financial literacy, residents of distressed neighborhoods are less likely to understand the terms of financing or to even read the documents thoroughly when they enter into financial transactions.

Third, residents in distressed neighborhoods tend to hold little wealth. Their weak and precarious economic condition makes their need for financing dire. Low-income households, with almost no cash reserves, are vulnerable to becoming victims of high-cost and predatory lenders.

Fourth, many residents in distressed neighborhoods have weak credit histories. They may not qualify for prime credit, as traditionally measured, owing to a lack of access to the traditional sources of credit. Many of the transactions in which they engage are not captured by traditional credit-scoring agencies, and some of the credit products they actually get to use have the effect of directly increasing their perceived and real credit risk.

Fifth, homes in lower-income minority and high-poverty neighborhoods often have little or no capital appreciation and are likely to experience even declining values. In these circumstances a homeowner can find him- or herself with a loan greater than the value of the home. In some of these neighborhoods, *any* homebuying would be ill-advised, unless accompanied by a serious neighborhood revitalization effort. Those who already own homes in such neighborhoods may find themselves prey to unfair and deceptive refinancing schemes whose effects actually exacerbate declining home values or lead to default and foreclosure.

Housing is the Centerpiece of Opportunity

Housing is the centerpiece of opportunity in America. It is not just shelter, a convenient or pleasant place to live. Housing is much more than that—it determines the opportunity structures on which a family or individual can rely. As is discussed above, housing is the key to asset accumulation for the typical American family. But housing is also the key by which to access quality education, good jobs, convenient transportation, valuable social networks, diverse and well-maintained recreational facilities, and quality physical and mental health centers. Social status and the general well-being of the family or individual are also significantly determined by housing.

Four chapters in this book further draw out the relationship between housing and key opportunity structures.

Housing and education: No one understands better the link between housing and schools than housing real estate agents. The quality of schools has for years been, arguably, the single most significant determinant of a quality housing market. The public schools that children in a family will attend are still predominantly decided by the location of housing. Hence, discrimination in housing and residential segregation grievously curtail the access of minority children to good-quality education. Chapter 4 in this book ("Housing and Education: The Inextricable Link" by Deborah McKoy and Jeffrey Vincent) draws out the link between housing and educational opportunity—the housing–school nexus. Housing opportunities can lead to better schooling opportunities as families move to school districts with better schools. Stable, affordable housing makes long-term uninterrupted attendance in the same school possible for children, thereby enhancing the learning experience for the individual child as well as the entire class. Socio-economic segregation becomes an important cause of educational inequality in a variety of ways, including its impact on local finances for schools. According to the authors, understanding the housing–schools nexus is an important first step. The chapter describes specific initiatives that have tried to leverage the connections between housing and schools in order to improve both.

Housing and jobs: Chapter 5 ("Residential Segregation and Employment Inequality" by Margery Austin Turner) examines the ways in which residential segregation contributes to employment inequality across racial and ethnic groups. It discusses the connections from housing and neighborhoods to job access, earnings, and job quality. Housing location has an immediate impact on access to jobs in terms of distance from jobs and commuting costs. In addition, labor-market outcomes are affected by education levels, skills, experience, attitudes, job-related information, referrals, prejudice, and discrimination—all of which are significantly influenced by the neighborhood of residence. For example, residents of neighborhoods that are far from employment centers (such as suburban job centers) may lack information about potential job opportunities. Also, community norms and expectations about education and good jobs tend to be lower in segregated minority neighborhoods; this possibly leads to worse labor market outcomes for the residents of these neighborhoods. This chapter highlights the empirical finding that although in recent years many minorities have gained access to suburban residential communities, these are often not the suburban jurisdictions that offer the most promising job opportunities. The chapter discusses a variety of policy responses, ranging from improving transportation between minority neighborhoods and job locations to expanding opportunities for minorities to live closer to suburban employment centers. The chapter advocates fair housing enforcement and inclusionary zoning as tools for opening up suburban jurisdictions to minorities.

Moreover, some studies indicate that African Americans have worse access to jobs than any other racial or ethnic group. According to economists Steven Raphael and Michael Stoll, despite some improvement in the proximity of African Americans to jobs during the 1990s, African Americans on average remain *more physically isolated from jobs than members of any other racial/ ethnic group.* Raphael and Stoll (2002) found that in metropolitan areas with higher levels of segregation, minorities faced larger spatial mismatches between jobs and housing. Employers are known to discriminate against job applicants on the basis of their address; job seekers living in lower-income, minority neighborhoods may be rejected because of where they live (Tilly *et al.*, 2001; Wilson, 1996).

Housing and health: Housing and neighborhood affect exposure to specific health hazards as well as the general health and well-being of residents. Chapter 6 ("Impacts of Housing and Neighborhoods on Health: Pathways, Racial/Ethnic Disparities, and Policy Directions" by Dolores Acevedo-Garcia and Theresa Osypuk) comprehensively examines the link between housing and health; it highlights the connections between housing deficiencies and health disparities across race/ethnicity. With a view to reducing inequalities in housing conditions, the chapter recommends that fair housing principles should be embedded in the regular practice and evaluation of housing assistance programs.

The link between housing and children's health is best known in the case of lead paint, which has harmful effects on the development of children. Housing features like grab bars can enhance the functionality of disabled or elderly members of the household (Kutty, 2000). Housing location also affects access to good hospitals or other healthcare facilities. Stability of housing tenure reduces stress and stress-related ailments. There is recent evidence that residents in neighborhoods with good walkability features have lower rates of obesity. Housing costs also determine the disposable income left over for the household to spend on health care and healthy foods and behaviors.

Housing and social networks: Housing design, neighborhood amenities, and neighborhood composition, in part, determine the social networks formed by members of a family. Some housing developments are designed to promote better interaction with neighbors, with features such as balconies, porches, community spaces, and planned community activities. Social networks can promote emotional well-being and a sense of safety, and can also open up a range of opportunities—economic, educational, and social. Chapter 7 ("Neighborhood Segregation, Personal Networks, and Access to Social Resources" by Rachel Garshick Kleit) examines the importance of social networks in providing access to social and economic opportunity, and the influence of different types of neighborhoods on social networks. Social networks act as social capital.

The chapter examines the influence of racial and economic segregation of neighborhoods on the nature of social networks. According to the author, segregated neighborhoods tend to offer social networks that are likely to be less useful for economic advancement. Other observations made in this chapter are that poor African American women tend to be spatially bounded in their social relations; hence, the composition of the neighborhood can have important implications for this group. According to the author, quality economic information is likely to be extremely limited in high-poverty neighborhoods, although social relations in such neighborhoods can be a rich source of social support. Planned communities can facilitate social interactions in proactive ways through site planning and design. The chapter cautions that desegregation alone will not improve social networks unless it is accompanied by social resources, which include certain social norms and levels of trust.

Since housing is the centerpiece of opportunity, housing-related programs can help promote access to economic opportunity. These programs can serve as vehicles for upward economic mobility for families currently living in disadvantaged communities.

Rethinking the Costs of Segregation

A Closer Look at the Definition and Meaning of Segregation

As America becomes more diverse, the concept of segregation also increases in complexity and is becoming more challenging to measure and understand. Today, segregation between African Americans and whites persists at high levels. Moreover, Latino–white segregation has increased in recent years. In 2000, major cities like New York, Chicago, Detroit, Milwaukee, and Newark experienced extremely high levels of segregation. By some measures, segregation has declined in recent decades. But where segregation has declined, it has generally been in relatively small Sunbelt communities with small African American populations. In older Northeastern and Midwestern industrial communities, traditional levels of segregation persist (Squires and Kubrin, 2006).

The complexity of the issues facing us is highlighted by a new form of integration that is occurring together with declines in segregation measured at the national level. That new form of integration, according to a study by John Iceland (2004), is increased exposure of blacks to Latinos. Studies also show that over the 1980s and 1990s the rate of exposure of Asians and Latinos to whites decreased (Briggs, 2005).

In fact, levels of segregation remain so high today that it is easy to understand the feeling of frustration among many that it will never end. In a recent article in the *New York Times*, columnist David Brooks (2007) speculates that perhaps the dream of an integrated society is unrealistic. In part, he concludes:

> [M]aybe integration is not in the cards. Maybe the health of a society is not measured by how integrated each institution within it is, but by how freely people can move between institutions. In a healthy

society, a person can live in a black neighborhood, send her kids to Catholic school, go to work in a lawyer's office and meet every Wednesday with a feminist book club. Multiply your homogenous communities and be fulfilled.

There are at least three major concerns with adopting this view with respect to residential segregation in America. First, much of today's segregation remains the result of illegal actions that deny families their rights to live in the communities of their choice. Failure to enforce the laws should not be rewarded with capitulation to illegal actions; rather, the laws should be enforced. Second, to adopt such a view would ignore a century of experience that has demonstrated that separate but equal does not work. As this book demonstrates, access to quality schools, good jobs, healthy financial markets, and more is directly correlated with residential location. The healthy society described by Brooks, in which blacks can be segregated residentially but receive equal access to society's opportunities, simply does not exist, nor has it ever existed in America. While joining a book club, for example, is voluntary, living in segregated black neighborhoods is rarely completely a result of free choice.

The purpose of integration, and the reason it is such a valued outcome by so many U.S. citizens, civil rights activists, policy makers, and scholars, is that it is a key route to expand access to opportunity for disadvantaged groups, and simultaneously limit opportunities for victimization of a minority population. If integration simply exposes lower-income minorities to each other, little is achieved. Many recent data suggest that a new form of resegregation of African Americans and other lower-income minorities is occurring, yet is being mistaken by some studies for a healthy integration.

Resegregation of the nation's public schools is a dramatic symptom of the negative impact of continued residential segregation. It is also a litmus test for the significance of studies that purport to show increased integration. The nation's public schools are resegregating (Orfield and Lee, 2004). By 2000, minority students, particularly Latinos and African Americans, were in schools with substantially fewer white students than was the case in 1990 (Orfield and Lee, 2004). And between 1992 and 2002 the number of minority students attending majority-minority schools also increased. During the same period, the share of minority students attending public schools with white students declined (Orfield and Lee, 2004).

The recent U.S. Supreme Court decision (issued June 2007) against certain policies to bring about school integration actually underscores the importance of fair housing enforcement. It has long been recognized that residential segregation directly contributes to segregated classrooms

(Squires, 2007). When neighborhoods become integrated, school integration is expected to follow.

Today, virtually all large school districts have greater levels of segregation of minority and low-income students than in 1986, despite there being modest progress toward desegregation in the 1970s (The Opportunity Agenda, 2006). Thus, although opinion polls show greater racial tolerance and acceptance of integration among white Americans, African American and Latino students today are less exposed to white students than they were in 1990.

Chapter 8 of this book ("Continuing Isolation: Segregation in America Today" by Ingrid Gould Ellen) highlights some recent segregation trends. This chapter examines possible causes of current levels of racial and ethnic segregation. It concludes that present-day segregation can be explained by the legacy of segregation and discrimination of the past and by current decisions of white households to avoid moving to racially integrated and largely minority communities. The chapter makes the assessment that residential segregation between African Americans and whites has declined over the past few decades, but it has changed only slowly; and levels of segregation remain high.

The Broader Significance of Eliminating Discrimination

By the middle of this century, half of the U.S. population will consist of people of color. Yet that fastest-growing share of the nation's population is the least well housed, has the most tenuous connections to labor and financial markets, has exceptionally low levels of wealth, and is becoming increasingly isolated from quality educational opportunities. These trends do not bode well for America. Minority households will grow as a share of the nation's labor force. Their ability to compete effectively in an increasingly competitive global marketplace will impact all Americans.

The influence of poorly educated students is already a growing concern for many business leaders and policy makers. According to a recent Blue Ribbon Commission on Higher Education, established by the National Conference of State Legislators (2006), the United States is not prepared for the dramatically changing demographic shifts in its populations. Latinos, African Americans, and recent immigrants are the fastest-growing, but lowest-participating, populations in the U.S. higher education system. Moreover, lower-income students, who are disproportionately minorities, are increasingly being priced out of college. The Commission noted that while America falls behind in educational attainment, other countries are outranking the United States and significantly improving their higher education performance.

In their chapter on trends in the U.S. economy (Chapter 9, "Trends in the

U.S. Economy: The Evolving Role of Minorities"), Dean Baker and Heather Boushey examine a number of recent developments in the economy and society, and project the implications of these trends if they continue unaddressed over the next two decades. The chapter notes that the past two decades have been marked by a sharp growth in wage inequality. This has meant that the bulk of the population, who get most of their income from working, have received little benefit from the economy's growth over the past quarter-century. Not surprisingly, they highlight that African Americans have felt a disproportionate impact of these trends. The chapter also highlights disturbing trends in the field of education—that in math, science, and literacy tests, students in the United States rank near the bottom among students from rich countries.

An interesting and often overlooked trend they highlight is the extra-ordinary number of people incarcerated in the United States, and the cost of the corrections system; both have increased rapidly over the past quarter-century. The United States already has the largest prison popula-tion and the highest rate of incarceration in the world. One in every 32 American adults was behind bars, on probation, or on parole at the end of 2005 (Bureau of Justice Statistics, 2006). Baker and Boushey point out that African Americans and Latinos enter the criminal justice system in grossly disproportionate numbers. Incarceration is expensive for the nation in at least two ways: it is costly to house and provide food and other necessities for prisoners, and incarcerated individuals do not contribute to the economy.

African Americans account for the largest share of the growth in the number of persons incarcerated over the past two decades. If present trends continue, by 2020 two out of three African American men between the ages of 18 and 24 will be in prison (Joel, 2000). The nation's failures in education, integration, and access to jobs have directly impacted the lives of families living in distressed neighborhoods. Residents of such neighborhoods are more likely to enter the criminal justice system, and, once having entered it, are likely to suffer from lifelong negative impacts.

The large and growing prison population in the United States represents a grievous waste of human resources and capital. The financial cost of incarceration in the nation's prison industry is so high that it actually costs more to incarcerate a person in a high-security federal prison for one year than to pay for four years of college tuition at many highly respected colleges and universities across the nation (Carr, 2002). Spending for state colleges and prisons comes from a state's general funds. The ever-expanding prison systems have reduced state funds available for programs that promote economic growth, such as higher education programs. According to William B. Harvey of the American Council on Education, "[I]t makes a lot more sense for us as a society to spend money developing people than incarcerating people. The payoff is dramatically positive over time in terms of earning potential and contribution to society" (Hocker, 2002). Baker and Boushey warn that the United States will face many serious challenges over the next two decades, and that while solutions to the problems the country currently faces are not easy, those problems will worsen if they are not addressed.

Successful Interventions Are Achievable

Americans are a feisty people. We are proud of our accomplishments and successes. Our zeal to compliment our achievements sometimes leads us to make inaccurate assumptions regarding the true pillars and foundations of our success. For example, we cherish the view that individual success is a result of our individual investments of time, energy, intelligence, and financial resources. And we often perceive that people who have failed have done so as a result of their own personal limitations. While there is some truth in both of these beliefs, there is also a fair amount of inaccuracy.

Much of our success as a nation is the result of carefully crafted policies that intentionally and directly helped to build the largest and most affluent middle-class society of any nation on earth. As Douglas Massey and others (Katznelson, 2005) point out, programs such as land grants, high-quality public education, a broad range of housing programs, and specially designed financial institutions, and unique legislation in times of particular need, are important pillars of our success. Our shortcoming as a nation was that access to those programs and initiatives was not shared equally among all Americans, and the negative results are clear.

Compensating for decades of denial of opportunity will not be easy. But, as this book points out, it is essential. Equally important, the solutions are not beyond our ability to identify and implement. The first step to redress segregation is to enforce fair housing laws. Failure to enforce the law is both unconscionable and increasingly harmful to society at large. A second step to redressing years of discrimination would be the institution of common-sense consumer financial protections to help financially vulnerable households better engage the financial markets (including home mortgage markets). A final component would be the expansion or creation of programs aimed at repairing the damage to financial markets in lower-income minority communities.

Enforcing Existing Fair Housing and Fair Lending Laws

Because housing is the centerpiece of opportunity in the United States, equal access to housing markets is central to achieve equal opportunity. Significant progress in providing equal access to housing markets can be made by simply enforcing current fair housing and fair lending laws. Each day, thousands of homeseekers enter the markets to relocate. They have worked hard, done all the right things. They have, as we like to say, pulled themselves up by their own bootstraps. But when they enter the housing markets—both rental and homeowner—their attempts at improving their living circumstances are stifled by illegal discrimination. Simply enforcing current nondiscrimination laws would result in higher minority homeownership rates, sustained and successful homeownership for minorities in the neighborhoods of their choice, reduced segregation, and elimination of the costs of housing discrimination (such as higher search costs) that minority families currently bear. This would lead to the indirect effects of better schools for minority children, better access to jobs, and better neighborhoods for minority families (National Community Reinvestment Coalition, 2006). Because of the critical link between housing and other opportunities, substantial progress can be made in improving social and economic equality.

As in the case of understanding and redressing segregation or enhancing opportunities in areas of concentrated poverty, enforcement of fair housing and fair lending laws presents its own unique challenges. In Chapter 10 ("Prospects and Pitfalls of Fair Housing Enforcement Efforts"), Gregory Squires addresses some current issues in fair housing enforcement. He examines the weaknesses of the present system of fair housing enforcement. He points out that in recent years the focus of fair housing enforcement has been on a number of protected classes, not just racial minorities. Legal protections now extend to religious minorities, families with children, persons with disabilities, and sexual orientation. The chapter raises the question of whether the diversity of protected classes is a boon or bane for fair housing enforcement.

While eliminating all forms of discrimination should be a national priority, the limited resources devoted to fair housing enforcement are increasingly spread so thinly that it is questionable whether any group benefits significantly from such efforts. Squires cautions that without an increase in fair housing resources, expanding the categories of protected classes undermines enforcement efforts for those minority households that have experienced the most severe and sustained housing discrimination. While admitting that it is difficult to argue against any action designed to remedy an inequity, Squires discusses trade-offs between alternative strategies for fair housing enforcement. Squires concedes that limited resources force an artificial and frustrating splintering in the fair housing movement, and pit one group against another.

The focus by Squires on the fair housing issues that largely affect African Americans is meant to be illustrative. Each ethnic group has unique concerns related to fair housing. For example, Latinos face barriers in the form of regulations that limit the size of the household allowed to occupy a unit, and rules that define "household" in a manner that excludes extended family members. The impact of such regulations falls disproportionately on Latinos. There is concern that household size is being used as a proxy for Latino ethnicity in order to specifically discriminate against Latino households. Also, fair housing issues related to Native Americans are dramatically different from those most frequently experienced by Latinos or African Americans.

Repairing Financial Markets

One of the enduring legacies of decades of discrimination is the dysfunctional nature of the financial markets in many lower-income, as well as moderate-income minority, communities. As was discussed earlier, check cashers, payday lenders, pawnshops, and subprime lenders heavily saturate these markets because of their large shares of financially vulnerable residents. In recent years, financial regulatory agencies have invested heavily in research and conferences to highlight the problems that exist in these areas. But there has been little federal investment in actual products or institutions designed to redress the market failure created by years of discriminatory practices.

Moreover, federal regulation of the principal financial services providers in distressed communities could be described in large part as nonexistent. There is no national regulation for alternative financial services providers, and state regulation is largely weak and inconsistent. The explosive growth in subprime lending to blacks and Latinos was driven principally by unregulated institutions. Simply put, the consumers who are in the greatest need of protection and support from financial regulatory agencies receive the least amount of help.

Much of the damage from excessive subprime lending could have been avoided with simple commonsense regulatory oversight. A handful of basic guidelines in the subprime lending market could have prevented the loss of billions of dollars of wealth from already financially marginal households. Requiring that borrowers be underwritten in a manner that ensures they qualify for, and have the financial resources to repay, the loans they receive; mandating that loans offered to consumers be suitable for the financial circumstances of the borrower; and requiring that brokers act in the best interest of the borrower they serve, are examples of commonsense regulations.

Moreover, a major limitation in distressed markets is a dearth of competition for financial services and asset-building products. As a result, promoting robust competition in mortgage lending to distressed communities is also key to ensuring fair and affordable housing finance. Inasmuch as public policy contributed significantly to the dysfunctional markets of many disstressed communities, a reasonable action for federal policy would be to support private institutions in the creation and implementation of new lines of financial products and institutions aimed at building wealth in lower-income and minority communities. Moreover, laws such as the Community Reinvestment Act, that are designed to ensure access to mainstream financial services in lower-income and minority communities, should be seriously enforced. And, key to their effective enforcement is the need to update or modernize those laws constantly to take into account fundamental changes in the financial services sector (National Community Reinvestment Coalition, 2007b).

Shifting the Investment Incentive Paradigm

One specific approach to changing the competitive landscape in disenfranchised communities is the development and implementation of investment products that place investors on the side of borrowers. The recent implosion of the subprime market was a reflection of the fact that sophisticated financial engineering allowed capital market investors to benefit significantly through unfair and deceptive and predatory mortgage products. We propose *a new investment incentive paradigm*—under which investors gain when consumers gain, and, in particular, when lower-income Americans gain. One idea in this arena might be a shared equity mortgage product. Shared equity mortgages (SEMs) are home mortgages that allow a homeowner to use both debt and equity to finance homebuying.

When investors in the financial sector take an equity stake in the mortgage, some of the mortgage risks are shifted to the financial sector, which is in a better position to manage the risks. Under SEMs the investor community has a vital stake in ensuring that the real estate markets in which its members have invested through SEMs are healthy, with appreciating property values. Wall Street investors with a stake in SEMs would have a direct interest in supporting policies to curb predatory lending, as well as other, more traditional forms of fair housing violations that could increase the risk of foreclosures. They would have a stake in supporting the creation of healthy, vital neighborhoods in what are currently distressed neighborhoods.

SEMs are not just a concept. Recently, the Fannie Mae Foundation sponsored the design of a new SEM product that provides stable investor returns while at the same time providing homeowners with a predictable and transparent cost of capital (Caplin *et al.*, 2007). The success of SEMs would naturally depend on the specific design of the product and the extent to which it has protections for the interests of the homeowner. Although implementing innovations such as SEMs would require changes in the regulatory structures relating to U.S. mortgages, it is clear that some changes are already long overdue. The federal government has an impressive track record in creating institutions to promote efficient financial markets. It has been particularly impressive in promoting long-term mortgage products that have helped America become the best-housed nation in the world. That commitment to ensure vibrant sustainable homeownership for the vast majority of Americans should now be aimed at those who have historically been excluded, so as to further enhance wealth accumulation and economic opportunity. Products that have the potential to dramatically change the investment paradigm so that investors gain when consumers benefit are not beyond our imagination or our ability to develop.

Conclusion

In the final chapter of this book, "Achieving a Just (and Economically Secure) Society" (by James H. Carr and Nandinee K. Kutty), we reframe the issues of fair housing and access to opportunity structures in the context of growing economic inequality in the nation and other challenges facing Americans today. Specifically, we argue that many of the programs or opportunities needed to promote economic mobility for historically disadvantaged groups (racial and ethnic minorities) are the same programs that would benefit most Americans. Good jobs, quality education, decent affordable housing, safe neighborhoods, comprehensive health care, access to mainstream financial services, and a reliable social safety network are keys to upward economic and social mobility. Ensuring these opportunities are available to all residents would empower both traditionally disadvantaged families as well as the broader society as a whole. America has a proud history and heritage of developing and implementing comprehensive public programs and innovative policies to promote upward mobility. Our recommendation is to draw on our past successes and meet the challenges that face us, with sound public policies, as we have done in the past, but this time, for the benefit of all Americans.

References

ACORN (Association of Community Organizations for Reform Now) (2004) *Separate and Unequal 2004: Subprime Lending in America*, Report, March. New York: Association of Community Organizations for Reform Now.

Apgar, William C., Mark Duda, and Rochelle Nawrocki Gorey (2005) "The Municipal Cost of Foreclosures: A Chicago Case Study," Housing Finance Policy Research Paper Number 2005-1, Homeownership Preservation Foundation.

Bair, Sheila (2005) *Low-Cost Payday Loan: Opportunities and Obstacles*. Baltimore, MD: The Annie E. Casey Foundation, June.

Briggs, Xavier de Souza (2005) "More *Pluribus*, Less *Unum*? The Changing Geography of Race and Opportunity." Chapter 2 in *The Geography of Opportunity*, edited by Xavier de Souza Briggs. Washington, DC: Brookings Institution, pp. 17–41.

Brookings Institution (2006) *From Poverty, Opportunity: Putting the Market to Work for Lower Income Families*. Washington, DC: Brookings Institution.

Brooks, David (2007) "The End of Integration," *New York Times*, July 6.

Bureau of Justice Statistics (2006) "One in Every 32 Adults Was in Prison, Jail, on Probation, or on Parole at the End of 2005," press release, November 30. Available at http://www.ojp.usdoj. gov/bjs/pub/press/pripropr.htm (accessed December 31, 2006).

Caplin, Andrew, James H. Carr, Frederick Pollock, and Zhong Yi Tong (2007) *Shared-Equity Mortgages, Housing Affordability, and Homeownership*. Washington, DC: Fannie Mae Foundation.

Carr, James, H. (2002) "Discrimination in a Time of National Crisis—Lessons from September 11," *Vital Speeches of the Day*, 68 (18).

Center for Responsible Lending (2003) "Predatory Mortgage Lending Robs Homeowners and Devastates Communities." Center for Responsible Lending Fact Sheet, Durham, NC. Available at http://www.responsiblelending.org (accessed November 17, 2006).

Center for Responsible Lending (2006) *Losing Ground: Foreclosures in the Subprime Market and Their Cost to Homeowners*. Durham, NC: Center for Responsible Lending.

Eakes, Martin (2007) "Preserving the American Dream: Predatory Lending Practices and Home Foreclosures," Testimony before the U.S. Senate Committee on Banking, Housing and Urban Affairs, February 7.

Ernst, Keith, John Farris, and Uriah King (2004) *Quantifying the Cost of Predatory Payday Lending*. Durham, NC: Center for Responsible Lending. Available at http://www.responsiblelending. org/pdfs/CRLpaydaylendingstudy121803.pdf (accessed January 5, 2007).

Gilbert, Charlene and Quinn Eli (2000) *Homecoming: The Story of African-American Farmers*. Boston: Beacon Press.

Hirsch, Arnold R. (1983) *Making the Second Ghetto: Race and Housing in Chicago, 1940–1960*. Cambridge: Cambridge University Press.

Hocker, Cliff (2002) "More Brothers in Prison than in College?" *Global Black News*, October 11. Available at http://www.globalblacknews.com/Jail.html (accessed December 25, 2006).

Iceland, John (2004) "Beyond Black and White: Metropolitan Residential Segregation in Multi-ethnic America," *Social Science Research*, 33, pp. 248–271.

Inside B&C Lending (2006) "Subprime Mortgage Origination Indicators," November 10.

Jackson, Kenneth T. (1985) *Crabgrass Frontier: The Suburbanization of the United States*. Oxford: Oxford University Press.

Jargowsky, Paul A. (2003) *Stunning Progress, Hidden Problems: The Dramatic Decline of Concentrated Poverty in the 1990s*. May. Washington, DC: Brookings Institution.

Jaynes, Gerald D. (forthcoming) "Two Evolutions: Black Affluence—Black Poverty," in Henry Louis Gates, Jr., *Handbook of African American Citizenship*. Oxford: Oxford University Press.

Joel, Dyer (2000) *The Perpetual Prison Machine: How America Profits from Crime*. Boulder, CO: Westview Press.

Joint Center for Housing Studies (2006a) *State of the Nation's Housing 2006*. Cambridge, MA: Joint Center for Housing Studies, Harvard University.

Joint Center for Housing Studies (2006b) Downloadable Excel tables for "State of the Nation's Housing 2006." Available at http://www.jchs.harvard.edu/publications/markets/son2006/ index.htm (accessed June 26, 2006).

Katz, Bruce (2004) *Neighborhoods of Choice and Connection: The Evolution of American Neighborhood Policy and What It Means for the United Kingdom*. Washington, DC: Brookings Institution.

Katznelson, Ira (2005) *When Affirmative Action Was White*. New York: W.W. Norton.

King, Uriah, Wei Li, Delvin Davis, and Keith Ernst (2005) "Race Matters: The Concentration of Payday Lenders in African American Neighborhoods in North Carolina." Durham, NC: Center for Responsible Lending.

Kingsley, Thomas G. and Kathryn L.S. Pettit (2002) *Population Growth and Decline in City Neighborhoods*. Washington, DC: Urban Institute. Available at http://www.urban.org/ url.cfm?ID=310594 (accessed January 19, 2006).

Kingsley, Thomas G. and Kathryn L.S. Pettit (2003) *Concentrated Poverty: A Change in Course*. May. Washington, DC: Urban Institute.

Kutty, Nandinee K. (2000) "Production of Functionality by the Elderly: A Household Production Function Approach," *Applied Economics*, 32, pp. 1269–1280.

Kutty, Nandinee K. (2005) "A New Measure of Housing Affordability: Estimates and Analytical Results," *Housing Policy Debate*, 16 (1), pp. 113–142.

LaCour-Little, Michael (2006) Conference Remarks at Credit Research Center (Georgetown University) Seminar on "Current Issues in Mortgage Pricing, Fair Lending, and Legislation to Prevent Predatory Lending," Washington, DC, June.

Laureau, Annette (2003) *Unequal Childhoods: Class, Race, and Family Life.* Berkeley, CA: University of California Press.

Library of Congress (2002) *The African American Odyssey: A Quest for Full Citizenship.* Library of Congress Exhibition. Available at http://memory.loc.gov/ammem/aaohtml/exhibit/aointro.html (accessed December 16, 2006).

Lui, Meizhu, Barbara J. Roblés, Betsy Leondar-Wright, Rose M. Brewer, and Rebecca Adamson, with United for a Fair Economy (2006) *The Color of Wealth: The Story behind the U.S. Racial Wealth Divide,* New York: The New Press.

Lunt, Penny (1993) "Banks Make Check-cashing Work," *ABA Banking Journal* (December), pp. 51–52.

Mahon, Chris (2005) "Texas Payday Lending," *Brownsville Herald,* September 18.

Massey, Douglas S. and Nancy A. Denton (1993) *American Apartheid: Segregation and the Making of the Underclass.* Cambridge, MA: Harvard University Press.

Mittal, Anaradha and Joan Powell (2000) "The Last Plantation," *Earth Island Journal* 15 (3). Available at http://www.earthisland.org/eijournal/fall2000/wr_fall2000lastplant.html (accessed January 5, 2007).

Morin, Richard (2001) "Misperceptions Cloud Whites' View of Blacks," *Washington Post,* July 11.

National Community Reinvestment Coalition (2006) *2005 Fair Lending Disparities: Stubborn and Persistent* 11 (May).

National Community Reinvestment Coalition (2007a) *Income Is No Shield against Racial Differences in Lending: A Comparison of High-Cost Lending in America's Metropolitan Areas* (July). Available at http://www.ncrc.org/pressandpubs/documents/NCRC %20metro %20study %20race %20and %20income %20disparity %20July %2007.pdf (accessed July 16, 2007).

National Community Reinvestment Coalition (2007b) *Are Banks on the Map? New Study Finds Banks Less Available to Working Class and Minority Communities* (March).

National Conference of State Legislators (2006) Blue Ribbon Commission on Higher Education in "Transforming Higher Education: National Imperative—State Responsibility." Washington, DC.

National Fair Housing Alliance (2004) *National Fair Housing Alliance 2004 Fair Housing Trends Report.* Washington, DC: National Fair Housing Alliance.

Oliver, Melvin L. and Thomas M. Shapiro (1995) *Black Wealth/White Wealth: A New Perspective on Racial Inequality.* New York: Routledge.

Opportunity Agenda, The (2006) *The State of Opportunity in America.* Report. Available at http://www.opportunityagenda.org/site/c.mwL5KkN0LvH/b.1405931/k.887C/State_of_Opportunity.htm (accessed December 15, 2006)

Orfield, Gary and Chungmei Lee (2004) *Brown at 50: King's Dream or Plessy's Nightmare.* Cambridge, MA: Harvard University Civil Rights Project.

Quercia, Roberto G., Michael A. Stegman, and Walter R. Davis (2004) "Assessing the Impact of North Carolina's Predatory Lending Law," *Housing Policy Debate,* 15 (3), pp. 573–601.

Quillian, Lincoln (2003) "How Long Are Exposures to Poor Neighborhoods? The Long-term Dynamics of Entry and Exit from Poor Neighborhoods," *Population Research and Policy Review,* 22, pp. 221–249.

Rant, Mark Robert (2005) *One Nation, Underprivileged.* New York: Oxford University Press.

Raphael, Steven and Michael A. Stoll (2002) *Modest Progress: The Narrowing Spatial Mismatch between Blacks and Jobs in the 1990s.* Washington, DC: Brookings Institution.

Roblés, Barbara J. (2007) *Wealth Building in Communities of Color: Economic Justice as a Civil and Human Right.* Center for Community Development and Civil Rights and School of Social Work, Arizona State University, June.

Ross, Stephen L. and John Yinger (2002) "Looking the Other Way: A Critique of the Fair-lending Enforcement System and a Plan to Fix It." Center for Policy Research Policy Brief No. 24/2002, Syracuse University (April).

Rusk, David (2001) "The Segregation Tax: The Cost of Racial Segregation to Black Homeowners." Washington, DC: Brookings Institution.

Shipler, David K. (2004) *The Working Poor: Invisible in America.* New York: Alfred A. Knopf.

Simmons, Patrick A. (2004) "A Tale of Two Cities: Growing Affordability Problems amidst Rising Homeownership for Urban Minorities." *Fannie Mae Foundation Census Note 14,* Washington, DC: Fannie Mae Foundation.

Snarr, Robert W., Jr. (2002) "No Cash 'til Payday: The Payday Lending Industry." *Compliance Corner*, Quarter 1. Supervision, Regulation and Credit Department of the Federal Reserve Bank of Philadelphia.

Squires, Gregory D. (2007) "Enforce Fair Housing Laws," *Seattle Post Intelligencer*, July 4.

Squires, Gregory D. and Charis E. Kubrin (2006) *Privileged Places: Race, Residence, and the Structure of Opportunity.* Boulder, CO: Lynne Rienner.

Stegman, Michael A. and Robert Farris (2001) *Welfare, Work, and Banking: The North Carolina Financial Services Survey.* Chapel Hill, NC: Center for Community Capitalism.

Stegman, Michael A. and Robert Farris (2005) "Welfare, Work, and Banking: The Use of Consumer Credit by Current and Former TANF Recipients in Charlotte, North Carolina," *Journal of Urban Affairs*, 27 (4), pp. 379–402.

Stegman, Michael A., Martha Rocha, and Walter Davis (2004) "The Accessibility of Self-service Banking Technology to Low-income and Minority Communities: Preliminary Results from a Spatial Analysis of Automated Teller Machines in the United States." Paper presented at the Community Development Finance Research Conference, Federal Reserve Bank of New York.

Tilly, Chris, Philip Moss, Joleen Kirschenman, and Ivy Kennelly (2001) "Space as a Signal: How Employers Perceive Neighborhoods in Four Metropolitan Labor Markets." In *Urban Inequality: Evidence from Four Cities*, edited by Alice O'Connor, Chris Tilly, and Lawrence D. Bobo. New York: Russell Sage Foundation.

Tough, Paul (2006) "What It Takes to Make a Student," *New York Times*, November 26.

Turner, Margery Austin, Stephen L. Ross, George Galster, and John Yinger (2002) *Discrimination in Metropolitan Housing Markets: National Results from Phase I of HDS2000.* Washington, DC: The Urban Institute.

U.S. Department of Housing and Urban Development (2000) *Unequal Burden: Income and Racial Disparities in Subprime Lending in America.* Washington, DC.

Wilson, William J. (1996) *When Work Disappears: The World of the New Urban Poor.* New York: Alfred A. Knopf.

Yinger, John (1995) *Closed Doors, Opportunities Lost: The Continuing Costs of Housing Discrimination.* New York: Russell Sage Foundation.

CHAPTER 2

Origins of Economic Disparities: The Historical Role of Housing Segregation

DOUGLAS S. MASSEY

The word "ghetto" means different things to different people. The word originated in sixteenth-century Venice and referred to the neighborhood where Jews were compelled to live. Later the word was generalized to refer to any city area in which Jews were isolated, and in the United States it eventually came to refer to a black residential area (see Wirth 1928). To many observers today the term still means a predominantly black neighborhood. To others it connotes not only a black area but one that is very poor and plagued by a host of social and economic problems. Because race and class are independent dimensions of social variation that interact in characteristic ways to determine a group's social environment, I have argued elsewhere that the two factors should not be confused when defining the black ghetto (Massey and Denton 1993). Hence, I generally define a ghetto solely on the basis of race. For my purposes here, a ghetto is a set of neighborhoods inhabited exclusively by members of one group and within which virtually all members of that group live.

According to this definition, only one ethnic or racial group in the history of the United States has ever experienced ghettoization even briefly. For urban blacks, the ghetto has been the paradigmatic residential configuration for nearly a century. The black ghetto did not happen by accident or as a coincidental by-product of other race-neutral processes occurring within U.S. housing markets. Rather, white Americans made a series of deliberate historical decisions to deny blacks full access to urban housing and to enforce their spatial isolation in society.

Through its deliberate decisions, white America consistently chose to build, support, and maintain a characteristic residential configuration known as the ghetto. Sometimes these decisions were individual, sometimes they were collective, and sometimes the powers and prerogatives of government were harnessed to maintain the residential color line. At critical points between the end of the Civil War in 1865 and the passage of the Fair Housing Act in 1968, white America successively and consistently chose to reinforce and strengthen the walls of black segregation to perpetuate the ghetto. Here I describe how high levels of racial segregation were achieved historically and how the ghetto came to dominate the residential experience of urban blacks.

Before the Ghetto

For a brief time after the Civil War, it seemed that blacks might actually assume their place as full citizens of the United States. During Reconstruction (1865–1876), former slaves throughout the South took advantage of the Thirteenth, Fourteenth, and Fifteenth Amendments to the Constitution and the presence of federal troops to enforce them to mobilize on a variety of fronts (Lieberson 1980; Foner 1990). Politically, they registered to vote in large numbers and sent black representatives to congress and statehouses. Socially, they took advantage of assistance from the Freedman's Bureau and private philanthropic efforts to found large numbers of schools, churches, and other civic organizations. Economically, they began to acquire land, establish businesses, and apply their free labor to achieve some measure of economic independence.

All this came to an end with the re-establishment of white supremacy throughout the South with the withdrawal of federal troops after 1876 (Lieberson 1980; Woodward 2001). The system that came to be known as Jim Crow, a set of laws and informal expectations that subordinated blacks to whites in all areas of social and economic life, disenfranchised them politically through subterfuges such as the grandfather clause, the poll tax, and literacy requirements (Woodward 2001). Jim Crow marginalized blacks socially through a system of legalized segregation wherein separate was not equal, and through a new system of sharecropping that left tenant farmers little better off than their slave forebears. Although conditions were not as harsh in the North, blacks were nonetheless confined to the lowest rungs of the occupational ladder by informal discrimination and *de facto* segregation.

During this period, American cities north and south were just beginning to throw off the trappings of the pre-industrial past. For the most part, patterns of urban social and spatial organization still reflected the needs of commerce, trade, and small-scale manufacturing. Public transportation systems were crude or nonexistent and production was largely carried out within households or small shops. People got around by walking or riding horses, so there was little geographic differentiation between places of work and residence. Land use was not highly specialized, real estate prices were low, and socially distinctive residential areas had not yet emerged. In the absence of structural steel, electricity, and efficient mechanical systems, building densities were low and urban population distribution was fairly uniform in most cities (see Massey 2005).

Such a spatial structure is not conducive to high levels of segregation by class, race, or ethnicity, and the small black population that inhabited northern cities before 1900 occupied a niche in the urban geography little different from that of other groups. Before 1900, blacks were not particularly segregated from whites, and although they were overrepresented in the most dilapidated housing and on the poorest streets, their residential status did not differ markedly from that of others in similar economic circumstances (Hershberg 1981; Hershberg *et al.* 1981).

If the disadvantaged residential condition of blacks in the nineteenth century could be attributed to prejudice and discrimination, it was to prejudice and discrimination in employment rather than housing. Since blacks were systematically excluded from most skilled trades and white-collar jobs, they were consigned to a low economic status that translated directly into poor housing. Those few blacks who were able to overcome these obstacles and achieve success in some profession or trade were generally able to improve their housing conditions and acquire a residence befitting their status in a white neighborhood. Studies of black residential life in northern cities around the time of the Civil War reveal little systematic exclusion from white neighborhoods on the basis of skin color (Kusmer 1976).

This view is verified by historical studies that report quantitative indexes of racial segregation. The most widely used measure of segregation is the index of dissimilarity, which measures the degree to which blacks and whites are evenly spread among neighborhoods in a city. Evenness is defined with respect to the racial composition of the city as a whole. If a city is 10 percent black, then an even residential pattern requires that every neighborhood be 10 percent black and 90 percent white. Thus, if a neighborhood is 20 percent black, the excess 10 percent of blacks must move to a neighborhood where the black percentage is under 10 percent to shift the residential configuration toward evenness. The index of dissimilarity gives the percentage of blacks who would have to move to achieve an even residential pattern—one where every neighborhood replicates the racial composition of the city.

A variety of historical studies have computed dissimilarity indexes for American cities c. 1860, and their findings are summarized in the first column of Table 2.1. These numbers measure the extent of black–white segregation across city wards, which are large spatial units of 6,000 to 12,000 people that are used to approximate neighborhoods in historical data. A simple rule of thumb for interpreting these indexes is that values under 30 are low, those between 30 and 60 are moderate, and anything above 60 is high.

According to these criteria, black–white segregation in northern cities was moderate around 1860. The average index was 46, meaning that on average just under half of urban blacks would have had to move to achieve an even

TABLE 2.1 Indices of Black–White Segregation (Dissimilarity) in Selected Northern and Southern Cities, *c.* 1860–1870, 1910, and 1940

	Free Blacks vs. Whites, *c.* 1860	Blacks vs. Native Whites, 1910	Nonwhites vs. whites, 1940
Northern Cities			
Boston	61.3	64.1	86.3
Chicago	50.0	66.8	95.0
Cincinnati	47.9	47.3	90.6
Cleveland	49.0	69.0	92.0
Indianapolis	57.2	–	90.4
Milwaukee	59.6	66.7	92.9
New York	40.6	–	86.8
Philadelphia	47.1	46.0	88.8
St. Louis	39.1	54.3	92.6
San Francisco	34.6	–	82.9
Wilmington	26.1	–	83.0
Average	45.7	59.2	89.2
Southern Cities			
Augusta	–	58.8	86.9
Baltimore	22.1	–	90.1
Charleston	23.2	16.8	60.1
Jacksonville	–	39.4	94.3
Louisville	20.2	–	81.7
Mobile	29.8	–	86.6
Nashville	43.1	–	86.5
New Orleans	35.7	–	81.0
Average	29.0	38.3	81.0

Source: Massey and Denton (1993).

or integrated city. Wilmington, Delaware, San Francisco, California, and St. Louis, Missouri, had especially modest indexes of around 26, 35, and 39 respectively. The only city that displayed a segregation index in the high range (just barely) was Boston, Massachusetts, which had a value of 61.3. Boston's segregation had been much lower earlier in the century—it had an index of just 44 in 1830. Moreover, even though segregation was relatively high in 1860, by 1890 it had gone back to a moderate level of 51, and racial segregation did not reach 60 again until 1910 (Kantrowitz 1979).

Black–white segregation scores in the 30 to 60 range are not terribly different from those observed for European immigrant groups in the same period. Before 1880, immigrants in the United States came principally from Ireland and Germany. According to a variety of studies, the level of segregation between these two European groups and native whites ranged from 20 to 45 in northern cities in 1850 and 1860 (Massey 1985). Thus, black segregation scores were only slightly greater than those typical of European immigrant groups in the same era (Hershberg *et al.* 1981).

Such modest levels of segregation, combined with small black populations, led to substantial contact between blacks and whites in northern cities. This conclusion derives from historical studies of black communities in nineteenth-century northern cities. In places such as Cleveland, Chicago, Detroit, and Milwaukee, small black communities were dominated by an elite composed of educated professionals, business owners, and successful tradespeople, most of whom were northern-born or migrants from border states (Massey and Denton 1993). Within the upper stratum, interracial contacts were frequent, cordial, and often intimate. Members of the elite were frequently of mixed racial origins themselves and tended to be light-skinned. Although the lower classes usually did not maintain such amicable interracial ties, they also interacted frequently with whites in their places of work and on the streets (see Osofsky 1963; Katzman 1973; Kusmer 1976; Philpott 1978; Trotter 1985).

A high degree of interracial contact in northern cities is confirmed by an analysis of racial composition within the neighborhoods inhabited by nineteenth-century blacks. Given racial breakdowns for ward populations, the percentage of blacks in the ward of the average black citizen can be computed. This average, known as the isolation index, measures the extent to which blacks live within neighborhoods that are predominantly black (see Massey and Denton 1988). A value of 100 percent indicates complete ghettoization and means that all blacks live in totally black areas; a value under 50 percent means that blacks are more likely to have whites than blacks as neighbors.

Stanley Lieberson (1980) made this calculation for blacks in seventeen northern cities between 1890 and 1930, and his results are reproduced in

Table 2.2. The first column shows that blacks in the North tended to live in predominantly white neighborhoods during the nineteenth century. In 1890 the most ghettoized city in America was Indianapolis, Indiana, where the average black lived in a neighborhood that was 13 percent black; at that time, blacks in three-quarters of American cities lived in neighborhoods that were less than 10 percent black. In other words, the typical black resident of a nineteenth-century northern city lived in a neighborhood that was upward of 90 percent white. Even in cities that later developed large black ghettos, such as Chicago, Cleveland, Detroit, Los Angeles, Newark, and New York, blacks were more likely to come into contact with whites than with other blacks.

There is also little evidence of ghettoization among southern blacks before 1900. Indeed, segregation levels in the South tend to be lower than those in

TABLE 2.2 Indices of Black Isolation within Wards of Selected Northern Cities, 1890–1930

	Isolation Indices by Year				
	1890	1900	1910	1920	1930
Boston	8.5	6.4	11.3	15.2	19.2
Buffalo	1.0	4.4	5.7	10.2	24.2
Chicago	8.1	10.4	15.1	38.1	70.4
Cincinnati	9.4	10.1	13.2	26.9	44.6
Cleveland	4.7	7.5	7.9	23.9	51.0
Detroit	5.6	6.4	6.8	14.7	31.2
Indianapolis	12.9	15.1	18.5	23.4	26.1
Kansas City	12.7	13.2	21.7	23.7	31.6
Los Angeles	3.3	3.2	3.8	7.8	25.6
Milwaukee	1.4	2.4	1.9	4.1	16.4
Minneapolis	1.6	1.6	1.7	2.1	1.7
Newark	4.1	5.5	5.4	7.0	22.8
New York	3.6	5.0	6.7	20.5	41.8
Philadelphia	11.7	16.4	15.7	20.8	27.3
Pittsburgh	8.1	12.0	12.0	16.5	26.8
St. Louis	10.9	12.6	17.2	29.5	46.6
San Francisco	1.4	1.1	0.7	1.0	1.7
Average	6.7	7.8	9.7	16.8	29.9

Source: Massey and Denton (1993) based on Lieberson (1980).

the North. Before the Emancipation Proclamation, urban slaves were intentionally dispersed by whites to prevent the formation of a cohesive black society (Wade 1971), although this policy broke down in the years before the Civil War, when free blacks and slaves who were living out gravitated toward black settlements on the urban periphery to escape white supervision. Historical studies are consistent in reporting a great deal of racial integration in housing before 1900 (Berlin 1974).

The bottom of Table 2.1 presents black–white dissimilarity indexes computed by several investigators to measure the extent of segregation between whites and free blacks in six southern cities c. 1860. Levels of racial segregation were considerably lower than those observed in the North. The average segregation score of 29 is some 17 points below the average for northern cities, and, by the criteria set forth earlier, four of the six cities had indexes in the low range (below 30). The most segregated southern city was Nashville, Tennessee, where 43 percent of free blacks would have had to leave their wards to have achieved an even residential configuration.

No study has systematically examined the degree of black isolation within neighborhoods of southern cities in the nineteenth century, but published data on ward populations in Louisville, Kentucky, in 1845 and in Charleston, South Carolina, in 1861 permit a calculation (see Taeuber and Taeuber 1965; Wade 1971). In Louisville the average free black lived in a neighborhood that was only 14 percent black, but in Charleston, the figure was 45 percent. The higher figure is attributable to the fact that blacks comprised 44 percent of Charleston's population in 1861, not to higher segregation; if blacks and whites had been evenly distributed throughout Charleston, every neighborhood would have been 44 percent black simply because of the number of blacks in the city. In any event, free blacks in both cities were more likely to share a ward with whites than with other blacks.

Free blacks were a minority of all blacks in the antebellum South, as most were slaves. The data from Louisville and Charleston reveal, however, that slaves were even less segregated from whites than were free blacks; in 1861 the slave–white dissimilarity index was 14.2 in Louisville in 1845 and 11.4 in Charleston. Thus, whether one considers slaves or free blacks, there is little evidence of a distinctive black ghetto in southern cities in the nineteenth century. Throughout the South, blacks were scattered widely among urban neighborhoods and were more likely to share neighborhoods with whites than with members of their own group.

In contrast to the situation in the North, residential integration in the postbellum South was not accompanied by a relatively open set of race relations among elites. As the Reconstruction era drew to a close, black–white relations came to be governed by the increasingly harsh realities of the Jim Crow system. However, the implementation of Jim Crow did not increase segregation or reduce the frequency of black–white contact; it simply governed the terms under which integration occurred and strictly regulated the nature of interracial social contacts.

Neighborhoods in many southern cities evolved a residential structure characterized by broad avenues interspersed with small streets and alleys (Demerath and Gilmore 1954). Large homes on the avenues contained white families who employed black servants, and laborers lived on the smaller streets. The relationship of master and slave was thus supplanted by one of master and servant or a paternalistic relationship between boss and worker. Despite their economic and social subjugation, however, blacks in southern cities continued to have direct personal contacts with whites, albeit on unequal terms. As in the North, the social worlds of the races overlapped.

Building the Ghetto

The era of integrated living and widespread interracial contact was rapidly dismantled in American cities after 1900 because of two developments: the industrialization of America and the concomitant movement of blacks from farms to cities. The pace of change was most rapid in the North, not only because industrialization was more rapid and complete there but also because the South's Jim Crow system provided an effective alternative to the ghetto in bringing about the subordination of blacks. Moreover, the interspersed pattern of black and white settlement in southern cities carried with it a physical inertia that retarded the construction of the ghetto (Roof et al. 1976).

Industrialization in the North unleashed a set of social, economic, and technological changes that dramatically altered the urban environment in ways that promoted higher levels of segregation between social groups. Before industrialization, production occurred primarily in the home or small shop. By the turn of the century, manufacturing had shifted decisively to large factories that employed hundreds of laborers, and individual plants clustered in extensive manufacturing districts, which together carried a demand for thousands of workers. Dense clusters of tenements and row houses were constructed near these districts to house the burgeoning workforce (Massey 2005).

The new demand for labor could not be met by native white urbanites alone, so employers turned to migrants of diverse origins. Before World War I the demand for unskilled labor was met primarily by immigrants from rural southern and eastern Europe (Erickson 1957; Perry 1978). Their immigration was guided and structured by social networks that connected them to relatives and friends who had arrived earlier. Drawing upon the ties of kinship and common community origin, the new immigrants obtained jobs and housing in U.S. cities, and in this way, members of specific ethnic groups were channeled to particular neighborhoods and factories (Massey 1985).

At the same time, the need to oversee industrial production—and to administer the wealth it created—brought about a new managerial class composed primarily of native white Americans. With their increasing affluence, the retail sector also expanded dramatically. Both administration and retail sales depended crucially on face-to-face interaction, which put a premium on proximity and high population densities (Massey 2005). The invention of structural steel and mechanical elevators allowed cities to expand upward with skyscrapers, which were grouped into central business districts that brought thousands of people into regular daily contact. The development of efficient urban rail systems permitted the city to expand outward, creating new residential districts in suburban areas to house the newly affluent class of middle-class managers and service workers (Warner and Burke 1962).

These developments brought about an unprecedented increase in urban social segregation. Not only was class segregation heightened, but more recent immigrants—Jews, Poles, Italians, Czechs—experienced far more segregation from native whites than did earlier immigrants, the Irish and Germans. Whereas the segregation of immigrants from Europe, as measured by the index of dissimilarity, rarely exceeded 50 before 1870, after the turn of the century values in the range from 50 to 65 were common (Lieberson 1963).

Southern blacks also formed part of the stream of migrants to American cities, but until 1890 the flow was relatively small; only 70,000 blacks left the South during the 1870s and 80,000 departed during the 1880s (Farley and Allen 1987: 113). In contrast, the number of European immigrants ran into the millions in both decades. Immigration, however, was cyclical and strongly affected by economic conditions abroad. When the demand for labor in European cities was strong, emigration to the United States fell, and when European demand flagged, emigration to the United States rose (Hatton and Williamson 1998).

This periodic ebb and flow of European immigration created serious structural problems for American employers, particularly when boom periods in Europe and America coincided. In this case, Europeans moved to their own industrial cities and U.S. factories had difficulty attracting new workers. Periodic labor shortages caused northern employers to turn to domestic sources of labor, such as migrants from American rural areas, particularly those in the South. Thus, black migration to northern cities oscillated inversely with the ebb and flow of European immigration (Thomas 1954).

By the turn of the twentieth century, northern employers had discovered another reason to employ southern blacks: their utility as strikebreakers.

Blacks were repeatedly employed in this capacity in northern labor disputes between 1890 and 1930; black strikebreakers were used seven times in New York between 1895 and 1916 and were employed in this capacity in Cleveland in 1896, Detroit in 1919, Milwaukee in 1922, and Chicago in 1904 and 1905 (Spear 1967; Osofsky 1963; Kusmer 1976; Trotter 1985; Zunz 1982). Poor rural blacks with little understanding of industrial conditions and no experience with unions were recruited in the South and transported directly to northern factories, often on special trains arranged by factory owners.

The association of blacks with strikebreaking was bound to earn them the enmity of white workers, but discrimination against blacks by labor unions cannot be attributed to this animosity alone. European groups also had been used as strikebreakers, but labor leaders overcame these attempts at union busting by incorporating each new wave of immigrants into the labor movement. Unions never employed this strategy with southern blacks, however. From the start, blacks suffered unusually severe discrimination from white unions simply because they were black (Grossman 1989).

Most of the skilled-crafts unions of the American Federation of Labor, for example, excluded blacks until the 1930s; and the Congress of Industrial Organizations accepted blacks only grudgingly, typically within segregated Jim Crow locals that received poorer contracts and lower priorities in job assignments. Being denied access to the benefits of white unions, blacks had little to lose from crossing picket lines, thereby setting off a self-perpetuating cycle of mutual hostility and distrust between black and white workers (Grossman 1989).

Black out-migration from the South grew steadily from the end of the nineteenth century into the first decades of the twentieth century. During the 1890s some 174,000 blacks left the South, and this number rose to 197,000 between 1900 and 1910 (Farley and Allen 1987). The event that transformed the stream into a flood, however, was the outbreak of World War I in 1914. In one fell swoop it increased the demand for U.S. industrial production and cut northern factories off from their traditional source of European labor. In response, employers began a spirited recruitment of blacks from the rural South (Grossman 1989).

The arrival of the recruiters in the South coincided with the coming of the Mexican boll weevil, which devastated Louisiana's cotton crop in 1906, before moving on to Mississippi in 1913 and Alabama in 1916. The collapse of southern agriculture was aggravated by a series of disastrous floods in 1915 and 1916, and low cotton prices up to 1914. In response, southern planters shifted production from cotton to food crops and livestock, both of which require fewer workers. Thus, the demand for black tenant farmers and day laborers fell just when the need for unskilled workers in northern cities skyrocketed (Grossman 1989).

This correspondence between push and pull factors increased the level of black out-migration to new heights and greatly augmented the black populations of Chicago, Detroit, Cleveland, Philadelphia, and New York. Between 1910 and 1920 some 525,000 blacks left their homes in the South and took up life in the North, and during the 1920s the outflow reached 877,000 (Farley and Allen 1987). With time, this migration acquired a dynamic of its own, as established migrants found jobs and housing for their friends and relatives back home. At the same time, northern black newspapers such as the *Chicago Defender*, which were widely read in the South, exhorted southern blacks to escape their oppression and move northward. As a result of this dynamic, black out-migration from the South continued at a substantial rate even during the Great Depression (Grossman 1989).

Northern whites viewed this rising tide of black migration with increasing hostility and considerable alarm. Middle-class whites were repelled by what they saw as the uncouth manners, unclean habits, slothful appearance, and illicit behavior of poorly educated, poverty-stricken migrants who had only recently been sharecroppers, and a resurgence of white racist ideology during the 1920s provided a theoretical, "scientific" justification for these feelings (Zuberi 2003). Working-class whites, for their part, feared economic competition from the newcomers; as first- or second-generation immigrants who were themselves scorned by native whites, they reaffirmed their own whiteness by oppressing a people that was even lower in the racial hierarchy (Ignatiev 1996).

As the composition of the black community shifted from northern to southern birth, and as the size of the population rose steadily after 1900, white racial views hardened and the relatively fluid and open period of race relations in the North drew to a close. Newspapers increasingly used terms such as "nigger" and "darky" in print and carried unflattering stories about black crimes and vice (Osofsky 1963; Kusmer 1976). After decades of relatively integrated education, moreover, white parents increasingly refused to enroll their students in schools that included blacks (Lieberson 1980; Grossman 1989). Doors that had permitted extensive interracial contact among the elite suddenly slammed shut as black professionals lost white clients, associates, and friends (Katzman 1973; Kusmer 1976).

The most dramatic harbinger of the new regime in race relations, however, was the upsurge in racial violence. In northern cities a series of communal riots broke out between 1900 and 1920 in the wake of massive black migration. Race riots struck New York City in 1900; Evansville, Indiana, in 1903; Springfield, Illinois, in 1908; East St. Louis, Illinois, in 1917; and Chicago in 1919 (Chicago Commission on Race Relations 1922; Rudwick 1964; Kusmer 1976; Bigham 1987). In each case, individual blacks were singled out for attack because of the color of their skin. Those living away from recognized black neighborhoods had their houses ransacked or burned. Those unlucky or unwise enough to be caught trespassing in white neighborhoods were beaten, shot, or lynched. Blacks on their way to work were pulled from trolleys and beaten. Rampaging bands of whites roamed the streets for days, attacking blacks at will. Although most of the rioters were white, most of those arrested and nearly all of the victims were black.

As the tide of violence rose in northern cities, blacks were increasingly divided from whites by a hardening color line in employment, education, and, especially, housing. Whites became increasingly intolerant of black neighbors, and fear of racial turnover and black invasion spread. Those blacks living away from recognized Negro areas were forced to move into expanding black belts, darkytowns, Bronzevilles, or Niggertowns. Well-educated, middle-class blacks of the old elite found themselves increasingly lumped together with poorly educated, impoverished migrants from the rural South; well-to-do blacks had progressively greater difficulty finding housing commensurate with their social status. In white eyes, black people belonged in black neighborhoods no matter what their social or economic standing; the color line grew increasingly impenetrable.

Thus, levels of residential segregation between blacks and whites began a steady rise at the turn of the twentieth century that would last for sixty years. The indexes shown in the second column of figures in Table 2.1 reveal the extent of this increase. By 1910 the average level of racial segregation in seven northern cities was 59 (compared to 46 in 1860), and four cases fell clearly within the high range (with index scores above 60). The initial stages of ghetto formation are most clearly revealed in Chicago (where the index increased from 50 to 67), Cleveland (with an increase of 49 to 69), Milwaukee (from 60 to 67), and St. Louis (from 39 to 54).

The progressive segregation of blacks continued in subsequent decades, and by World War II the foundations of the modern ghetto had been laid in virtually every northern city. The last column of Table 2.1 presents dissimilarity indices computed by Taeuber and Taeuber (1965) for 1940. Some caution must be exercised in interpreting these figures because they are based on block statistics rather than ward data. Blocks are substantially smaller than wards, and the degree of segregation that can be measured tends to increase as the geographic size of the units falls; what may appear to be an integrated ward actually may be quite segregated on a block-by-block basis (Van Valey and Roof 1976).

The shift from wards to blocks adds at least 10 points to the dissimilarity indexes (and probably more), but even making a liberal allowance for this artifact of the neighborhood unit used, it is clear that the level of black–white segregation rose substantially after 1910. At the block level the degree of black–white segregation in northern cities reached an average value of 89 by

1940, with indexes varying narrowly in the range from 80 to 100; this implies a range of about 70 to 90 using ward data, with an average around 80. It is safe to surmise, therefore, that by 1940 at least 70 percent of northern black city dwellers would have had to move to achieve an even residential configuration in northern cities (compared to a figure of only 46 percent in 1860).

With a rapidly growing black population being accommodated by an ever smaller number of neighborhoods and an increasingly uneven residential configuration, the only possible outcome was an increase in the spatial isolation of blacks. As Table 2.2 shows, levels of racial isolation in northern cities began to move sharply upward after 1900, especially after 1910. By 1930, blacks were well on their way to experiencing a uniquely high degree of spatial isolation in American cities, with Chicago leading the way. Its isolation index increased from only 10 percent in 1900 to 70 percent 30 years later. Thus, as of 1930 the typical black Chicagoan lived in a neighborhood that was over two-thirds black. The level of black racial isolation also rose in other cities, indicating the growth of incipient ghettos—from 8 percent to 51 percent in Cleveland, from 5 percent to 42 percent in New York, and from 13 percent to 47 percent in St. Louis.

The increasing ghettoization of blacks was not simply a result of their growing numbers. Stanley Lieberson (1980) has clearly demonstrated that the segregation of blacks in the urban North increased after 1900 not only because their share of the population grew but because the same racial composition led to more isolation than it had during earlier periods. As the new century wore on, areas of acceptable black residence became increasingly circumscribed, and the era of the ghetto had begun.

Migration and industrial development also segregated the new European immigrant groups, of course, but recent studies have made it clear that immigrant enclaves in the early twentieth century were in no way comparable to the black ghettos that formed in most northern cities by 1940 (Philpott 1978). To be sure, certain neighborhoods could be identified as Italian, Polish, or Jewish, but these ethnic enclaves differed from black ghettos in three fundamental ways.

First, unlike black ghettos, immigrant enclaves were never homogeneous and always contained a wide variety of nationalities, even if they were publicly associated with a particular national origin group. In Chicago's Magyar district of 1901, twenty-two different ethnic groups were present and only 37 percent of all family heads were Magyar (26 percent were Polish) (Philpott 1978: 136). Similarly, an 1893 color-coded block map of Chicago's West Side prepared by the U.S. Department of Labor showed the location of European ethnic groups using eighteen separate colors. The result was a huge rainbow in which no block contained a single color. The average number of colors per block was eight, and four out of five lots within blocks were mixed. In none of the Little Italys identified on the map was there an all-Italian block (Philpott 1978: 137).

The myth of the immigrant ghetto was perpetuated by Ernest Burgess, a founder of the Chicago school of urban sociology. In 1933 he published what has become a well-known map showing the spatial locations of Chicago's various immigrant groups. He identified specific German, Irish, Italian, Russian, Polish, Swedish, and Czech ghettos. A closer examination of these data by Thomas Philpott, however, revealed that Burgess's immigrant ghettos were more fictional than real. The average number of nationalities per ghetto was 22, ranging from 20 in ostensibly Italian and Czech neighborhoods to 25 in areas that were theoretically Irish, German, and Swedish. In none of these ghettos did the ghettoized group constitute even a bare majority of the population, with the sole exception of Poles, who comprised 54 percent of their enclave. In areas that Burgess identified as being part of the black ghetto, however, blacks comprised 82 percent of the population (Philpott 1978: 139–141).

A second crucial distinction is that most members of European ethnic groups did not live in immigrant ghettos, as ethnically diluted as they were. Indeed, Burgess's Irish ghetto contained only 3 percent of Chicago's Irish population, and only 50 percent of the city's Italians lived in the Little Italys he identified. Only among Poles did a majority (61 percent) live in neighborhoods that were identified as being part of the Polish enclave. In contrast, 93 percent of Chicago's black population lived within the black ghetto (Philpott 1978: 141–142).

Thus, even at the height of their segregation early in the twentieth century, European ethnic groups did not experience a particularly high degree of isolation from American society—even in 1910, at the end of the peak decade of European immigration. Among the 100 or so indexes that Stanley Lieberson (1980) computed for seven European ethnic groups in seventeen cities in 1910, only seven cases had isolation indexes above 25 percent, and all but two were under 40 percent. The highest recorded levels of spatial isolation were for Italians in Boston (44 percent), Buffalo, New York (38 percent), and Milwaukee (56 percent), and for Russians (i.e., Jews) in New York (34 percent). In contrast, black isolation exceeded 25 percent in eleven of the seventeen cities Lieberson (1980) examined in 1930 (see Table 2.2), and what is truly startling about this fact is that black ghettos were still in their formative stages in 1930 and had not yet begun to approach their maximum isolation.

The last difference between immigrant enclaves and black ghettos is that whereas ghettos became a permanent feature of black residential life, ethnic enclaves proved to be a fleeting, transitory stage in the process of immigrant assimilation. Thus, the degree of segregation and spatial isolation among European ethnic groups fell steadily after 1910, as American-born children of immigrants experienced less segregation than their parents, and as spatial isolation decreased progressively with socioeconomic advancement (Lieberson 1963). For European immigrants, enclaves were places of absorption, adaptation, and adjustment to American society and served as springboards for broader mobility in society. Blacks were trapped behind an increasingly impenetrable color line.

The emergence of severe racial segregation in the North was not primarily a reflection of black housing preferences or a natural outcome of migration processes. On the contrary, as the ghetto walls grew thicker and higher, well-to-do blacks complained bitterly and loudly about their increasing confinement within crowded, dilapidated neighborhoods that were inhabited by people well below their social and economic status (Spear 1967; Kusmer 1976; Zunz 1982; Ballard 1984; Bigham 1987). Although they fought the construction of the ghetto as best they could, blacks found the forces arrayed against them to be overwhelming. The ghetto was created deliberately by whites who exercised power to enforce their preferences for racial separation in housing.

First and foremost among the tools that whites used to construct the ghetto was violence. The initial impetus for ghetto formation was a wave of racial violence that swept over northern cities in the period between 1900 and 1920. These disturbances were communal in nature, and victims were singled out for attack strictly on the basis of skin color. As history has repeatedly shown, during periods of communal strife the only safety is in numbers. Blacks living in integrated or predominantly white areas proved to be extremely vulnerable to white attack.

Black homes and apartments away from the main areas of black settlement were systematically ransacked and destroyed, and their occupants terrorized (Osofsky 1963; Rudwick 1964; Bigham 1987; Kusmer 1976). Many lives were lost when individual blacks were caught traveling through white neighborhoods to their homes. Those blacks who survived these attacks were loath to return to their former dwellings because they feared (correctly) that they would be subject to further violence. Following the riots, there was an outflow of blacks from outlying neighborhoods into the emerging ghetto, as the old integrated elite resigned itself to the new realities of racial segregation. Blacks who had been contemplating a move to better housing in white areas before the riot thought better of the idea afterward.

Racial violence did not end when the riots ceased in 1920; it simply assumed new, more controlled forms. As the black settlement pattern imploded, and scattered areas of black residence were eliminated or consolidated, a contiguous core of solidly black neighborhoods formed in most northern cities during the first decades of the century. By the time black migration quickened during the 1920s, new arrivals had to be accommodated within a very compact and spatially restricted area that was not open to easy expansion.

After 1920 the pattern of racial strife shifted from one of generalized communal violence aimed at driving blacks out of white neighborhoods, to a pattern of targeted violence concentrated along the periphery of an expanding ghetto. As migration continued and housing pressures within the ghetto became intolerable, and as health, sanitary, and social conditions deteriorated, middle-class black families were eventually driven across the color line into white neighborhoods adjacent to the ghetto, setting off an escalating cycle of racial violence (Drake and Cayton 1945; Spear 1967; Kusmer 1976; Philpott 1978; Zunz 1982).

The cycle typically began with threatening letters, personal harassment, and warnings of dire consequences to follow. Sometimes whites, through their churches, realtors, or neighborhood organizations, would take up a collection and offer to buy the black homeowner out, hinting at less civilized inducements to follow if the offer was refused. If these entreaties failed to dislodge the resident, spontaneous mobs, formed from neighborhood meetings or barroom discussions, would surround the house, hurling rocks and insults and sometimes storming and ransacking it. Periodic outbursts of mob violence would be interspersed with sporadic incidents of rock throwing, gun firing, cross burning, and physical attacks.

If the escalating violence failed to produce the desired result, bombing ensued, a step guaranteed to attract the attention not only of the homeowner but of the entire black community. During and after World War I, a wave of bombings followed the expansion of black residential areas in cities throughout the North. In Chicago, fifty-eight black homes were bombed between 1917 and 1921, one every twenty days (Drake and Cayton 1945). Black real estate agent Jesse Binga had his home and office bombed seven times in one year (Spear 1967). In Cleveland a wealthy black doctor who constructed a new house in an exclusive white suburb had his house surrounded by a violent mob and subsequently dynamited twice when he failed to leave (Kusmer 1976). Bombings were also reported to be a common means of combating the expansion of Detroit's ghetto (Zunz 1982).

The wave of violence and bombings crested during the 1920s, although the sporadic use of these techniques has continued up to the present (see Lukas 1985; Rieder 1985). Violence, however, is problematic as a strategy for maintaining the residential color line. Although whites of all classes initially resorted to violence, those in the middle and upper classes eventually realized its limitations. Not only did violent actions often destroy property within the neighborhood being defended, but injuries or death could bring legal charges and unfavorable publicity that decreased an area's stability. After the 1920s, middle-class whites increasingly turned to more "civilized" and institutionalized methods to build the ghetto.

A typical organizational solution to the threat of black residential expansion was the formation of neighborhood improvement associations. Although ostensibly chartered for the purpose of promoting neighborhood security and property values, their principal *raison d'être* was the prevention of black entry. On Chicago's South Side the Hyde Park Improvement and Protective Club and the Woodlawn Society were formed implicitly to rid their neighborhoods of unwanted black settlers and to prevent future black entry (Spear 1967; Philpott 1978). In New York, whites banded together in Harlem's Property Owners' Improvement Corporation and Brooklyn's Gates Avenue Association for the same reasons (Osofsky 1963; Connolly 1977). In other cities, similar organizations dedicated themselves to checking the expansion of black settlement along a ghetto's frontier (DeGraaf 1970; Trotter 1985; Bauman 1987).

These voluntary associations employed a variety of tools to preserve the racial homogeneity of threatened neighborhoods. They lobbied city councils for zoning restrictions, and for the closing of hotels and rooming houses that attracted blacks; they threatened boycotts of real estate agents who sold homes to blacks; they withdrew their patronage from white businesses that catered to black clients; they agitated for public investments in the neighborhood in order to increase property values and keep blacks out by economic means; they collected money to create funds to buy property from black settlers or to purchase homes that remained vacant for too long; and they offered cash bonuses to black renters who agreed to leave the neighborhood. In the exclusive Chicago suburb of Wilmette a committee of citizens went so far as to ask wealthy homeowners to lodge all maids, servants, and gardeners on the premises, or else to fire all blacks in their employ (Spear 1967).

One of the most important functions of the neighborhood associations was to implement restrictive covenants (Massey and Denton 1993). These documents were contractual agreements among property owners stating that none would permit a black to own, occupy, or lease their property. Those signing the covenant bound themselves and their heirs to exclude blacks from the covered area for a specified period of time. In the event of the covenant's violation, any party to the agreement could call upon the courts for enforcement and could sue the transgressor for damages. As typically employed, covenants took effect when some fixed percentage of property owners in a given area had signed, whereupon the remaining nonsignatories were pressured to sign also. A typical covenant lasted twenty years and required the assent of 75 percent of the property owners to become enforceable.

Before 1900, such covenants did not exist. Legal restrictions on the transfer of property to blacks took the form of deed restrictions, which covered single parcels and did not solve the problem of massive black entry into white neighborhoods. Deed restrictions also did not lend themselves to forceful collective action. After 1910 the use of restrictive covenants spread widely throughout the United States, and they were employed frequently and with considerable effectiveness to maintain the color line until 1948, when the Supreme Court declared them unenforceable and contrary to public policy (Jackson 1985).

Local real estate boards often took the lead in establishing restrictive covenants and arranging their widespread use. In 1927, for example, the Chicago Real Estate Board devised a model covenant that neighborhood organizations could adapt for their own use; the Board then organized a special drive to ensure its adoption by all of the better neighborhoods in the city (Philpott 1978). Although Chicago's local Board may have been unusually active in defending the color line, these actions were consistent with official policies of the National Association of Real Estate Brokers, which in 1924 adopted an article in its code of ethnics stating that "a Realtor should never be instrumental in introducing into a neighborhood . . . members of any race or nationality . . . whose presence will clearly be detrimental to property values in that neighborhood," a provision that remained in effect until 1950 (Helper 1969: 201).

The maintenance of a rigid color line in housing through violence and institutionalized discrimination paradoxically also created the conditions for ghetto expansion. Rapid black migration into a confined residential area created an intense demand for housing within the ghetto, which led to a marked inflation of rents and home prices. The racially segmented market generated real estate values in black areas that far exceeded anything in white neighborhoods, and this simple economic fact created great potential for profits along the color line. This led to some real estate agents specializing in opening up new areas to black settlement (Drake and Cayton 1945; Molotch 1972; Philpott 1978; Grossman 1989).

White real estate boards attempted to forestall such actions by threatening with expulsion agents who violated the color line, but since black agents were excluded from real estate boards, this threat had little effect on them. Furthermore, the potential profits were great enough that many whites were willing to face public opprobrium. In the end the real estate industry settled on a practical compromise of keeping "blacks from moving into white residential areas haphazardly and to see to it that they filled a block solidly before being allowed to move into the next one" (Helper 1969). Essentially this strategy represented a policy of containment and tactical retreat before an advancing color line. For some, it proved to be a very profitable compromise.

The methods that realtors used to open neighborhoods to black entry and to reap profits during the transition came to be known as blockbusting (Philpott 1978; Hirsch 1983). The expansion of the ghetto generally followed the path of least resistance, slowing or stopping at natural boundaries such as rivers, railroad tracks, or major thoroughfares, and moving toward low-status rather than high-status areas (Hoyt 1939). Blockbusting agents would select a promising area for racial turnover, most often an area adjacent to the ghetto that contained older housing, poorer families, aging households, and some apartment buildings. Agents would then quietly acquire a few homes or apartments in the area and rent or sell them to carefully chosen black families.

The inevitable reaction of white violence and resistance would then be countered with deliberate attempts to increase white fears and spur black demand (Philpott 1978; Zunz 1982). Agents would go door to door warning white residents of the impending invasion and offering to purchase or rent homes on generous terms. They often selected ostentatiously lower-class blacks to be the first settlers in the neighborhood in order to heighten fears and encourage panic; at times, these settlers were actually confederates of the realtor. In neighborhoods of family homes, a realtor might divide up the first black-occupied house into small units, which were intentionally rented to poor southern arrivals who were desperate for housing and willing to pay high rents for cramped rooms of low quality. While white panic spread, the realtors would advertise widely within the black community, pointing out the availability of good housing in a newly opened neighborhood, and thereby augmenting black demand.

Given the intensity of black demand and the depths of white prejudice, the entry of a relatively small number of black settlers would quickly surpass the threshold of white tolerance and set off a self-perpetuating cycle of racial turnover (Duncan and Duncan 1957; Morrill 1965). No white renters or homebuyers would enter an area under the cloud of a black invasion, and as the rate of white departures accelerated, each departing white family would be replaced with one or more black families. As the threat of violence subsided and whites gave up defending the neighborhood, black demand soared, and agents reaped substantial profits because the new entrants were willing to pay prices much higher than those previously paid by whites.

In neighborhoods of single family homes, the initial black entrants tended to be middle- and upper-class families seeking to escape the deplorable conditions of the ghetto (Duncan and Duncan 1957; Taueber and Taeuber 1965). Like other middle-class people, they sought more agreeable surroundings, higher-quality schools, lower crime rates, bigger houses, larger properties, and a better class of people. Since white banks did not make loans to black applicants, realtors were able to augment their profits by acting as bankers, as well as sales agents, and, given the racially segmented credit market, they were able to charge interest rates and demand down payments well above those paid by whites (Helper 1969; Hirsch 1983).

The attempts of black middle-class families to escape the ghetto were continually undermined by real estate agents seeking quick profits. Often they sold homes to black families who needed quality housing but were in no position to pay for it. As both seller and lender, the agent would collect a cash advance and several months of mortgage payments before the buyer defaulted; when the family was evicted, the house was sold to another family under similar terms. In this way, agents could sell a home several times in the course of a year and generate extra profits. Frequently, agents bought homes in single-family neighborhoods, subdivided them into rooming houses, and then leased the resulting kitchenette apartments at high rents to poor families (Drake and Cayton 1945; Spear 1967).

The prevalence of these quick-profit schemes meant that the ghetto constantly followed the black middle class as it sought to escape from the poverty, blight, and misery of the black slum. Following resegregation, neighborhoods fell into progressive neglect and disrepair as owners were shuffled into and out of homes that sat vacant between sales. With many settlers paying rents and mortgages beyond their means, they could not afford repairs and routine maintenance, which led to housing dilapidation. In addition, the illegal subdivision of single family homes brought the very poor into what were originally middle-class areas. Complaints to city inspectors by black homeowners usually went unheard. Typically, real estate agents were careful to pay off local officials, who were then only too happy to turn a blind eye to problems in the black community.

During the 1920s and 1930s, black ghettos expanded behind a leading edge of middle-class pioneers who were subsequently swamped by an influx of poor families. This caused the progressive deterioration of the neighborhood. As the decline accelerated, affluent families sought new homes in adjacent white neighborhoods, beginning a new cycle of neighborhood transition and decay. This process, when repeated across neighborhoods, yielded a distinct class gradient in the ghetto, with the poorest families being concentrated toward the center in the worst, most crowded, and least desirable housing, and the middle and upper classes progressively increasing their share of the population as one moved from the core toward the periphery of the ghetto (Frazier 1937; Drake and Cayton 1945; Duncan and Duncan 1957; Taueber and Taeuber 1965).

As the black ghetto became denser and more spatially concentrated, a struggle for power, influence, and ideological control emerged within the black community between the old elite and the new Negroes of the 1920s and 1930s (Osofsky 1963). The latter were politicians and, to a lesser extent, business owners who benefited from the spatial concentration of black demand within a racially segmented market. In ideological terms the struggle was symbolized by the debate between the adherents of W.E.B. Du Bois and the followers of Booker T. Washington. The former argued that blacks should fight white injustice and demand their rightful share of the fruits of American society, and the latter advocated accommodating white racism while building an independent black economic base.

The rise of the ghetto, more than anything else, brought about the eclipse of the old elite of integrationist blacks who dominated black affairs in northern cities before 1910. These professionals and tradesmen who catered to white clients and aspired to full membership in American society were supplanted by a class of politicians and entrepreneurs whose source of power and wealth lay in the black community itself. Rather than being caterers, barbers, doctors, and lawyers who served a white or racially mixed clientele, the new elite were politicians and business owners with a self-interested stake in the ghetto. With their ascendancy, the ideal of an integrated society and a fight against racial segregation went into a long remission (Frazier 1968).

These new Negroes included real estate tycoons, such as Chicago's Jesse Binga and New York's Philip A. Payton, who specialized in opening new areas for black settlement and made millions in the process (Drake and Cayton 1945; Osofsky 1963; Spear 1967). Publishing newspapers for a black audience brought wealth and influence to Robert S. Abbott, who built the *Chicago Defender* into the most important black newspaper in the country, and P.M.H. Savory, who published the *Amsterdam News* from the 1920s until his death in 1965 (Grossman 1989). With the concentration of the black population came the concentration of black votes and buying power, and a new generation of politicians and business owners came to the fore—people like Oscar DePriest, who became Chicago's first black alderman and the first black elected to Congress from the North (Spear 1967), and New York's Madame C.J. Walker, who made a fortune with a line of black cosmetics and hair-straightening products (Osofsky 1963). The interests of these new economic and political leaders were tied to the ghetto and its concerns rather than to the pursuit of an integrated life within mainstream American society.

Meanwhile, in the South, conditions for urban blacks were considerably less tolerant than in the North. The Jim Crow system of race relations was at its most powerful during the early years of the twentieth century. Its paternalistic system of race relations guaranteed the subordination of blacks and, paradoxically, lessened the need for a rigid system of housing segregation. Among older southern cities, in particular, the traditional grid pattern of white avenues and black alleys kept segregation levels relatively low.

Although direct evidence on the degree of racial segregation in southern cities is limited, the few available studies suggest that it was less severe in the early twentieth century than in the emerging ghettos of the North.

The three southern cities shown in Table 2.1 had an average black–white dissimilarity score of only 38 in 1910—21 points lower than the average in the North. In Charleston, South Carolina, the level was particularly low at about 17; although this value appears to represent an increase since the nineteenth century, it is an artifact of the exclusion of slaves from the earlier computation. When they are included in the 1860 calculation, the index falls to 11 (Taeuber and Taeuber 1965). Of the three cities shown in 1910, none displays indexes in the range generally accepted as high.

Southern whites were not completely immune to threats posed by black urbanization. After 1910, black populations also began to rise in southern cities, for essentially the same reasons as in the North, and whites similarly became alarmed at the influx of black migrants. In the context of Jim Crow, the reaction of southern whites never reached the same extremes of panic and fear as in the North. Rather, given the tradition of legally enforced segregation in other spheres, southern whites simply turned to the law to promote greater separation between the races in housing. The movement toward legally enforced residential segregation began in 1910, when Baltimore's city council passed an ordinance establishing separate white and black neighborhoods in the city. Additional laws to establish legal segregation in housing were passed in Virginia between 1911 and 1913, with Ashland, Norfolk, Portsmouth, Richmond, and Roanoke adopting ordinances emulating Baltimore's. By 1913 the movement had spread southward to Winston-Salem and Greenville, North Carolina, and Atlanta, Georgia. By 1916, Louisville, St. Louis, Oklahoma City, and New Orleans had passed laws establishing separate black and white districts (Rice 1968). As the movement gathered steam, some northern cities began to consider the possibility of adopting similar ordinances to resolve their racial difficulties (Drake and Cayton 1945).

In 1916 the National Association for the Advancement of Colored People filed a suit in the federal court to block the implementation of Louisville's segregation law, and one year later the Supreme Court declared it unconstitutional (Rice 1968). The movement toward legally sanctioned housing segregation ended. Thereafter, racial segregation in southern cities was accomplished by the same means as in the North—through violence, collective antiblack action, racially restrictive covenants, and discriminatory real estate practices. Segregation, nonetheless, continued to develop at a slower pace than in northern cities owing to the slower pace of industrialization, the unique spatial organization of southern cities, and the greater social control of blacks afforded by Jim Crow.

The 1940 black–white segregation indexes shown in Table 2.1 conceal the lower segregation in the South because they rely on block rather than ward data. Although the average score of 81 is eight points lower than in the North, it is still quite high. The use of blocks rather than wards interacts with classic white avenue–black alley settlement patterns to produce a misleading picture of segregation in the south. When ward tabulations are used, the level of segregation in Charleston, South Carolina, falls from 60 to 27 (compared to a ward-level index of only 17 in 1910) while that in Jacksonville, Florida, drops from 94 to 47 (thirty years earlier it had been 39). Although the walls of the ghetto were rising in the South by 1940, they had not yet reached the height of those in the North, particularly in the older cities (Taeuber and Taeuber 1965).

Shoring the Walls of the Ghetto

The outlines and form of the modern black ghetto were in place in most northern cities by the outbreak of World War II. Events unleashed by the war would not change the frontiers of black settlement so much as fill in the gaps. Once World War II was over, an unprecedented boom ushered in a new economic order that dramatically transformed the social and spatial organization of cities, creating sprawling, decentralized metropolises where compact settlements once stood. This new urban political economy mixed the public and private sectors to an unprecedented degree; the distinguishing feature of racial segregation in the postwar era is the unprecedented role that government played not only in maintaining the color line but in reinforcing and strengthening the walls of the ghetto.

By 1930 the perimeters of black settlement were well established in most cities and the level of black–white residential dissimilarity had stabilized at a very high level. Blacks were nearly as unevenly distributed in American cities as they would ever be, but within the circumscribed areas that had been ceded to black settlement lived a significant number of whites as late as 1930 (Lieberson 1980). The Great Depression and World War II eliminated this residual white population and made northern ghettos the homogeneously black communities they are today. The Depression brought widespread unemployment to blacks in the North, but as bad as economic conditions were in the North, they were worse in the South. Given the self-perpetuating dynamics inherent in mass migration, the movement from South to North continued, and from 1930 to 1940 some 400,000 black migrants left the South for northern cities (Farley and Allen 1987). When they arrived, they faced unusually bleak residential circumstances because the Depression had virtually ended new residential construction after 1929. Although housing construction began to pick up by 1940, the entry of the United States into

World War II once again brought home construction to a halt. During the 1930s and 1940s, therefore, black migrants entered an urban environment with an essentially fixed and very limited supply of housing.

At first the newcomers took the place of whites departing from racially changing neighborhoods located near the fringe of the ghetto. Once these neighborhoods had become all black, further ghetto expansion proved to be difficult because the housing shortage meant that there was nowhere for whites on the other side of the color line to go. As whites in adjacent neighborhoods stood firm and blocked entry, the expansion of the ghetto slowed to a crawl, and new black arrivals were accommodated by subdividing housing within the ghetto's boundaries. Apartments were carved out of bedrooms, closets, garages, basements, and sheds. As population densities within the ghetto rose, black spatial isolation increased (Drake and Cayton 1945; Duncan and Duncan 1957; Lieberson 1980).

The entry of the United States into World War II brought full war mobilization and a shortage of factory workers in the North. In response to the new demand for labor, black migration from South to North soared during the 1940s. The new migrants arrived in cities plagued by intense housing shortages and vacancy rates under 1 percent, even in white areas. During the 1940s, population densities within the ghetto increased to new and often incredible heights, a phenomenon that Otis and Beverly Duncan appropriately labeled *piling up* (Duncan and Duncan 1957). This stage in the process of ghetto formation increased black isolation to new extremes, and from this time forward, blacks in large northern cities were effectively removed—socially and spatially—from the rest of American society.

World War II brought recovery from the economic malaise of the Depression, but four years of full employment combined with wartime consumer shortages produced a large surplus of savings and a tremendous demand for housing. Additional capital for homeownership was soon made available through new loan programs at the Federal Housing Administration and the Veterans Administration. The mix of surplus capital and frustrated demand ignited an unparalleled postwar boom in residential home construction.

As home construction skyrocketed during the late 1940s and 1950s, men and women began to marry and have babies at remarkable rates. After postponing marriage and childbearing during the hard times of the Depression and through the disruptions of war, American couples sought to make up for lost time; the baby boom was on. The growing families of the 1950s sought large houses on spacious lots in areas with good schools and plenty of room for supervised play. These conditions were most easily met by constructing new homes on inexpensive land located outside of central cities. The suburbanization of America proceeded at a rapid pace and the white middle class deserted inner cities in massive numbers. While only one-third of U.S. metropolitan residents were suburban dwellers in 1940, by 1970 suburbanites constituted a majority within metropolitan America.

In making this transition from urban to suburban life, middle-class whites demanded and got massive federal investments in highway construction that permitted rapid movement to and from central cities by car. The surging demand for automobiles accelerated economic growth and contributed to the emergence of a new decentralized spatial order. Whereas early industrialism was based on steam power, rail transportation, and rudimentary communications (e.g., the telegraph and surface mail), the new political economy grew up around electric power, automotive transport, and advanced telecommunications (Massey 2005).

Steam and rail technology had encouraged spatial concentration in human activities. Factories were built compactly to conserve mechanical power and agglomerated to use common steam plants, rail lines moved large numbers of people along fixed routes to a single point, and crude communications put a premium on face-to-face interaction. In the new post-industrial order, the substitution of electricity for steam power eliminated the impetus for centralized manufacturing districts, and a growing reliance on transport by truck made congested cities undesirable as centers of manufacturing and shipping. Widespread commuting by automobile extended residential development in all directions around the central city, not just along fixed rail lines. As workers and factories took advantage of the new technologies and moved to the suburbs, retail activities followed (Massey 2005).

This period of rapid economic growth and growing spatial deconcentration was accompanied by relatively low levels of immigration; with the expansion of educational opportunities and the rise of service employment, the children of earlier immigrants increasingly left the ranks of manual workers. Employers once again turned to black migrants from the rural South to fill the demand for labor in manufacturing, heavy industry, and low-wage services. Within the South a wave of mechanization and capital investment spread through southern agriculture; this put an end to the sharecropping system and constricted the demand for rural labor (Fligstein 1981). As in earlier times, the coincidence of push and pull factors led to extensive black out-migration, with the net flow totaling 1.5 million during the 1950s and 1.4 million during the 1960s (Farley and Allen 1987).

Despite this rapid transformation of American cities, one feature of urban geography remained unchanged: the black ghetto. The institutional practices and private behaviors that had combined to maintain the color line before the World War II remained to support it afterward, with one significant change. Although whites were still highly resistant to racial integration in housing, withdrawal to the suburbs provided a more attractive alternative to the defense of threatened neighborhoods, leading to a prevalence of flight over fight among whites in racially changing areas (Frey 1979, 1980). The combination of rapid white suburbanization and extensive black in-migration led to an unprecedented increase in the physical size of the ghetto during the 1950s and 1960s.

In the postwar years the percentage of blacks within northern cities shifted dramatically and rapidly upward. Between 1950 and 1970 the percentage of blacks more than doubled in most large northern cities, going from 14 percent to 33 percent in Chicago, from 16 percent to 38 percent in Cleveland, from 16 percent to 44 percent in Detroit, and from 18 percent to 34 percent in Philadelphia. In the space of two decades, Gary, Indiana, Newark, New Jersey, and Washington, DC were transformed from predominantly white to predominantly black cities; Gary reached 53 percent black in 1970, while Newark and Washington reached levels of 54 percent and 71 percent black, respectively (Massey and Denton 1993).

What is striking about these transformations is how effectively the color line was maintained despite the massive population shifts. The white strategy of ghetto containment and tactical retreat before an advancing color line, institutionalized during the 1920s, was continued after 1945; the only change was the rate at which the leading edge of the ghetto advanced. In a few short years, vast areas of Chicago's south and west sides went black, as did Cleveland's east side, Philadelphia's north and west sides, and most of central-city Newark, Detroit, Baltimore, and Washington. All the while, however, the residential segregation of blacks was maintained (Taeuber and Taeuber 1965).

In cities receiving large numbers of black migrants, the cycle of racial turnover was so regular and pervasive that most neighborhoods could be classified by their stage in the transition process: all white, invasion, succession, consolidation, or all black. In six northern cities studied by Taeuber and Taeuber, 90 percent of all neighborhoods inhabited by blacks in 1960 were either all black or clearly moving in that direction, a pattern that prevailed through 1970 (see Massey and Mullan 1984).

The remarkable persistence of segregation despite the massive redistribution of whites and blacks is confirmed by Table 2.3, which presents indexes of residential dissimilarity calculated at the block level for thirty U.S. cities from 1940 through 1970. These measures show that racial segregation became a permanent structural feature of the spatial organization of American cities in the years after World War II. In the three decades after 1940, black–white segregation remained high and virtually constant, averaging over 85 at all times in all regions. Segregation levels in the North peaked in 1950 and then edged slightly downward by 1970. Southern cities

TABLE 2.3 Block-Level Indices of Nonwhite–White Segregation for Thirty Cities, 1940–1970

	Segregation Indices by Year			
	1940	1950	1960	1970
Northern Cities				
Boston	86.3	86.5	83.9	79.9
Buffalo	87.9	89.5	86.5	84.2
Chicago	95.0	92.1	92.6	88.8
Cincinnati	90.6	91.2	89.0	83.1
Cleveland	92.0	91.5	91.3	89.0
Columbus	87.1	88.9	85.3	84.1
Detroit	89.9	88.8	84.5	80.9
Gary	88.3	93.8	92.8	82.9
Indianapolis	90.4	91.4	91.6	88.3
Kansas City	88.0	91.3	90.8	88.0
Los Angeles	84.2	84.6	81.8	78.4
Milwaukee	92.9	91.6	88.1	83.7
Newark	77.4	76.9	71.6	74.9
New York	86.8	87.3	79.3	73.0
Philadelphia	88.0	89.0	87.1	83.2
Pittsburgh	82.0	84.0	84.6	83.9
St. Louis	92.6	92.9	90.5	89.3
San Francisco	82.9	79.8	69.3	55.5
Average	87.0	88.4	85.6	81.7
Southern Cities				
Atlanta	87.4	91.5	93.6	91.5
Baltimore	90.1	91.3	89.6	88.3
Birmingham	86.4	88.7	92.8	91.5
Dallas	80.2	88.4	94.6	92.7
Greensboro	93.1	93.5	93.3	91.4
Houston	84.5	91.5	93.7	90.0
Memphis	79.9	86.4	92.0	91.8
Miami	97.9	97.8	97.9	89.4
New Orleans	81.0	84.9	86.3	83.1
Norfolk	96.0	95.0	94.6	90.8
Tampa	90.2	92.5	94.5	90.7
Washington	81.0	80.1	79.7	77.7
Average	87.3	90.1	91.9	89.1

Source: Massey and Denton (1993).

peaked in 1960. Only San Francisco experienced a significant long-term decline in the level of racial segregation. By 1970 at least 70 percent of blacks would have had to move to achieve an even residential configuration in most cities, and in many places the figure was closer to 90 percent.

Such persistently high levels of segregation imply that blacks and whites occupied separate and wholly distinct neighborhoods at each point between 1940 and 1970. Given the fact that northern cities received about 4.5 million black migrants during the period, the only possible outcome was a substantial increase in degree of black spatial isolation. Although no studies have computed decade-by-decade isolation indices for U.S. cities, census data

TABLE 2.4. Indices of Black Isolation within Neighborhoods of Thirty Cities, 1930 and 1970

Northern Cities			Southern Cities	
City	1930	1970	City	1970
Boston	19.2	66.1	Atlanta	88.0
Buffalo, New York	24.2	75.2	Baltimore	84.8
Chicago	70.4	89.2	Birmingham, Alabama	57.9
Cincinnati	44.6	63.9	Dallas	82.0
Cleveland	51.0	86.6	Greensboro, N. Carolina	62.0
			Houston	72.1
Columbus, Ohio	–	65.2		
Detroit	31.2	77.1	Memphis	82.9
Gary, Indiana	–	83.2	Miami	81.5
Indianapolis	26.1	65.5	New Orleans	75.6
Kansas City	31.6	75.6	Norfolk, Virginia	79.8
			Tampa, Florida	62.3
Los Angeles	25.6	73.9	Washington	88.1
Milwaukee	16.4	74.5		
New York	41.8	60.2	Average	76.4
Newark, New Jersey	22.8	78.3		
Philadelphia	27.3	75.6		
Pittsburgh	26.8	70.8		
St. Louis	46.6	85.1		
San Francisco	1.7	56.1		
Average	31.7	73.5		

Source: Massey and Denton (1993)

allow us to carry out this task for 1970. Table 2.4 presents our results for thirty cities, along with Lieberson's 1930 isolation indices, which indicate long-term trends.

Among northern cities, the average level of black spatial isolation more than doubled between 1930 and 1970, going from 32 percent to nearly 74 percent. Whereas a typical northern black resident was likely to live in a neighborhood dominated by whites in 1930 (only Chicago and Cleveland were exceptions), by 1970 the situation had completely reversed. Now blacks in all northern cities were more likely to live with other blacks than with whites, and in four cities (Chicago, Cleveland, Gary, and St. Louis) the average black person lived in a neighborhood that was over 80 percent black. Unless they worked in the larger mainstream economy, blacks in these cities were very unlikely to have any contact with whites.

Although we lack an earlier reference point to discern long-term trends in the South, black isolation was clearly an accomplished fact in southern cities by 1970 as well. The average level of black isolation within southern cities was slightly higher than in the North (76 percent versus 74 percent), and the index exceeded 80 percent in six cases (Atlanta, Baltimore, Dallas, Memphis, Miami, and Washington, DC). In all cities, blacks were very unlikely to share a neighborhood with members of other racial groups. Indeed, the lowest isolation index was 58 percent (in Birmingham), so that blacks throughout the South tended to live in residential areas where the vast majority of residents were black. Patterns for 1970, therefore, represent a complete reversal of conditions during the late nineteenth century, when residential contact between southern blacks and whites was the rule.

Throughout the United States the ghetto had become an enduring, permanent feature of the residential structure of black community life by 1940, and over the next thirty years the spatial isolation of blacks increased to historically unprecedented levels. The highest isolation index ever recorded for any ethnic group in any American city was 56 percent (for Italians in Milwaukee, Wisconsin, in 1910), but by 1970 the lowest level of spatial isolation observed for blacks was 56 percent in San Francisco (see Lieberson 1980).

The universal emergence of the black ghetto in American cities after 1940 rests on a foundation of long-standing white racial prejudice. Although attitudes cannot be studied directly before 1940, when opinion polls become available, they confirm the depth of white prejudice against blacks in the area of housing. For example, in 1942, 84 percent of white Americans polled answered "yes" to the question "Do you think there should be separate sections in towns and cities for Negroes to live in?" (Allport 1958); in 1962, 61 percent of white respondents agreed that "white people have a right to keep blacks out of their neighborhoods if they want to, and blacks should respect that right"; it was not until 1970 that even a bare majority of white respondents (53 percent) disagreed with the latter statement (Schuman *et al.* 1998).

From 1940 to 1970 there was widespread support among whites for racial discrimination in housing and for the systematic exclusion of blacks from white neighborhoods. As a result, whites continued to resist any attempt at black entry through acts of harassment and violence, and if entry was achieved, the neighborhood was avoided by subsequent white homeseekers, guaranteeing racial turnover and resegregation (Massey and Mullan 1984). The only difference from earlier times was that the racial turnover and the ghetto's physical expansion were accomplished more quickly, but blacks remained in a ghetto nonetheless.

The institutionalization of discrimination within the real estate industry continued in the postwar era. Although racially restrictive covenants were declared unenforceable by the Supreme Court in 1948, a comprehensive study by Helper (1969) of real estate policies in the 1950s revealed a pervasive pattern and practice of discrimination against blacks in most American cities. In a survey of real estate agents in Chicago, Helper found that 80 percent of agents refused to sell blacks property in white neighborhoods, and 68 percent refused to rent them such property. Moreover, among those agents who did sell or rent to blacks, half said they would do so only under restrictive conditions, such as when a significant number of blacks had already entered the area. Another survey of Chicago's real estate agents, conducted by Molotch (1972) in the mid-1960s, found that only 29 percent of agents were willing to rent to blacks unconditionally (regardless of local market conditions or racial compositions), and half of these open-minded agents were themselves black.

Helper (1969) presented similar findings from studies of housing discrimination in other cities during the 1950s. One study carried out in suburban New York identified forty-six separate techniques used by white realtors to exclude blacks from neighborhoods, and Helper identified twenty-six different methods in her Chicago survey. Most of the techniques could be classified as either flat refusal or subterfuge (falsely saying a property was unavailable), with 56 percent of agents using the first technique and 24 percent using the latter. When handling properties in black areas, 22 percent said they were more careful screening black applicants than whites, 14 percent said they required security deposits of blacks but not whites, and 25 percent said they charged higher rents to blacks.

In their personal views, the realtors studied by Helper (1969) appeared to share the prejudices of their white clients. Some 59 percent of her respondents rejected racial integration in principle, and 84 percent espoused an ideological stance that supported the exclusion of blacks from white neighborhoods. Some 65 percent said they believed that the entry of blacks was bad for neighborhoods, and among realtors who were members of Chicago's Real Estate Board, support for the exclusion of blacks was even stronger, with 91 percent holding views consistent with an exclusionary ideology.

In her interviews with realtors, Helper (1969) also uncovered considerable evidence of discrimination by banks and savings institutions in denying loans to black homeseekers. Among realtors offering information on the issue, 62 percent felt that few or very few banks were willing to make loans to blacks, and half of the agents confirmed that banks would not make loans to areas that were black, turning black, or threatened with the possibility of black entry.

In summary, there is considerable evidence pointing to the persistence of prejudice against blacks in the postwar period and to the widespread translation of this sentiment into systematic, institutionalized racial discrimination within urban housing markets. These private beliefs and actions were not the only forces shoring up the walls of ghettos between 1940 and 1970, for what was new and utterly exceptional about the postwar era was the extent to which the federal government became involved in perpetuating racial segregation.

Beginning in the 1930s, the federal government launched a series of programs designed to increase employment in the construction industry and make homeownership widely available to the American public. The Home Owners Loan Corporation (HOLC) was the first of these programs, and it served as a model for later efforts. Passed in the Depression year of 1933, it provided funds for refinancing urban mortgages in danger of default and granted low-interest loans to former owners who had lost their homes through foreclosure, enabling them to regain their properties.

Unfortunately for blacks, the HOLC also initiated and institutionalized the practice of redlining (Jackson 1985). This discriminatory practice grew out of a ratings system HOLC developed to evaluate the risks associated with loans made to specific urban neighborhoods. Four categories of neighborhood quality were established, and the lowest was coded with the color red; it and the next-lowest category virtually never received HOLC loans. The vast majority of mortgages went to the top two categories, the highest of which included areas that were "new, homogeneous, and in demand in good times and bad" (to HOLC this meant areas inhabited by "American business and professional men"); the second category consisted of areas that had reached their peak, but were still desirable and could be expected to remain stable.

The HOLC's rating procedures systematically undervalued older central-city neighborhoods that were racially or ethnically mixed. Jewish areas were generally placed in category two if their economic status was high enough, but if they were working class or located near a black settlement, they would fall into the third category because they were "within such a low price or rent range as to attract an undesirable element." Black areas were invariably rated as fourth grade and redlined. As Jackson (1985) points out, the HOLC did not invent these standards of racial worth in real estate—they were already well established by the 1920s—but simply bureaucratized them and applied them on an unprecedented scale. It lent the power, prestige, and support of the federal government to the systematic practice of racial discrimination in housing.

According to Jackson (1985), HOLC underwriters were far more concerned about the location and movement of blacks than any other demographic trend. He cites a confidential 1941 HOLC survey of real estate prospects in the St. Louis area that repeatedly mentions "the rapidly increasing Negro population" and the consequent "problem in the maintenance of real estate values." Every neighborhood analysis in the report includes maps of the density of black settlement. Black neighborhoods are always coded red, and even those with small percentages of black residents were usually rated as hazardous and placed in the lowest category.

Through this discriminatory ratings system, HOLC mortgage funds were invariably channeled away from established black areas and were usually redirected from neighborhoods that looked as though they might include blacks in the future. Funds distributed through the HOLC program were modest, and the agency's major role in shoring up the walls of the ghetto lay in its role as a model for both private and public credit institutions.

During the 1930s and 1940s, private banks relied heavily on the HOLC system to make their own loan decisions, and the agency's residential security maps were widely circulated throughout the lending industry (Jackson 1985). Banks adopted the HOLC's procedures (and prejudices) in constructing their own maps and ratings, thereby institutionalizing and disseminating the practice of redlining. As late as 1970, examiners for the Federal Home Loan Bank Board were redlining zip code areas that showed any signs of racial change (Hays 1985). The HOLC not only channeled federal funds away from black neighborhoods but also was responsible for a much larger and more significant disinvestment in black areas by private institutions.

By far the greatest effect of the HOLC rating system came from its influence on the underwriting practices of the Federal Housing Administration (FHA) and the Veterans Administration (VA) during the 1940s and 1950s. The FHA loan program was created by the National Housing Act in 1937, and the VA program was authorized by the Servicemen's Readjustment Act of 1944 (Jackson 1985). These loan programs together completely reshaped the residential housing market of the United States and pumped millions of dollars into the housing industry during the postwar era. Loans made by the FHA and VA were a major impetus for the rapid suburbanization of the United States after 1945.

The FHA program operated by guaranteeing the value of collateral for loans made by private banks. Before this program, mortgages generally were granted for no more than two-thirds of the appraised value of a home, so buyers needed to acquire at least 33 percent of the value of a property to make a down payment; frequently, banks required that a prospective owner have half the assessed value of a home before making a loan. The FHA program, in contrast, guaranteed over 90 percent of the value of collateral so that down payments of 10 percent became the norm. The FHA also extended the repayment period to twenty-five or thirty years, which resulted in low monthly payments, and insisted that all loans be fully amortized. The greater security afforded by FHA guarantees virtually eliminated the risk to banks, and induced banks to lower the interest rates they charged borrowers. When the VA program was established, it followed practices established by the earlier FHA program (Jackson 1985).

As purchasing a house became less difficult and costly, homeownership was within reach of most Americans for the first time. Between 1934 and 1969 the percentage of families living in owner-occupied dwellings increased from 44 percent to 63 percent. During the 1940s and 1950s, FHA financing and the advent of new construction techniques made it cheaper to buy new suburban homes than to rent comparable older dwellings in the central city. As a result, FHA and VA practices contributed significantly to the decline of the inner city by encouraging the selective out-migration of middle-class whites to the suburbs.

This bias toward suburbia was evident in FHA practices and regulations, which favored the construction of single family homes but discouraged the building of multifamily units (Jackson 1985). In addition, FHA loans for the remodeling of existing structures were small and had a short amortization period, making it easier and cheaper for a family to purchase a new house than to renovate an older one. But the most important factor encouraging white suburbanization and reinforcing the segregation of blacks was the FHA requirement for an unbiased professional appraisal of insured properties, which naturally included a rating of the neighborhood.

In rating a home, the FHA established minimum standards for lot size, setbacks, and separation from existing structures that essentially rendered many inner-city dwellings, notably row houses and attached dwellings, ineligible (Jackson 1985). In evaluating neighborhoods, the agency followed the HOLC's earlier lead in racial matters, manifesting an obsessive concern with the presence of what the 1939 FHA Underwriting Manual called "inharmonious racial or nationality groups." According to the manual, "if a neighborhood is to retain stability, it is necessary that properties shall continue to be occupied by the same social and racial classes" (Jackson 1985).

In the late 1940s the FHA recommended the use of racially restrictive covenants as a means of ensuring the security of neighborhoods, and it did not change this recommendation until 1950, two years after the Supreme Court declared covenants unenforceable and contrary to public policy (Jackson 1985). Like the HOLC, the FHA compiled maps and charts showing the location and movement of black families, and it frequently drew updated versions of the HOLC Residential Security Maps to determine the suitability of neighborhoods for FHA loans.

As a result of these policies, the vast majority of FHA and VA mortgages went to white middle-class suburbs, and very few were awarded to black neighborhoods in central cities. It is difficult to determine the full extent of the resulting disinvestment in black neighborhoods, however, because the FHA did not publish loan statistics below the county level, which is curious, given the agency's obsessive concern with neighborhood data before making loans. Jackson (1985) has partially overcome this limitation by focusing on cases where cities and counties are coterminous.

St. Louis County, Missouri, is a suburban area that surrounds the city of St. Louis. From 1934 to 1960 the county received five times as many FHA mortgages as did the city, and nearly six times as much loan money; per capita mortgage spending was 6.3 times greater. Jackson (1985) observed similar differentials in the dispersal of FHA mortgages among Washington, DC, and its suburbs. Most startling was the case of New York City and its suburbs. Per capita FHA lending in Nassau County, New York (i.e., suburban Long Island), was 11 times that in Kings County (Brooklyn) and 60 times that in Bronx County (the Bronx).

As the new postindustrial urban order developed, the disinvestment in central cities at the expense of suburbs increasingly meant the disinvestment in blacks as opposed to whites (Jackson 1985). Sometimes FHA procedures rendered whole cities ineligible for FHA-guaranteed loans simply because of a minority presence, thereby accelerating their decline. In 1966 the FHA had no mortgages in either Paterson or Camden, New Jersey, both older cities where non-Hispanic whites were declining in number during the 1950s (and actually became minorities in the 1970s). Given the importance of the FHA in the residential housing market, such blanket redlining sent strong signals to private lending institutions, which followed suit and avoided making loans within the affected areas. The lack of loan capital flowing into minority areas made it impossible for owners to sell their homes, leading to steep declines in property values and a self-perpetuating cycle of disrepair, deterioration, vacancy, and abandonment (Frey 1979).

Thus, by the late 1950s many central cities were locked into a self-perpetuating cycle of decline that was directly encouraged and largely supported by federal housing policies. As poor blacks from the South entered cities in large numbers, middle-class whites fled to the suburbs to escape them and to insulate themselves from the social problems that accompanied the rising tide of poor (Massey 1994). As the growing demand for city services—particularly social services—drove up the cost of local government, politicians were forced to raise taxes, which further accelerated the flight of the white middle class, creating additional pressures for tax increases.

Despite this vicious cycle of decline, most central cities were not completely stripped of their middle and upper classes. Whites associated with a variety of elite institutions, including universities, hospitals, libraries, foundations, businesses, were often tied physically to the city by large capital investments, spatially immobile facilities, and long-standing traditions. Faced with a steady decline in the physical stock of the city and the progressive encroachment of the black ghetto, these powerful interests turned to the federal government for relief.

They received it from Congress in the form of the Housing Acts of 1949 and 1954, which provided federal funds to local authorities to acquire slum properties, assemble them into large parcels, clear them of existing structures, and prepare them for redevelopment. But in order to qualify for federal funding, local redevelopment authorities had to guarantee that an adequate supply of replacement housing would be made available to displaced families at rents within their means. To satisfy the latter provision, local planning agencies turned to public housing (Hirsch 1983; Bauman 1987).

During the 1950s and 1960s, local elites manipulated housing and urban renewal legislation to carry out widespread slum clearance in growing black neighborhoods that threatened white business districts and elite institutions. Public housing was pressed into service to house black families displaced by the razing of neighborhoods undergoing renewal. Although liberal planners often tried to locate the projects away from ghetto areas, white politicians and citizens mobilized to block the construction of projects within their neighborhoods; white city councils and mayors usually obtained the right of veto over any proposed project site (Hirsch 1983). As a result, projects were typically built on cleared land within or adjacent to existing black neighborhoods (Goldstein and Yancey 1986; Massey and Kanaiaupuni 1993). In order to save money, maximize patronage jobs, and house within the ghetto as many blacks as possible, local authorities constructed multiunit projects of extreme high density.

The razing of neighborhoods near threatened areas did check the spread of urban blight, and saved many areas, but black critics complained that urban renewal simply meant Negro renewal. The evidence largely bears them out (White 1980). As black neighborhoods adjacent to threatened white areas were torn down and converted to other uses, thereby blocking the expansion of the ghetto in that direction, public housing for displaced residents had to be constructed elsewhere. For political reasons, projects could only be built in ghetto areas, so other black neighborhoods were razed and high-density units constructed there to accommodate the residents of both neighborhoods.

In the end, urban renewal almost always destroyed more housing than it replaced (Hirsch 1983). As a result, many poor blacks were permanently displaced into other crowded ghetto neighborhoods, contributing to their instability and further decline. Moreover, delays between the time when neighborhoods were torn down and new projects were erected displaced many others into the ghetto on a temporary basis. Frequently, urban renewal programs only shifted the problems of blight, crime, and instability from areas adjacent to elite white neighborhoods to locations deeper inside the black ghetto.

Established black neighborhoods could not absorb all the families displaced by urban renewal and public housing construction, and some were forced to seek housing in working-class white neighborhoods located at points along the ghetto's periphery. Thus, an important secondary effect of urban renewal was to accelerate racial turnover, expand the ghetto, and shift the threat of ghetto expansion from elite white districts to working-class white neighborhoods (Bauman 1987).

After two decades of urban renewal, public housing projects in most large cities had become black reservations by 1970, highly segregated from the rest of society and characterized by extreme social isolation (Massey and Bickford 1991). The replacement of low-density slums with high-density towers of poor families also reduced the class diversity of the ghetto and brought about a geographic concentration of poverty that was previously unimaginable (Massey and Kanaiaupuni 1993). This new segregation of blacks—economically as well as socially—was the direct result of an unprecedented collaboration between local and national government (Hirsch 1983).

This unholy marriage came about when private actions to maintain the color line were overwhelmed by the massive population shifts of the 1950s and 1960s. The degree of racial segregation in public housing is directly and unambiguously linked to the differential growth of black and white urban populations in the postwar era. Today, blacks are most segregated in public housing precisely where their numbers were growing most rapidly compared to those of whites during the 1960s (Hirsch 1983). Public housing, in the words of historian Arnold Hirsch, represents a new, federally sponsored "second ghetto," one "solidly institutionalized and frozen in concrete," where "government took an active hand not merely in reinforcing prevailing patterns of segregation but in lending them a permanence never seen before" (Hirsch 1983: 252–254).

Separate and Unequal

By the late 1960s, virtually all American cities with significant black populations had come to house large ghettos characterized by extreme segregation and historically unprecedented levels of spatial isolation. In other words, the average black city dweller lived in a neighborhood where the vast majority of his or her neighbors were also black. Before 1940, no racial or ethnic group in American history had ever experienced an isolation index above 60 percent, but by 1970 this level was normal for blacks in large American cities.

Not only was the segregation of European ethnic groups lower, it was also temporary. Whereas Europeans' isolation indexes began to drop shortly after 1920, the spatial isolation characteristic of blacks had become a permanent feature of the residential structure of large American cities by 1940. This profound segregation reversed nineteenth-century patterns, where neighborhoods were racially integrated and the social worlds of blacks and whites overlapped. Under the residential configurations prevailing in 1970, meaningful contact between blacks and whites outside the workforce would be extremely unlikely; this created the structural conditions for the emergence of separate cultural worlds, the geographic concentration of poverty, and the alienation of blacks from the values and institutions of U.S. society.

These conditions arose because of deliberate actions taken by whites to deny blacks access to urban housing markets and to exclude them from white neighborhoods. Throughout the postwar era, whites displayed a high degree of prejudice against black neighbors, and this sentiment was repeatedly expressed in violence directed at blacks who attempted to leave the ghetto. Restrictive covenants and deed restrictions were employed by neighborhood improvement associations to exclude blacks from housing outside the ghetto, boycotts were organized to punish merchants or agents who sold to blacks, and social pressure was applied to realtors, property owners, and public officials who did not adhere to the principle of racial exclusion. Discrimination in the real estate industry was institutionalized from 1920 onward.

After 1940 the federal government was drawn into the defense of the residential color line. Federally sponsored mortgage programs systematically channeled funds away from minority neighborhoods, bringing about a wholesale disinvestment in black communities during the 1950s and 1960s. Meanwhile, local officials using funds from the HUD carried out systematic slum clearance in ghetto neighborhoods adjacent to threatened white districts, and then built large blocks of high-density public housing in other black neighborhoods to contain black families displaced by this *renewal*. The result was a new, more permanent, federally sponsored second ghetto in which blacks were isolated by class as well as race.

The systematic segregation of blacks within inner cities during the twentieth century had profound effects on their social and economic well-being. The racial segmentation of housing markets excluded black homeseekers from the expanding suburbs and diverted most housing demand away from inner-city markets, causing the value of black-owned homes to languish and impairing the ability of black families to accumulate wealth (Oliver and Shapiro 1995; Conley 1999). About half of the black–white wealth gap may be attributed to the direct effects of residential segregation (Yinger 1993). At the same time, the transformation of the central city from manufacturing to services and the suburbanization of employment isolated black workers from stable, high-paying jobs and separated them from the dynamic locus of employment creation (Wilson 1996). The consequent decline of earnings and employment among black males reduced the incentives for marriage and led, in turn, to a proliferation of female-headed families and welfare dependency (Wilson 1987).

The economic deprivation, social isolation, and psychological alienation produced by decades of segregation bore bitter fruit in a series of violent urban riots during the 1960s. The violence began in Birmingham, Alabama, in the summer of 1963, but the real bellwether was the Los Angeles riot of August 1965, which did $35 million worth of damage and left 4,000 injured and 34 dead (U.S. National Advisory Commission on Civil Disorders 1988). After sporadic violence in Chicago and Cleveland during the summer of 1966, a convulsive wave of mob violence erupted during July and August of 1967, when black ghettos in sixty U.S. cities exploded in a cataclysm of frustration and rage. The violence was particularly destructive in Detroit, Newark, and Milwaukee; Chicago's inferno followed Martin Luther King's assassination in April 1968.

Unlike the communal race riots of the early 1900s, these disturbances arose from within the black community itself and were *commodity riots* directed at property rather than people (Janowitz 1969). Outside of confrontations with police and guardsmen, there was little black-on-white or white-on-black violence (Meier and Rudwick 1969). Attacks were confined largely to the ghetto and were directed at white property, institutions, or authority symbols. Looting became the characteristic act of the disturbances. White people were not singled out for assault, and black rioters did not attempt to leave the ghetto. The participants did not express a racial hatred of whites but an anger with the conditions of racial oppression and economic deprivation that had been allowed to fester in the ghetto for sixty years.

In the wake of the violence and destruction, President Johnson appointed a national commission of elected officials and public figures chaired by Illinois governor Otto Kerner. The Kerner Commission issued its report in March 1968 and firmly concluded that the riots stemmed from the simple fact that "our nation is moving toward two societies, one black, one white—separate and unequal" (U.S. National Advisory Commission on Civil Disorders 1988). The growing inequality was attributed to the persistence of discrimination and a legacy of disadvantages in employment, education, and welfare, but segregation was clearly identified by the commissioners as underlying all other social and economic problems.

A point "fundamental to the commission's recommendations" was that

> federal housing programs must be given a new thrust aimed at overcoming the prevailing pattern of racial segregation. If this is not done, those programs will continue to concentrate the most impoverished and dependent segments of the population into central-city ghettos, where there is already a critical gap between the needs of the population and the public resources to deal with them.
>
> (U.S. National Advisory Commission on Civil Disorders 1988: 28)

To accomplish this aim the commission recommended that the federal government "enact a comprehensive and enforceable open housing law to cover the sale or rental of all housing," and that it "reorient federal housing programs to place more low and moderate income housing outside of ghetto areas" (U.S. National Advisory Commission on Civil Disorders 1988: 28).

Within months of the commission's report in March 1968, the nation seemed to be moving decisively toward the implementation of these recommendations. In April the Fair Housing Act was passed by Congress and signed into law by the president; it banned discrimination in the sale or rental of housing. The following year, Dorothy Gautreaux and her fellow plaintiffs won their lawsuit, which alleged that the Chicago Housing Authority (CHA) had discriminated against blacks in the location of its public housing projects; the judge ordered the CHA to locate the next 700 units and 75 percent of all subsequent units in predominantly white areas (Vernarelli 1986). Given these new tools in the fight against residential segregation, observers looked forward to the dismantling of the ghetto during the 1970s, and to a reversal of historical trends toward segregation. Unfortunately, that did not happen.

References

Allport, Gordon W. 1958. *The Nature of Prejudice.* Garden City, NY: Doubleday Anchor.

Ballard, Allen B. 1984. *One More Day's Journey: The Story of a Family and a People.* New York: McGraw-Hill.

Bauman, John F. 1987. *Public Housing, Race, and Renewal: Urban Planning in Philadelphia, 1920–1974.* Philadelphia: Temple University Press.

Berlin, Ira. 1974. *Slaves without Masters: The Free Negro in the Antebellum South.* New York: Pantheon.

Bigham, Darrel. 1987. *We Ask Only a Fair Trial: A History of the Black Community of Evansville, Indiana.* Bloomington: Indiana University Press.

Chicago Commission on Race Relations. 1922. *The Negro in Chicago: A Study of Race Relations and a Race Riot.* Chicago: University of Chicago Press.

Conley, Dalton. 1999. *Being Black, Living in the Red: Race, Wealth, and Social Policy in America.* Berkeley: University of California Press.

Connolly, Harold X. 1977. *A Ghetto Grows in Brooklyn.* New York: New York University Press.

DeGraaf, Lawrence B. 1970. "The City of Black Angels." *Pacific Historical Review* 39: 323–352.

Demerath, N.J., and H.W. Gilmore. 1954. "The Ecology of Southern Cities." Pp. 120–125 in Rupert B. Vance and N.J. Demerath, eds., *The Urban South.* Chapel Hill: University of North Carolina Press.

Drake, St. Clair, and Horace R. Cayton. 1945. *Black Metropolis: A Study of Life in a Northern City.* New York: Harcourt, Brace.

Duncan, Otis D., and Beverly Duncan. 1957. *The Negro Population of Chicago: A Study of Residential Succession.* Chicago: University of Chicago Press.

Erickson, Charlotte. 1957. *American Industry and the European Immigrant, 1860–1885.* Cambridge, MA: Harvard University Press.

Farley, Reynolds, and Walter R. Allen. 1987. *The Color Line and the Quality of Life in America.* New York: Russell Sage.

Fligstein, Neil. 1981. *Going North: Migration of Blacks and Whites from the South, 1900–1950.* New York: Academic Press.

Foner, Eric. 1990. *A Short History of Reconstruction.* New York: Perennial Press.

Frazier, E. Franklin. 1937. "Negro Harlem: An Ecological Study." *American Journal of Sociology* 43: 72–88.

——. 1968. "Human, All Too Human: The Negro's Vested Interest in Segregation." Pp. 283–291 in G. Franklin Edwards, ed., *E. Franklin Frazier on Race Relations.* Chicago: University of Chicago Press.

Frey, William H. 1979. "Central City White Flight: Racial and Nonracial Causes." *American Sociological Review* 44: 425–448.

——. 1980. "Black In-migration, White Flight, and the Changing Economic Base of the Central City." *American Journal of Sociology* 85: 1396–1417.

Goldstein, Ira, and William L. Yancey. 1986. "Public Housing Projects, Blacks, and Public Policy: The Historical Ecology of Public Housing in Philadelphia." Pp. 262–289 in John M. Goering, ed., *Housing Desegregation and Federal Policy.* Chapel Hill: University of North Carolina Press.

Grossman, James R. 1989. *Land of Hope: Chicago, Black Southerners, and the Great Migration.* Chicago: University of Chicago Press.

Hatton, Timothy J., and Jeffrey G. Williamson. 1998. *The Age of Mass Migration.* Oxford: Oxford University Press.

Hays, R. Allen. 1985. *The Federal Government and Urban Housing: Ideology and Change in Public Policy.* Albany: State University of New York Press.

Helper, Rose. 1969. *Racial Policies and Practices of Real Estate Brokers.* Minneapolis: University of Minnesota Press.

Hershberg, Theodore. 1981. "Free Blacks in Antebellum Philadelphia: A Study of Ex-slaves, Freeborn, and Socioeconomic Decline." Pp. 368–391 in Theodore Hershberg, ed., *Philadelphia: Work, Space, Family, and Group Experience in the 19th Century.* New York: Oxford University Press.

Hershberg, Theodore, Alan N. Burstein, Eugene P. Ericksen, Stephanie W. Greenberg, and William L. Yancey. 1981. "A Tale of Three Cities: Blacks, Immigrants, and Opportunity in Philadelphia, 1850–1880, 1930, 1970." Pp. 461–491 in Theodore Hershberg, ed., *Philadelphia: Work, Space, Family, and Group Experience in the 19th Century.* New York: Oxford University Press.

Hirsch, Arnold R. 1983. *Making the Second Ghetto: Race and Housing in Chicago, 1940–1960.* Cambridge: Cambridge University Press.

Hoyt, Homer. 1939. *The Structure and Growth of Residential Neighborhoods in American Cities.* Washington, DC: U.S. Government Printing Office.

Ignatiev, Noel. 1996. *How the Irish Became White.* New York: Routledge.

Jackson, Kenneth T. 1985. *Crabgrass Frontier: The Suburbanization of the United States.* New York: Oxford University Press.

Janowitz, Morris. 1969. "Patterns of Collective Racial Violence." Pp. 412–444 in Hugh Davis Graham and Ted Robert Gurr, eds., *Violence in America: Historical and Comparative Perspectives.* New York: New American Library.

Kantrowitz, Nathan. 1979. "Racial and Ethnic Segregation in Boston: 1830–1970." *Annals of the American Academy of Political and Social Science* 441: 41–54.

Katzman, David. 1973. *Before the Ghetto: Black Detroit in the Nineteenth Century.* Urbana: University of Illinois Press.

Kusmer, Kenneth L. 1976. *A Ghetto Takes Shape: Black Cleveland 1870–1930.* Urbana: University of Illinois Press.

Lieberson, Stanley. 1963. *Ethnic Patterns in American Cities.* New York: Free Press.

——. 1980. *A Piece of the Pie: Blacks and White Immigrants since 1880.* Berkeley: University of California Press.

Lukas, J. Anthony. 1985. *Common Ground: A Turbulent Decade in the Lives of Three American Families.* New York: Vintage.

Massey, Douglas S. 1985. "Ethnic Residential Segregation: A Theoretical Synthesis and Empirical Review." *Sociology and Social Research* 69: 315–350.

——. 1994. "The Age of Extremes: Concentrated Affluence and Poverty in the 21st Century." *Demography* 33: 395–412.

——. 2005. *Strangers in a Strange Land: Humans in an Urbanizing World.* New York: Norton.

Massey, Douglas S., and Adam Bickford. 1991. "Segregation in the Second Ghetto: Racial and Ethnic Segregation in American Public Housing, 1977." *Social Forces* 69: 1011–1038.

Massey, Douglas S., and Nancy A. Denton. 1988. "The Dimensions of Residential Segregation." *Social Forces* 67: 281–315.

——. 1993. *American Apartheid: Segregation and the Making of the Underclass.* Cambridge, MA: Harvard University Press.

Massey, Douglas S., and Shawn M. Kanaiaupuni. 1993. "Public Housing and the Concentration of Poverty." *Social Science Quarterly* 74: 109–123.

Massey, Douglas S., and Brendan P. Mullan. 1984. "Processes of Hispanic and Black Spatial Assimilation." *American Journal of Sociology* 89: 836–873.

Meier, August, and Elliot Rudwick. 1969. "Black Violence in the 20th Century: A Study in Rhetoric and Retaliation." Pp. 399–412 in Hugh Davis Graham and Ted Robert Gurr, eds., *Violence in America: Historical and Comparative Perspectives.* New York: New American Library.

Molotch, Harvey L. 1972. *Managed Integration: The Dilemmas of Doing Good in the City.* Berkeley: University of California Press.

Morrill, Richard L. 1965. "The Negro Ghetto: Problems and Alternatives." *Geographical Review* 55: 339–361.

Oliver, Melvin, and Thomas Shapiro. 1995. *Black Wealth/White Wealth: A New Perspective on Racial Inequality.* New York: Routledge.

Osofsky, Gilbert. 1963. *Harlem: The Making of a Ghetto: Negro New York 1890–1930.* New York: Harper and Row.

Perry, J.M. 1978. *The Impact of Immigration on Three American Industries, 1865–1914.* New York: Arno Press.

Philpott, Thomas. 1978. *The Slum and the Ghetto: Neighborhood Deterioration and Middle-class Reform, Chicago, 1880–1930.* New York: Oxford University Press.

Rice, Roger L. 1968. "Residential Segregation by Law, 1910–1917." *Journal of Southern History* 64: 179–199.

Rieder, Jonathan. 1985. *Canarsie: The Jews and Italians of Brooklyn against Liberalism.* Cambridge, MA: Harvard University Press.

Roof, Wade Clark, Thomas L. Van Valey, and Daphne Spain. 1976. "Residential Segregation in Southern Cities: 1970." *Social Forces* 55: 59–71.

Rudwick, Elliot. 1964. *Race Riot at East St. Louis: July 2, 1917.* Urbana: University of Illinois Press.

Schuman, Howard, Charlotte Steeh, Lawrence Bobo, and Maria Krysan. 1998. *Racial Attitudes in America: Trends and Interpretations.* Cambridge, MA: Harvard University Press.

Spear, Allan H. 1967. *Black Chicago: The Making of a Negro Ghetto, 1890–1920.* Chicago: University of Chicago Press.

Taeuber, Karl E., and Alma F. Taeuber. 1965. *Negroes in Cities: Residential Segregation and Neighborhood Change.* Chicago: Aldine.

Thomas, Brinley. 1954. *Migration and Economic Growth: A Study of Great Britain and the Atlantic Economy.* Cambridge: Cambridge University Press.

Trotter, Joe William. 1985. *Black Milwaukee: The Making of an Industrial Proletariat, 1915–1945.* Urbana: University of Illinois Press.

U.S. National Advisory Commission on Civil Disorders. 1988. *The Kerner Report.* New York: Pantheon Books.

Van Valey, Thomas L., and Wade Clark Roof. 1976. "Measuring Residential Segregation in American Cities: Problems of Intercity Comparison." *Urban Affairs Quarterly* 11: 453–468.

Vernarelli, Michael J. 1986. "Where Should HUD Locate Assisted Housing? The Evolution of Fair Housing Policy." Pp. 214–234 in John M. Goering, ed., *Housing Desegregation and Federal Policy.* Chapel Hill: University of North Carolina Press.

Wade, Richard C. 1971. "Residential Segregation in the Ante-bellum South." Pp. 10–14 in John H. Brace, Jr., August Meier, and Elliot Rudwick, eds., *The Rise of the Ghetto.* Belmont, CA: Wadsworth.

Warner, Sam Bass Jr., and Colin B. Burke. 1968. *Streetcar Suburbs: The Process of Growth in Boston.* Cambridge, MA: Harvard University Press.

White, Michael J. 1980. *Urban Renewal and the Residential Structure of the City.* Chicago: Community and Family Studies Center.

Wilson, William Julius. 1987. *The Truly Disadvantaged: The Inner City, the Underclass, and Public Policy.* Chicago: University of Chicago Press.

———. 1996. *When Work Disappears: The World of the New Urban Poor.* New York: Knopf.

Wirth, Louis. 1928. *The Ghetto.* Chicago: University of Chicago Press.

Woodward, C. Vann. 2001. *The Strange Career of Jim Crow.* New York: Oxford University Press.

Yinger, John. 1993. *Closed Doors, Opportunities Lost: The Continuing Costs of Housing Discrimination.* New York: Russell Sage.

Zuberi, Tukufu. 2003. *Thicker than Blood: How Racial Statistics Lie.* Minneapolis: University of Minnesota Press.

Zunz, Olivier. 1982. *The Changing Face of Inequality: Urbanization, Industrial Development, and Immigrants in Detroit, 1880–1920.* Chicago: University of Chicago Press.

CHAPTER 3

From Credit Denial to Predatory Lending: The Challenge of Sustaining Minority Homeownership

KATHLEEN C. ENGEL AND PATRICIA A. MCCOY

Homeownership is the main vehicle for accumulating wealth for most Americans.[1] In the past, legally sanctioned discrimination impeded minorities' efforts to purchase homes. Such discrimination, while illegal today, is far from eradicated. Indeed, discrimination in lending continues in the form of credit denials and excessive interest rates and fees. As a result, people of color still do not have the same opportunities as whites to own homes and build wealth. In recent years the federal government has successfully implemented policies designed to increase minority homeownership. However, lenders have undermined these hard-won gains by making home purchase and refinance loans with predatory features to people of color.[2] Soaring interest payments on loans now imperil homeownership among black, Hispanic, and Native American households.

Abusive lenders exploit inequalities resulting from past discrimination to target people of color with predatory loans. Generations of inadequate schools and exclusion from the financial mainstream have made it difficult for many minority households to acquire the financial knowledge and awareness they need to protect themselves from unfair lenders.[3] At the same time, persistent lending discrimination has prevented minorities from attaining the financial milestones they need to qualify for low-cost loans. Finally, lingering vestiges of spatial discrimination, including the absence of low-cost lenders and the rise of fringe financial services providers in predominantly minority neighborhoods, result in minority consumers being disproportionately served by unscrupulous lenders.

It is not enough for minority families to attain homeownership if they are overcharged for mortgages and ultimately forced to default on their loans. This chapter argues that sustaining homeownership for minorities is just as important as attaining homes in the first place. In the first section, we describe homeownership among people of color and its value in helping minorities build wealth and financial security. The second section describes how the home mortgage market evolved from one dominated by credit discrimination and shortages to one that freely grants credit. In the same section we also explain how changes in the lending market fostered predatory lending and the concentration of predatory lending in communities of color. In the third section we describe how predatory lending impairs minority borrowers' ability to retain their homes and harms their surrounding communities. Finally, in the fourth section we propose policies to make minority homeownership sustainable.

Minority Home Ownership: Acquisition and Retention

The Value of Homeownership

For people of color, their homes are their most important asset and vehicle for accumulating wealth.[4] This makes sense for several reasons. Almost every household has to pay for housing, in the form of either rent or mortgage payments. By trading mortgage payments for rent, people can invest in assets that are likely to appreciate. In addition, no other investment allows a household to leverage a small investment as effectively as buying a house. Today it is possible to buy a house with a small down payment or even zero percent down. A family that puts 5 percent down to buy a house will earn a 100 percent return on the investment every time the house appreciates 5 percent.[5] Favorable tax treatment compounds the effects of leveraging because when it comes time to sell a home, up to $250,000 in profit from the sale ($500,000 for married couples) will be excluded from taxation on the sale if the homeowner lived in the home for at least two years.[6]

The wealth effects of this leveraging depend on the movement in a home's value. Homes are like other equity investments: they can rise or fall in value. Whether it is more profitable to own or rent involves chance, because profitability largely depends on whether house prices go up or down while the home is owned.[7] Nonetheless, the aggregate effects of homeownership on wealth for minority households are so impressive that homeownership is worthwhile if accomplished in an affordable and sustainable manner.

Homeownership Initiatives

During the past fifteen years, federal policy makers have expanded home-ownership opportunities for low- and moderate-income people, including millions of people of color. Some of these initiatives are designed to increase the demand for affordable loans. For example, federal policy makers revamped the Federal Housing Administration (FHA) loan guaranty program for low- and moderate-income homebuyers[8] to court minority purchasers. Similarly, the American Dream Downpayment Act of 2003[9] authorizes subsidies to as many as 40,000 lower-income families annually to help defray down payments and closing costs.

Other federal initiatives focus on increasing the private-sector supply of residential mortgages to lower-income homeowners. For instance, in 1992, Congress enacted federal housing goals that require Fannie Mae and Freddie Mac to devote a large percent of their loan purchases to those made to low- and moderate-income home buyers.[10] The Community Reinvestment Act requires federal bank regulators to publicly grade banks and thrifts on their records of lending to low- and moderate-income neighborhoods and to consider those records in deciding whether to approve regulatory applications by individual banks and thrifts.[11]

Homeownership and Wealth among People of Color

In the 1990s, minority homeownership rates began to rise. Between 1994 and 2003 the black homeownership rate rose nearly 15 percent while Hispanic homeownership rose over 13 percent. Together, black and Hispanic homeownership rates grew nearly twice as fast as white homeownership rates over that decade.[12] Despite that progress, a gap persists between white and minority homeownership rates. In 2003, only 48.8 percent of black and 46.7 percent of Hispanic households owned their homes, while 75.4 percent of whites were homeowners. Put differently, the white homeownership rate in 2004 exceeded the black and Hispanic rate by nearly 50 percent.[13]

Just as people of color have lower rates of homeownership, their financial assets are less than those of whites. In 2004, white households had a median net worth of $140,700, more than five times that of nonwhite and Hispanic households (Table 3.1). Similarly, in 2004 the median total assets of white households ($224,500) outstripped those of non-white and Hispanic households ($59,600) by almost four to one.

Substantial percentages of minority households have almost no assets (see Table 3.2). In 2004, minority households were more than five times more likely than whites to have no financial assets (15 versus 2.8 percent) and eight times more likely to have no assets at all (5.6 versus 0.7 percent). These wealth disparities were even worse among black and Hispanic renters, half of whom had almost zero net wealth.[14]

These data are significant to any discussion of home acquisition and retention. Having financial assets—usually cash—is a prerequisite to purchasing a home. Lenders often require down payments and up-front points

TABLE 3.1 Median Household Net Worth and Assets in Dollars, 2004

	Net Worth	Financial Assets	Primary Residence (for Home-owners)	Total Assets
White Non-Hispanic	$140,700	$36,000	$165,000	$224,500
Nonwhite or Hispanic	$24,800	$5,000	$130,000	$59,600

Source: Brian K. Bucks, Arthur B. Kennickell, and Kevin B. Moore, "Recent Changes in U.S. Family Finances: Evidence from the 2001 and 2004 Survey of Consumer Finances," *Federal Reserve Bulletin* (2006): A1–A38, A8, A14, and A23.

Note. The first three columns of figures do not add up to the total median assets reported in the fourth column. This is because the total median assets data reflect the assets of homeowners and non-homeowners.

TABLE 3.2 Households with No Assets in 2004

	No Assets of Any Sort	No Financial Assets such as Bank Account or Retirement Savings	No Nonfinancial Assets such as a Car or Home
White Non-Hispanic	0.7%	2.8%	4.2%
Nonwhites and Hispanics	5.6%	15.0%	16.0%

Source: Brian K. Bucks, Arthur B. Kennickell, and Kevin B. Moore, "Recent Changes in U.S. Family Finances: Evidence from the 2001 and 2004 Survey of Consumer Finances," *Federal Reserve Bulletin* (2006): A13 and A22.

and fees. To the extent that people of color have reduced financial assets, they have less access to the money needed to obtain home purchase loans. Having financial assets can also have an effect on individuals' ability to retain their homes. Borrowers invariably face unanticipated financial shocks, from furnaces that die and roofs that begin leaking to job loss and unexpected healthcare expenditures. For people of color, who are less likely to have adequate financial buffers, such emergencies can ultimately lead them to default on their mortgages and lose their homes.[15]

The Fragility of Minority Homeownership Gains
Strides in minority homeownership rates have proven transitory. Black and Hispanic homeownership rates slipped in the 1980s before reversing course

in the 1990s.[16] More recently, black homeownership rates topped out in 2005 and then began to fall.[17]

If society is serious about closing the wealth gap between white and minority citizens, it must come to grips with the reasons why home-ownership rates among people of color recently surged, only to hit a wall. The answer has to do, in part, with the emergence of the subprime residential mortgage market, which offers high-cost loans designed for people with less than perfect credit histories.

Subprime loans have helped fuel minority homeownership rates; however, they can contain terms that are unfair and burdensome. People of color, who are far more likely than white households to obtain subprime loans, are disproportionately subject to the abuses in the subprime market. As a result, they may pay more for loans than they should, given their credit profiles, and are more likely to have loans on terms that they cannot afford. When borrowers pay high interest rates, especially if their payments exceed what they can reasonably afford, their homes are at risk, particularly when their interest rates are reset or financial emergencies strike.[18]

Emergence of the Subprime Market: From Credit Denial to Abusive Loans

Long-standing Discrimination in the Home Mortgage Market and Responses

Historically, minorities faced significant barriers to obtaining home loans. Until outlawed in 1968, *de jure* discrimination was practiced by private entities and the federal government. Redlining by lenders and insurers, racially restrictive covenants, and discriminatory FHA loans combined to deny minority families needed home loans.[19]

De jure discrimination was not the only force limiting homeownership among people of color during this period. Rigidities in the credit markets also worked to their disadvantage. Up through the 1980s, lenders had limited funds, and the demand for loans exceeded the supply of available money for loans.[20] Because credit was tight and profit margins were low,[21] bankers only granted loans to people they perceived to be the best credit risks, a category that rarely included people of color.

As a consequence, generations of black and Hispanic families could not obtain home loans, with devastating results that persist today. By denying credit to qualified minority applicants, banks and other lenders prevented those applicants from accumulating the wealth that typically accompanies homeownership, thereby perpetuating poverty. Additionally, loan denials bred disillusionment that made minorities suspicious of banks and reluctant to maintain checking and savings accounts. With every discriminatory act and loan denial, banks pushed people of color out of the financial mainstream.

Until the late 1960s there was no federal law prohibiting lending discrimination against minorities. With Martin Luther King's assassination in April 1968, riots exploded in inner-city neighborhoods across the country, prodding Congress into action. Today, there are two federal laws prohibiting discrimination in lending, and comparable laws in every state.

With Title VIII of the Civil Rights Act of 1968 (the Fair Housing Act, FHA), Congress banned discrimination in residential mortgages.[22] Congress later passed the Equal Credit Opportunity Act of 1974 (ECOA),[23] which prohibits discrimination in any aspect of a credit transaction. Both laws proscribe lending discrimination based on race, color, religion, sex, familial status, and national origin. The laws further forbid retaliation against individuals who enforce federal antidiscrimination laws.[24] The FHA also bans credit discrimination based on handicap, while the ECOA separately proscribes lending discrimination based on marital status, age, or receipt of public assistance.[25] Lawsuits by victims of lending discrimination and by state and federal authorities are the enforcement mechanism for both acts.[26]

Although Congress prohibited *de jure* lending discrimination against minorities in Title VIII and the ECOA, those laws have had limited effect. Private plaintiffs have filed relatively few lending discrimination suits and won fewer still. There are various explanations for the paucity of successful lending discrimination claims. Some minorities who are discouraged from applying for loans on prohibited grounds may not know that such discouragement is illegal. Others who apply for loans and are turned down may suspect discrimination but not be able to assemble sufficient proof. That is a particular problem when victims need, but lack access to, the lender's individual loan files to prove they were subject to disparate treatment. Even when victims can surmount these hurdles, the cost of expert testimony can be prohibitive. Finally, damages in lending discrimination cases are often low and subject to limits on punitive damages under Title VIII and on civil penalties under the ECOA. The prospect of low damages discourages lawyers from accepting these cases.[27]

The federal government, which can use its subpoena powers and bank examinations to assemble evidence of suspected discrimination, has successfully pursued fair lending claims. To date, most government efforts have focused on discriminatory denials of credit to people of color, not on claims that lenders are providing credit on discriminatory terms.

In the 1990s the U.S. Department of Justice (DOJ) brought a series of high-profile lawsuits against large and small home mortgage lenders, alleging that they had engaged in a "pattern or practice" of denying people mortgage loans based on race.[28] In 1992 the DOJ filed the first such suit against Decatur Federal Savings and Loan in the Atlanta metropolitan area, four years after the *Atlanta Journal and Constitution* published a Pulitzer Prize-winning exposé of local lending discrimination in a series of articles titled "The Color of Money."[29] Ultimately, Decatur Federal Savings and Loan signed a consent decree agreeing to make 1 million dollars' worth of loans to previously rejected black applicants.[30]

In 1992 the Federal Reserve Bank of Boston conducted a study of discriminatory credit denials by examining home loan approval rates in Boston. After controlling for more than twenty indicators of creditworthiness, they found that black and Hispanic loan applicants were 60 percent more likely than comparably qualified whites to be turned down for loans.[33] These results brought the issue of mortgage redlining to the forefront of policy debates across the country.

Between 1992 and 2000 the DOJ vigorously pursued a series of cases alleging lending discrimination. Some cases were spurred by press reports of loan discrimination. Others stemmed from fair lending examinations by federal banking regulators that were ultimately referred to the DOJ for prosecution. The DOJ had an enviable success rate, settling virtually all of the cases on favorable terms.[31] The Clinton-era Department of Housing and Urban Development (HUD) also successfully prosecuted a number of credit discrimination claims.[32]

Government enforcement is subject to political vagaries, as subsequent events demonstrated. After George W. Bush won the presidential election in 2000, the DOJ prosecuted no new lending discrimination cases.[34] And even under the Clinton administration, staffing limitations and the laborious, costly task of amassing statistical proof for pattern-and-practice cases hampered the DOJ's ability to sue.[35] As a result, the laws prohibiting lending discrimination have had only limited success.

The Transformation of the Residential Loan Market

In the late 1970s the home mortgage market began undergoing unprecedented changes that made it possible for people of color to obtain credit. These changes also created opportunities for lenders to exploit financially inexperienced borrowers. These developments included securitization, a sophisticated technique that taps bond markets to finance residential loans.[36] Securitization helped increase credit to minorities by expanding the supply of credit. At the same time, securitization provided financing to a new breed of marginal nonbank lenders who were willing to serve (and exploit) people who had been historically shut out of the credit market.

In the early 1980s federal deregulation further paved the way for credit to be extended to minorities. In 1980 Congress liberalized the usury laws by removing interest rate caps on first-lien residential mortgages; this opened the door to high-cost subprime loans. Subprime loans are designed for people at increased risk of default. Lenders have not, however, marketed these loans solely to high-risk borrowers. Rather, they have taken advantage of less sophisticated prime-eligible borrowers and saddled them with costly subprime loans.

In 1982 Congress enacted legislation permitting adjustable-rate mortgages, interest-only loans, and balloon clauses. This has allowed lenders to entice cash-strapped borrowers into loans by offering them lower monthly payments on the front end in exchange for onerous payments on the back end that borrowers often cannot afford. These new loan products typically contain a bewildering array of complex terms that few borrowers can adequately evaluate.[37]

Another development, automated underwriting, made it possible to pinpoint credit risks more accurately, which resulted in loan approvals to people who previously could not qualify for loans. Before automated underwriting, underwriters manually analyzed residential loan applications for approval, using their personal experience, intuition, and rigid underwriting conventions such as maximum debt-to-income ratios. Once automated underwriting became available, lenders discovered that traditional underwriting requirements such as a 20 percent down payment, savings equal to two to three months' worth of expenses, stable employment for one to two years, perfect credit histories, stringent debt ratios, and detailed documentation were not essential for prompt repayment. Eventually, automated underwriting gave lenders confidence to offer home loans with low or no down payments, lower points and fees, reduced cash reserve requirements, relaxed debt-to-income ratios, low or no documentation, hybrid interest rates, and liberal employment standards.[38] This underwriting flexibility proved especially important for minorities, many of whom could not qualify for home loans under manual underwriting guidelines.[39]

That said, automated underwriting is not necessarily race blind. In fact, it is possible for lenders to devise underwriting formulas that contain variables that directly or indirectly discriminate against people of color. In this way, automated underwriting can mask discriminatory lending practices.

Taken together, these developments culminated in a sea change for minorities, turning what had been a scarcity into an abundance of credit. In contrast to the small, constrained lending industry of two decades ago, the mortgage market came to enjoy a constant infusion of capital orchestrated by Wall Street firms.[40] These changes made it possible for more people of color to purchase, rehabilitate, and borrow against their homes. At the same time, the new market realities created opportunities for the subprime lending industry to exploit naïve borrowers.

The Subprime Lending Industry

Two decades ago, when subprime lenders surfaced, they were regarded as shady operators. Since then, subprime lenders have gone mainstream, with large national firms entering the subprime market and driving out smaller, local subprime lenders. In the past ten years the identity of the top subprime originators changed almost completely because of acquisitions, exit, and market entry by conventional prime lenders. Of the top ten originators in 1996, only one—Household—remained on the top ten list in 2003. In the process, the makeup of the subprime lending industry tilted away from thinly capitalized independent mortgage companies to mortgage subsidiaries of large national banks and better-capitalized independent lenders with assets of $5 billion or more. The subprime market also became more concentrated. Thus, in 1995 the top twenty-five subprime loan originators controlled 39.3 percent of the market; by 2003 the top twenty-five originators controlled 93.4 percent of the market.[41]

Subprime lenders use three distinct channels for mortgage lending: retail, correspondent, and broker. In retail lending, the lender directly recruits loan applicants and underwrites and funds the loans. A retail lender may sell its loans on the secondary market or hold them in portfolio. In contrast, in correspondent lending a smaller lender known as the correspondent performs the same three functions but immediately sells its loans to a larger wholesale lender at a prenegotiated price.[42]

In the last channel, the brokerage channel, mortgage brokers, typically working with numerous lenders, directly market loan products to potential applicants. Mortgage brokers function free of federal banking regulation[43] and often fall outside the ambit of other federal and state regulatory schemes.[44] This lack of oversight is particularly problematic because the structure for compensating brokers raises serious consumer protection concerns. Mortgage brokers are only compensated for loans made and are paid through upfront fees. As a consequence, brokers have heightened incentives to maximize their profits at the expense of borrowers.[45]

Predatory Lending Practices

The practices that subprime lenders use to exploit borrowers range from loans with per se abusive terms, such as yield-spread premiums, to loans that borrowers cannot reasonably be expected to repay. Even when borrowers can afford loans and the terms are not abusive per se, the loan pricing may not be competitive with loans that are offered to other, comparably qualified applicants. Together, these loan abuses comprise predatory lending. We define predatory lending as a syndrome of abuses that benefit the various actors involved with loan origination to the detriment of borrowers.[46] These abuses fall into six categories.

1. Loans structured to result in seriously disproportionate net harm to
   borrowers. When lenders make subprime loans that are substantially
   likely to result in serious harm to borrowers and their communities,
   those loans are predatory. Such harm can consist of asset-based
   lending, which is the making of loans to borrowers who cannot
   afford the monthly payments but have high equity in their homes
   that could be seized in foreclosure. Similarly, the repeated refinancing of loans at short intervals, designed to allow brokers and lenders
   to extract large fees, is rarely in borrowers' best interests. Pushing
   borrowers to take on more debt than they would otherwise choose,
   steering borrowers to subprime loans when they could obtain prime
   loans, and refinancing low-interest loans at higher rates can also
   cause seriously disproportionate net harm to borrowers.[47]
2. Rent seeking. Many subprime lenders, aware that lower-income and
   minority borrowers are often less savvy about loan transactions,
   charge fees and interest rates that exceed the risk the borrowers
   present. This exertion of market power constitutes rent seeking.
   Examples include steering, double billing for the same services,
   billing for services that were never rendered, and imposing prepayment penalties or points without lowering the interest rate as
   the prime market would do.[48]
3. Loans involving illegal fraud or deception. Predatory lending also
   frequently involves fraud or deception by brokers or lenders. For
   example, brokers or lenders may misrepresent loan terms or make
   promises that they have no intention of keeping, such as assurances
   to refinance in the future on better terms.[49]
4. Other forms of nontransparency that do not amount to fraud.
   Lenders may also withhold information in a manner that falls short
   of fraud but that nevertheless results in unfair loan terms. Foremost
   is the use of price lists (called rate sheets) that inform brokers of
   the interest rates for which borrowers qualify. Brokers and lenders
   keep rate sheets secret from borrowers because they do not want
   borrowers to know the lenders' minimum acceptable loan terms.
   Unwitting borrowers may pay more in interest rates and fees, which
   results in greater profits for the lenders and brokers.[50] While the
   Truth in Lending Act[51] and the Real Estate Settlement Procedures
   Act[52] require certain pricing disclosures, these laws do not compel
   the disclosure of other pricing practices such as rate sheets that
   would be of direct interest to borrowers.[53] This lack of transparency
   is another example of a predatory practice.
5. Loans requiring borrowers to waive meaningful legal redress. Subprime loans typically contain mandatory arbitration clauses that

require borrowers to take any disputes to arbitration and preclude them from participating in class action litigation. These provisions bar borrowers from access to the courts.[54]

6. Servicing abuses. Once loans are consummated and securitized, an entity known as a servicer typically becomes responsible for collecting the loan payments and distributing the proceeds. Some servicers have engaged in abusive servicing practices, including charging unjustified fees, taking actions that push borrowers into default, and employing abusive collection methods.[55]

Predatory lending can have devastating consequences for homeowners because it strips home equity to the benefit of brokers and lenders. Not only do predatory practices increase the cost of credit and put borrowers' homes at risk, but they also reduce the ability of borrowers to escape onerous loans. Victims of predatory lending who have lost their home equity and ruined their credit scores in the process often find it impossible to refinance on more favorable terms.[56] The bulk of subprime loans contain large prepayment penalties[57] that can make refinancing nearly impossible unless lenders refinance the prepayment penalties through new loans—a practice that further depletes borrowers' home equity. For borrowers who cannot meet their loan obligations when balloon payments come due or variable rates rise, a downward spiral is practically inevitable. In such situations, lenders often resurface with new, exploitative offers to refinance. While the new loans may temporarily stave off foreclosure, the lenders take the opportunity to strip out more equity by charging additional fees that are added to the loans' principal. Often, after several such loan flippings, borrowers have spent all of the equity in their homes to pay for back interest and financed fees.[58]

It is difficult to assess the percentage of subprime loans that are predatory. Researchers who have studied foreclosure filings have found that predatory terms pervade loans that have gone into foreclosure.[59] A study by The Reinvestment Fund found that almost half of all subprime loans made in lower-income black neighborhoods in Philadelphia involved loan flipping.[60] A study of subprime first-lien refinance loans that originated in 1999 and subsequently were sold on the secondary market found that nearly 60 percent of those loans had a predatory feature—in the form of either a balloon clause or a prepayment penalty of at least three years or both.[61] Other studies of terms in subprime loans have also found evidence of predatory lending.[62]

Subprime Lenders' Penetration of Minority Neighborhoods

Researchers who have examined geographic lending patterns in recent years have found that subprime lending is concentrated in predominantly minority neighborhoods. A study of seven cities by economists at the Federal

Reserve Board and Wharton found that the likelihood of receiving a subprime home loan increased as the percentage of blacks in a census tract
increased, after controlling for credit risk at the census tract level.[63] A similar
study of ten cities by the National Community Reinvestment Coalition found
that subprime lending rose along with the proportion of black and elderly
residents in a neighborhood, even after holding credit risk and housing stock
characteristics constant at the census tract level.[64] Another study of neighborhoods in the Chicago area found that subprime lending rates in middle-
income neighborhoods varied by race. In predominantly black areas,
subprime refinance loans constituted 48 percent of the lending activity; in
comparable white areas, only 8 percent of loans were subprime.[65] Other
studies have documented similar findings.[66]

Recent research reports on the pricing of subprime loans have concluded
that even when income and/or credit risk are controlled for, people of color
pay more for home loans. A seminal 2000 study found that blacks, Native
Americans, Asians, and Hispanics pay higher rates than whites for home
mortgage loans, even after borrower income, debt, and credit history have
been controlled for. The authors concluded, "[T]he simple observation that
[b]lack home buyers are more likely to obtain more expensive mortgages
than [w]hites with similar credit-risk factors, including location and credit
history, is troubling and merits further investigation."[67]

In 2005 and 2006, Federal Reserve Board economists issued reports echo-
ing the conclusions of other studies finding that black and Hispanic borrowers
pay more for home purchase and refinance loans than their white counterparts.[68] In the 2005 report, the economists concluded that borrower-related
factors were "insufficient to account fully for racial or ethnic differences in
the incidence of higher-priced lending; significant differences remain
unexplained."[69] It is noteworthy that the authors found that prices charged
by particular individual lenders drove much of the observed pricing disparity.
A study by the Center for Responsible Lending (CRL) in 2006 found that black
borrowers were more likely than whites to receive loans with higher interest
rates and prepayment penalties, even after controlling for credit risk. The same
study found that Latino borrowers were more likely than similarly qualified
whites to receive subprime home purchase loans at higher rates.[70]

Researchers have generated the same results using different data sets and
statistical tools. One study of lenders found that blacks and Hispanics were
at least twice as likely to have subprime loans as their white counterparts with
the same incomes.[71] These disparities widened as income increased.[72]
Another study of subprime refinancings found that lower-income blacks had
subprime loans 2.4 times as often as similarly situated whites; among upper-
income homeowners, blacks were three times as likely to end up in the subprime market as whites with comparable incomes.[73] The same study found

that lower-income Hispanics received 1.4 times as many subprime loans as whites with similar incomes. Upper-income Hispanics were 2.2 times as likely to receive subprime loans as upper-income whites.[74] A third study of Chicago borrowers concluded that "[black] and Hispanic borrowers are more likely than white borrowers to get subprime loans at all income levels."[75] As one would expect, the same disparities hold true in reverse when looking at data on prime loans. Thus, the odds of obtaining a prime loan were the same for white borrowers with incomes below 80 percent of the area median and black borrowers with incomes exceeding 120 percent of the area median.[76] These numbers are only getting worse over time. Since the 1990s the percentage of Hispanics and blacks with high-cost loans has been rising while the rate for whites has remained constant.[77]

The evidence that subprime lenders dominate the home mortgage market for minorities accords with evidence that subprime lenders target minority residents.[78] Conversely, the presence of high rates of prime lending in white communities and the low rates of prime loans in predominantly minority communities suggests that prime lenders focus their lending efforts on white borrowers.

When people of color are in the market for home loans, they often do not look beyond subprime lenders and mortgage brokers. One reason is a lingering mistrust of banks. Many continue to deeply mistrust banks, especially if they or family members personally experienced discrimination at the hands of a bank.[79] This legacy of discrimination, combined with past credit denials for legitimate reasons, often deters them from approaching depository institutions for loans.

Convenience and familiarity also explain why many underserved individuals turn to subprime lenders. In lower-income and predominantly minority neighborhoods, subprime lenders and mortgage brokers often accept loan applications at nearby storefront offices. Other subprime lenders and brokers directly solicit borrowers by distributing leaflets, making phone calls, or going door to door.

Practicalities present further impediments to shopping for credit on favorable terms. Unlike many subprime lenders, most bank branches do not have evening hours and may not be easily accessible by public transportation.[80] The physical structure of large banks, which is designed to give depositors confidence in banks' financial stability, can be imposing and intimidating to others.[81] The Internet, which could lead to alternative sources of funding, requires a computer and some knowledge about navigating the Web. Even for computer-savvy loan applicants, if they do not fit neatly within traditional underwriting criteria (for example, some of their income is in cash), they might need to locate a lender who employs manual underwriting techniques. For senior citizens and people with disabilities, these transportation and technological hurdles can be even higher.

For Hispanic consumers, who like blacks are disproportionately more likely to use subprime lenders,[82] language barriers may explain that pattern. Mortgage brokers are more likely than bank loan officers to be bilingual and able to communicate easily with and translate documents for Spanish-speaking customers.[83] Cultural, racial, or neighborhood affinity may also play a role. If the broker or loan officer serving applicants is from the same community, frequents the same institutions, speaks the same language, goes to the same church, or looks like the borrowers, borrowers may believe that the broker or lender will represent their best interests.[84]

Push marketing—that is, marketing that is targeted to people who are not actively shopping for credit—is one more reason why people in lower-income and minority neighborhoods are more likely to end up with subprime loans. In theory, people in lower-income neighborhoods are free to contact multiple lenders or mortgage brokers. In reality, inexperienced consumers frequently are unaware that they are even eligible for credit until a broker or a lender approaches them.[85] In this situation, the instinct is to accept whatever loan terms are offered out of fear that the offer could vanish.[86]

Subprime lenders and brokers are acutely aware that poor schooling and exclusion from the financial mainstream have left many minority consumers unsophisticated about the mortgage process. In a Fannie Mae survey of blacks and Spanish Hispanics (defined as Hispanics who speak primarily Spanish in their homes) in 2003, sizable numbers of those surveyed had misconceptions about the mortgage market, misconceptions that lenders could exploit to their advantage. These misconceptions include:[87]

- that mortgage lenders are required by law to give borrowers the best possible rates on loans (64 percent of blacks and 75 percent of Spanish Hispanics);[88]
- that loan applicants need perfect credit ratings to qualify for a mortgage (43 percent and 78 percent);
- that loan applicants need to have had the same job for five years to qualify for a mortgage (59 percent and 61 percent); and
- that applicants who have not always paid their bills on time or who carry some debt will not qualify for a mortgage (51 percent and 71 percent).

The mistaken belief that brokers and lenders owe borrowers a duty to offer loans on the best possible terms is particularly troubling. It raises the concern that minority consumers will unduly trust lending personnel who have incentives to market loans with inflated terms. Similarly, when borrowers mistakenly believe that their credit or employment histories render them ineligible for loans, they are more likely to jump at the first offer of a loan, regardless of its terms. Opportunities for loan abuses arise if brokers and lenders know that borrowers believe they are ineligible for credit.

Even when loan representatives are not using hard-sell tactics to push borrowers to enter loans, borrowers often do not shop elsewhere for loans on better terms, and with good reason.[89] Even the most sophisticated borrowers cannot make informed comparisons in the subprime market because of the baffling array and complexity of subprime loan terms[90] and the fact that subprime loan terms are not advertised. Unable to understand the complex loan terms, borrowers tend to focus on the amount of the monthly payments at origination rather than the overall cost of credit.[91] Furthermore, even when borrowers grasp subprime loan terms such as adjustable rates, balloon payments, and prepayment penalties, current disclosures make it virtually impossible for them to calculate the cost and effect of those terms.[92]

Lenders and brokers also exploit the fact that most borrowers have psychological blocks that lead them—regardless of wealth—to minimize the possibility of future negative events, such as loan defaults.[93] Such blocks affect practically everyone but have a more serious effect on lower-income borrowers, who have fewer financial resources to call upon if their mis-understanding of loan terms and miscalculation of risk result in default.[94]

Unlike financially unsophisticated subprime borrowers, lenders and brokers know the financial consequences of loan terms and know which terms will yield the greatest profits. This information asymmetry, coupled with built-in incentives to maximize profits by increasing the amount that borrowers pay in fees and interest,[95] explains the penetration of subprime lenders in communities of color.

Banks' Failure to Meet the Needs of Minority Communities

Given the paucity of affordable, prime-rate loans in minority areas, one might expect banks to rush in and seize the competitive advantage. That has not been the case. Instead, as subprime mortgage lenders, payday lenders, and check cashers have eclipsed bank branches in minority neighborhoods, it has become increasingly apparent that banks do not market the financial services that residents need, such as high-quality home loans,[96] free check cashing, inexpensive wire transfers, and short-term, unsecured loans.[97]

Most banks restrict free check cashing to their depositors. To the extent that banks provide unsecured short-term loans, those loans are limited to credit card advances or lines of credit drawn on checking accounts or home equity.[98] These services are often unavailable to people with lower incomes,[99] many of whom are unbanked[100] and do business strictly in the cash economy, cut off from conventional credit.[101] The idea that banks are not serving the needs of consumers is bolstered by evidence that the boom in alternative financial services coincided with a decline in the number of banked households.[102]

Banks and thrifts often find it unpalatable to make home loans in lower-income neighborhoods, partly because many residents pose higher credit risk because of past financial troubles and unverifiable or low incomes. Making loans to those individuals might subject banks to scrutiny by state or federal banking regulators because of safety and soundness concerns.[103] In addition, because many of those borrowers may only qualify for subprime loans, lending to them at subprime rates could expose banks to charges of unfairness. This is especially true if the borrowers default and the banks initiate foreclosure actions.[104] These reputational concerns are heightened in predominantly minority neighborhoods, where high interest rates and loan collections could trigger charges of racial bias.[105]

Even when banks seek to lend to lower-income borrowers, it is difficult for them to compete effectively with subprime lenders. For one thing, credit histories of lower-income loan applicants often fall outside the boilerplate underwriting criteria that banks apply.[106] Manual underwriting is one route around this problem, but banks are ill equipped to engage in this type of individualized underwriting. Banks that do employ manual underwriting may take longer to process applications than subprime mortgage brokers. Borrowers may opt to use a mortgage broker if they hear that bank processing is slower. Another limitation arises if banks cannot readily obtain information on property values. Property sales, which provide information on property values, are less frequent in lower-income neighborhoods. As a result, banks have little sales information on which to assess the quality of the collateral backing mortgage loans.[107] For all of these reasons, mortgage lenders in underserved neighborhoods tend to be nonbank subprime lenders, who are often, but not always, subject to different and more lax regulatory regimes.

High-cost and Predatory Loans Threaten the Stability of Minority Homeownership and Neighborhoods

The emergence of the subprime market helped numerous minority families acquire homes. However, in too many cases, that homeownership proved short-lived. The high debt burden of subprime loans has forced disproportionate numbers of minority homeowners to relinquish their homes and return to renting. Subprime loans also inflict damage on surrounding neighborhoods, in the form of ill-kept homes, foreclosures, and blight.

Abusive Loans Jeopardize the Sustainability of Minority Homeownership and Wealth Accumulation

High-cost loans increase the likelihood that people of color will lose their homes. Foreclosure is one more area in which the minority experience has been worse than that of whites. A study by the Department of Housing and Urban Development (HUD) found that even after a wide array of economic and demographic variables had been controlled for, black households terminated homeownership 30 percent more often than comparable white households.[108] The record was only slightly better for Hispanics.[109] Specifically, the average first-time black homebuyer remained a homeowner for only 9.5 years—versus 16.1 years for the average white—before reverting to renting or moving in with relatives. For the average first-time Hispanic homebuyer, homeownership lasted only 12.5 years.[110]

Why is homeownership more precarious for blacks and Hispanics than for whites? Racial disparities in subprime lending are a leading explanation. As already discussed, black and Hispanic borrowers are substantially more likely to end up with predatory subprime loans, which put them at greater risk of losing their homes. A recent study found that as the initial interest rate on mortgages rose one percentage point, the probability that a household would terminate homeownership rose 16 percent annually thereafter.[111]

Having an adjustable-rate, interest-only, or option-payment mortgage makes matters worse. For the past eight years, adjustable-rate mortgages (ARMs) have been the product of choice for subprime lenders. Four-fifths of subprime loans were ARMs by September 2005. The most widespread innovation has been hybrid ARMs that reset to higher interest rates in two to three years (referred to as 2/28 or 3/27 mortgages). Many of these hybrid ARMs feature low initial teaser rates. Once the introductory period on these loans expires and the rate resets, borrowers can be shocked to find their monthly payments doubling overnight. While, in theory, borrowers could avoid this payment shock by refinancing into a cheaper product before the rate resets, rising interest rates, falling home values, deteriorating credit scores, and stiff prepayment penalties make refinancing impossible for many borrowers. Indeed, so many hybrid ARMs have ended up in foreclosure that critics dub them "exploding mortgages."[112]

The magnitude of this problem can be seen from research showing that even a small rate reset of one percentage point substantially jeopardizes homeownership. Once the rate on an ARM adjusts, each percentage point increase makes it 30 percent more likely that a household will terminate homeownership.[113] Many recent subprime hybrid ARMs with low teaser rates have initial resets of 6 percentage points (600 basis points), which increases the risk of losing one's home by 180 percent.

Subprime ARMs are more prevalent among people of color than whites. A recent study by the Consumer Federation of America found that black and Hispanic borrowers "were more likely ... to prefer [adjustable rate mortgages], but they were less likely to understand the risks." Blacks and Hispanics were also more likely to have option-payment and interest-only mortgages.[114]

The destabilizing effect of high-cost loans on minority homeownership can be seen in the skyrocketing rates of home foreclosure in the United States. By the first quarter of 2007 the percentage of U.S. foreclosure starts had reached its highest level in over fifty years. That quarter alone, 2.43 percent of all subprime mortgages went into foreclosure. The percentage for subprime ARMs that quarter was even higher, equaling 3.23 percent. These numbers only provide a snapshot; the longitudinal numbers are even worse. Historically, in the first five years after origination, 18 to 20 percent of all subprime loans have gone into foreclosure and the number is expected to rise. The subprime foreclosure rate is so high that subprime loans caused a net loss in the number of new homeowners every year from 1998 through 2006.[115]

Subprime mortgages are substantially more likely than prime mortgages to go into foreclosure. A Philadelphia study found that subprime borrowers were six times more likely than prime borrowers to go into foreclosure within two years of origination.[116] In 2006, Harvard's Joint Center for Housing Studies reached the conclusion that default rates for subprime borrowers were seven times those for prime borrowers.[117] The risk of foreclosure becomes worse when borrowers have subprime loans with predatory features. Subprime loans containing terms associated with predatory lending, such as extended prepayment penalties and balloon payments, are 20 to 50 percent more likely to result in foreclosure.[118]

Because people of color disproportionately hold subprime loans, subprime foreclosures are concentrated in minority communities.[119] In recent years, predominantly minority neighborhoods in Cleveland, Chicago, Atlanta, and Philadelphia suffered spikes in foreclosure rates that substantially exceeded foreclosure rates in white neighborhoods.[120] Authors of a study of Chicago neighborhoods found that foreclosures went up as the percentage of black residents in a census tract increased.[121] A 2002 study of one Arizona county concluded that 34.7 percent of the homes in foreclosure were owned by Hispanic borrowers, even though Hispanic borrowers represented only 11.9 percent of the home loans in the county.[122] Among Native Americans, foreclosure rates also appear to be elevated. In one survey, 35 percent of the respondents knew of someone who had lost his or her home because of foreclosure.[123]

When unaffordable loans end up in foreclosure, the affected families almost always lose their most important asset, their homes. For many, losing their home has far-flung consequences. Their children may have to change schools and adjust to new teachers, expectations, and curricula. Because educational attainment is positively correlated with residential stability,[124] the consequences of dislocation can last a lifetime.[125] Parents and children lose important social networks that can give a sense of belonging, and connections to jobs and positive social relationships. Losing one's home and having to relocate can also lead to physical and psychological ill health.[126]

Those homeowners with high-cost loans who manage to keep their homes are not free of financial woes. They may have to delay car or credit card payments, which can damage their credit ratings and thus limit their ability to obtain credit that could help them to refinance onerous loans.[127] Others may have to reduce or eliminate expenditures for food, child care, or health insurance.[128] As these borrowers sink more money into retaining their homes, their families' health may decline, their children's safety may be compromised, and even their ability to maintain employment may be jeopardized if they cannot afford transportation. For people in this situation, there is no buffer in the event of a major financial crisis, such as a job layoff, serious illness, or the need for a new furnace.[129]

One researcher has labeled this progression housing-induced poverty.[130] Minority homeowners have an especially high incidence of housing-induced poverty. In 2000, for example, 45.7 percent of Latino homeowners and 11.6 percent of black homeowners spent 50 percent of their income or more on their home mortgage payments. The same figure for non-Latino white households that year was 6.7 percent. Between the inception of the subprime market in 1990 and 2000, the number of black and Latino homeowners paying more than half of their incomes for housing grew by 39 and 98 percent respectively.[131]

One study on housing-induced poverty asked whether low-income individuals would have amassed more wealth by owning a home or renting and investing the difference. The study found that "low-income home owners who paid rates even two percentage points over prime and did not refinance when interest rates fell would have done better renting far more than half the time for three-, five-, and seven-year-holding periods" in all four cities studied.[132] What makes this finding especially disturbing is that the cheapest A– subprime loans generally cost two percentage points over prime.[133] Borrowers who pay for even costlier B, C, or D grade subprime loans are even worse off. Affordable loans can help eliminate the Hobson's choice between having to rent or losing wealth to subprime loans.

Even when borrowers are able to keep their homes and support their families, if they are paying inflated prices for loans, they have lost opportunities for accumulating wealth.[134] Less money is available to save for college or retirement or to pay down mortgage debt. For those with adjustable-rate mortgages, the opportunities for wealth accumulation decrease as interest rates rise.

The Community Effects of Abusive Lending

Subprime lending also jeopardizes communities. High-cost lending is clustered in predominantly minority urban and inner-ring suburban neighborhoods[135] that are economically vulnerable because of commercial disinvestment, white flight, and outward job migration. When subprime lending boosts default risks in already unstable neighborhoods, it threatens those communities with blight.[136]

Many households in predominantly minority neighborhoods struggle to make their mortgage payments and have difficulty maintaining their homes. As neighborhoods begin to look shabby, local property values fall. When homeowners are so strapped that they default and the holders of their loans foreclose, the values of both the foreclosed homes and nearby homes decline. A recent study of low- and moderate-income neighborhoods in Chicago estimated that homes decline in value between 1.44 and 1.8 percent for each foreclosed home within one-eighth of a mile.[137] Similarly, when property tax delinquencies rise, property values decline. A Cleveland study found that for each 1 percent increase in neighborhood property-tax delinquencies, sales prices fell $778 per home.[138] Although the actual amount of the decline varies from neighborhood to neighborhood, it is indisputable that property values decline in low- and moderate-income neighborhoods when foreclosures and property-tax delinquencies rise.

Mounting foreclosures fuel fears of neighborhood decline and a downward spiral of neighborhood blight and homeowner flight.[139] As abandoned and foreclosed properties multiply, remaining homeowners lose motivation to invest in their properties as they may not be able to recover the costs of any improvements if they sell their homes.[140] Worse yet, homeowners may decide to flee the neighborhood altogether. When this happens, previously owner-occupied housing often becomes rental housing, with the attendant problems. Crime and fires increase as homes go into foreclosure and the proportion of rental units rises,[141] causing residents to feel unsafe and isolated.[142] Neighborhoods become dirty and less desirable to potential homebuyers and businesses.[143]

Cities that for decades invested significant amounts of money combating urban blight and revitalizing neighborhoods not only lose their investments in these communities but also valuable tax revenues as properties depreciate or are abandoned. At the same time, city expenditures for police, fire, and safety go up with increased foreclosures. Cities also bear the cost of demolishing blighted abandoned homes and pursuing tax delinquency foreclosures. Studies calculating the costs to cities of resolving abandoned and foreclosed residential properties find that they range from $430 to $40,000 per home.[144]

As borrowers struggle with unmanageable monthly loan payments or lose their homes, cities may also experience greater demand for social welfare programs. More residents may turn to cities for assistance with heating costs, food, and shelter. The educational system can feel the effect as well. When children lose their homes, they often switch schools, which strains urban school systems that are already strapped for resources.

In sum, lending abuses have serious negative implications for minority homeownership and communities. By targeting blacks, Hispanics, and other minorities with overpriced loans, lenders and brokers undermine home-ownership and revitalization initiatives, and borrowers lose opportunities to build wealth. In the worst situations, borrowers lose their homes to fore-closure, with devastating consequences for the homeowners, their families, and their communities. As the authors of a HUD-sponsored study con-cluded, "just as there is public concern about the gap in homeownership rates between whites and minorities, there should be concern about the gap in the duration of stay in owned homes between whites and minorities."[145]

Making Minority Homeownership Sustainable

As recent research findings make clear, it is not enough to help minority renters buy homes. Society also needs to ensure that homeownership is sustainable. To date, federal homeownership initiatives have focused on improving opportunities for people of color to acquire homes but have paid scant attention to home retention. As climbing default rates and foreclosures testify, ignoring sustainability is shortsighted.

In this final section of the chapter we sketch some initial ideas for tackling the challenge of sustainability. In doing so we seek to achieve two goals: to help future minority homebuyers avoid exploitative loans and provide relief to homeowners who are already saddled with predatory loans.

Making Suitable Loans

As noted, loan terms can determine whether homeowners are able to retain their homes. Homeowners can lose their homes when lenders misrepresent loan terms or borrowers cannot anticipate their future payment obligations because of the complexity of their loans. To prevent these situations from arising requires imposing a duty of suitability on lenders. Previously, we proposed federal legislation that would make it illegal for a subprime broker or lender to make a loan that is unsuitable for a particular borrower. A duty of suitability would put the burden of avoiding abusive lending on brokers and lenders, who are in the best position to avoid unfair lending practices.[146] Originators who violated suitability standards would be liable for loan reformation, damages, attorneys' fees, and cram-downs.

While suitability encompasses a number of standards,[147] above all, suitability means that lenders and brokers should not make loans unless the borrowers can repay them out of current income and have sufficient income left for necessities and emergencies.[148] While this standard is important for all subprime loans, it has special urgency in the case of traditional adjustable-rate, interest-only, and option-payment mortgages, which dominate the subprime market.[149] Payments for principal and interest remain the same over the life of fixed-rate mortgages, but monthly payments on adjustable-rate, interest-only, and option-payment products can, and generally do, go up—often sharply. Too many lenders granted those loans when borrowers could make the initial monthly payments, regardless of their ability to afford the payments once the interest rose. For borrowers who were already financially strapped, this was a recipe for disaster. And for hybrid ARMs with lower teaser rates, the payment shock was so severe that even many financially comfortable borrowers could not afford the payments following reset. Under a suitability rule, lenders would be required to calculate borrowers' ability to make the highest possible monthly loan payments allowed under the loan note. In addition, low-documentation and no-documentation loans need to be prohibited or severely restricted and replaced with a rule requiring lenders to obtain written verification of borrowers' ability to pay. Lenders must also be liable for encouraging—or ignoring—inflated appraisals.[150]

Finally, legislators need to address abuses by brokers more vigorously and ban yield spread premiums. Too many brokers exploit the trust that minority consumers place in them to deliver the best interest rates, while accepting back-door yield spread premiums that drive up the borrowers' cost of loans. Brokers typically lack capital and insurance, which not only makes them judgment-proof but also eliminates any incentive for aggrieved borrowers to sue them. States should eliminate the problem of judgment-proof brokers by requiring insurance or bonding. The law should also prevent brokers who have been "caught" engaging in fraud from reestablishing their businesses in different jurisdictions. A national database on mortgage brokers and any sanctions against them would be a step in that direction. Lastly, prosecutors on the state and federal level need to use their investigatory and prosecutorial powers to pursue brokers that have engaged in fraud. Stopping broker abuse is nothing more than commonsense consumer protection.

Homeownership Counseling

In many minority neighborhoods, nonprofits and government agencies offer independent, prepurchase counseling for people who want to buy homes.

The content, duration, delivery, and quality of that counseling vary enormously. Moreover, prepurchase counseling has its limitations. Counselors generally lack legal training, rarely have the opportunity to review actual loan documents before closing, and are hesitant to recommend or advise against specific lenders. Nevertheless, independent counseling programs can be valuable.

At their best, counseling programs can help people locate suitable loans, improve their credit scores to qualify for cheaper mortgages, accumulate savings, teach borrowers how to budget, match them with subsidized loans, assess their creditworthiness, and inform them how to avoid abusive loans.[151] Likewise, postpurchase counseling can assist homeowners in refinancing to better loans while steering clear of predatory refinance loans. It has been demonstrated that refinancing to a cheaper loan will improve a homeowner's chance of retaining his or her home.[152] Understanding the value of refinancing is particularly important for black and Hispanic borrowers, who are less likely than white borrowers to refinance when interest rates drop.[153]

Making the Prime Market More Accessible by Improving Automated Underwriting

Borrowers maximize their investment in their homes when they obtain the best possible price for credit. Likewise, the lower borrowers' monthly mortgage payments, the greater their financial cushion. In the prime and Alt-A markets, automated underwriting by Fannie Mae and Freddie Mac has substantially increased affordable mortgage loans to people of color.[154] Nevertheless, automated underwriting has limitations that block some creditworthy minority households from obtaining prime credit.[155]

Automated underwriting is only as good as the data that it captures. When evaluating creditworthiness, automated underwriting typically considers an applicant's past use of conventional credit, such as mortgages and credit cards.[156] Numerous minority households do not use conventional credit. Instead, they frequent check-cashing agencies and payday lenders that almost never report to credit bureaus.[157] Similarly, standard credit histories do not reflect regular rent payments, utility payments, and overseas remittances that could evince creditworthiness.[158] As a result, up to 54 million Americans have credit histories that are too sparse to score, or no credit histories at all.[159] A disproportionate number of these individuals are minorities and cannot be processed through automated underwriting unless the underwriting has a manual review component that takes into account less conventional evidence of credit history.[160]

In addition, vagaries and gaps in credit reporting can artificially depress credit scores. Normally, creditors have no legal obligation to report prompt payments. When creditors report delinquencies and omit prompt payments, applicants' credit records are skewed and make them appear less qualified.[161] Subprime lenders have increased motivation to report only delinquencies because this impairs borrowers' ability to refinance into cheaper prime loans.

Even for minority households who do use conventional credit, the use of credit scores in automated underwriting can have a disparate effect on their ability to secure the best-priced loans. This is because people of color tend to receive lower relative scores on certain factors that determine credit ratings.[162] For example, the fact that blacks and Hispanics have lower average incomes than whites drives down their credit scores and can make them ineligible for prime loans, but under manual review the same borrowers might be deemed prime eligible. Similarly, credit-rating agencies base credit scores partially on the number of times finance companies have made inquiries about an applicant and the applicant's highest revolving credit limit. Lower-income loan applicants and people of color often receive lower scores on these factors. One study has found that risk assessment models employing those factors are more likely to result in credit denials than manual review systems.[163] To the extent that the factors used in automated underwriting have a disparate effect on people of color, automated underwriting actually contributes to lending discrimination.

Automated underwriting also fails to correct the thick file–thin file syndrome that arises when loan officers coach white applicants more than comparably qualified blacks and Hispanics on how to boost their credit scores with written explanations of delinquencies.[164] A HUD-sponsored study found that mortgage lenders and brokers provided less information about financing options and less coaching to black and Hispanic testers than to white testers, who provided similar information about their finances.[165]

Although automated underwriting has reduced the cost of credit and is race blind, failure to consider certain credit factors, excess emphasis on other factors, failure to report good credit histories, and racially biased coaching of applicants can limit the access people of color have to prime loans. When borrowers then turn to subprime lenders, they may well pay rates that exceed the actual credit risk they present.

Initiatives such as PayRentBuildCredit (PRBC) that collect data on rent and utility payments are a step in the right direction, but they are in their infancy.[166] Progress has been hampered by a lack of standardized data, irregular reporting, state laws prohibiting the disclosure of utility payments, the absence of a central data repository, and weak incentives for landlords and utilities to report payments voluntarily.[167]

In the meantime, lenders could help address deficiencies in automated underwriting by adding pilot projects to their affordable lending programs that take into account regular remittances or prompt rent or utility payments when underwriting loans.[168] Data from those loans could then be used to judge whether prompt payments of this sort accurately predict credit risk.[169] Similarly, mining data from loans rated as somewhat risky but approved by Freddie Mac and Fannie Mae could help assess the default risks among borrowers who do not satisfy traditional underwriting criteria.[170]

Making Subprime Prices Competitive

When borrowers pay too much for loans, the added debt burden puts home-ownership at risk. There is no evidence that subprime loans are accurately priced for risk. To the contrary, many subprime borrowers overpay for loans.

In the prime market, loans with comparable features have similar prices and are based on average pricing—that is, the risk presented by the average prime borrower, not the specific loan applicant in question.[171] Prime prices are roughly comparable, even though many prime borrowers have spots on their credit histories and vary in risk.[172] In contrast, subprime prices vary widely for loans with identical features. In general, B borrowers pay more than A– borrowers for the same loan, while C borrowers pay more than B borrowers, etc.

Because subprime price buckets are often ordered according to risk, the subprime market gives the appearance of risk-based pricing. However, that is not true of risk-based pricing. In theory, risk-based pricing should tailor the price that borrowers pay to the default risk that each individual presents. In subprime there is no such attempt to calibrate prices to the precise risk individuals present. Instead, overpricing is endemic. For example, a study of subprime prices in the A– market found that the loans examined charged a full 100 basis points—1 percent—more on average than the actual risk borrowers presented.[173] Similarly, numerous people who are actually eligible for prime loans are steered to costlier subprime loans.[174] Finally, the persistent pricing gap of over 200 basis points between A and A– loans is incompatible with the smooth pricing curve that one would expect with risk-based pricing.[175]

To tackle the problem of subprime overpricing, policy makers need to proceed on multiple fronts. The lack of price competition in the subprime industry needs to be addressed,[176] as do the lack of true transparency and the ability to comparison-shop.

Any serious effort to increase competition must also grapple with the ill effects of marketing targeted at gullible consumers. One policy solution would be to require loan applicants to obtain quotes from at least two lenders or undergo mandatory independent counseling before closing. Alternatively, lenders could be required to process every home loan application through an independent automated underwriting program, such as Freddie Mac's Loan Prospector or Fannie Mae's Desktop Underwriter, and make loan offers based on borrowers' eligibility under these underwriting standards. Finally, equipping independent housing counselors with Fannie Mae or Freddie Mac automated underwriting systems would help counselors assess whether individuals qualify for prime loans and advise them accordingly.[177]

Helping Minorities Survive Financial Shocks

When minority homeowners terminate homeownership, generally it is because of income shocks (such as unemployment, illness, death, or divorce) or budget shocks (such as unmanageable interest rates on mortgages or spiraling energy, home repair, healthcare, or credit card bills).[178] For low- and moderate-income families, who lack financial cushions, competitive loan pricing alone may not provide adequate resources to permit them to retain their homes when faced with unexpected expenses. Programs ranging from subsidized savings plans and loans for home repairs to affordable insurance against falling house prices[179] and loss of income could provide needed safety nets.[180] Among these programs, subsidized savings plans are of paramount importance. Many minority homeowners, particularly lower-income homeowners, lack sufficient savings to survive financial blows.

In many cases, lower-income homeowners exhaust their meager savings at closing to pay for the closing costs and down payment. Matched savings programs such as Individual Development Accounts (IDAs) can help cash- poor minority families build savings by matching every dollar they save. Today, the federal government's Assets for Independence program and the American Dream Demonstration provide matching funds with support from foundations.[181] Initial research has found IDAs successful in increasing savings, especially for blacks.[182]

However, these programs are not a panacea. IDA programs serve a limited number of families, are not available in every locale, and tend to focus on buying a first home instead of sustaining homeownership. IDA architects have emphasized qualifying for home loans and neglected the continued need for savings once financially stretched individuals become homeowners. Expanding and revamping IDA programs to encourage saving after buying a home could provide a significant boon to sustainability.

In addition, better tax incentives for lower-income homeowners could free up income that owners need for home maintenance and other expenses. Under current federal tax law, lower-income households cannot enjoy the full benefit of the mortgage interest deduction because they are less likely to itemize. Even when they do itemize, the fact that they are taxed at lower marginal rates makes their deductions worth less. Both circumstances reduce the tax advantage of lower-income homeownership.[183] Putting lower-income homeowners on equal tax footing with more affluent homeowners in terms of a tax credit for mortgage interest would boost their financial returns from owning a home.

Make It Easier for Private Plaintiffs to Prove Lending Discrimination

The continued systematic evidence of lending discrimination that academic and government researchers have uncovered contrasts with the paltry record of success private plaintiffs have had in lending discrimination cases. This disparity underscores the need to revamp federal discrimination laws to enable borrowers who have suffered lending discrimination to secure the relief they need, including loan reformation and damages.

Three needed reforms are of the utmost importance. First, it is unconscionable to require injured borrowers to assemble proof of discrimination in advance of discovery when lenders possess the crucial evidence. Lawyers representing victims of lending discrimination face a catch-22. On the one hand, if they assert that a lender engaged in discrimination but do not have the loan files to support such an allegation, they can be in violation of procedural and ethical rules, and subject themselves and their clients to sanctions. On the other hand, if they fail to sufficiently allege lending discrimination in complaints, the cases can be dismissed for failure to state cognizable claims.

Borrowers who suspect they have been victims of discrimination should be able to request that the federal government subpoena the relevant evidence, analyze it, and issue an order for probable cause in support of a private lawsuit for relief if the evidence supports such a claim. Given the federal government's history of complicity in perpetuating lending discrimination, it should take a more active role in reviewing evidence of discrimination and providing victims easier access to the courts.

Second, borrowers who can prove that lenders used a prohibited category such as race or ethnicity as a proxy for lack of creditworthiness should be awarded full relief without further proof of injury. As the law stands now, to recover the full panoply of damages in disparate treatment claims, borrowers must prove that if lenders had not engaged in discrimination, they would have been treated more favorably—that is, not been denied a loan or obtained a loan on better terms. If borrowers cannot adduce this proof, they can, at best, only recover damages for emotional distress and injunctive relief. For example, the court could prohibit the lender from using race as a factor in determining creditworthiness and loan terms. These borrowers cannot obtain damages based on the loan denial or loan terms. Use of race, ethnicity, or any other prohibited category as a proxy for creditworthiness is so repugnant that the law should not countenance that practice by limiting the available relief. Rather, if lenders engage in statistical discrimination, borrowers should be entitled to damages in the principal amount of the loans they sought without having to generate further proof of injury.

Because there are no federal laws or regulations that require lenders to disclose data on applicants' credit profiles, it is difficult for government agencies and researchers to acquire data necessary to study lending discrimination. Federal banking regulators should consider amending the Home Mortgage Disclosure Act and Community Reinvestment Act regulations to require that applicants' credit scores be reported to the federal government.[184] Most lenders retain borrowers' scores from the leading credit-scoring companies. Ideally, the law would require lenders to provide these scores for each applicant from each credit-scoring agency. Making the data publicly available could give rise to privacy issues; however, there are confidentiality rules and statistical tools that the government could employ to make the data available without compromising applicants' privacy. For example, the Census Bureau allows academics and government agencies access to highly confidential census data through Research Data Centers. The census researchers are carefully screened and must comply with rigid confidentiality rules.[185] A similar approach could be taken with lending data.[186]

Conclusion

During the past two decades, opportunities for people of color to purchase homes and obtain mortgage loans have increased exponentially. Changes in the financial market, federal deregulation, antidiscrimination laws, and homeownership initiatives have combined to make this possible. Unfortunately, some of these same forces have fostered abusive lending, which threatens the homeownership gains that minorities have made in recent years. It is imperative that policy makers couple their homeownership agenda with policies aimed at sustaining homeownership.

Acknowledgments

Our thanks go to Corryn Firis, Tom Fitzpatrick, and Jessica Mathewson for their invaluable research assistance. In addition, we are grateful to Jim Carr for inspiring us to think more broadly about challenges in increasing and sustaining minority homeownership.

Notes

1. Joint Center for Housing Studies of Harvard University, *The State of the Nation's Housing 2006*: 19.
2. High interest rate loans are more common in refinancing than home purchase transactions, perhaps because of the federal home purchase programs. Christopher E. Herbert and Eric S. Belsky, *The Homeownership Experience of Low-Income and Minority Families* (HUD Office of Policy Development and Research, February 2006): 36.
3. Consumers who use subprime lenders tend to have lower levels of education. Howard Lax, Michael Manti, Paul Raca, and Peter Zorn, "Subprime Lending: An Investigation of Economic

Efficiency," *Housing Policy Debate* 15 (2004): 533–571, 547; Paul S. Calem, Jonathan E. Hershaff, and Susan M. Wachter, "Neighborhood Patterns of Subprime Lending: Evidence from Disparate Cities," *Housing Policy Debate* 15 (2004): 603–622, 611–618.

4. For whites, home equity represents 39 percent of net worth; for blacks, the number rises to 51 percent. For Hispanics, homeownership accounts for 63 percent of net worth. Eric Belsky and Allegra Calder, "Credit Matters: Low-Income Asset Building Challenges in a Dual Financial Service System," in *Building Assets, Building Credit: Creating Wealth in Low-Income Communities* (Washington, DC: Brookings Institution Press, 2005): 14.

5. Eric S. Belsky and Nicolas P. Retsinas, "New Paths to Building Assets for the Poor," in *Building Assets, Building Credit: Creating Wealth in Low-Income Communities* (Washington, DC: Brookings Institution Press, 2005): 4 n.4.

6. 26 U.S.C. § 121.

7. Eric S. Belsky, Nicolas P. Retsinas, and Mark Duda, "The Financial Returns to Low-Income Homeownership" (Joint Center for Housing Studies of Harvard University Working Paper No. W05-9, Sept. 2005): 15–16.

8. FHA insurance encourages lenders to make loans to underserved borrowers by reimbursing them for most costs associated with default, including the cost of foreclosure and sale, property taxes, maintenance, and accrued interest from the date of default. Terrence M. Clauretie and Mel Jameson, "Interest Rates and the Foreclosure Process: An Agency Problem in FHA Mortgage Insurance," *Journal of Risk and Insurance* 57 (1990): 701, 701–702. Although FHA is committed to lending to minorities, it is facing mounting competition and losing market share to prime and subprime lenders. General Accountability Office, "Federal Housing Administration Modernization Proposals Would Have Program and Budget Implications and Require Continued Improvements in Risk Management" (GAO-07-708 June 2007); Joint Center for Housing Studies of Harvard University, *The State of the Nation's Housing 2006*: 18.

9. Pub. L. No. 108-186, tit. I, § 102, 117 Stat. 2686 (2003) (codified at 42 U.S.C. § 12821).

10. Federal Housing Enterprise Financial Safety and Soundness Act 1992, 12 U.S.C. §§ 4501–4641. These affordable housing goals are established by HUD. Under those goals, for 2005 through 2008, at least 52 percent of all mortgages purchased by Fannie Mae and Freddie Mac must be loans to low- and moderate-income homebuyers. In addition, both of these government-sponsored entities must expand their purchases of mortgages from low-income census tracts. HUD's Joint Goals for the Federal National Mortgage Association (Fannie Mae) and the Federal Home Loan Mortgage Corporation (Freddie Mac) for the Years 2005, 2008 and Amendments to HUD's Regulation of Fannie Mae and Freddie Mac, Final Rule, 69 Fed. Reg. 63580, 63639 (Nov. 2, 2004) (codified at 24 C.F.R. § 81.12(c)(1)).

11. 12 U.S.C. §§ 2902(1)–(3), 2903(a)(2). Examples of such applications include applications for a federal bank or thrift charter, for federal deposit insurance, to open or close a branch, to relocate a home office or branch, to enter into a merger, acquisition or consolidation, to assume another depository institution's liabilities, or to acquire the shares or assets of an insured bank or thrift.

12. In comparison, homeownership by non-Hispanic white households grew by only 7.7 percent between 1994 and 2003. HUD's Joint Goals for the Federal National Mortgage Association (Fannie Mae) and the Federal Home Loan Mortgage Corporation (Freddie Mac) for the Years 2005, 2008 and Amendments to HUD's Regulation of Fannie Mae and Freddie Mac, Final Rule, 69 Fed. Reg. 63580, 63585 (Nov. 2, 2004); Edward M. Gramlich, *America's Second Housing Boom* (Urban Institute, Feb. 2007): 1–3.

13. HUD's Joint Goals for the Federal National Mortgage Association (Fannie Mae) and the Federal Home Loan Mortgage Corporation (Freddie Mac) for the Years 2005, 2008 and Amendments to HUD's Regulation of Fannie Mae and Freddie Mac, Final Rule, 69 Fed. Reg. 63580, 63585 (Nov. 2, 2004); Christopher E. Herbert, Donald R. Haurin, Stuart S. Rosenthal, and Mark Duda, "Homeownership Gaps among Low-Income and Minority Borrowers and Neighborhoods" (HUD Working Paper, March 2005): vii, www.huduser.org/Publications/pdf/HomeownershipGapsAmongLow-IncomeAndMinority.pdf. More recent data on Hispanic homeownership rates estimate that 50 percent of Hispanics own their own homes. HUD, *Improving Homeownership Opportunities for Hispanic Families* (2006): 19, n.11.

14. Christopher E. Herbert *et al.*, "Homeownership Gaps among Low-Income and Minority Borrowers and Neighborhoods" (HUD Working Paper, March 2005): vii, www.huduser.org/

Publications/pdf/HomeownershipGapsAmongLow-IncomeAndMinority.pdf. In 2004, black homeowners had median net wealth of $81,581, versus $1,810 for black renters. That same year, Hispanic homeowners had median net wealth of $86,400, versus $3,100 for Hispanic renters. The comparable figures for whites were substantially higher, at $213,700 for homeowners and $6,200 for renters. Joint Center for Housing Studies of Harvard University, *The State of the Nation's Housing* 2006: 19 and tbl. W-11.

15. Researchers have found that race and ethnicity are stronger predictors of foreclosures than income. Christopher E. Herbert and Eric S. Belsky, *The Homeownership Experience of Low-Income and Minority Families* (HUD Office of Policy Development and Research, Feb. 2006): 48–49. This could be because people of color have fewer assets to rely on during financial hard times.

16. The U.S. Census Bureau reports the following homeownership rates for blacks and Hispanics since 1950:

Year	Black homeownership rate	Hispanic homeownership rate
1950	34.5%	Not reported
1960	Not reported	Not reported
1970	41.6%	43.7%
1980	44.4%	43.4%
1990	43.4%	42.4%
2000	46.3%	45.7%

Source: http://www.census.gov/hhes/www/housing/census/historic/.

17. According to the Census Bureau, black homeownership fell from 49.7 percent in 2004 to 48.8 percent in 2005. Vikas Bajaj and Ron Nixon, "For Minorities, Signs of Trouble in Foreclosures," *New York Times*, Feb. 22, 2006; Joint Center for Housing Studies of Harvard University, *The State of the Nation's Housing 2006*: tbl. A-5.

18. Vikas Bajaj and Ron Nixon, "For Minorities, Signs of Trouble in Foreclosures," *New York Times*, Feb. 22, 2006; Joint Center for Housing Studies of Harvard University, *The State of the Nation's Housing 2006*.

19. Benjamin Howell, "Exploiting Race and Space: Concentrated Subprime Lending as Housing Discrimination," *California Law Review* 94 (2006): 101–147, 107–109.

20. John V. Duca and Stuart S. Rosenthal, "Do Mortgage Rates Vary Based on Household Default Characteristics? Evidence on Rate Sorting and Credit Rationing," *Journal of Real Estate Finance and Economics* 8 (1994): 99–113; Joseph E. Stiglitz and Andrew Weiss, "Credit Rationing in Markets with Imperfect Information," *American Economic Review* 71 (1981): 393–410.

21. Lewis S. Ranieri, "The Origins of Securitization, Sources of Its Growth, and Its Future Potential," in *A Primer on Securitization* (Cambridge, MA: MIT Press, 1996): 31–43.

22. Pub. L. No. 90-284, 82 Stat. 81 (1968) (codified as amended at 42 U.S.C. §§ 3601–3631); Frank Lopez, "Using the Fair Housing Act to Combat Predatory Lending," *Georgetown Journal on Poverty, Law and Policy* 6 (1999): 73–109.

23. Pub. L. No. 93-495, 88 Stat. 1500, 1521–1525 (1974) (codified as amended at 15 U.S.C. §§ 1691–1691f).

24. 15 U.S.C. § 1691(a); 42 U.S.C. §§ 3604(b)–(c), 3605(a), (b)(1), 3617; Patricia A. McCoy, *Banking Law Manual: Federal Regulation of Financial Holding Companies, Banks and Thrifts* § 8.02[2] (LEXIS 2nd ed. 2000).

25. 15 U.S.C. § 1691(a); Patricia A. McCoy, *Banking Law Manual: Federal Regulation of Financial Holding Companies, Banks and Thrifts* § 8.02[1] (LEXIS 2nd ed. 2000). Many states have passed laws that are analogous to FHA and ECOA. Victor M. Goode and Conrad A. Johnson, "Emotional Harm in Housing Discrimination Cases," *Fordham Urban Law Journal* 30 (2003): 1143–1213, 1143.

26. 15 U.S.C. § 1691e; 42 U.S.C. §§ 3612(o), 3613.

27. Kathleen C. Engel, "Moving up the Residential Hierarchy: A New Remedy for an Old Injury Arising from Housing Discrimination," *Washington University Law Quarterly* 77 (1999): 1153–1198, 1188–1191; Patricia A. McCoy, *Banking Law Manual: Federal Regulation of Financial Holding Companies, Banks and Thrifts* § 8.04[2] (LEXIS 2nd ed. 2000).

28. This is a type of intentional discrimination claim that the DOJ can pursue when statistical evidence of disparities gives rise to an inference of intentional discrimination.

29. Bill Dedman, "The Color of Money," *Atlanta Journal-Constitution* (May 1988).
30. Robert G. Schwemm, "Introduction to Mortgage Lending Discrimination Law," *John Marshall Law Review* 28 (1995): 317–332, 322; Anthony D. Taibi, "Banking, Finance, and Community Economic Empowerment: Structural Economic Theory, Procedural Civil Rights, and Substantive Racial Justice," *Harvard Law Review* 107 (1994): 1463–1545.
31. Katharine Fraser, "Fair-Lending Suit Will Cost Tenn. Banking Company $3M," *American Banker* 30 (Sept. 1999): 1–2; Willy E. Rice, "Race, Gender, 'Redlining,' and the Discriminatory Access to Loans, Credit, and Insurance: An Historical and Empirical Analysis of Consumers Who Sued Lenders and Insurers in Federal and State Courts, 1950–1995," *San Diego Law Review* 33 (1996): 583–569; Ali Sartipzadeh, "Justice Department Sues Credit Card Bank for Alleged Discrimination against Hispanics," *BNA Banking Report* 5 (April 1999): 630; Ali Sartipzadeh, "Problems Persist in Sub-Prime Loan Area, Minority Denials Still High, DOJ's Lee Says," *BNA Banking Report* 21 (Sept. 1998): 436; Jaret Seiberg, "U.S. Imposes Record Fine of $9 Million in Bias Case," *American Banker* 11 (Aug. 1997): 1–2; Anthony D. Taibi, "Banking, Finance, and Community Economic Empowerment: Structural Economic Theory, Procedural Civil Rights, and Substantive Racial Justice," *Harvard Law Review* 107 (1994): 1463–1545, 1477 and n.53.
32. Ali Sartipzadeh, "HUD Unveils Huge Mortgage Bias Settlement; Company Takes Issue With Characterization," *BNA Banking Report* 25 (Jan. 1999): 166.
33. Alicia H. Munnell, Geoffrey M. B. Tootell, Lynn E. Browne, and James McEneaney, "Mortgage Lending in Boston: Interpreting HMDA Data," *American Economic Review* 86 (1996): 25–53. For discussion of critiques of the Boston Fed study and subsequent studies confirming its basic findings, see, for example, James H. Carr and Isaac F. Megbolugbe, "The Federal Reserve Bank of Boston Study on Mortgage Lending Revisited," *Journal of Housing Research* 4 (1993): 277–313; Keith N. Hylton and Vincent D. Rougeau, "Lending Discrimination: Economic Theory, Econometric Evidence, and the Community Reinvestment Act," *Georgetown Law Journal* 85 (1996): 237–294, 273–274; Peter P. Swire, "The Persistent Problem of Lending Discrimination: A Law and Economics Analysis," *Texas Law Review* 73 (1995): 787–869, 808–809; and Stephen L. Ross and John Yinger, *The Color of Credit* (Cambridge, MA: MIT Press, 2002): 107–167.
34. www.usdoj.gov/crt/housing/documents/casesummary.htm#alt. Recent exceptions have been *United States v. The Mortgage Super Center, Inc.*, Complaint (D. Ariz., filed Dec. 24, 2004) and *United States v. First National Bank*, Complaint (N.D. Miss., filed Apr. 27, 2006).
35. Robert G. Schwemm, "Introduction to Mortgage Lending Discrimination Law," *John Marshall Law Review* 28 (1995): 317–332, 322–323; Willy Rice, "Race, Gender, 'Redlining,' and the Discriminatory Access to Loans, Credit, and Insurance: An Historical Empirical Analysis of Consumers Who Sued Lenders and Insurers in Federal and State Courts," *San Diego Law Review* 33 (1996): 638–639.
36. Also known as "structured finance," securitization takes pools of residential mortgages, turns the cash flows from each pool into bonds of different maturities that are secured by the underlying mortgages, and sells the bonds to investors. Tamar Frankel, "Securitization (Asset-Backed Securities and Structured Financing)," ch. 4 in *Financial Product Fundamentals: A Guide for Lawyers* (New York: PLI, 1999).
37. Office of Thrift Supervision, Responsible Alternative Mortgage Lending, 65 Fed. Reg. 17,811, 17,812–17,814 (Apr. 5, 2000); Donna S. Harkness, "Predatory Lending Prevention Project: Prescribing a Cure for the Home Equity Loss Ailing the Elderly," *Boston University Public Interest Law Journal* 10 (2000): 1–61.
38. Eric S. Belsky and Nicolas P. Retsinas, "New Paths to Building Assets for the Poor," in *Building Assets, Building Credit: Creating Wealth in Low-Income Communities* 5 (Washington, DC: Brookings Institution Press, 2005).
39. Stuart S. Rosenthal, "Eliminating Credit Barriers to Increase Homeownership: How Far Can We Go?" (Research Institute for Housing America Working Paper No. 01-01, 2001); www.freddiemac.com/sell/factsheets/fm100.htm; Prepared Remarks for Paul Peterson, Former Chief Operating Officer, Freddie Mac, Feb. 27, 2004, www.freddiemac.com/speeches/peterson/pp022704.html.
40. William C. Apgar and Allegra Calder, "The Dual Mortgage Market: The Persistence of Discrimination in Mortgage Lending," in *The Geography of Opportunity: Race and Housing Choice in Metropolitan America* (Washington, DC: Brookings Institution Press, 2005): 101–123, 103–106.

41. Glenn B. Canner and Wayne Passmore, "The Role of Specialized Lenders in Extending Mortgages to Lower-Income and Minority Borrowers," *Federal Reserve Bulletin* 85 (1999): 709, 717–718; *Mortgage Market Statistics Annual,* 2004 (Inside Mortgage Finance Publications, Inc., 2004); "Subprime Residential Lending Volume Leaders Q2 2005," *National Mortgage News,* Sept. 5, 2005, 1 (in the second quarter of 2005, the top twenty-five subprime lenders made $142 billion in subprime residential loans, comprising 76 percent of that market); Elvin K. Wyly, Mona Atia, and Daniel J. Hammel, "Has Mortgage Capital Found an Inner-City Spatial Fix?," *Housing Policy Debate* 15 (2004): 623–685, 652–663.

42. William C. Calder and Allegra Calder, "The Dual Mortgage Market: The Persistence of Discrimination in Mortgage Lending," in *The Geography of Opportunity: Race and Housing Choice in Metropolitan America* (Washington, DC: Brookings Institution Press, 2005): 101–123, 105; Elizabeth Renuart, "An Overview of the Predatory Mortgage Lending Process," *Housing Policy Debate* 15 (2004): 467–502, 470.

43. Dan Immergluck, "Stark Differences: Explosion of the Subprime Industry and Racial Hypersegmentation in Home Equity Lending," *Housing Policy in the New Millennium Conference Proceedings* (HUD, 2001): 235–255, 240; John P. Caskey, *Fringe Banking: Check-Cashing Outlets, Pawnshops, and the Poor* (Russell Sage Foundation, 1994): 10.

44. Lawrence Hansen, "In Brokers We Trust: Mortgage Licensing Statutes Address Predatory Lending," *Journal of Affordable Housing* 14 (2005): 332–364, 338.

45. Kathleen C. Engel and Patricia A. McCoy, "A Tale of Three Markets: The Law and Economics of Predatory Lending," *Texas Law Review* 80 (2002): 1255–1381, 1363–1364.

46. Kathleen C. Engel and Patricia A. McCoy, "A Tale of Three Markets: The Law and Economics of Predatory Lending," *Texas Law Review* 80 (2002): 1255–1381, 1259–1370.

47. Freddie Mac, *Automated Underwriting: Making Mortgage Lending Simpler and Fairer for America's Families* (1996): ch. 5, text accompanying notes 5–6; Howard Lax, Michael Manti, Paul Raca, and Peter Zorn, "Subprime Lending: An Investigation of Economic Efficiency," *Housing Policy Debate* 15 (2004): 533–571, 540–544.

48. Keith S. Ernst, *Borrowers Gain No Interest Rate Benefits from Prepayment Penalties on Subprime Mortgages* (Center for Responsible Lending Research Report, Jan. 2005); Howard Lax, Michael Manti, Paul Raca, and Peter Zorn, "Subprime Lending: An Investigation of Economic Efficiency," *Housing Policy Debate* 15 (2004): 533–571, 547; Mark Shroder, "The Value of the Sunshine Cure: Efficacy of the RESPA Disclosure Strategy" (Working Paper, 2000): 14–15, fig. 2, tbl. 4; Alan M. White, "Risk-Based Mortgage Pricing: Present and Future Research," *Housing Policy Debate* 15 (2004): 503–531.

49. Board of Governors of the Federal Reserve System, *Expanded Interagency Guidance on Subprime Lending* (2001): 19; Department of the Treasury and Department of Housing and Urban Development, *Curbing Predatory Home Mortgage Lending* (2000): 24, 79–90, www.huduser.org/publications/hsgfin/curbing.html.

50. Alan M. White, "Risk-Based Mortgage Pricing: Present and Future Research," *Housing Policy Debate* 15 (2004): 503–531.

51. 15 U.S.C. §§ 1601 et seq.

52. 15 U.S.C. §§ 2601 et seq.

53. Kathleen C. Engel and Patricia A. McCoy, "A Tale of Three Markets: The Law and Economics of Predatory Lending," *Texas Law Review* 80 (2002): 1255–1381, 1305–1307.

54. Shelly Smith, Student Note, "Mandatory Arbitration Clauses in Consumer Contracts: Consumer Protection and the Circumvention of the Judicial System," *DePaul Law Review* 50 (2001): 1191–1251, 1192–1193.

55. Kurt Eggert, "Limiting Abuse and Opportunism by Mortgage Servicers," *Housing Policy Debate* 15 (2004): 753–784, 756–761.

56. ACORN, *Predatory Lending in America* (2004): 7.

57. Depending on the data set and period studied, researchers have found that 40–98 percent of subprime mortgages have prepayment penalties. Less than 2 percent of prime mortgages have prepayment penalties. John Farris and Christopher A. Richardson, "The Geography of Subprime Mortgage Prepayment Penalty Patterns," *Housing Policy Debate* 15 (2004): 687–714, 691; Debbie Gruenstein Bocian and Richard Zhai, *Borrowers in Higher Minority Areas More Likely to Receive Prepayment Penalties on Subprime Loans* (Center for Responsible Lending, 2005): 5.

58. Department of the Treasury and Department of Housing and Urban Development, *Curbing Predatory Home Mortgage Lending* (2000): 74, www.huduser.org/publications/hsgfin/curbing.html.

59. Ellen Schloemer *et al.*, *Losing Ground: Foreclosures in the Subprime Market and Their Cost to Homeowners* (Center for Responsible Lending, 2006); Richard D. Stock, *Predation in the Sub-Prime Lending Market: Montgomery County* (Miami Valley Fair Housing Center, 2001): 7; Lynne Dearborn, "Mortgage Foreclosures and Predatory Lending in St. Clair County, Illinois" (Working Paper, 2003); Steven C. Bourassa, *Predatory Lending in Jefferson County: A Report to the Louisville Urban League* (Louisville Urban League, 2003).

60. The Reinvestment Fund, *Predatory Lending: An Approach to Identify and Understand Predatory Lending* (2004).

61. Roberto G. Quercia, Michael A. Stegman, and Walter R. Davis, "The Impact of Predatory Loan Terms on Subprime Foreclosures: The Special Case of Prepayment Penalties and Balloon Payments" (Working Paper, Jan. 2005): 25, 22–23 and tbls. 4–6.

62. Dan Immergluck and Geoff Smith, "Risky Business: An Econometric Analysis of the Relationship between Subprime Lending and Neighborhood Foreclosures" (Working Paper, 2004).

63. Paul S. Calem, Jonathan E. Hershaff, and Susan M. Wachter, "Neighborhood Patterns of Subprime Lending: Evidence from Disparate Cities," *Housing Policy Debate* 15 (2004): 603–622, 613–615, 619–620.

64. National Community Reinvestment Coalition, "The Broken Credit System: Discrimination and Unequal Access to Affordable Loans by Race and Age" (Working Paper, 2003): 31–34, www.ncrc.org/policy/cra/documents/ncrcdiscrimstudy.pdf.

65. Department of Housing and Urban Development, *Unequal Burden in Chicago: Income and Racial Disparities in Subprime Lending* (2000): 6–7.

66. Jim Campen, *Borrowing Trouble? V: Subprime Mortgage Lending in Greater Boston, 2000–2003* (Massachusetts Community and Banking Council, 2005); Marsha J. Courchane, Brian J. Surette, and Peter M. Zorn, "Subprime Borrowers: Mortgage Transitions and Outcomes," *Journal of Real Estate Finance and Economics* 29 (2004): 365–392, 372–373; Joint Center for Housing Studies of Harvard University, *The State of the Nation's Housing 2006*: 18 and fig. 24; ACORN, *Predatory Lending in America* (2004); Elvin K. Wyly *et al.*, "American Home: Predatory Mortgage Capital and Neighborhood Spaces of Race and Class Exploitation in the United States" (Working Paper, 2005): 1617; Kenneth Harney, "Study Finds Race, Ethnicity Affect Quotes on Mortgages," *Baltimore Sun*, June 17, 2006, 9C; *National Community Reinvestment Coalition v. Allied Home Mortgage Capital Corp.*, Complaint (Dept. of Housing and Urban Development, filed June 14, 2006), www.ncrc.org/pressandpubs/press_releases/documents/2006/HUDComplaint.pdf.

67. Anthony Pennington-Cross, Anthony Yezer, and Joseph Nichols, "Credit Risk and Mortgage Lending: Who Uses Subprime and Why?" (Research Institute for Housing America Working Paper, No. 00-03, 2000): 13, 16.

68. Robert B. Avery, Kenneth P. Brevoort, and Glenn B. Canner, "Higher-Priced Home Lending and the 2005 HMDA Data," *Federal Reserve Bulletin* (2006): A123–A166, A159; Robert B. Avery, Glenn B. Canner, and Robert E. Cook, "New Information Reported under HMDA and Its Application in Fair Lending Enforcement," *Federal Reserve Bulletin* (summer 2005): 344–394, 376–381.

69. Robert B. Avery, Glenn B. Canner, and Robert E. Cook, "New Information Reported under HMDA and Its Application in Fair Lending Enforcement," *Federal Reserve Bulletin* (summer 2005): 344–394, 379. At the Board's request, the private-sector Credit Research Center analyzed loans for a limited set of eight lenders from the Board's larger data set using credit controls provided from a separate lender-created proprietary data set and concluded that some of the differences detected in the analysis of the HMDA data could be explained by borrower characteristics that HMDA did not capture. Ibid., 385–387. For at least two reasons, these findings should be viewed with some skepticism. First, the proprietary data set represents only a handful of large lenders and less than one-quarter of all subprime loans made, raising serious questions about sample bias. More importantly, the owners of the data would not permit independent researchers or even the Federal Reserve Board to evaluate and analyze the data.

70. Debbie Gruenstein Bocian, Keith S. Ernst, and Wei Li, *Unfair Lending: The Effect of Race and Ethnicity on the Price of Subprime Mortgages* (Center for Responsible Lending Research Report, May 31, 2006): 16–19. In a similar vein, two previous studies by the Center for Responsible Lending found that subprime borrowers in predominantly minority neighborhoods had significantly higher odds than subprime borrowers in predominantly white neighborhoods of having prepayment penalties in their loans. John Farris and Christopher A. Richardson, "The Geography of Subprime Mortgage Prepayment Penalty Patterns," *Housing Policy Debate* 15 (2004): 687–714, 708–708; Debbie Gruenstein Bocian and Richard Zhai, *Borrowers in Higher Minority Areas More Likely to Receive Prepayment Penalties on Subprime Loans* (Center for Responsible Lending, 2005): 6.

71. California Reinvestment Coalition, *Who Really Gets Home Loans? Year Eleven* (2005): 11.

72. California Reinvestment Coalition, *Who Really Gets Home Loans? Year Eleven* (2005): 12.

73. Calvin Bradford, *Risk or Race? Racial Disparities in the Subprime Refinance Market* (Center for Community Change, 2002): 8.

74. Calvin Bradford, *Risk or Race? Racial Disparities in the Subprime Refinance Market* (Center for Community Change, 2002): 8; *Homeownership and Wealth Building Impeded* (National Community Reinvestment Coalition, April 2006).

75. Woodstock Institute, *Reinvestment Alert: New Mortgage Pricing Data Sheds Light on Subprime Market* (2005): 2.

76. William C. Apgar and Allegra Calder, "The Dual Mortgage Market: The Persistence of Discrimination in Mortgage Lending," in *The Geography of Opportunity: Race and Housing Choice in Metropolitan America* (Washington, DC: Brookings Institution Press, 2005): 101–123, 110.

77. Christopher E. Herbert and Eric S. Belsky, *The Homeownership Experience of Low-Income and Minority Families* (HUD Office of Policy Development and Research, Feb. 2006): 34–35.

78. William C. Apgar and Allegra Calder, "The Dual Mortgage Market: The Persistence of Discrimination in Mortgage Lending," in *The Geography of Opportunity: Race and Housing Choice in Metropolitan America* (Washington, DC: Brookings Institution Press, 2005): 101–123, 109–111; Dan Immergluck, "Stark Differences: Explosion of the Subprime Industry and Racial Hypersegmentation in Home Equity Lending," *Housing Policy in the New Millennium Conference Proceedings* (HUD, 2001): 235–255, 250–251; Daniel Immergluck and Marti Wiles, *Two Steps Back: The Dual Mortgage Market, Predatory Lending, and the Undoing of Community Development* (Woodstock Institute, 1999): 40.

79. Keith N. Hylton and Vincent D. Rougeau, "Lending Discrimination: Economic Theory, Econometric Evidence, and the Community Reinvestment Act," *Georgetown Law Journal* 85 (1996): 237–294, 258; Anthony Pennington-Cross, Anthony Yezer, and Joseph Nichols, *Credit Risk and Mortgage Lending: Who Uses Subprime and Why?* (Research Institute for Housing America Working Paper, No. 00-03, 2000): 16.

80. There is conflicting evidence whether bank hours and locations explain why people fail to obtain checking accounts. Jeanne M. Hogarth and Kevin H. O'Donnell, "Banking Relationships of Lower-Income Families and the Governmental Trend toward Electronic Payment," *Federal Reserve Bulletin* (1999): 459–473; Christopher Berry, "To Bank or Not to Bank? A Survey of Low-Income Households" (Working Paper, 2004): 89; John P. Caskey, *Fringe Banking: Check-Cashing Outlets, Pawnshops, and the Poor* (Russell Sage Foundation, 1994). Even if accessibility does not deter people from obtaining checking accounts, it could be a factor impeding people from seeking mortgage loans from banks.

81. Robert E. Litan et al., *The Community Reinvestment Act after Financial Modernization: A Baseline Report* (U.S. Dept. of the Treasury, 2000): 18–19.

82. William H. Greene, Sherrie L.W. Rhine, and Maude Toussaint-Comeau, "The Importance of Check-Cashing Businesses to the Unbanked: Racial/Ethnic Differences" (Working Paper, 2003): 14; Ana M. Aizcorbe, Arthur B. Kennickell, and Kevin B. Moore, "Recent Changes in U.S. Family Finances: Evidence from the 1998 and 2001 Survey of Consumer Finances," *Federal Reserve Bulletin* (Jan. 2003): 1–32, 10.

83. Janis Bowdler, *Jeopardizing Hispanic Homeownership: Predatory Practices in the Homebuying Market* (National Council of La Raza, 2005): 6; John Leland and Tom Zeller, "Mortgage Suit Says 'Trust Us' Led to Fleecing," *New York Times*, Sept. 28, 2006.

84. Janis Bowdler, *Jeopardizing Hispanic Homeownership: Predatory Practices in the Homebuying Market* (National Council of La Raza, 2005): 12; Kyle Smith, *Predatory Lending in Native American Communities* (Native Assets Research Center, 2003): 6.

85. Department of the Treasury and Department of Housing and Urban Development, *Curbing Predatory Home Mortgage Lending* (2000): 18, www.huduser.org/publications/hsgfin/curbing.html. An AARP study found that over half of older borrowers who refinanced loans through mortgage brokers did not initiate their loans; rather, the brokers approached the borrowers. Kellie Kim-Sung and Sharon Hermanson, *Experiences of Older Refinance Mortgage Loan Borrowers: Broker- and Lender-Originated Loans* (AARP, 2003).

86. Kathleen C. Engel and Patricia A. McCoy, "A Tale of Three Markets: The Law and Economics of Predatory Lending," *Texas Law Review* 80 (2002): 1255–1381, 1297–1298; Department of the Treasury and Department of Housing and Urban Development, *Curbing Predatory Home Mortgage Lending* (2000): 79, www.huduser.org/publications/hsgfin/curbing.html.

87. Fannie Mae, *Understanding America's Homeownership Gaps*, Fannie Mae National Housing Survey (2003): 7.

88. Except in rare circumstances, currently there is no legal requirement that subprime lenders lend to prime-eligible borrowers at prime rates. Eric Belsky and Allegra Calder, "Credit Matters: Low-Income Asset Building Challenges in a Dual Financial Service System," in *Building Assets, Building Credit: Creating Wealth in Low-Income Communities* (Washington, DC: Brookings Institution Press, 2005).

89. Eric Belsky and Allegra Calder, "Credit Matters: Low-Income Asset Building Challenges in a Dual Financial Service System," in *Building Assets, Building Credit: Creating Wealth in Low-Income Communities* (Washington, DC: Brookings Institution Press, 2005); American Association of Retired Persons, *AARP Consumer Home Equity/Home Improvement Lending Survey* (2000): 4; Richard Hynes and Eric A. Posner, "The Law and Economics of Consumer Finance" (Working Paper, 2001): 6; Howard Lax, Michael Manti, Paul Raca, and Peter Zorn, "Subprime Lending: An Investigation of Economic Efficiency," *Housing Policy Debate* 15 (2004): 533–571, 552; Marsha J. Courchane, Brian J. Surette, and Peter M. Zorn, "Subprime Borrowers: Mortgage Transitions and Outcomes," *Journal of Real Estate Finance and Economics* 29 (2004): 365–392, 372.

90. William C. Apgar and Allegra Calder, "The Dual Mortgage Market: The Persistence of Discrimination in Mortgage Lending," in *The Geography of Opportunity: Race and Housing Choice in Metropolitan America* (Washington, DC: Brookings Institution Press, 2005): 101–123, 103–106; Brian Bucks and Karen Pence, "Do Homeowners Know Their House Values and Mortgage Terms?" (Federal Reserve Board, Jan. 2006): 19, papers.ssrn.com/sol3/papers.cfm?abstract_id=899152; Allen J. Fishbein and Patrick Woodall, *Exotic or Toxic? An Examination of the Non-Traditional Mortgage Market for Consumers and Lenders* (Consumer Federation of America, May 2006): 10–11, www.consumerfed.org/pdfs/Exotic_Toxic_Mortgage_Report0506.pdf; Alan M. White, "Risk-Based Mortgage Pricing: Present and Future Research," *Housing Policy Debate* 15 (2004): 503–531, 509–512; Department of the Treasury and Department of Housing and Urban Development, *Curbing Predatory Home Mortgage Lending* (2000): 60, www.huduser.org/publications/hsgfin/curbing.html; Ira Goldstein, "Bringing Subprime Mortgages to Market and the Effects on Lower-Income Borrowers" (Working Paper, 2004): 19–20.

91. Susan Block-Lieb and Edward J. Janger, "The Myth of the Rational Borrower: Rationality, Behavioralism and the Misguided Reform of Bankruptcy Law," *Texas Law Review* 84 (2006): 1481–1565, 1539.

92. Government Accounting Office, *Alternative Mortgage Products: Impact on Defaults Remains Unclear, but Disclosure of Risks to Borrowers Could Be Improved* (September 2006): 21–22, 29–30; Patricia A. McCoy, "Rethinking Disclosure in a World of Risk-Based Pricing," *Harvard Journal on Legislation* 44 (2007): 123–166.

93. Patricia A. McCoy, "A Behavioral Analysis of Predatory Lending," *Akron Law Review* 38 (2005): 725–739; Lauren E. Willis, "Decisionmaking and the Limits of Disclosure: The Problem of Predatory Lending," *Maryland Law Review* 65 (2006): 707–840.

94. Rakesh Kochar, *The Wealth of Hispanic Households: 1996–2002* (Pew Hispanic Center, 2004).

95. Kathleen C. Engel and Patricia A. McCoy, "What Does Wall Street Have to Do with Predatory Lending?" *Housing Policy Debate* 15 (2004): 715–751, 737; William C. Apgar and Allegra Calder, "The Dual Mortgage Market: The Persistence of Discrimination in Mortgage Lending," in *The Geography of Opportunity: Race and Housing Choice in Metropolitan America* (Washington, DC: Brookings Institution Press, 2005): 101–123, 102–103.

96. Daniel Immergluck and Marti Wiles, *Two Steps Back: The Dual Mortgage Market, Predatory Lending, and the Undoing of Community Development* (Woodstock Institute, 1999): 41–44.
97. Another explanation for the boom in alternative financial service providers is that banks have been exiting low- and moderate-income neighborhoods. Robert E. Litan *et al.*, *The Community Reinvestment Act after Financial Modernization: A Baseline Report* (U.S. Dept. of the Treasury, 2000): 56–57; John P. Caskey, "Bank Representation in Low-Income and Minority Urban Communities," *Urban Affairs Quarterly* 29 (1994): 617–638, 630–631. Recent studies refute this explanation. Raphael W. Bostic and Glenn B. Canner, "Consolidation in Banking: How Recent Changes Have Affected the Provision of Banking Services," *Neighborworks Journal* 18 (2000): 22–25. At least one author has found, separate from the question of bank exit, that people living in black and Hispanic neighborhoods are less likely to have a nearby bank than people living in white communities. Caskey, "Bank Representation in Low-Income and Minority Urban Communities," 618.
98. John P. Caskey, *The Economics of Payday Lending* (Filene Research Institute, 2002): 26.
99. John P. Caskey, *Fringe Banking: Check-Cashing Outlets, Pawnshops, and the Poor* (Russell Sage Foundation, 1994): 61.
100. By unbanked, we mean not having a savings or checking account. Minority households are significantly more likely than whites to be unbanked. The numbers are telling: in 2001, 32.9 percent of African Americans were unbanked, although African Americans comprised only 12.2 percent of the U.S. population. Likewise, 19.6 percent of Latinos were unbanked, even though Latinos comprised 13.7 percent of the population. Federal Reserve Board, "The Unbanked—Who Are They?," *Capital Connections* 3(2) (spring 2001); Information Policy Institute, "Giving Underserved Consumers Better Access to the Credit System: The Promise of Non-Traditional Data" (Working Paper, July 2005); William H. Greene, Sherrie L.W. Rhine, and Maude Toussaint-Comeau, "The Importance of Check-Cashing Businesses to the Unbanked: Racial/Ethnic Differences," *Review of Economics and Statistics* 88 (2006): 146–157; Ana M. Aizcorbe, Arthur B. Kennickell, and Kevin B. Moore, "Recent Changes in U.S. Family Finances: Evidence from the 1998 and 2001 Survey of Consumer Finances," *Federal Reserve Bulletin* (Jan. 2003): 1–32, 10; Brian K. Bucks, Arthur B. Kennickell, and Kevin B. Moore, "Recent Changes in U.S. Family Finances: Evidence from the 2001 and 2004 Survey of Consumer Finances," *Federal Reserve Bulletin* (2006): A1–A38, A13.
101. Eric Belsky and Allegra Calder, "Credit Matters: Low-Income Asset Building Challenges in a Dual Financial Service System," in *Building Assets, Building Credit: Creating Wealth in Low-Income Communities* (Washington, DC: Brookings Institution Press, 2005).
102. John P. Caskey, *Fringe Banking: Check-Cashing Outlets, Pawnshops, and the Poor* (Russell Sage Foundation, 1994): 84–106.
103. Keith N. Hylton, "Banks and Inner Cities: Market and Regulatory Obstacles to Development Lending," *Yale Journal on Regulation* 17 (2000): 197–251, 200; Robert B. Avery, Glenn B. Canner, and Robert E. Cook, "New Information Reported under HMDA and Its Application in Fair Lending Enforcement," *Federal Reserve Bulletin* (summer 2005): 344–394, 381.
104. Keith N. Hylton and Vincent D. Rougeau, "Lending Discrimination: Economic Theory, Econometric Evidence, and the Community Reinvestment Act," *Georgetown Law Journal* 85 (1996): 237–294, 258. Similar concerns may make banks disinclined to offer short-term loans and other financial services that people on reduced incomes need. John P. Caskey, *The Economics of Payday Lending* (Filene Research Institute, 2002): 42.
105. John V. Duca and Stuart S. Rosenthal, "Do Mortgage Rates Vary Based on Household Default Characteristics? Evidence on Rate Sorting and Credit Rationing," *Journal of Real Estate Finance and Economics* 8 (1994): 99–113.
106. Robert E. Litan *et al.*, *The Community Reinvestment Act after Financial Modernization: A Baseline Report* (U.S. Dept. of the Treasury, 2000): 87–88; Keith N. Hylton, "Banks and Inner Cities: Market and Regulatory Obstacles to Development Lending," *Yale Journal on Regulation* 17 (2000): 197–251, 209–210; Janis Bowdler, *Jeopardizing Hispanic Homeownership: Predatory Practices in the Homebuying Market* (National Council of La Raza, 2005): 7.
107. William W. Lang and Leonard I. Nakamura, "A Model of Redlining," *Journal of Urban Economics* 33 (1993): 223–234; David C. Ling and Susan M. Wachter, "Information Externalities and Home Mortgage Underwriting," *Journal of Urban Economics* 44 (1998): 317–332; Paul S. Calem, "Mortgage Credit Availability in Low- and Moderate-Income Minority Neighborhoods: Are Information Externalities Critical?," *Journal of Real Estate*

Finance and Economics 13 (1996): 71–89; Robert B. Avery, Patricia E. Beeson, and Mark S. Sniderman, "Neighborhood Information and Home Mortgage Lending," *Journal of Urban Economics* 45 (1999): 287–310.

108. Donald R. Haurin and Stuart S. Rosenthal, *The Growth Earnings of Low Income Households and the Sensitivity of Their Homeownership Choices to Economic and Socio-Demographic Shocks* (U.S. Dept. of Housing and Urban Development, April 2005): vi, 16, 19 www.huduser.org/Publications/pdf/EarningsOfLow-IncomeHouseholds.pdf; Donald R. Haurin and Stuart S. Rosenthal, *The Sustainability of Homeownership: Factors Affecting the Duration of Homeownership and Rental Spells* (U.S. Dept. of Housing and Urban Development, Dec. 2004): vii, www.huduser.org/Publications/pdf/homeownsustainability.pdf.

109. Donald R. Haurin and Stuart S. Rosenthal, *The Sustainability of Homeownership: Factors Affecting the Duration of Homeownership and Rental Spells* (U.S. Dept. of Housing and Urban Development, Dec. 2004): vii, www.huduser.org/Publications/pdf/homeownsustainability.pdf.

110. Donald R. Haurin and Stuart S. Rosenthal, *The Sustainability of Homeownership: Factors Affecting the Duration of Homeownership and Rental Spells* (U.S. Dept. of Housing and Urban Development, Dec. 2004): vii, www.huduser.org/Publications/pdf/homeownsustainability.pdf.

111. Donald R. Haurin and Stuart S. Rosenthal, *The Growth Earnings of Low Income Households and the Sensitivity of Their Homeownership Choices to Economic and Socio-Demographic Shocks* (U.S. Dept. of Housing and Urban Development April 2005): vii, www.huduser.org/Publications/pdf/EarningsOfLow-IncomeHouseholds.pdf.

112. Patricia A. McCoy, "Rethinking Disclosure in a World of Risk-Based Pricing," *Harvard Journal on Legislation* 44 (2007): 123–166, 145; Roberto G. Quercia, Michael A. Stegman, and Walter R. Davis, "The Impact of Predatory Loan Terms on Subprime Foreclosures: The Special Case of Prepayment Penalties and Balloon Payments" (Working Paper, Jan. 2005): 23, 29–30; Statement of Michael Calhoun, Testimony before the U.S. Senate Committee on Banking, Housing and Urban Affairs, Subcommittee on Housing, Transportation, and Community Development (June 26, 2007): 4, http://www.responsiblelending.org/policy/testimony/page.jsp?itemID=33152423. For a description of interest-only and option payment (often known as option ARM) mortgages, see Allen J. Fishbein and Patrick Woodall, *Exotic or Toxic? An Examination of the Non-Traditional Mortgage Market for Consumers and Lenders* (Consumer Federation of America, May 2006): 3–9, 10–11, www.consumerfed.org/pdfs/Exotic_Toxic_Mortgage_Report0506.pdf.

113. Donald R. Haurin and Stuart S. Rosenthal, *The Growth Earnings of Low Income Households and the Sensitivity of Their Homeownership Choices to Economic and Socio-Demographic Shocks* (U.S. Dept. of Housing and Urban Development, April 2005): 18, www.huduser.org/Publications/pdf/EarningsOfLow-IncomeHouseholds.pdf; Christopher L. Cagan, *Mortgage Payment Reset: The Rumor and the Reality* (First American Real Estate Solutions, Feb. 8, 2006), www.firstamres.com/pdf/MPR_White_Paper_FINAL.pdf; Allen J. Fishbein and Patrick Woodall, *Exotic or Toxic? An Examination of the Non-Traditional Mortgage Market for Consumers and Lenders* (Consumer Federation of America, May 2006): 10–11, www.consumerfed.org/pdfs/Exotic_Toxic_Mortgage_Report0506.pdf.; Ruth Simon, "Late Payments on Mortgages Rise," *Wall Street Journal*, May 18, 2006: D1.

114. Allen J. Fishbein and Patrick Woodall, *Exotic or Toxic? An Examination of the Non-Traditional Mortgage Market for Consumers and Lenders* (Consumer Federation of America, May 2006): 10–11, 24 (citing Consumer Federation of America, Lower-Income and Minority Consumers More Likely to Prefer and Underestimate the Risks of Adjustable Rates Mortgages (July 2004)), www.consumerfed.org/pdfs/Exotic_Toxic_Mortgage_Report0506.pdf.

115. Christopher L. Cagan, *Mortgage Payment Reset: The Rumor and the Reality* (First American Real Estate Solutions Working Paper, No. 2006), http://www.firstamres.com/pdf/MPR_White_Paper_FINAL.pdf; Center for Responsible Lending, *Subprime Lending: A Net Drain on Homeownership* (CRL Issue Paper, No. 14, March 27, 2007): 2, http://www.responsiblelending.org/pdfs/Net-Drain-in-Home-Ownership.pdf; Dina El Boghdady and Nancy Trejos, "Foreclosure Rate Hits Historic High," *Washington Post*, June 15, 2007; Mortgage Bankers Association, *Delinquencies Decrease in Latest MBA National Delinquency Survey*, June 14, 2007, http://www.mortgagebankers.org/NewsandMedia/PressCenter/55132.htm; Ellen Schloemer, Wei Li, Keith Ernst, and Kathleen Keest, *Losing Ground: Foreclosures in the Subprime Market and Their Cost to Homeowners* (Center for Responsible Lending, Dec. 2006): 15, http://www.mortgagebankers.org/NewsandMedia/PressCenter/55132.htm. See also *Home Insecurity*

2004: Foreclosure Growth in Ohio (Policy Matters Ohio, Aug. 2004); *Predatory Lending in South Central Pennsylvania: A Review of Rising Foreclosure Filings and the Relationship to Predatory Lending* (Acorn Fair Housing, 2003); Steven C. Bourassa, *Predatory Lending in Jefferson County: A Report to the Louisville Urban League* (Louisville Urban League, 2003); Toshiko Nagazumi et al., *Preying on Neighborhoods: Subprime Mortgage Lending and Chicagoland Foreclosures* (National Training and Information Center, 1999); *Monroe County Foreclosure Study and the Commonwealth's Response* (The Reinvestment Fund, 2004).

116. Ira Goldstein, "Bringing Subprime Mortgages to Market and the Effects on Lower-Income Borrowers" (Joint Center for Housing Studies of Harvard University Working Paper, 2004): 14.

117. Joint Center for Housing Studies of Harvard University, *The State of the Nation's Housing 2006*: 18. Other studies have documented high rates of foreclosure among homeowners with subprime home loans. *Home Insecurity 2004: Foreclosure Growth in Ohio* (Policy Matters Ohio, Aug. 2004); *Predatory Lending in South Central Pennsylvania: A Review of Rising Foreclosure Filings and the Relationship to Predatory Lending* (Acorn Fair Housing, 2003); Debbie Gruenstein and Christopher Herbert, *Analyzing Trends in Subprime Originations and Foreclosures: A Case Study of the Boston Metro Area* (Abt Associates, 2000); Paul Bellamy, *The Expanding Role of Subprime Lending in Ohio's Burgeoning Foreclosure Problem* (Coalition on Homelessness and Housing in Ohio, undated); Dan Immergluck and Geoff Smith, *Risky Business: An Econometric Analysis of the Relationship between Subprime Lending and Neighborhood Foreclosures* (Center for Responsible Lending, March 2004); Ken Zimmerman, Elvin Wyly, and Hilary Botein, *Predatory Lending in New Jersey: The Rising Threat to Low-Income Homeowners* (New Jersey Institute for Social Justice, 2002); Toshiko Nagazumi et al., *Preying on Neighborhoods: Subprime Mortgage Lending and Chicagoland Foreclosures* (National Training and Information Center, 1999); Dan Immergluck and Geoff Smith, "Measuring the Effect of Subprime Lending on Neighborhood Foreclosures: Evidence from Chicago," *Urban Affairs Review* 40 (2005): 362–389; Roberto G. Quercia, Michael A. Stegman, and Walter R. Davis, "The Impact of Predatory Loan Terms on Subprime Foreclosures: The Special Case of Prepayment Penalties and Balloon Payments" (Working Paper, Jan. 2005): 25; *Losing the American Dream: A Report on Residential Mortgage Foreclosures and Abusive Lending Practices in Pennsylvania* (Pennsylvania Department of Banking, 2005); Debbie Gruenstein and Christopher Herbert, *Analyzing Trends in Subprime Originations and Foreclosures: A Case Study of the Atlanta Metro Area* (Abt Associates, 2000); Richard Rhey and Ari Posner, *The American Dream Lost: Foreclosures in Pima County, Arizona* (Southwest Fair Housing Council, 2004).

118. Roberto G. Quercia, Michael A. Stegman, and Walter R. Davis, "The Impact of Predatory Loan Terms on Subprime Foreclosures: The Special Case of Prepayment Penalties and Balloon Payments" (Working Paper, Jan. 2005): 25, 27; Morgan J. Rose, "Foreclosures of Subprime Mortgages in Chicago: Analyzing the Role of Predatory Lending Practices" (Office of the Comptroller of the Currency Working Paper No. 2006-1, Aug. 2006): 26–27.

119. *Losing the American Dream: A Report on Residential Mortgage Foreclosures and Abusive Lending Practices in Pennsylvania* (Pennsylvania Department of Banking, 2005): 25.

120. Vikas Bajaj and Ron Nixon, "For Minorities, Signs of Trouble in Foreclosures," *New York Times*, Feb. 22, 2006; Joint Center for Housing Studies of Harvard University, *The State of the Nation's Housing 2006*.

121. Nathan Benefield et al., *The Southwest Foreclosure Project* (Southwest Organizing Project, 2003): 17–18. Foreclosures rates by density of Hispanic residents, in contrast, were negatively correlated.

122. Richard Rhey and Ari Posner, *The American Dream Lost: Foreclosures in Pima County, Arizona* (Southwest Fair Housing Council, 2004): 11.

123. *High Cost Lending on Indian Reservations: Watch Out if You Are Buying a Home* (National American Indian Housing Council and the National Community Reinvestment Coalition, 2003): 6.

124. Daniel Aaronson, "A Note on the Benefits of Homeownership," *Journal of Urban Economics* 47 (2000): 354–384, 356; William M. Rohe, Shannon Van Zandt, and George McCarthy, "The Social Benefits and Costs of Homeownership" (Joint Center for Housing Studies of Harvard University Working Paper, 2001): 20–21.

125. Christopher E. Herbert and Eric S. Belsky, *The Homeownership Experience of Low-Income and Minority Families* (HUD Office of Policy Development and Research, February 2006): 103–106.

126. Christopher E. Herbert and Eric S. Belsky, *The Homeownership Experience of Low-Income and Minority Families* (HUD Office of Policy Development and Research, Feb. 2006): 111–116.

127. Low- and moderate-income borrowers, especially African American and Hispanic home-owners, spend disproportionate amounts of their income meeting their mortgage payment obligations. Using 2000 census data, one study found that 14 percent of African American homeowners and 12 percent of Hispanic homeowners devote at least half their income to paying their mortgage loans. Patrick A. Simmons, *A Tale of Two Cities: Growing Affordability Problems amidst Rising Homeownership for Urban Minorities* (Fannie Mae Foundation, June 2004): 6.

128. Joint Center for Housing Studies of Harvard University, *The State of the Nation's Housing 2006*: 26–27; Kathleen C. Engel, "Do Cities Have Standing? Redressing the Externalities of Predatory Lending," *Connecticut Law Review* (2006): 355–391, 375.

129. *Losing the American Dream: A Report on Residential Mortgage Foreclosures and Abusive Lending Practices in Pennsylvania* (Pennsylvania Department of Banking, 2005): 10–12.

130. Nandinee K. Kutty, "A New Measure of Housing Affordability: Estimates and Analytical Results," *Housing Policy Debate* 16 (2005): 113–142, 127–128, 136–137.

131. Patrick A. Simmons, *A Tale of Two Cities: Growing Affordability Problems amidst Rising Homeownership for Urban Minorities* (Fannie Mae Foundation, June 2004): 5–6 and App. A; Joint Center for Housing Studies of Harvard University, *The State of the Nation's Housing 2006*: 3, 25–26.

132. Eric S. Belsky, Nicolas P. Retsinas, and Mark Duda, "The Financial Returns to Low-Income Homeownership" (Joint Center for Housing Studies of Harvard University Working Paper, No. W05-9, Sept. 2005): 17.

133. Howard Lax, Michael Manti, Paul Raca, and Peter Zorn, "Subprime Lending: An Investigation of Economic Efficiency," *Housing Policy Debate* 15 (2004): 533–571, 567–569; Alan M. White, "Risk-Based Mortgage Pricing: Present and Future Research," *Housing Policy Debate* 15 (2004): 503–531, 512–513.

134. This is true for all financial services. Whenever consumers pay excess rates for credit, their opportunities to move up the wealth ladder decline. John P. Caskey, *Fringe Banking: Check-Cashing Outlets, Pawnshops, and the Poor* (Russell Sage Foundation, 1994): 147.

135. Allen J. Fishbein and Patrick Woodall, *Subprime Cities: Patterns of Geographic Disparity in Subprime Lending* (Consumer Federation of America, 2005): 12; Woodstock Institute, *Reinvestment Alert: New Mortgage Pricing Data Sheds Light on Subprime Market* (2005): 3; Jonathan Hershaff, Susan Wachter, and Karl Russo, "Subprime Lending: Neighborhood Patterns over Time in US Cities" (Working Paper, 2005): 6, papers.ssrn.com/sol3/papers.cfm?abstract_id=920847.

136. Kathe Newman and Elvin K. Wyly, "Geographies of Mortgage Market Segmentation: The Case of Essex County, New Jersey," *Housing Studies* 19 (2004): 53–83, 54.

137. Dan Immergluck and Geoff Smith, "There Goes the Neighborhood: The Effect of Single-Family Mortgage Foreclosures on Property Values" (Working Paper, 2005): 9. A study in Rochester likewise found that foreclosures had a negative impact on home values. *Residential Foreclosure in Rochester, New York* (The Housing Council, 2003): 10.

138. Robert A. Simons, Roberto G. Quercia, and Ivan Maric, "The Value Impact of New Residential Construction and Neighborhood Disinvestment on Residential Sales Price," *Journal of Real Estate Research* 15 (1998): 147–161, 158–159.

139. Remarks by Governor Edward M. Gramlich, Federal Reserve Board Governor, before the Financial Services Roundtable Annual Housing Policy Meeting, Chicago (May 21, 2004).

140. Keith N. Hylton, "Banks and Inner Cities: Market and Regulatory Obstacles to Development Lending," *Yale Journal on Regulation* 17 (2000): 197–251, 219–220; "Homeownership and Its Benefits," HUD Urban Policy Brief No. 2 (2001): 5–6; Edward L. Glaeser and Denise DiPasquale, "Incentives and Social Capital: Are Homeowners Better Citizens?," *Journal of Urban Economics* 45 (1999): 354–384.

141. Gregory D. Squires and Charis E. Kubrin, "Privileged Places: Race, Uneven Development and the Geography of Opportunity in Urban America," *Urban Studies* 42 (2005): 47–68, 54; Dan Immergluck and Geoff Smith, "The Impact of Single-Family Mortgage Foreclosures on Neighborhood Crime," *Housing Studies* 21 (2006): 851–866; William C. Apgar and Mark Duda, *Collateral Damage: The Municipal Impact of Today's Mortgage Foreclosure Boom* (Homeownership Preservation Foundation, 2005): 6; William M. Rohe, Shannon Van Zandt,

and George McCarthy, "The Social Benefits and Costs of Homeownership" (Joint Center for Housing Studies of Harvard University Working Paper, 2001): 14.

142. Alan Mallach, "Bringing Buildings Back: Turning Abandoned Properties into Community Assets" (Working Paper, 2005): 7–8; Dan Immergluck and Geoff Smith, "The Impact of Single-Family Mortgage Foreclosures on Neighborhood Crime," *Housing Studies* 21 (2006): 851–866.

143. Alan Mallach, "Bringing Buildings Back: Turning Abandoned Properties into Community Assets" (Working Paper, 2005): 7–8; William C. Apgar and Mark Duda, *Collateral Damage: The Municipal Impact of Today's Mortgage Foreclosure Boom* (Homeownership Preservation Foundation, 2005): 7.

144. William C. Apgar and Mark Duda, *Collateral Damage: The Municipal Impact of Today's Mortgage Foreclosure Boom* (Homeownership Preservation Foundation, 2005): 10–15; *Cost Effectiveness of Mortgage Foreclosure Prevention* (Family Housing Fund, 1995): 16–17.

145. Donald R. Haurin and Stuart S. Rosenthal, *The Sustainability of Homeownership: Factors Affecting the Duration of Homeownership and Rental Spells* (U.S. Dept. of Housing and Urban Development, 2004): viii; Joint Center for Housing Studies of Harvard University, *The State of the Nation's Housing 2006*: 51.

146. Kathleen C. Engel and Patricia A. McCoy, "A Tale of Three Markets: The Law and Economics of Predatory Lending," *Texas Law Review* 80 (2002): 1255–1381, 1318–1358.

147. Kathleen C. Engel and Patricia A. McCoy, "A Tale of Three Markets: The Law and Economics of Predatory Lending," *Texas Law Review* 80 (2002): 1255–1381, 1343–1344.

148. Michael E. Stone, "What Is Housing Affordability? The Case for the Residual Income Approach," *Housing Policy Debate* 17 (2006): 151–184, 175–178.

149. Joint Center for Housing Studies of Harvard University, *The State of the Nation's Housing 2006*: 1–2, 17.

150. On July 10, 2007, federal banking regulators released a final guidance on subprime mortgage lending that requires subprime loans to be underwritten at the fully indexed rate, assuming a fully amortizing repayment schedule. The guidance also bans no-documentation and low-documentation loans unless mitigating factors clearly minimize the need for direct verification of the borrower's ability to repay. Department of the Treasury *et al.*, Final Guidance—Statement on Subprime Mortgage Lending, 72 Fed. Reg. 37,569 (July 10, 2007). The guidance is a major step in the right direction. However, it has its limitations. The guidance only applies to federally insured depository institutions and their affiliates, and even for those lenders the guidance is not binding. Independent nonbank lenders and mortgage brokers do not need to heed the guidance at all except where their state regulators have adopted the guidance. Finally, the guidance falls short of requiring subprime ARMs to be underwritten to the maximum interest rate. Generally, the fully indexed rate is only the initial reset rate. The interest rate on most ARMs can and often does rise above the fully indexed rate to the maximum interest rate ceiling over the life of the loan.

151. Abdighani Hirad and Peter M. Zorn, "A Little Knowledge Is a Good Thing: Empirical Evidence of the Effectiveness of Pre-Purchase Homeownership Counseling" (Joint Center for Housing Studies of Harvard University Working Paper, No. LIHO-01.4, Aug. 2001): 13–15, www.jchs.harvard.edu/publications/homeownership/liho01-4.pdf; George McCarthy and Roberto Quercia, *Bridging the Gap between Supply and Demand: The Evolution of the Homeownership Education and Counseling Industry* (The Research Institute for Housing America Report 00-01, May 2000); Department of Housing and Urban Development, *Improving Homeownership Opportunities for Hispanic Families* (2006): 80–87; Edward M. Gramlich, *America's Second Housing Boom* (Urban Institute, February 2007): 1–3.

152. Eric S. Belsky, Nicolas P. Retsinas, and Mark Duda, "The Financial Returns to Low-Income Homeownership" (Joint Center for Housing Studies of Harvard University Working Paper, No. W05-9, Sept. 2005): 17.

153. Yongheng Deng and Stuart Gabriel, "Enhancing Mortgage Credit Availability among Underserved and Higher Credit-Risk Populations: An Assessment of Default and Prepayment Option Exercise among FHA-Insured Borrowers" (Working Paper, 2002): 11, 13–14, 17–19 and tbl. 1; Anthony Pennington-Cross, "Credit History and the Performance of Prime and Nonprime Mortgages," *Journal of Real Estate Finance and Economics* 27 (2003): 279, 280–281, 289, 292–294, 296–297, 300; Robert Van Order and Peter M. Zorn, "The Performance of Low-Income and Minority Mortgages: A Tale of Two Options" (Freddie Mac Working Paper,

2001): 23; R. Russell Hurst, "Securities Backed by Closed-End Home Equity Loans," in *The Handbook of Mortgage-Backed Securities* (Frank J. Fabozzi, ed., 5th ed. 2001): 281, 292.

154. Susan Wharton Gates, Vanessa Gail Perry, and Peter M. Zorn, "Automated Underwriting in Mortgage Lending: Good News for the Underserved?," *Housing Policy Debate* 13 (2002): 369–391; Susan Wharton Gates, Cindy Waldron, and Peter Zorn, "Automated Underwriting: Friend or Foe to Low-Mod Households and Neighborhoods?" (Freddie Mac Working Paper, Nov. 2003); John W. Straka, "A Shift in the Mortgage Landscape: The 1990s Move to Automated Credit Evaluations," *Journal of Housing Research* 11 (2000): 207–232.

155. James H. Carr, "Risk-Based Pricing: Automation's Benefits Are Not Automatic," *The NeighborWorks Journal* 17 (summer 1999): 11; Department of Housing and Urban Development, *Improving Homeownership Opportunities for Hispanic Families* (2006): 63–70; Department of Housing and Urban Development, *Review of Selected Underwriting Guidelines to Identify Barriers to Hispanic Homeownership* (2006): 3–6.

156. Eric S. Belsky and Nicolas P. Retsinas, "New Paths to Building Assets for the Poor," in *Building Assets, Building Credit: Creating Wealth in Low-Income Communities* (Washington, DC: Brookings Institution Press, 2005): 1–9.

157. Eric Belsky and Allegra Calder, "Credit Matters: Low-Income Asset Building Challenges in a Dual Financial Service System," in *Building Assets, Building Credit: Creating Wealth in Low-Income Communities* (Washington, DC: Brookings Institution Press, 2005).

158. M. Cary Collins, Keith D. Harvey, and Peter J. Nigro, "The Influence of Bureau Scores, Customized Scores, and Judgmental Review on the Banking Underwriting Decisionmaking Process," *Journal of Real Estate Research* 24 (2002): 129–152; Information Policy Institute, "Giving Underserved Consumers Better Access to the Credit System: The Promise of Non-Traditional Data" (Working Paper, July 2005).

159. Information Policy Institute, "Giving Underserved Consumers Better Access to the Credit System: The Promise of Non-Traditional Data" (Working Paper, July 2005).

160. Federal Reserve Board, "The Unbanked—Who Are They?," *Capital Connections* 3 (spring 2001); Allen J. Fishbein, *Going Subprime: Will Low-Income Homebuyers Gain or Lose when Fannie Mae and Freddie Mac Move into the Subprime Lending Market?* (National Housing Institute, October 2002).

161. Robert B. Avery, Paul S. Calem, and Glenn B. Canner, "An Overview of Consumer Data and Credit Reporting," *Federal Reserve Bulletin* (Feb. 2003): 47–73; Eric Belsky and Allegra Calder, "Credit Matters: Low-Income Asset Building Challenges in a Dual Financial Service System," in *Building Assets, Building Credit: Creating Wealth in Low-Income Communities* (Washington, DC: Brookings Institution Press, 2005).

162. Michael A. Stegman, Roberto G. Quercia, and Jennifer S. Lobenhofer, "Automated Underwriting: Getting to 'Yes' for More Low-Income Applicants" (presented before the 2001 Conference on Housing Opportunity, Research Institute for Housing America, April 2001).

163. M. Cary Collins, Keith D. Harvey, and Peter J. Nigro, "The Influence of Bureau Scores, Customized Scores, and Judgmental Review on the Banking Underwriting Decisionmaking Process," *Journal of Real Estate Research* 24 (2002): 129–152, 108–109.

164. Alicia H. Munnell, Geoffrey M.B. Tootell, Lynn E. Browne, and James McEneaney, "Mortgage Lending in Boston: Interpreting HMDA Data," *American Economic Review* 86 (1996): 25–53; James H. Carr, *Risk-Based Pricing: Are There Fair Lending Implications?* (Fannie Mae Foundation, summer 1999).

165. Margery Austin Turner *et al.*, *All Other Things being Equal: A Paired Testing Study of Mortgage Lending Institutions* (HUD, 2002): 36.

166. Anna Afshar, "Uses of Alternative Credit Data Offers Promise, Raises Issues," *New England Community Developments* (Federal Reserve Bank of Boston 3rd Qtr., 2005): 1–6; Eric Belsky and Allegra Calder, "Credit Matters: Low-Income Asset Building Challenges in a Dual Financial Service System," in *Building Assets, Building Credit: Creating Wealth in Low-Income Communities* (Washington, DC: Brookings Institution Press, 2005); "Renters Can Build Credit," *Shelterforce Online* 125 (Sept./Oct. 2002), www.nhi.org/issues/125/goingsubprime.html.

167. Information Policy Institute, "Giving Underserved Consumers Better Access to the Credit System: The Promise of Non-Traditional Data" (Working Paper, July 2005).

168. A recent HUD study offers additional prescriptions for adapting underwriting standards to increase lending opportunities for consumers who do not fall within conventional

underwriting criteria. Department of Housing and Urban Development, *Improving Homeownership Opportunities for Hispanic Families* (2006): 93–94.

169. Susan W. Gates, Cindy Waldron, and Peter Zorn, "Automated Underwriting: Friend or Foe to Low-Mod Households and Neighborhoods?" (Working Paper, 2003); Prepared Remarks for Paul Peterson, Former Chief Operating Officer, Freddie Mac, Feb. 27, 2004, www.freddie mac.com/speeches/peterson/pp022704.html; Michael A. Stegman, Roberto G. Quercia, and Jennifer S. Lobenhofer, "Automated Underwriting: Getting to 'Yes' for More Low-Income Applicants" (presented before the 2001 Conference on Housing Opportunity, Research Institute for Housing America, April 2001).

170. Prepared Remarks for Paul Peterson, Former Chief Operating Officer, Freddie Mac, Feb. 27, 2004; Michael A. Stegman, Roberto G. Quercia, and Jennifer S. Lobenhofer, "Automated Underwriting: Getting to 'Yes' for More Low-Income Applicants" (presented before the 2001 Conference on Housing Opportunity, Research Institute for Housing America, April 2001).

171. Allen J. Fishbein, "Going Subprime: Will Low-Income Homebuyers Gain or Lose when Fannie Mae and Freddie Mac Move into the Subprime Lending Market?," *Shelterforce Online* 125 (Sept./Oct. 2002), www.nhi.org/issues/125/goingsubprime.html.

172. The Federal Reserve Bank of Boston, for example, concluded that up to 80 percent of home loan applicants had blemished credit records. Alicia H. Munnell, Geoffrey M.B. Tootell, Lynn E. Browne, and James McEneaney, "Mortgage Lending in Boston: Interpreting HMDA Data," *American Economic Review* 86 (1996): 25–53.

173. Howard Lax, Michael Manti, Paul Raca, and Peter Zorn, "Subprime Lending: An Investigation of Economic Efficiency," *Housing Policy Debate* 15 (2004): 533–571.

174. In 1996 a Freddie Mac study determined that up to 35 percent of subprime borrowers actually qualified for prime-rate loans. Freddie Mac, *Automated Underwriting: Making Mortgage Lending Simpler and Fairer for America's Families* (Sept. 1996): ch. 5, www.freddiemac.com/corporate/reports/moseley/mosehome.html; John W. Straka, "A Shift in the Mortgage Landscape: The 1990s Move to Automated Credit Evaluations," *Journal of Housing Research* 11 (2000): 207–232, 222–223; Howard Lax, Michael Manti, Paul Raca, and Peter Zorn, "Subprime Lending: An Investigation of Economic Efficiency," *Housing Policy Debate* 15 (2004): 533–571, 565; Department of Housing and Urban Development, *HUD's Joint Goals for the Federal National Mortgage Association (Fannie Mae) and the Federal Home Loan Mortgage Corporation (Freddie Mac) for the Years 2005, 2008 and Amendments to HUD's Regulation of Fannie Mae and Freddie Mac*, Final Rule, 69 Fed. Reg. 63580, 65053 (Nov. 2, 2004); Diana Henriques and Lowell Bergman, "A Special Report: Profiting from Fine Print with Wall Street's Help," *New York Times*, March 15, 2000, A1.

175. Howard Lax, Michael Manti, Paul Raca, and Peter Zorn, "Subprime Lending: An Investigation of Economic Efficiency," *Housing Policy Debate* 15 (2004): 533–571, 567; Alan M. White, "Risk-Based Mortgage Pricing: Present and Future Research," *Housing Policy Debate* 15 (2004): 503–531.

176. Kathleen C. Engel and Patricia A. McCoy, "A Tale of Three Markets: The Law and Economics of Predatory Lending," *Texas Law Review* 80 (2002): 1255–1381, 1297–1298.

177. Prepared Remarks for Paul Peterson, Former Chief Operating Officer, Freddie Mac, Feb. 27, 2004.

178. Peter J. Elmer and Steven A. Seelig, "Insolvency, Trigger Events, and Consumer Risk Posture in the Theory of Single-Family Mortgage Default," *Journal of Housing Research* 10 (1999): 1–25; Donald R. Haurin and Stuart S. Rosenthal, "The Growth Earnings of Low Income Households and the Sensitivity of Their Homeownership Choices to Economic and Socio-Demographic Shocks" (HUD Working Paper, April 2005): 12–13, 16–19, www.huduser.org/Publications/pdf/EarningsOfLow-IncomeHouseholds.pdf; Donald R. Haurin and Stuart S. Rosenthal, *The Sustainability of Homeownership: Factors Affecting the Duration of Homeownership and Rental Spells* (U.S. Dept. of Housing and Urban Development, 2004): viii; Joint Center for Housing Studies of Harvard University, *The State of the Nation's Housing 2006*: 8–9.

179. William N. Goetzmann *et al.*, "Home Equity Insurance: A Pilot Project" (Working Paper, May 2003).

180. Eric S. Belsky, Nicolas P. Retsinas, and Mark Duda, "The Financial Returns to Low-Income Homeownership" (Joint Center for Housing Studies of Harvard University Working Paper, No. W05-9, Sept. 2005): 18.

181. Center for Community Capitalism, "Financial Institutions and Individual Development Accounts: Results of a National Survey" (Working Paper, Oct. 2003).

182. Ray Boshara, "Individual Development Accounts: Policies to Build Savings and Assets for the Poor," *Brookings Institution Policy Brief* 32 (March 2005): 1–8.

183. Eric S. Belsky, Nicolas P. Retsinas, and Mark Duda, "The Financial Returns to Low-Income Homeownership" (Joint Center for Housing Studies of Harvard University Working Paper, No. W05-9, Sept. 2005): 4–5, 15–16.

184. Department of Housing and Urban Development, *Improving Homeownership Opportunities for Hispanic Families* (2006): 96.

185. 13 U.S.C. § 23; U.S. Census Center for Economic Studies, Research Program, http://www.ces.census.gov/index.php/ces/1.00/researchprogram.

186. Similarly, if banking regulators made their findings in fair lending examinations more transparent, borrowers and the public would have greater access to potential evidence of lending discrimination. For a description of the fair lending exams, see Office of the Comptroller of the Currency, Federal Deposit Insurance Corporation, Federal Reserve Board, Office of Thrift Supervision, and National Credit Union Administration, Interagency Fair Lending Examination Procedures.

CHAPTER 4

Housing and Education: The Inextricable Link

DEBORAH L. MCKOY AND JEFFREY M. VINCENT

Introduction

As researchers begin to explore the impacts of nonschool factors on educational quality and student achievement, evidence suggests that housing issues play a key role. For several decades, metropolitan areas have experienced changes in residential housing patterns. At the same time, the quality of urban public schools has become increasingly problematic, suggesting a possible connection between residential trends and educational quality. However, knowledge about the specific impacts of housing on education remains limited. Most often, planning and redevelopment efforts are undertaken with little consideration for their potential impacts on local schools, while educational reforms and school facility construction rarely relate to broader urban revitalization activities. Government actions often exacerbate the problem, for example, by failing to promote mixed-income and affordable family housing such that both schools and neighborhoods can become more socioeconomically integrated. This chapter seeks to describe several major connections between housing and schools, identify specific school and housing initiatives that have tried to leverage the connections between the two to improve both, and to identify some of the challenges in integrating housing and educational policy, research, and development.

The complex relationship between housing and education—the "housing–schools nexus"—is found across the United States in varying degrees. As increasing evidence reveals that housing values rise and fall with test scores, real estate agents say that the quality of schools is now a central driving force behind the country's most expensive housing markets.[1] As a result, families with the resources to consider the many housing and school options available have been moving into newer suburbs where recent development provides access to higher-quality housing and good schools. Or, if families remain in older neighborhoods, they often opt out of the public system for private or alternative schools. As middle- and high-income families leave for the suburbs, urban neighborhoods deteriorate.[2] Areas of increasing poverty develop, where residents too poor to leave—the majority being black and Latino—send their children to local, poverty-concentrated schools. In addition, the recent National Fair Housing Alliance Study revealed continued racial discrimination against blacks and Latinos in the rental and sales markets, steering families toward neighbors with poverty-concentrated schools.[3]

What does this situation mean for those schools? The departure of middle-income residents erodes the tax base of cities and inner-ring suburbs, leaving them with fewer resources and greater challenges, including aging school buildings, students whose social and educational needs are greater owing to the environment of poverty, and often a rising population of new immigrants with limited English proficiency. As a result, urban and increasingly inner-ring suburban school districts are left to cope with a complex set of issues that they are often ill equipped to handle. As has been repeatedly pointed out, "bad schools and decaying neighborhoods are a familiar and disheartening combination seemingly locked together."[4] One consistent finding in educational research is that socioeconomic conditions largely predict student achievement and that poverty concentration is correlated highly with school and student failure.[5] Despite this evidence, little research has been directed at the question: What impact do residential patterns and housing trends have on education?

Two interrelated trends are particularly noteworthy in understanding the housing–schools nexus. First, on a regional level, decades of metropolitan expansion and demographic change have led to increasing racial and economic segregation in both older neighborhoods and their schools, with a bifurcated public education system of "good" suburban schools and "failing" city schools. However, more recently the situation continues to change; the conventional "city versus suburb" dichotomy is less the case. The proportion of high-poverty census tracts in the suburbs rose from 11 percent in 1980 to 15 percent in 2000.[6] By 2002 about the same number of low-income people lived in suburban cities as lived in central cities.[7] Still, higher-income families continue to move to suburbs farther out. Public schools are feeling this impact. The problems typically associated with urban schools—racial tension, violence, economic disparities, new immigrants—are an increasing reality for some suburban communities.

Second, affordable housing, even in inner cities and first-ring suburbs, is becoming scarce, often because of rising housing costs, new immigration, and/or gentrification. As a result, residential mobility rates often increase for low-income families when they find themselves priced out of the markets where they live.[8] This means that many low-income students move frequently, and the disruption of their academic experience plays a major role in low achievement levels and high dropout rates; the impact is felt not only on their education, but on the experience of their classmates.

The Housing–Schools Nexus

Neighborhoods and School Change

The effects of a half-century of metropolitan expansion and demographic change have been increasing racial and economic segregation, with poverty concentrated in older neighborhoods and their schools. On the housing side of the equation, although more neighborhoods now are considered racially integrated than a decade ago, many communities remain almost exclusively composed of households of one race or ethnicity. Neighborhoods that had black majorities in 1990 were more likely to gain black residents than to become more racially integrated by 2000. More than half of all people living in concentrated poverty are black, and concentrated suburban poverty is increasing. In terms of public schools, a January 2005 report titled *Brown At 50: King's Dream or Plessy's Nightmare* concludes that fifty years after the Supreme Court's *Brown v. Board of Education of Topeka* (1954) ruling made legally sanctioned racial segregation in public schools unconstitutional, "desegregation efforts are largely failing and . . . the nation's public schools are actually re-segregating."[9] Between 1992 and 2002 the number of minority students attending majority-minority schools increased. During the same time, the proportion of minority students attending public schools with white students declined. Thus, by 2000, minorities, particularly Latino and black students, were in schools with substantially fewer white students than was the case in 1990.[10]

Efforts to dismantle segregation were hampered by the Supreme Court's 1974 *Milliken v. Bradley* ruling, which found that suburban districts were not legally mandated to take part in cross-district desegregation efforts. School district boundaries, along with the traditional assignment of students to schools in their neighborhood, are the mechanism by which neighborhood demographics are translated into school demographics.[11] As a result, separate suburban school districts have been created within virtually all metropolitan regions. Homebuyers have access to a wealth of data about public schools; through their housing decisions, they sort themselves into school districts they view as acceptable, and the most commonly researched factors are test scores and racial and economic composition of the student body.[12] Middle- and higher-income households move out of urban districts, where the quality of schools continues to decline, contributing to deteriorating neighborhoods.[13] Since many families, especially middle- and higher-income families, use educational quality as a key factor in choosing where to live, entire communities have developed around demand for high-quality public schools. When the American Planning Association/American Institute of Certified Planners (APA/AICP) 2000 Millennium Survey asked voters in suburbs and small to medium cities what might lead them to live in a more urban setting, better schools ranked first.[14] Also, the 2002 Public Policy Institute of California Statewide Survey on Land Use found schools to be the third most important factor Californians considered in choosing neighborhoods to live in.[15]

Parents who have the resources are willing to pay for better schools by paying more for housing. One study found that parents will pay an additional 2.5 percent in housing costs for a 5 percent increase in test scores at the local public school,[16] whereas another study found that the distinction between an A and a B on a school report card is valued in the housing market at 7 percent.[17] School closures can also impact real estate: the loss of a neighborhood school can reduce home values by nearly 10 percent.[18] Thus, schools and their quality—both real and perceived—greatly impact residential choices and the housing market.

Community and school desegregation efforts are further hampered by discrimination in the real estate market. The National Fair Housing Alliance (NFHA) estimates that at least 3.7 million instances of housing discrimination occur annually against blacks and Latinos in the rental and sales markets.[19] The NFHA study also provides evidence of the education connection, finding that schools are being used as a proxy for the racial or ethnic composition of neighborhoods. Generally, white testers were asked whether they had children, and if they said yes, most agents discussed the importance of schools and selected homes to show them on the basis of schools—schools in districts that were overwhelmingly white. Agents rarely brought up the issue of schools with black and Latino testers who had children. In fact, the white testers were told to avoid the same schools that served the homes selected for black and Latino testers, schools predominantly composed of children of color.

Discriminatory practices like these have a range of consequences for public schools. By 2050, public school enrollment is expected to reach nearly 60 percent nonwhite (from 36 percent in 1996).[20] Between 1992 and 2002 the likelihood increased that black and Latino students would be enrolled in schools with fewer white students.[21] Whereas geographic concentrations of poverty decreased in the past decade,[22] the level of concentrated poverty in public schools grew.[23] Among the public school student population, race and income are closely linked, as are race and the likelihood of being enrolled in a high-poverty school.[24] More than 60 percent of black and Latino students attend high-poverty schools (in which more than half the families are below the poverty line), compared with 30 percent of Asian students and only 18 percent of whites. Most white and Asian students attend schools where less than 30 percent of families are below the poverty line. Additionally, the spectrum of languages spoken constitutes one of the greatest pressures on urban systems. In 1979 only 9 percent of schoolchildren came from homes where English was not spoken, but today around 20 percent of children do so, largely as a result of Latino population increases throughout the country.[25] The share of school-age children with immigrant parents rose from 6 percent in 1970 to nearly 20 percent by 2000.[26]

Schools in low-income communities are left with the difficult and unfair task of overcoming the obstacles of poverty. This places enormous pressure on schools not only to educate children but also to battle symptoms of poverty such as the lack of health care, nutrition, and quality housing for their students. Further, when low-income children are concentrated and isolated, they are denied not only school resources but also connections to social networks that can help them escape poverty by linking to the world of economic and social success.[27] The racial isolation in schools stems from the prevailing history of urban policies and residential preference linked to family income.[28] As one author notes, "What we may actually be seeing is not racial and ethnic separation but economic sorting."[29]

Concentrations of race and poverty found in neighborhoods manifest themselves in schools and classrooms. Richard Rothstein, in *Class and Schools*, argues that because minorities are more likely to be segregated into areas of concentrated poverty,

> their communities usually reflect conditions of distress—housing inadequacy and decay, weak and failing infrastructure, and critical lack of mentors and jobs – all of which adversely affect school resources but also connections to networks that can help them out of the neighborhood of poverty into the world of economic and social success.[30]

As two prominent researchers note, "Socio-economic segregation is a stubborn, multidimensional and deeply important cause of educational inequality."[31]

IMPACTS ON STUDENTS AND FAMILIES

Educational achievement is strongly impacted by the racial and income composition of the student body. Majority-white schools have high graduation rates, whereas schools with large minority and low-income populations tend to have high dropout rates. In 2002, for example, one-third of high schools that were 50 percent or more minority graduated less than half their class, while only 2 percent of schools that were less than 10 percent minority did.[32] Two-thirds of schools that were 90 percent or more minority had a dropout rate of 40 percent or greater.

The average black or Latino student in elementary, middle, or high school currently achieves at about the same level as a white student in the lowest quartile of white achievement.[33] Gains made by black and Latino students from the late 1970s to the late 1980s on national measures eroded in the 1990s. These declines occurred despite aggressive school reform. It is also significant that black students are much less likely than white students to graduate from high school, acquire a college or advanced degree, or earn a living that places them in the middle class.

Living in the poor-quality housing common in low-income urban neighborhoods has numerous costs for families. Research has shown that stable and quality housing can help foster good parenting by providing families with a sense of control, choice, and well-being.[34] Conversely, housing in poor condition, with amenities in constant disrepair, reduces the quality of children's lives and hinders academic development by impeding their ability to learn or develop good study habits. Inadequate heat, lack of air conditioning, inoperable plumbing, or rodent infestation—common conditions in substandard housing—can be disruptive to any learner. Evidence suggests that neighborhood quality has profound effects on student outcomes.[35]

IMPACTS ON TEACHERS AND CLASSROOMS

Teachers and classrooms in communities of concentrated poverty face unequal burdens compared to their counterparts in wealthier areas. One of the greatest discrepancies is access to instructional resources such as multimedia and other technologies. Schools in wealthier communities offer a range of educational resources that help teachers enhance traditional classroom practices. At the other extreme, many high-poverty school districts tend to have older books, out-of-date computers, and other old or failing technology. Higher pupil-to-teacher ratios, which typically result in poorer learning experiences, are often found in these schools. To make matters worse, teachers in high-priced housing markets are often in need of affordable housing for themselves.

Students living in poverty often require the largest amount of school-centered nutrition and healthcare intervention.[36] In the poorest school districts, funds for school nurses and counselors are the first cuts in school budgets, and some students attend even though they are sick, potentially risking the health of their peers and teachers. With little confidence that their students will be able to get support for homework, or even have a quiet place to study, teachers in urban schools often assign less homework than peers in wealthier school districts, leading to significant consequences for academic achievement.

Given all this, it is not surprising that urban school districts often have trouble attracting and retaining quality teachers, negatively impacting student outcomes. In Charlotte, North Carolina, for example, one study found that almost one-third of teachers in high-poverty schools left the profession each year during the early 2000s.[37] Research demonstrates that high-poverty schools have more teachers without credentials and are the first to recruit from alternative teacher preparation and placement programs such as Teach For America. A 2004 U.S. Department of Education report found that schools with 75 percent low-income students had three times as many uncertified, out-of-field teachers in both English and science. In an environment where the challenges are great, the compensation small, and collegial support or collaborative opportunities are rare, constant teacher turnover and increasingly low teacher morale are a consistent problem, one that greatly hinders school stability and consistent school reform.[38]

IMPACTS ON SCHOOLS AND SCHOOL DISTRICTS

For public schools district administrators, changing demographics present complex and intertwined challenges: student populations decline; school funding is reduced; and new demands are placed on basic school operations. Historically, local property taxes have been the major source of funding for public schools, so the relative wealth or poverty of the surrounding community has a direct impact on school funding.[39] State contributions to school district funding are determined by student enrollment and average daily attendance (ADA) calculations, so in communities losing students, state funding decreases and alternatively, where student population is growing, state funding increases.

Dealing with significant changes in budget and population directly affects the day-to-day operation of school districts across metropolitan areas. With fewer resources, high-poverty schools must cut school activities and services such as sports, art, music, healthcare, and security guards. In addition, the federal No Child Left Behind Act provides financial incentives for schools to focus more on test preparation than on elective classes such as art and music. The reduced school curriculum and limited extracurricular activities offered at urban schools are a central concern for many middle-class families seeking a rich and well-rounded education for their children.[40]

Population growth and neighborhood change put additional pressures on school districts in terms of providing adequate school facilities for students. Growth areas look to build schools while areas with student declines often look to close schools. In high-growth communities, housing developers are often charged impact fees for public infrastructure such as school facilities. Additionally, developers will often set aside land for a new school. However, this land often tends to be less than optimal in terms either of development potential or of proximity to adjacent neighborhoods. Districts with declining enrollments look to close schools, but risk losing scarce and expensive land should student populations rebound.

In urban communities undergoing redevelopment, efforts to replace high-density public housing with lower-density mixed-income housing is reducing student population in the lowest-income communities. It is also contributing to gentrification of neighborhoods and further reducing density. In cities such as San Francisco, Washington, DC, New York, and Boston, land values are rapidly rising such that there is demand for public school land for real estate development.

Housing Affordability, Mobility, and Student Achievement

In addition to the demographic shifts discussed above, another trend impacting schools is frequent student transfers due to the lack of affordable housing, even in the inner cities and first-ring suburbs, owing to rising costs, gentrification, and immigration. Steering on the basis of race or ethnicity worsens the affordability problem. According to NFHA, steering inflates the value of homes in certain majority-white school districts and limits demand for homes and schools in minority districts.[41] This artificial manipulation of the market depresses home values, and to compensate, these areas must raise taxes, providing a reason for agents to steer whites away.

Changes in the housing market put pressure on low-income families. A 2000 census study found that 51 percent of the 41.5 million people surveyed in the United States changed residences in 1999.[42] Thirty percent moved for positive housing reasons, such as moving from rental units to homeownership (11.5 percent) or to a new or better home (18.5 percent). However, nearly 10 percent, at least 2.3 million people, moved as a result of negative housing conditions, primarily the need for a better and safer neighborhood or cheaper housing. Overcrowded housing, in poor condition or with health hazards, puts enormous stress on families and can often lead to unplanned or unwanted moves. Moreover, when home prices and rents increase, families may be forced to move frequently. Too often, student mobility results from market forces that push families to poor or poorer neighborhoods and schools.

The issue of student mobility has received increasing attention in both educational and housing research. The *Journal of Negro Education* released a special edition in 2003 titled "Student Mobility: How Some Children Get Left Behind."[43] A growing literature investigates the impact of mobility on educational administration and student achievement. Researchers and practitioners alike agree that school instability is largely a function of residential instability.[44]

Finding an acceptable *and* affordable place to live is becoming difficult for many public school families. In 2000 the U.S. Department of Housing and Urban Development (HUD) reported that an all-time high of about 5.4 million households either live in severely inadequate housing or pay more than half their income on housing.[45] Recent reports by both the Center for Housing Policy and the Joint Center for Housing Studies at Harvard University also found that more than three-quarters of America's working families spend more than half their income on housing, compared to 20 percent in the 1960s.[46] The one-third of all U.S. households that rent their housing are especially affected. One analysis found that while the rent burden has increased only modestly in the past few decades, the most pronounced increases were borne by poor households.[47] Lack of affordable housing has increased residential mobility rates among low-income families, who are priced out of their neighborhoods.

Homeownership is also an important issue that relates to student mobility. Families owning homes tend to be more stable over time. Nearly 70 percent of Americans own their homes, but the rate of homeownership for working families with children is lower than in 1978, according to a study by the Center for Housing Policy.[48] The study indicates that the trend is being driven by a combination of factors: soaring housing costs that have overshot wage increases; higher healthcare bills; and a rise in the number of single parents. Hispanic and black working families with children have struggled the most; their homeownership rate has stagnated at about 45 percent, far below that of white families (71 percent) as of 2003.[49]

The affordability of housing also affects the residential choices of new immigrants. Although this is beginning to change, new immigrant families tend to reside, at least initially, in lower-cost central city and older inner-ring suburban neighborhoods.[50] This trend places newly arriving school-age students—especially Latino and Asian students—in schools already troubled by declining resources.

IMPACTS ON STUDENTS AND FAMILIES

In many urban centers, high housing costs often force parents to spend more time working to pay the rent or mortgage, with less time available to help their children with homework or be involved in their child's school. Study after study demonstrates the importance of parental involvement and how difficult this is to achieve in under-resourced, largely low-income schools.[51] Additionally, research has shown that stable and good-quality housing can help foster good parenting by providing families with a sense of control, choice, and well-being.[52]

As pressures from rising housing costs push vulnerable families from residence to residence, moving from school to school affects students' social and emotional life as well as their academic achievement.[53] Making new friends and learning new social expectations and norms are difficult tasks, demanding more time than frequent transfers allow. Student misbehavior and violence can also result from high mobility. A longitudinal study tracking 4,500 adolescents in California and Oregon from seventh grade demonstrated that violence increased by 20 percent among students who moved frequently in their elementary school years.[54] In the worst-case scenario, housing prices may force families with children to become homeless. As students in local schools, these children are at much greater risk of illness, injury, malnutrition, abuse, neglect, violence, separation from family, and delays in cognitive and language development.[55]

IMPACTS ON TEACHERS AND CLASSROOMS

When students are moving into and out of local schools, teachers are continuously getting to know new students as well as their learning needs and abilities. One of the most difficult aspects of student mobility is assigning transfer students to specific classes at their new schools. Inappropriate or incorrect ability grouping is particularly critical for mobile students; students with special needs or those who require individual education programs or English language accommodation can be misplaced.[56] The new teacher has limited information about mobile students, and discovering that students have been incorrectly placed can take weeks or even months. This crucial decision will influence not only how much the student will learn but also classroom placement for future years.[57]

High student mobility rates make it harder for *all* students to be prepared adequately for testing. A California study revealed that even nonmobile students had significantly lower average test scores in high schools that had high student mobility rates.[58] Those students who move frequently are particularly affected. Unless they attend for a certain percentage of days, mobile students simply "don't count": their scores are not considered in schools' reporting statistics. Because they are held accountable for test scores under the federal No Child Left Behind (NCLB) legislation, teachers may feel less incentive to focus their attention on transferring students whose scores do not matter. On the other hand, teachers may find themselves held responsible for the academic progress of students who were not in their class for the entire year but nevertheless met the score-reporting cutoff. Research indicates that high student mobility leads to teacher burnout and even resignation, creating more problems for schools.[59]

IMPACTS ON SCHOOLS AND SCHOOL DISTRICTS

School administrators are challenged to track the educational needs of students as they move into and out of the system. Transcripts rarely follow students in a timely fashion. Additionally, schools in low-income, high-mobility areas are often unable to rely on consistent participation from parents. Many of the transient families are poor or newly immigrated. Compared with parents in more privileged and better-resourced districts, lower-income parents tend to experience numerous barriers to effective school participation activities such as decision making, fund raising, or parent advocacy.[60] Language differences also increase the challenges of these relationships between parents and schools. The number and diversity of students from families speaking a language other than English rose rapidly in the 1990s; the number of children who speak a language other than English at home more than doubled from 5.1 to 10.6 million between 1980 and 2000.[61] Many of them are found in low-income urban schools.

Innovations at the Housing–Schools Nexus

Recognizing the linkage between the quality of housing and the quality of local schools, innovative leaders in both areas have developed a variety of strategies for improving educational outcomes and providing quality affordable housing. Some of these involve uncoupling urban schools from the poor neighborhoods through different assignment policies. This provides ways for students in the worst neighborhoods to get a quality education, as well as ways to even out the resources available to all schools, regardless of neighborhood. Other solutions link schools to residential and commercial development in ways that are designed to improve their resources and educational environment.

Alternative School Assignment Policies

With school assignments traditionally based on school districts and neighborhood of residence, families living in poverty have had limited school options. To remedy this situation, a number of school assignment policies and practices have changed the traditional school and neighborhood relationship, providing opportunities for minority and low-income families. School districts have instituted policies to increase racial and economic integration in their schools. One of the least popular of these was "bussing," started in 1973. For the most part, it was court-ordered and designed to eliminate the institutional segregation that had defined public education. A more popular approach has been the use of magnet schools, introduced in the 1970s. A magnet school often features a specialized or unique curriculum or evaluation strategy to attract students of various social, racial, and economic backgrounds. In 2001, high numbers of magnet schools were found in Chicago, New York City, Puerto Rico, and Los Angeles.[62] Parents from the entire district, regardless of their residence within the district, may apply to send their children to a magnet school.

Another example of a school policy designed to foster better economic and racial integration is San Francisco's "Diversity Index." San Francisco Unified School District's Diversity Index was adopted to guide school assignment, with the goal of achieving economic integration among students. The district uses a formula incorporating sixteen student measures to determine school assignment. Race is the last variable, and school assignments are often determined well before race comes into the equation. Students are assigned on the basis of a determination of optimal and acceptable diversity for a school. However, this policy has been very controversial in its implementation.

Charter schools offer another alternative. Developed in the mid-1990s, public charter schools are publicly funded, but controlled through charters to independent entities that operate a public school. Charter schools have school district boundaries, but are generally open by lottery or other broad-based access system to any student from the district.

A number of cities, including Washington, DC, Milwaukee, and Cleveland are using school vouchers. In theory, vouchers provide maximum access to choice among public schools or private schools, empowering families to choose the best educational option for their children. School choice proponents assert that free market forces on public education will improve all schools, public and private, because consumer demand will force schools to meet the standards of their customers. While choice has been hailed as a way to empower families and inject competition into the educational field, studies have shown mixed results.[63] One central critique is that school vouchers give additional advantage to already advantaged students, further fueling patterns of economic and racial segregation in schools.[64]

Research has yet to determine how these newer types of school assignment policies have affected housing patterns and prices and whether housing policies have taken new school assignment options for families into account.

Rather than try to counter residential patterns through school assignment integration policies, another approach seeks to reinvigorate neighborhood schools to build stronger connections between families, schools, and communities. In this approach, neighborhood schools—ones that draw their students locally—become neighborhood centers of recreational, educational, and health services and support, with the goal of not only improving student achievement but also strengthening families and communities.

For example, community schools (sometimes called full-service schools) seek to bring educational, recreational, and health services together under one roof, particularly in disadvantaged neighborhoods, to better meet the wide variety of needs for children and their families.[65] The Coalition for Community Schools promotes this model as the vehicle for strengthening schools, families, and communities so that together they can improve student learning.[66] The result is a push away from desegregation policies that uncouple family residence and school assignment; instead, the link is reinvigorated, fostering neighborhood, family, and school cohesion. Some have argued that neighborhood schools are positively correlated with student achievement.[67] In particular, advocates believe that neighborhood schools will increase parental involvement, permit students to walk to and from school, and create local community social capital.

Alternative Housing Policies

One way to increase integration within schools and to improve educational opportunities for low-income children is to give their families an opportunity to relocate to districts with higher-quality schools. A variety of housing policies have attempted to alleviate patterns of racial and economic segregation, with mixed results.

The first effort—and one of the best-known—was the Gautreaux program, which relocated public housing families into different parts of the Chicago metropolitan area. Studies of the children involved show that, over a period of seven to ten years, those who moved to the suburbs had lower dropout rates (5 versus 20 percent) and higher rates of college attendance (54 versus 21 percent) than those who moved somewhere else within the city.[68] While the evidence is not decisive, the schools in suburban neighborhoods to which the students relocated had greater racial and economic integration.

In 1992 the U.S. Department of Housing and Urban Development launched the Moving to Opportunity for Fair Housing Demonstration Program (MTO), attempting to replicate the Gautreaux project's results. This effort sought to uncover what happens when very poor families have the opportunity to move out of subsidized housing in the poorest neighborhoods of Baltimore, Boston, Chicago, Los Angeles, and New York.

The findings have been mixed. In Baltimore, one study found that elementary schoolchildren who moved from high-poverty to low-poverty neighborhoods had improved reading and math scores.[69] Other studies have not detected significant impacts on educational achievement.[70] One study found that many participating children actually remained at their original school rather than switching to a "better" school.[71] This may explain the insignificant improvement, and it points to a flaw in the policy. While gaining access to better schools by moving to a better neighborhood is one of the project's goals, policy mechanisms failed to encourage or assist families in transferring their students to these schools.

Another housing policy demonstrating a potentially positive impact is the federal HOPE VI urban revitalization program. The Urban Institute has shown very hopeful outcomes for low-income students enrolled in this program. The ongoing HOPE VI Panel Study showed that families who received Section 8 housing vouchers moved to neighborhoods with better schools, although residents who were simply reassigned to other public housing developments did not find better schools.[72] Key factors in better performance were having parents who have high school diplomas themselves, who are more engaged with their children's education, and who do not suffer from depression. In addition, the better-performing students were found to have higher levels of self-efficacy and social competence. While not conclusive, these findings indicate that, in addition to housing, social and health-related conditions correlate positively with a child's success in school.

An earlier study of Albuquerque, New Mexico, also revealed positive outcomes when low-income children in public housing are moved to high-income communities and schools. Metro Albuquerque has one dominant city government and one unified school system. As a result, public housing families live in a greater variety of neighborhoods, and a high percentage of the city's children attend the public schools (more than 92 percent at the time of this study in 1994). According to the study:

> Despite their family circumstances, children from public housing households living in middle-class neighborhoods and attending middle-class schools show measurable improvement in their academic performance over children of similar individual and family characteristics living in low-income neighborhoods and attending low-income schools.[73]

Linking School Improvement to Housing Redevelopment

Neighborhood revitalization strategies are beginning to include schools in a more comprehensive approach to redevelopment. One survey showed that more than 200 community organizations are linking their work to school reform in a range of ways.[74] According to some researchers, "If urban school reform in the United States is to be successful, it must be linked to the revitalization of the communities around our schools."[75] Turnham and

Khadduri conducted case studies of six revitalization programs, in Baltimore, Philadelphia, Washington, DC, Atlanta, St. Louis, and North Richmond, California.[76] Each case had a focus on different housing and educational strategies, ranging from public housing redevelopment and affordable housing improvements to greater homeownership opportunities. Some programs sought to attract middle-income families to a community by improving schools and offering better housing opportunities, whereas others sought to create more affordable housing and homeownership opportunities for local residents.

Developers working on impoverished sections of Baltimore, St. Louis, and Atlanta have formally coordinated school improvement, new housing development, and community services, with the particular goal of retaining old residents in the new diverse mixed-income communities.[77] In 1989 The Enterprise Foundation, now called Enterprise Community Partners, led by developer Jim Rouse, teamed up with the City of Baltimore, churches, and local community organizations to launch the Neighborhood Transformation Initiative. This has brought education reform to center stage in the Sandtown–Winchester neighborhood. The goal was to "cement a relationship between community and school" as part of nearby housing renovation and construction in a seventy-two-block neighborhood about a mile and a half from downtown Baltimore. At the three elementary schools affected by the project, the percentage of students performing at a satisfactory level on the Grade 5 comprehensive state tests increased at a higher rate than in the city's public schools as a whole. At the same time, homeownership rates have risen, vacancy has declined, crime rates fell in all categories between 1997 and 2000, and real estate values increased during the 1990s.

Richard Baron, a well-known mixed-income housing developer, has had similar success in St. Louis and Atlanta. He recognizes school as being at "the center of virtually every residential real estate decision made in America."[78] In the 1990s he began working with the St. Louis Public Housing Authority and the U.S. Department of Housing and Urban Development (HUD) to renovate old public housing developments and the low-performing Jefferson Elementary School, raising an additional $3.5 million for the latter. Baron called for specific school reforms and a new principal, along with mixed-income development. As with the Baltimore example, these school reforms were meant to reinforce the new redevelopment and guide schools to play a central role in the process of revitalizing the neighborhood. A diverse set of residents and children are now socializing in the neighborhood and at school. Because the housing is attractive, well built, and formally linked to school reform, family mobility has been reduced, and children tend to stay at their school longer, reducing classroom disruptions.

Baron developed a similar project in Atlanta, known on Centennial Place. His partners were the federal HOPE VI redevelopment program, the Atlanta Housing Authority, the Atlanta Public School District, and the Integral Group, a local developer. Residents and the community helped to plan the transformation of a former public housing development into a mixed-income "community of choice." Their identified needs were (1) improved education, (2) day care, and (3) job opportunities.

In return for the developers' renovation of the public elementary school, the local school district agreed to make it a neighborhood school—that is, the school would draw its students primarily from nearby neighborhoods. By 2001, students at the Centennial Place Elementary School exceeded the standards in all categories tested by the State of Georgia. In the 2002–2003 school year, 93 percent of students met or exceeded math testing standards, and 98 percent of students met or exceeded standards in reading. The environment for learning had improved dramatically.

Against these positive findings, some research has found that redevelopment strategies can do harm to low-income households and to communities of color. In analyzing the Chicago Public Housing Transformation Program, which demolished many of the public housing developments in Chicago and relocated residents throughout the city, Pauline Lipman argues that the result has been gentrification of city neighborhoods. Along with local advocates, she argues that the gentrification was strategically—and purposefully—linked to one of the largest school reforms efforts in the United States: sixty low-achieving schools have been closed, and 100 new smaller schools were added, two-thirds of them run by charters or private contractors. Lipman argues that the combination of housing demolition, gentrification, and school reform is "concretely and symbolically linked to pushing out low-income people of color and destroying their communities."[79] Even if this outcome was not intentional, a negative potential exists. While mixed-income housing may initially include units that are affordable, as schools improve, housing costs are likely to increase. A key challenge is to ensure that housing remains affordable as the quality of education rises.

Two other housing policies show an increasing, although indirect, connection to education: (1) infill housing, which is residential development on small parcels of land surrounded by already developed areas; and (2) inclusionary zoning polices, which require specific percentages of affordable housing in new development. A recent study for the State of California found that school quality was one of the leading reasons families would be willing to relocate to an infill housing site—a strategy to attract families back to denser urban areas.[80] Regarding the latter innovation, former mayor and urban researcher David Rusk studies and advocates inclusionary zoning as a vehicle to bring more affordable housing to low-income families across regions. In effect, he positions inclusionary zoning as education policy.[81] An estimated 100 cities and counties have enacted inclusionary zoning laws that if adequately enforced would provide opportunities for more public school families to live in higher-income neighborhoods and attend higher-income schools.[82] However, inclusionary zoning often goes unenforced, and targeted goals remain unmet in most localities.

Building New Schools

Several efforts by neighborhood revitalization organizations have focused on creating new schools, both to attract new middle-income residents and to retain diverse families already in the community. In Baltimore the Patterson Park Community Development Corporation was formed in 1996 to address disinvestment in the community. Working in partnership with a local Catholic school and a local foundation, it provided school subsidies to families who bought homes through a special program designed to attract residents to the neighborhood.[83] The neighborhood went on to plan a neighborhood-based public charter school in hopes of creating an economically and racially diverse student body. Program designers used enrollment boundaries to draw students from local families because they hoped that local residents would contribute to the revitalization and integration of the neighborhood. The effort has been led by many of the 125 families who bought houses as part of the homeownership program.

There are community-based organizations (CBOs) that are creating charter schools as a way to expand their current services and provide "one-stop shopping" for the communities they serve. CBOs recognize that as neighborhood schools improve, fewer younger urban middle-income parents leave cities seeking areas with better schools.[84] They find, as other studies do, that with more middle-income families, classrooms become more diverse, and the economic base remains strong.[85] In many of these projects, local organizers conceive of charter schools before they have a building in place. This allows CBOs to purchase or lease vacant, dilapidated properties and renovate them, often into schools and community centers. In turn, the whole neighborhood is improved. Examples of CBO-driven charter schools are found at local and national levels.

A well-recognized example of improving a public school in conjunction with housing development is the community-managed public–private partnership between the District of Columbia James F. Oyster Bilingual Elementary School and a private developer.[86] The school was located on 1.67 acres of highly desirable land in Woodley Park, an upper-income residential area that nevertheless had a racially and economically mixed student body in the late 1980s. Understanding both the city's lack of financial resources and the value of the land that the school was on, Oyster School parents came up with the idea of selling part of the school's land to developers to pay for the necessary school improvements. These parents then started the 21st Century School Fund and in 1998 managed the process whereby the school district entered into an agreement with LCOR, a private property development firm, to build an apartment house on a portion of this land. In exchange for land and in lieu of property taxes, LCOR paid the debt service on a bond to design, construct, and furnish a new Oyster school. The agreement led to benefits for the whole city school system; the company also agreed to set aside $445,000 to fund other school modernization projects in the city.

Another example of innovation is found in San Diego. The city and school district teamed up on two redevelopment projects in the densely populated City Heights neighborhood. Nearly complete, the ten city block City Heights Urban Village has a pedestrian-friendly town square surrounded by retail, community, and educational facilities.[87] Already completed are a police substation, community gymnasium, elementary school, library, community service center, recreation center, continuing education center, and retail center. Still under construction are townhomes and an office center. Partners on this public–private project include the City of San Diego, San Diego Unified School District, CitiLink Investment Corporation, and Price Charities, among others.

Success breeds more innovation. The city and the school district are now working on another project in City Heights, the San Diego Model School Development. Again using an "urban village" concept, the smaller model school redevelopment site includes a new elementary school, new mixed-income family housing units, and community services. By forming a Joint Powers Authority (JPA) between local agencies, the goal is to work collaboratively to site a much-needed new school that takes up less space and provides a wide range of community amenities.[88]

Smart Growth and Other New Initiatives

The Smart Growth movement, a major recent urban planning strategy, has also increasingly focused on the role of schools in urban growth and development. The smart growth agenda seeks to curb low-density development that leads to urban sprawl and to conserve resources and land in the process.[89] Affordable housing is a critical component, and advocates are interested in how changes in traditional school planning can foster sounder and healthier neighborhoods.[90] In particular, the Smart Growth-Smart Schools Initiative launched in 2004 by the Kellogg Foundation hopes to link an urban housing agenda to the movement for educational equity.[91]

Tied to smart growth issues is the notion of "schools as centers of community"—that is, that schools should be strategically located in neighborhoods so that they are easy to get to and act as central public spaces for events and community building, not just quality learning.[92] Planners, architects, and developers have been touting the role civic buildings, housing, and especially public schools can play in the life of a neighborhood, as both social and physical centerpieces. Many argue that the development (or redevelopment) of smaller schools on smaller sites can save time and money, put schools and homes closer together, and allow schools to better serve as centers of their communities.[93]

Additionally, there are new governance structures connecting housing and schools. In several states undergoing population growth, such as California and Ohio, governments are creating new administrative bodies. The Cities, Counties, Schools Partnership of California, for example, brings different actors together for dialogue across these policy divides.[94] The goal of these new structures is to align school planning with larger housing and metropolitan planning so that policy makers can share information, data, and projections and so that school districts and cities can better coordinate their development needs.

Challenges to Integrating Housing and Education

Housing and education have always been organically connected, yet rarely has policy or practice in either field addressed the connection. Through specific project efforts, educators and housing polity makers are beginning to experiment with how to leverage these natural connections to the advantage of residential development and of public schools. However, the policy and research communities need to help develop a better understanding of the relationship between housing and schools for this to be a success. Following this, policy makers need to use the findings from practice and research to create a new policy framework for targeting the housing–school nexus effectively.

Research Needs

Significant research voids exist at the housing–schools nexus. Specifically, we need to better understand the impact of mixed-income housing and other policies that seek to integrate communities on existing residents. For example, how does displacement affect student achievement? Research must explore the academic successes in mixed-income redevelopments to determine whether higher scores on standardized tests are due to improvements made by students who lived in these communities prior to redevelopment, or if they are attributable to an influx of higher-income students through gentrification. Finding this out is complicated by the fact that, as part of the federal NCLB policy, improvement is measured at the school level rather than the student level. Thus, the focus on improving failing schools may provide a subtle incentive for schools and cities to push out poorly performing students via school transfer or gentrification. Another impediment lies in the very nature of mixed-income housing—that is, that there is a need to sustain some level of affordable housing. As schools improve, market-rate developers may build housing that is expensive and out of reach for many of the families the school improvements were intended to help. Remembering that housing costs typically rise as school quality improves, how can housing remain affordable? There is little research to show that mixed-income housing programs actually lead to better and more economically integrated housing for all residents. Moreover, programs are unlikely to succeed if middle-income families avoid mixed-income communities because of deep racial biases.

On a related issue, while neighborhoods and schools become more diverse through mechanisms such as magnet schools or other reform efforts, internal problems may remain. For example, in Berkeley, California, one of the most celebrated models of racially integrated schools in the country, schools are overwhelmingly segregated inside their walls. While the overall student population is diverse, the more advanced college-prep classes are overwhelmingly filled with white and Asian students, while black and Latino students are tracked into less rigorous classes for those not expected to attend college.[95] This phenomenon, well known in the educational literature as tracking, remains a formidable hurdle for educational equity. Overall, research is needed to understand whether and how mixed-income housing leads to better and economically integrated housing for all residents, and how these actions ultimately impact schools. This work will form the basis for appropriate policy responses.

Connecting Policy and Practice

There is a structural disconnect between the education and housing sectors that presents a key barrier to successfully addressing the goals of advocates on both sides. School districts generally act autonomously from municipal authority, which makes it difficult to align plans, processes, and budgets for housing and school development.[96] Successful collaboration between the two sectors has often relied on the personal connections of individuals, rather than on formal established relationships between housing and education administrators. Although there have been a few successful efforts by actors such as New Schools, Better Neighborhoods, an organization that works to connect communities and schools in the Los Angeles area through housing and school facilities development, there are still considerable obstacles to aligning planning for building housing and schools. There is a general lack of understanding across disciplines and the absence of formal governance structures to sustain coordination across housing and education sectors.[97] Practitioners have voiced concern that the challenges to succeeding at collaboration often outweigh the possible rewards.[98]

More specifically, housing and education have different administrative practices, especially relating to funding, development regulations, and operational timelines. Though both the housing and education sectors are faced with inadequate funding, they may deal with this challenge differently. For example, developers may focus on the construction of housing that is designed to attract households without children so that they can avoid neighborhood opposition on the grounds that new construction will require increased taxes for education. Collaboration is further stymied by competing and noncomplementary regulations. Education is predominantly a public resource; whereas housing development occurs primarily in the private sector, driven by market forces.[99] This means that housing development can respond more quickly to demand, but school development is often slowed by more rigid funding structures. Furthermore, schools operate on a fixed and slow-moving academic schedule and are subject to project completion deadlines, while housing can be developed quickly and with more flexibility. In the private sector time is money, while in the public sector plans must go through mandatory approval processes that often take significant time.

Conclusion

Tremendous socioeconomic change has occurred in America's cities since the 1950s. During this time, both housing and public schools in older urban areas have experienced increasingly severe—and intertwined—problems. Yet rarely have policy responses been aimed at addressing the housing–schools nexus. As is shown in this chapter, the evidence has grown clearer: issues of housing and schools are far more interrelated and mutually dependent than previously acknowledged. Neighborhoods with poor housing too often have low performing schools while areas with good housing have higher per-forming schools. The first to notice, perhaps, were middle-income families, who now largely flood into the suburbs seeking not just a nice house at a reasonable price but also a fine education and promising future for their children—a goal that all families deserve to pursue.

While innovative housing developers, cities, and community organiza-tions are beginning to recognize the importance of high-quality schools to overall revitalization efforts, there are few formal mechanisms to institu-tionalize practices that address the housing–school nexus. Any effort to integrate education and housing policies and programs will face several challenges, most of them rooted in the way policy makers and practitioners historically think and act. Better understanding the housing–school nexus is an important first step.

Notes

1. For example, Lloyd, Carol. 2005. The Home School Conundrum: Parents' Real Estate Decisions Often Based on Kids' Education Needs. *San Francisco Chronicle*, March 25; Ginsberg, Marsha. 2004. Educated Buyers; Test Scores, School Ratings Drive Decisions as Much as Floor Plans and City. *San Francisco Chronicle*, February 15, page G1.

2. Orfield, Myron. 2002. *American Metropolitics: The New Suburban Reality.* Washington, DC: Brookings Institution Press.

3. National Fair Housing Alliance. 2006. *Unequal Opportunity: Perpetuating Housing Segregation in America*, 2006 Fair Housing Trends Report. Washington, DC: National Fair Housing Alliance.

4. Stone, Clarence, Kathryn Doherty, Cheryl Jones, and Timothy Ross. 1999. Schools and Disadvantaged Neighborhoods. In *Urban Problems and Community Development*, edited by Ronald F. Ferguson and William T. Dickens. Washington, DC: Brookings Institution Press.

5. Coleman, James, Ernest Q. Campbell, Carol J. Hobson, James McPartland, Alexander M. Mood, Frederick D. Weinfeld, and Robert G. York. 1966. *Equality of Educational Opportunity.* Washington, DC: U.S. Government Printing Office; Rothstein, Richard. 2004. *Class and Schools: Using Social, Economic, and Educational Reform to Close the Black–White Achievement Gap.* Washington, DC: Economic Policy Institute.

6. Kingsley, G. Thomas and Kathryn L.S. Pettit. 2003. *Concentrated Poverty: A Change in Course.* Washington, DC: Urban Institute; Swanstrom, Todd, Colleen Casey, Robert Flack, and Peter Dreier. 2004. *Pulling Apart: Economic Segregation among Suburbs and Central Cities in Major Metropolitan Areas.* Washington, DC: The Living Cities Census Series, Brookings Institution.

7. Berube, Alan and William H. Frey. 2002. *A Decade of Mixed Blessings: Urban and Suburban Poverty in Census 2000.* Washington, DC: Brookings Institution.

8. U.S. Department of Health and Human Services. 2001. *Geographical Mobility, Population Characteristics: March 1999 to March 2000.* Washington, DC: U.S. Department of Health and Human Services, Office of the Assistant Secretary for Planning and Evaluation.

9. Orfield, Gary and Chungmei Lee. 2004. *Brown at 50: King's Dream or Plessy's Nightmare?* Cambridge, MA: Civil Rights Project, Harvard University.

10. Orfield, Gary and Chungmei Lee. 2005. *Why Segregation Matters: Poverty and Educational Inequality.* Cambridge, MA: Civil Rights Project, Harvard University.

11. Orfield, Myron. 2002. *American Metropolitics: The New Suburban Reality.* Washington, DC: Brookings Institution Press.

12. Crone, Theodore M. 1998. *Housing Prices and the Quality of Public Schools: What Are We Buying?* Federal Reserve Bank of Philadelphia.

13. Orfield, Myron. 2002. *American Metropolitics: The New Suburban Reality.* Washington, DC: Brookings Institution Press.

14. American Planning Association and American Institute of Certified Planners. 2000. *The Millennium Survey: A National Poll of American Voters' View on Land Use.* Washington, DC: American Planning Association and American Institute of Certified Planners.

15. Baldassare, Mark. 2002. *Public Policy Institute of California Statewide Survey: Special Survey on Land Use.* San Francisco: Public Policy Institute of California.

16. Black, Sandra E. 1999. Do Better Schools Matter? Parental Valuation of Elementary Education. *Quarterly Journal of Economics* 114(2): 577–599.

17. Figlio, David. 2002. What's In a Grade? School Report Cards and House Prices. University of Florida, Department of Economics Working Paper.

18. Bogart, William T. and Brian A. Cromwell. 1997. How Much Is a Good School District Worth? *National Tax Journal* 50(2): 215–232.

19. National Fair Housing Alliance. 2006. *Unequal Opportunity: Perpetuating Housing Segregation in America*, Fair Housing Trends Report. Washington, DC: National Fair Housing Alliance. This measure does not include instances of discrimination against other protected classes, and discrimination in lending, insurance, planning, and zoning. Rental market discrimination is

most common, with private fair housing groups reporting 12,651 complaints in 2005 against apartment owners and managers.

In the same year, 747 complaints related to home sales were made. In an enforcement project involving 145 paired tests conducted in twelve major cities across the United States, the NFHA found evidence of steering on the basis of race or ethnicity in 87 percent of cases. Black and Latino testers were denied service or provided limited service by real estate agents in about 20 percent of instances, even though all black and Latino testers were better qualified for home purchase than their white counterparts. While white testers were shown an average of eight homes per test, black and Latino testers were shown an average of five homes per test. More often than their white counterparts, black and Latino testers were required to provide confirmation from a lender before being showed any homes.

20. Orfield, Myron. 2002. *American Metropolitics: The New Suburban Reality.* Washington, DC: Brookings Institution Press.
21. Orfield, Gary and Chungmei Lee. 2005. *Why Segregation Matters: Poverty and Educational Inequality.* Cambridge, MA: Civil Rights Project, Harvard University.
22. Rawlings, Lynette, Laura Harris, Margery Austin Turner, and Sandra Padilla. 2004. *Race and Residence: Prospects for Stable Neighborhood Integration.* Washington, DC: Urban Institute.
23. Orfield, Gary and Chungmei Lee. 2005. *Why Segregation Matters: Poverty and Educational Inequality.* Cambridge, MA: Civil Rights Project, Harvard University.
24. Rothstein, Richard. 2004. *Class and Schools: Using Social, Economic, and Educational Reform to Close the Black–White Achievement Gap.* Washington, DC: Economic Policy Institute.
25. Orfield, Myron. 2002. *American Metropolitics: The New Suburban Reality.* Washington, DC: Brookings Institution Press.
26. Van Hook, Jennifer and Michael Fix. 2000. A Profile of the Immigrant Student Population. In *Overlooked and Underserved: Immigrant Children in U.S. Secondary Schools*, edited by J.R. De Velasco, M. Fix, and T. Clewell. Washington, DC: The Urban Institute.
27. Briggs, Xavier de Sousa. 1998. Brown Kids in White Suburbs: Housing Mobility and the Many Faces of Social Capital. *Housing Policy Debate* 9(1): 177–221; Cattel, Vicky. 2001. Poor People, Poor Places, and Poor Health: The Mediating Role of Social Networks and Social Capital. *Social Science and Medicine* 52(10): 1501–1516.
28. Thernstrom, Abigail and Stephen Thernstrom. 2003. *No Excuses: Closing the Racial Gap in Learning.* New York: Simon & Schuster.
29. Foster-Bey, John A. 2004. Aiming for Integration? 50 Years after Brown. *National Review Online.* Available at http://www.nationalreview.com/comment/fosterbey200404150851.asp (accessed March 6, 2006).
30. Rothstein, Richard. 2004. *Class and Schools: Using Social, Economic, and Educational Reform to Close the Black–White Achievement Gap.* Washington, DC: Economic Policy Institute.
31. Orfield, Gary and Chungmei Lee. 2005. *Why Segregation Matters: Poverty and Educational Inequality.* Cambridge, MA: Civil Rights Project, Harvard University.
32. Ellen, Ingrid Gould and Margery Austin Turner. 1997. Does Neighborhood Matter? Assessing Recent Evidence. *Housing Policy Debate* 8(4): 833–866.
33. Rothstein, Richard. 2004. *Class and Schools: Using Social, Economic, and Educational Reform to Close the Black–White Achievement Gap.* Washington, DC: Economic Policy Institute.
34. Bartlett, Sheridan. 1998. Does Inadequate Housing Perpetuate Children's Poverty? *Childhood* 5: 405–428.
35. Ellen, Ingrid Gould and Margery Austin Turner. 1997. Does Neighborhood Matter? Assessing Recent Evidence. *Housing Policy Debate* 8(4): 833–866; Brooks-Gunn, Jeanne, Greg J. Duncan, and J. Lawrence Aber, eds. 1997. *Neighborhood Poverty: Contexts and Consequences for Children* (volume 1). New York: Russell Sage Foundation.
36. Rothstein, Richard. 2004. *Class and Schools: Using Social, Economic, and Educational Reform to Close the Black–White Achievement Gap.* Washington, DC: Economic Policy Institute.
37. Boger, John Charles. 2005. *The Socioeconomic Composition of the Public Schools: A Crucial Consideration in School Assignment Policy.* Chapel Hill, NC: Center for Civil Rights.
38. Holloway, L. 2000. Turnover of Teachers and Students Deepens the Troubles of Poor Schools. *The New York Times*, May 28: A29.
39. While starting in the 1980s courts have ordered state governments to devise new ways to fund public schools more equitably, school finance systems today are still very decentralized and look dramatically different from state to state. Illinois and New Jersey, as well as many other

states, depend somewhat on state funds but still rely most heavily on local property taxes. A few states, most notably California and Michigan, have state-controlled school finance systems. Hawaii is unique in that it has one statewide school district. Recent litigation across the country has challenged the notion of "adequacy" in school resources and conditions between districts.

40. Saulny, Susan. 2005. Middle Class, Signs of Anxiety on School Efforts. *New York Times*, December 27.

41. National Fair Housing Alliance. 2006. *Unequal Opportunity: Perpetuating Housing Segregation in America*, Fair Housing Trends Report. Washington, DC: National Fair Housing Alliance.

42. U.S. Department of Health and Human Services. 2001. *Geographical Mobility, Population Characteristics: March 1999 to March 2000*. Washington, DC: U.S. Department of Health and Human Services, Office of the Assistant Secretary for Planning and Evaluation.

43. *Journal of Negro Education*. 2003. Special Edition: "Student Mobility: How Some Children Get Left Behind." 72(1).

44. Rumberger, Russell W., K.A. Larson, R.K. Ream, and G.J. Palardy. 1999. *The Educational Consequences of Mobility for California Students and Schools*. Berkeley, CA: Policy Analysis for California Education; Crowley, Sheila. 2003. The Affordable Housing Crisis: Residential Mobility of Poor Families and School Mobility of Poor Children. *Journal of Negro Education* 72(1): 22–38.

45. U.S. Department of Housing and Urban Development. 2000. *The State of the Cities 2000: Megaforces Shaping the Future of America's Cities*. Washington, DC: HUD.

46. Lipman, Barbara J. 2005. The Housing Landscape for America's Working Families 2005. *New Century Housing* 5(1). Center for Housing Policy; Joint Center for Housing Studies at Harvard University. 2004. *The State of the Nation's Housing 2004*. Boston: Joint Center for Housing Studies at Harvard University. Between 1960 and 1970 the median renter devoted 20 percent of income to rent. Most government housing assistance programs subsidize housing costs such that housing expenditures of recipients do not exceed 30 percent of household income.

47. Quigley, John M. and Steven Raphael. 2004. Is Housing Unaffordable? Why Isn't It More Affordable? *Journal of Economic Perspectives* 18(1): 191–214.

48. Lipman, Barbara J. 2005. The Housing Landscape for America's Working Families 2005. *New Century Housing* 5(1). Center for Housing Policy.

49. Lipman, Barbara J. 2006. *Locked Out: Keys to Homeownership Elude Many Working Families with Children*. Washington, DC: Center for Housing Policy.

50. Frey, William H. 2006. *Diversity Spreads Out: Metropolitan Shifts in Hispanic, Asian, and Black Populations since 2000*. Washington, DC: Brookings Institution.

51. Cotton, Kathleen and Karen Reed Wikelund. 1990. *Parent Involvement in Education*. School Improvement Research Series. Boston: Northwest Regional Laboratory.

52. Bartlett, Sheridan. 1998. Does Inadequate Housing Perpetuate Children's Poverty? *Childhood* 5: 405–428.

53. Scanlon, E. and K. Devine. 2001. Residential Mobility and Youth Well-Being: Research, Policy, and Practice Issues. *Journal of Sociology and Social Welfare* 28(1): 119–138.

54. Ellickson, P.L. and K.A. McGuigan. 2000. Early Predictors of Adolescent Violence. *American Journal of Public Health* 90(4): 566–572.

55. Molnar, J.M., W.R. Rath, and T.P. Klein. 1990. Constantly Compromised: The Impact of Homelessness on Children. *Journal of Social Issues* 46(4): 109–124; National Coalition for the Homeless. 2005. Education of Homeless Children and Youth: Factsheet No. 10. Washington, DC: National Coalition for the Homeless.

56. Schneider, Barbara, Christopher B. Swanson, and Catherine Riegle-Crumb. 1998. Opportunities for Learning: Course Sequences and Positional Advantages. *Social Psychology of Education* 2: 25–53.

57. Gamoran, Adam. 1986. Instructional and Institutional Effects of Ability Grouping. *Sociology of Education* 59(4): 185–198.

58. Rumberger, Russell W., K.A. Larson, R.K. Ream, and G.J. Palardy. 1999. *The Educational Consequences of Mobility for California Students and Schools*. Berkeley, CA: Policy Analysis for California Education.

59. Cohen, Deborah. 1994. Moving Images. Education Week on the Web. Available at http://www.edweek.org (accessed March 6, 2006).

60. Dauber, Susan L. and Joyce L. Epstein. 1993. Parents' attitudes and practices of involvement

in inner-city elementary and middle schools. In *Families and Schools in a Pluralistic Society*, edited by N.F. Chavkin. Albany: State University of New York.

61. Fix, Michael and Jeffrey S. Passel. 2003. *U.S. Immigration: Trends and Implications for Schools*. Washington, DC: The Urban Institute.

62. U.S. Department of Education, National Center for Education Statistics, Common Core of Data, "Public Elementary/Secondary School Universe Survey," 2001–2002, Version 1a. Washington, DC: U.S. Department of Education.

63. Apple, Michael and Gerald Bracey. 2001. School Vouchers: An Education Policy Project Briefing Paper. Milwaukee: University of Wisconsin–Milwaukee School of Education, Center for Education Research, Analysis, and Innovation; Moe, Terry M. 2001. *Schools, Vouchers and the American Public*. Washington, DC: Brookings Institution Press.

64. Henig, Jeffrey R. 1994. *Rethinking School Choice: Limits of the Market Metaphor*. Princeton, NJ: Princeton University Press.

65. Dryfoos, Joy, Jane Quinn, and Carol Barkin. 2005. *Community Schools in Action: Lessons from a Decade of Practice*. Oxford: Oxford University Press; Blank, Martin, Atelia Melaville, and Bela P. Shah. 2003. *Making the Difference: Research and Practice in Community Schools*. Washington, DC: Coalition for Community Schools.

66. See http://www.communityschools.org.

67. Blank, Martin, Atelia Melaville, and Bela P. Shah. 2003. *Making the Difference: Research and Practice in Community Schools*. Washington, DC: Coalition for Community Schools.

68. Rubinowitz, Leonard and James Rosenbaum. 2000. *Crossing the Class and Color Lines: From Public Housing to White Suburbia*. Chicago: University of Chicago Press.

69. Ladd, Helen and Jens Ludwig. 2003. The Effects of MTO on Educational Outcomes in Baltimore: Early Evidence. In *Choosing a Better Life*, edited by John Goering and Judith Feins. Washington, DC: Urban Institute Press, pp. 117–152.

70. For example, Sanbonmatsu, Lisa, Jeffrey R. Kling, Greg J. Duncan, and Jeanne Brooks-Gunn. 2006. Neighborhoods and Academic Achievement: Results from the Moving to Opportunity Experiment. *Journal of Human Resources* 41(4): 649–691.

71. Popkin, Susan J., Laura E. Harris, and Mary K. Cunningham. 2002. *Families in Transition: A Qualitative Analysis of the MTO Experience*. Washington, DC: U.S. Department of Housing and Urban Development.

72. Eisman, Michael, Elizabeth Cove, and Susan J. Popkin. 2005. Resilient Children in Distressed Neighborhood: Evidence from the HOPE VI Panel Study. Metropolitan Housing and Communities Center, Urban Institute. Brief 7.

73. Rusk, David. 1994. *The Academic Performance of Public Housing Children: Does Living in Middle-Class Neighborhoods and Attending Middle-Class Schools Make a Difference?* Washington, DC: Urban Institute.

74. Mediratta, Kavitha, Norm Fruchter, and Anne Lewis. 2002. *Organizing for School Reform: How Communities Are Finding Their Voices and Reclaiming Their Public Schools*. Institute for Educational and Social Policy, New York University.

75. Warren, Mark. 2005. Communities and Schools: A New View of Urban Education Reform. *Harvard Educational Review* 75(2): 133–173.

76. Turnham, Jennifer and Jill Khadduri. 2004. *Integrating School Reform and Neighborhood Revitalization: Opportunities and Challenges*. Cambridge, MA: Abt Associates.

77. Proscio, Tony. 2004. *Schools, Community and Development: Erasing the Boundaries*. Columbia, MD: The Enterprise Foundation.

78. Baron, Richard. 2003. The 2003 Rouse Lecture on the American City. Fannie Mae Foundation. Available at http://www.fanniemaefoundation.org/news/signature_events/rouse/rouse-index.shtml (accessed March 9, 2006).

79. Lipman, Pauline. 2004. *High Stakes Education: Inequality, Globalization, and Urban School Reform*. New York: Routledge.

80. Landis, John and Heather Hood. 2005. *California State Infill Housing Study Report*. Berkeley, CA: Institute of Urban and Regional Development, University of California.

81. Rusk, David. 2003. Housing Policy Is School Policy: Remarks to the 44th Annual Meeting of Baltimore Neighborhoods, Inc. May 6. Available at http://www.gamaliel.org/DavidRusk/BNI percent20talk.pdf (accessed March 9, 2006).

82. Burchell, Robert, C. Kent Conine, Richard Dubin, David Flanagan, Catherine C. Galley, Eric Larsen, David Rusk, Ann B. Schnare, Bernard Tetreault, and Richard Tustian. 2000.

Inclusionary Zoning: A Viable Solution to the Affordable Housing Crisis? *New Century Housing* 1(2). The Center for Housing Policy.

83. Turnham, Jennifer and Jill Khadduri. 2004. *Integrating School Reform and Neighborhood Revitalization: Opportunities and Challenges.* Cambridge, MA: Abt Associates.

84. Halsband, Robin. 2003. Charter Schools Benefit Community Economic Development. *Journal of Housing and Community Development* November/December: 34–38.

85. Kahlenberg, Richard D. 2001. *All Together Now: Creating Middle-Class Schools through Public School Choice.* Washington, DC: Brookings Institution Press.

86. 21st Century School Fund. n.d. *Building Outside the Box.* Washington, DC: 21st Century School Fund.

87. City of San Diego Redevelopment Agency. Available at http://www.sandiego.gov/redevelopment-agency/majorproj.shtml (accessed March 9, 2006).

88. City of San Diego Redevelopment Agency. 2002. San Diego Model School Program in City Heights: Fact Sheet. The City of San Diego—its Housing Authority and Redevelopment Agency—and the school district entered into a joint powers of agreement that formed the San Diego Model School Development Agency.

89. Smart Growth Network. http://www.smartgrowth.org/about/overview.asp (accessed March 9, 2006).

90. Council of Educational Facility Planners International, Inc. and U.S. Environmental Protection Agency. 2004. *Schools for Successful Communities: An Element of Smart Growth.* Scottsdale, AZ: Council of Educational Facility Planners International; Smart Growth Network. 2001. *Affordable Housing and Smart Growth: Making the Connection.* Washington, DC: Smart Growth Network.

91. See http://www.smart-schools.org/.

92. U.S. Department of Education. 2000. *Schools as Centers of Community: A Citizen's Guide to Planning and Design.* Washington, DC: U.S. Department of Education.

93. Beaumont, Constance E. with Elizabeth G. Pianca. 2002. *Historic Neighborhoods in the Age of Sprawl: Why Johnny Can't Walk to School.* Washington, DC: National Trust for Historic Preservation.

94. See http://www.ccspartnership.org.

95. Noguera, Pedro. 2003. *City Schools and the American Dream: Reclaiming the Promise of Public Education.* New York: Teachers College Press.

96. Vincent, Jeffrey M. 2006. Public Schools as Public Infrastructure: Roles for Planning Researchers. *Journal of Planning Education and Research* 25: 433–437.

97. McKoy, Deborah L. and Jeffrey M. Vincent. 2005. The Center for Cities and Schools: Connecting Research and Policy Agendas. *Berkeley Planning Journal* 18: 57–77.

98. Vincent, Jeffrey M. 2006. Planning and Siting New Public Schools in the Context of Community Development: The California Experience. Unpublished dissertation. Department of City and Regional Planning, University of California, Berkeley.

99. Only an estimated 1 percent of the total housing stock in the nation is publicly owned.

CHAPTER 5

Residential Segregation and Employment Inequality

MARGERY AUSTIN TURNER

Despite substantial gains during much of the past half-century, employment outcomes for blacks and Hispanics still fall short of outcomes for whites. Blacks and Hispanics are less likely to have jobs and, if they are employed, earn lower wages on average. Differences between minorities and whites in education, skills, and experience explain part of the gap in employment outcomes but not all of it. Even after education and achievement have been controlled for, blacks and Hispanics—particularly men—do not enjoy as much success in the labor market as whites. This chapter reviews current theory and evidence on the contribution of residential segregation to persistent inequality in employment outcomes and presents new, exploratory analysis of 2000 census data on the isolation of minority neighborhoods from centers of employment opportunity.

Persistence of Employment Inequality

During the 1960s and 1970s, disparities between minorities and whites narrowed significantly, suggesting that the nation was making real progress toward more equitable employment opportunities. However, during the 1980s the gap between minorities and whites in both employment and wages widened again because of economic restructuring, the loss of manufacturing jobs, and the relative decline in wages for low-skill jobs (Smith 2001; Holzer 2001; Conrad 2001). The prosperity of the 1990s brought increases in employment for virtually all segments of the U.S. population, and the wage gap between white and minority men narrowed. However, the gap in employment rates between white and minority men continued to widen during the 1990s. For women, the opposite pattern prevailed during the past decade, with differences in employment narrowing while differences in wages narrowed. This pattern is probably attributable to the increase in employment among low-skilled women because of welfare reform (Holzer *et al.* 2004).

Thus, near the start of the twenty-first century, blacks and Hispanics are still at a substantial disadvantage relative to whites. As is illustrated in Table 5.1, the share of all blacks who are working (the employment to population ratio) falls substantially below that of either whites or Hispanics. The share of people who are actively seeking work but unable to find it (the unemployment rate) is roughly twice as high for blacks as for whites, and almost 50 percent higher for Hispanics than for non-Hispanic whites.

Considerable research has focused on identifying the causes of these racial and ethnic disparities in employment and wages. Clearly, differences between minorities and whites in education and experience—differences that stem in part from past discrimination—provide part of the explanation. However, these factors explain the wage gap more than the gap in employment rates and the gap between white and minority women more than between white and minority men (Smith 2001; Holzer 2001; Conrad 2001).

Outright discrimination against minorities in the labor market also plays a role. Paired-testing studies find that young black and Hispanic men applying for entry-level jobs are less likely than comparably qualified whites to be invited to apply, interviewed, or offered a position. In addition, they experience significant levels of unfavorable treatment with respect to information, encouragement, and terms of employment (Turner *et al.* 1991;

TABLE 5.1 Current Disparities in Employment by Race and Ethnicity (percentages)

	2001	2002	2003	2004
Ratio of employment to population				
Whites	63.7	66.5	66.4	63.2
Blacks	58.5	57.6	56.9	57.0
Hispanics	64.3	63.4	63.0	63.9
Unemployment rate				
Whites	4.9	5.1	5.1	4.6
Blacks	9.8	10.6	10.6	10.8
Hispanics	7.4	7.9	7.1	6.7

Source: Seasonally adjusted fourth-quarter estimates from the Current Population Survey.

Cross *et al.* 1990). More recent employment testing studies have used matched résumés for which the names of the fictitious job applicants were selected to provide explicit cues as to race or ethnicity.[1] These studies find that résumés with white-sounding names were 50 percent more likely to generate callbacks from employers than those with black-sounding names. Moreover, having better credentials significantly improved the rate of call-backs for the résumés with white-sounding names but not for the résumés with black-sounding names (Bertrand and Mullainathan 2003).

The Spatial Mismatch Hypothesis

Beginning in the late 1960s, labor-market analysts have considered the possibility that segregated housing patterns might also contribute to persistent employment inequalities. Specifically, John Kain (1968) argued that the concentration of blacks in segregated central-city neighborhoods limited their access to employment, as growing numbers of jobs moved to predominantly white suburban locations. In effect, this spatial mismatch hypothesis posits that demand for labor has shifted away from the neigh-borhoods where blacks are concentrated, that discrimination in housing and mortgage markets prevents blacks from moving to communities where job growth is occurring, and that information and transportation barriers make it difficult to find and retain jobs in these distant locations.

William Julius Wilson (1987) expanded this basic hypothesis, arguing that the exodus of jobs from central-city locations, combined with the persistence of residential segregation, contributed to rising unemployment among black men during the 1980s, as well as to worsening poverty and distress in black neighborhoods. A recent review finds that most empirical studies support the spatial mismatch hypothesis. Specifically, of twenty-eight studies reviewed, twenty-one confirm the hypothesis, and the seven that reject it are methodologically flawed. In fact, the review authors conclude that the impact of residential location on job outcomes may be even greater than most studies estimate. However, these impacts may vary significantly across metropolitan regions, with the biggest effects occurring in large metropolitan areas that are highly segregated (Ihlanfeldt and Sjoquist 1998).

However, over the past decade, conditions in both housing and labor markets have changed quite dramatically in many metropolitan areas. These changes raise questions about whether the traditional formulation of the spatial mismatch hypothesis still applies. Specifically, although discrimina-tion in metropolitan housing markets persists, its incidence is declining (Turner *et al.* 2002). As is discussed elsewhere in this book, data from the 2000 census indicate that residential segregation is declining, albeit slowly, and that growing numbers of blacks and Hispanics are moving to suburban communities (Pastor 2001). Moreover, the number (and population) of high-poverty central city neighborhoods declined during the 1990s (Jargowsky 2003; Kingsley and Pettit 2003), and at least some central cities began to experience economic revitalization, with expanding employment opportunities in previously distressed neighborhoods (Raphael and Stoll 2002).

While these changes have by no means eliminated the spatial separation between neighborhoods where minorities live and centers of expanding employment opportunity, they have certainly changed—and complicated—the picture. A recent analysis explores the extent of this change using 1990 and 2000 census data to track the extent of spatial mismatch between people of different races and ethnicities and jobs in all U.S. metropolitan areas (Raphael and Stoll 2002). This analysis constructs dissimilarity indexes, which are widely used to measure the extent of segregation between racial and ethnic groups, to quantify the spatial separation between people and jobs. As of 2000, the dissimilarity index between population and employment is highest for blacks (53 on a scale where 100 represents complete segregation), lower for Asians (43) and Hispanics (44), and lowest for whites (33).

During the 1990s the index declined for blacks and Hispanics, remained essentially unchanged for Asians, and increased slightly for whites. These improvements appear to result primarily from changes occurring within metropolitan regions and not from people moving between regions. Reductions in spatial mismatch for blacks were biggest in the Midwest and West, smaller in the South, and smallest in the Northeast. Moreover, improvements were the most dramatic in metropolitan areas where the black share of the population was lowest. The extent of mismatch remains greatest where black–white residential segregation is highest, and reductions in spatial mismatch are associated with declines in segregation levels.

There is strong evidence that residential segregation continues to separate minorities from centers of employment opportunity and that this separation contributes to unequal employment outcomes. However, the traditional image of minorities trapped in central city neighborhoods while jobs are located in more and more distant suburban locations is probably too simplistic. Both minority suburbanization and central city revitalization have complicated the reality of spatial mismatch, and there is good reason to suspect that patterns may vary significantly across metropolitan areas, which necessitates different policy remedies.

Current Patterns of Residential and Employment Location

To help us understand these emerging patterns better, this chapter presents a new, exploratory analysis of residential and employment locations in six metropolitan areas—Atlanta, Georgia; Boston, Massachusetts; Houston, Texas; Philadelphia, Pennsylvania; Seattle, Washington; and Washington,

DC.[2] Tables 5.2a and 5.2b present key characteristics of these metropolitan areas, which have very different demographic, housing, and labor market conditions. The six metropolitan regions range in population from about 2 million to just over 5 million, with the central cities accounting for dramatically different shares of the total. At one extreme, Washington, DC is home to only 12 percent of its region's total population, while at the other, Houston is home to 46 percent. In general, these regions are growing faster, in terms of both population and employment, than their central cities. Atlanta grew the fastest during the 1990s, with its population increasing 39 percent in the region but only 6 percent in the central city. The Philadelphia and Boston regions grew much more slowly, and the city of Philadelphia actually lost both population and jobs.

TABLE 5.2a Demographic and Economic Characteristics for Selected Metros

	Atlanta		Boston		Houston	
	City	Metro	City	Metro	City	Metro
Population, 2000	421,000	2,223,000	589,000	3,406,000	1,935,000	4,178,000
% Black	61%	29%	26%	7%	25%	18%
% Hispanic	4%	6%	14%	6%	37%	30%
% Foreign born	7%	10%	26%	15%	26%	20%
% Poor	25%	9%	29%	9%	19%	14%
% Unemployed	14%	5%	7%	4%	8%	6%
% Adults in mngmnt./ prof. occs.	26%	25%	26%	30%	20%	22%
Population change, 1990–2000	6%	39%	3%	6%	15%	26%
Employment change, 1990–2000	5%	34%	–1%	3%	4%	18%
Avg. family income	$73,000	$85,000	$62,000	$89,000	$60,000	$69,000
Avg. owner-occupied house value	$241,000	$173,000	$240,000	$289,000	$121,000	$127,000

TABLE 5.2b Demographic and Economic Characteristics for Selected Metros

	Philadelphia		Seattle		Washington, DC	
	City	Metro	City	Metro	City	Metro
Population, 2000	1,518,000	5,101,000	563,000	2,415,000	572,000	4,923,000
% Black	43%	20%	10%	5%	61%	27%
% Hispanic	8%	5%	5%	5%	8%	9%
% Foreign born	9%	7%	17%	14%	13%	17%
% Poor	23%	11%	12%	8%	20%	7%
% Unemployed	11%	6%	5%	4%	11%	4%
% Adults in mngmnt./ prof. occs.	16%	22%	32%	27%	29%	33%
Population change, 1990–2000	–4%	4%	9%	19%	–6%	17%
Employment change, 1990–2000	–11%	0%	13%	17%	–14%	8%
Avg. family income	$48,000	$73,000	$84,000	$80,000	$78,000	$91,000
Avg. owner-occupied house value	$72,000	$147,000	$315,000	$273,000	$252,000	$226,000

Source: Urban Institute tabulations of 1990 and 2000 Census data.

The racial and ethnic diversity of U.S. metropolitan areas is well represented by these six metropolitan areas. For example, the Atlanta and Washington, DC regions both have quite large black populations and smaller Hispanic populations. In contrast, both blacks and Hispanics account for much smaller shares of the total population in the Boston and Seattle metropolitan areas. In the Houston area, Hispanics account for three of every ten residents. The share of metro area residents who are foreign born also varies widely, from a low of only 7 percent in Philadelphia to a high of 20 percent in Houston.

Economic conditions also differ significantly across the six metropolitan areas. Poverty and unemployment were lowest in the Washington, DC, and Seattle regions, and considerably higher in the Houston area. Not surprisingly, both poverty and unemployment were substantially higher in the central cities than in the suburbs, even in the most prosperous metropolitan areas. Finally, average family incomes range from a low of $69,000 in Houston, where only about one in five workers has a managerial or professional position, to a high of $91,000 in the Washington, DC metropolitan area, where one-third of all workers are managers or professionals.

Residential Location by Race and Ethnicity

Residential segregation is quite high in all six of these metropolitan areas, even among high-wage workers. Overall levels of residential segregation are consistently highest for blacks, ranging from a low of 51 in Seattle, where the black population is very small, to a high of 68 in Philadelphia. In Atlanta, Houston, Philadelphia, and Washington, DC, levels of segregation are slightly lower for high-wage blacks than for low-wage blacks. The dissimilarity index in these four metropolitan areas ranges from 59 to 67, even for workers earning over $75,000 annually. Segregation levels are actually higher among high-wage workers than among low-wage workers in Seattle and Boston.

Levels of residential segregation for Hispanics are generally lower and more variable across the six metropolitan areas, ranging from a low of 30 in Seattle to a high of 57 in Boston. In Atlanta, Houston, and Washington, DC, levels of segregation generally decline as wage rates increase, but in Boston, Philadelphia, and Seattle the opposite pattern prevails, with substantially higher levels of residential segregation for high-wage Hispanics than for low-wage Hispanics.

In all six metropolitan areas, blacks and Hispanics are more likely to live in the central cities, while whites are more likely to live in suburban communities (see Table 5.3).[3] However, it would be a mistake to think of the suburbs in any of these metropolitan areas as exclusively white. In fact, a majority of blacks live in the suburbs of all but the Houston and Philadelphia metropolitan areas, and a majority of Hispanics live in the suburbs in all but Houston. In general, low-wage blacks are especially likely to live in central city jurisdictions. Even so, a very substantial share of low-wage blacks and Hispanics now live in suburban jurisdictions.

However, patterns of residential location within the suburbs are dramatically different for blacks and Hispanics than for whites. In general, minorities are overrepresented in the inner ring of suburban communities, while whites are more likely to live in the outer ring. In several metropolitan areas, suburban minorities are clustered in one or two counties. In the Washington, DC region, for example, only 21 percent of blacks and 11 percent of

TABLE 5.3 Residential Location by Race and Ethnicity in Selected Metros (Percentages)

		All Workers			Low-Wage Workers			High-Wage Workers		
		City	Inner Suburbs	Outer Suburbs	City	Inner Suburbs	Outer Suburbs	City	Inner Suburbs	Outer Suburbs
Atlanta	White	7.1	39.2	53.6	5.3	36.6	58.1	12.6	49.2	38.2
	Black	18.4	62.4	19.2	24.8	55.8	19.4	17.8	61.5	20.7
	Hispanic	10.1	53.7	36.3	10.7	55.2	34.0	9.7	52.0	38.3
Boston	White	7.7	49.1	43.2	7.7	45.2	47.0	7.0	60.3	32.6
	Black	47.5	32.6	19.9	48.4	31.0	20.6	32.5	51.4	16.1
	Hispanic	29.5	45.5	25.0	30.6	44.8	24.6	20.3	57.2	22.5
Houston	White	28.0	37.4	34.6	25.7	36.2	38.0	33.0	36.3	30.7
	Black	60.6	23.2	16.3	65.7	18.2	16.1	44.1	28.8	27.1
	Hispanic	52.5	30.5	17.0	57.6	26.8	15.6	40.5	35.8	23.6
Philadelphia	White	15.4	62.7	21.9	17.4	61.5	21.0	8.1	66.3	25.6
	Black	53.9	32.2	14.0	58.8	27.6	13.6	34.8	48.8	16.4
	Hispanic	37.0	43.5	19.4	39.5	40.9	19.7	18.4	57.7	23.9
Seattle	White	16.4	41.3	42.2	16.0	37.6	46.4	19.7	51.5	28.8
	Black	26.8	33.6	39.6	28.2	29.5	42.3	27.7	44.3	28.0
	Hispanic	19.0	44.8	36.3	20.0	43.6	36.3	16.2	55.9	27.9
Washington, DC	White	6.7	56.8	36.5	6.2	49.2	44.6	8.9	70.2	20.9
	Black	20.9	65.2	13.9	25.5	59.4	15.1	16.2	72.4	11.4
	Hispanic	10.8	74.7	14.6	12.4	75.0	12.6	12.2	74.5	13.3

Hispanics live in the central city. The vast majority of those who have located in the suburbs live in the inner suburban communities, while a much larger share of whites live in the outer suburbs. Specifically, 37 percent of whites live in outer suburban communities, compared to only 14 percent of blacks and 15 percent of Hispanics. Even among the highest-wage workers, a substantially larger share of whites live in the outer ring of suburbs.

Moreover, within the inner suburbs, patterns of residence vary dramatically by race (see Annex Table 5.A, p. 176). Specifically, more than two-thirds of all the blacks who live in the inner suburbs of the Washington, DC metropolitan area are clustered in a single county: Prince George's County, Maryland, which was 62 percent black as of 2000. Hispanics living in the inner suburbs are considerably less geographically clustered, but they are still far less likely than non-Hispanic whites to live in the region's outer suburbs.

To some extent, variations in residential location by race and ethnicity are attributable to income levels. Even among high-wage workers, blacks and Hispanics are more likely to live in the central city and inner suburbs, while whites are more likely to live in the outer suburbs. For example, in the Washington, DC region, 21 percent of white workers who earn more than $75,000 annually live in outer suburban communities, compared to 11 percent of blacks and 13 percent of Hispanics in the same wage range. Moreover, within the inner suburbs 32 percent of high-wage whites live in Fairfax County, Virginia, compared to only 12 percent of high-wage blacks but 30 percent of high-wage Hispanics (again, Annex Table 5.A).

Employment Location by Race and Ethnicity

Blacks and Hispanics are segregated from whites not only in their places of residence but also in their places of work. The rate of workplace segregation is lower than residential segregation but, as is illustrated in Figures 5.1a and 5.1b, blacks and Hispanics in all six metropolitan areas work in quite separate locations than whites. Specifically, black–white dissimilarity indexes by place of work range from 27 in Houston to 39 in Boston. In Atlanta, Houston, and Washington, DC, higher-wage black workers are considerably less segregated from their white counterparts, but in Boston, Philadelphia, and Seattle levels of segregation vary much less by wage level. Levels of workplace segregation for Hispanics from non-Hispanic whites are somewhat lower, ranging from 15 in Seattle to 29 in Philadelphia. For Hispanics, we see a clear pattern of rising levels of segregation as wage rates rise.

Consistent with the basic spatial mismatch hypothesis, blacks and Hispanics are more likely to work in the central cities, while whites are more likely to work in suburban areas (see Table 5.4). In all six metropolitan areas the share of blacks working in the central city is substantially higher than the

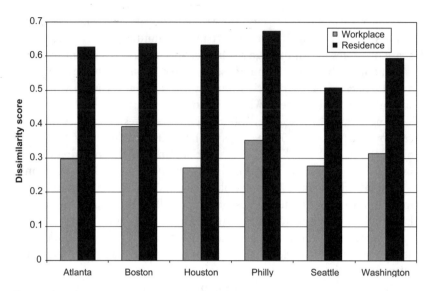

Figure 5.1a White–black segregation at work and home.

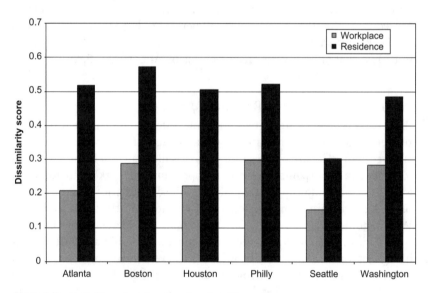

Figure 5.1b Anglo–Hispanic segregation at work and home.

TABLE 5.4 Employment Location by Race and Ethnicity in Selected Metros (Percentages)

		All Workers			Low-Wage Workers			High-Wage Workers		
		City	Inner Suburbs	Outer Suburbs	City	Inner Suburbs	Outer Suburbs	City	Inner Suburbs	Outer Suburbs
Atlanta	White	20.6	43.1	36.2	13.2	41.0	45.8	29.8	45.8	24.4
	Black	35.9	46.3	17.8	34.0	46.4	19.6	38.1	45.6	16.3
	Hispanic	23.1	44.7	32.2	22.2	44.2	33.7	25.0	50.2	24.8
Boston	White	15.8	48.4	35.8	10.6	45.8	43.6	23.0	54.5	22.4
	Black	45.6	38.7	15.8	42.9	38.3	18.8	46.1	44.1	9.9
	Hispanic	28.1	48.4	23.5	26.0	49.2	24.9	35.6	48.6	15.9
Houston	White	51.3	25.7	23.0	39.3	29.8	30.9	66.4	19.5	14.1
	Black	69.3	17.0	13.7	67.0	17.0	16.1	68.0	18.2	13.8
	Hispanic	61.9	23.0	15.2	61.5	22.8	15.7	62.3	24.2	13.4
Philadelphia	White	20.2	57.5	22.3	17.7	61.1	21.2	22.2	53.7	24.1
	Black	48.1	36.7	15.2	47.5	37.6	14.9	43.1	39.2	17.7
	Hispanic	33.3	47.2	19.6	32.9	47.7	19.4	28.7	46.2	25.1
Seattle	White	25.3	42.5	32.2	20.6	39.7	39.6	32.5	48.8	18.6
	Black	35.5	31.5	33.1	32.6	29.2	38.2	41.0	35.7	23.2
	Hispanic	27.0	42.3	30.7	25.3	41.4	33.3	29.3	52.0	18.8
Washington, DC	White	20.5	55.4	24.0	11.7	49.8	38.5	25.0	59.5	15.5
	Black	39.4	51.9	8.7	32.6	54.4	13.0	45.5	49.2	5.3
	Hispanic	23.3	64.8	11.9	19.2	68.0	12.8	33.8	57.1	9.1

share of whites. This pattern holds regardless of the relative size of city and suburban labor markets. In Boston, for example, only 16 percent of whites work in the central city, compared to 46 percent of blacks. In Houston, where about half of non-Hispanic whites work in the central city (51 percent), the percentage of blacks is almost 20 percentage points higher (69 percent). Hispanic workers are also more likely than non-Hispanic whites to work in the central city, although the gap is generally not as wide. In Atlanta, Seattle, and Washington, DC, the share of Hispanics working in central-city locations is only slightly higher than the share of whites.

Although minorities are more likely than whites to work in central cities, a majority of both blacks and Hispanics hold suburban jobs. The only exception to this rule is Houston, where the central city accounts for 57 percent of the region's total jobs. Thus, it would clearly be a mistake to argue that minorities are excluded from suburban employment opportunities. However, we see significant differences within the suburbs based on race and ethnicity. Just as blacks are more likely to live in the inner-ring suburbs, they are more likely to work there as well; while whites are more likely to work in the outer suburbs. Of the six metropolitan areas, Seattle is the only one in which roughly equal shares of whites, blacks, and Hispanics work in the outer suburbs. In contrast, whites in Boston are more than twice as likely as blacks to work in the outer suburbs and 1.5 times as likely as Hispanics. In Houston, even though the suburbs account for a much smaller share of jobs, whites are 1.7 times more likely than blacks and 1.5 times more likely than Hispanics to hold jobs in the outer suburbs.

Not only are members of minorities less likely to work in the outer suburbs but blacks are typically underrepresented in white suburban counties that are particularly rich in employment opportunities (Annex Table 5.B). For example, the Atlanta region's Gwinnett County, which is 70 percent white, accounts for about 18 percent of all suburban jobs and 43 percent of jobs in the outer ring. About 15 percent of all white workers are employed in Gwinnett County, compared to only 9 percent of black workers. In contrast, 22 percent of employed blacks in the Atlanta region work in DeKalb County, which is only 35 percent white, compared to only 12 percent of employed whites. We see a very similar pattern in the Washington, DC region. Fairfax County, Virginia, which is 67 percent white, accounts for one in five employed whites in the region compared to only one in ten employed blacks. In contrast, Prince George's County, Maryland, which is 25 percent white, accounts for 19 percent of the region's black employment but only 9 percent of white employment (Annex Table 5.C).

The picture is quite different for Hispanic workers in the suburbs. In the Atlanta region, Hispanics are just as likely as non-Hispanic whites to work in predominantly white Gwinnett County and much less likely than blacks to work in DeKalb County. Similarly, in the Washington, DC region, Hispanics are just as likely as non-Hispanic whites to work in Fairfax County and half as likely as blacks to work in Prince George's County. In the Houston region, where Hispanics account for a much larger share of the minority population, only 12 percent of Hispanics work in the predominantly white outer suburbs, compared to 23 percent of non-Hispanic whites (Annex Table 5.D).

How do these patterns of employment location vary by wage levels? As we have seen, Houston is the only one of our six metropolitan areas where a majority of all jobs are located in the central city. In Atlanta, Philadelphia, Seattle, and Washington, DC, roughly three-quarters of the region's jobs are located in the suburbs, and in Boston the suburbs account for more than eight of every ten jobs. However, as is illustrated in Figure 5.2, in five of the six metropolitan areas considered here, high-wage jobs remain more concentrated in central cities than low-wage jobs. More specifically, the share of high-wage jobs located in the central city is generally about ten percentage points higher than the share of low-wage jobs. This differential is greatest in the Washington, DC region, where one-third of all high-wage jobs are located in the central city, compared to only 18 percent of low-wage jobs.

In the Atlanta, Boston, Houston, Seattle, and Washington, DC regions, high-wage suburban jobs are more likely to be located in clusters than low-wage jobs. More than one-third of the Atlanta region's low-wage jobs are

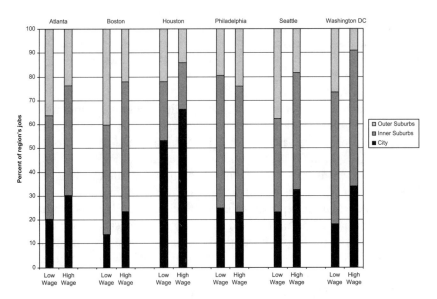

Figure 5.2 Spatial distribution of low-wage and high-wage jobs in selected metropolitan areas.

located throughout the outer suburbs, while less than a quarter of high-wage jobs are. In the Washington, DC region, fewer than one in ten high-wage jobs are located in the outer suburbs, as compared to more than one in four low-wage jobs. The Philadelphia area is different: it has a slightly higher share of high-wage jobs in the suburbs than in the central city and a slightly higher share in the outer suburbs than in the inner suburbs.

In some respects it appears that the geographic distribution of high-wage jobs aligns relatively well with minority residential locations. However, the suburban areas where high-wage jobs are concentrated are among the most predominantly white, while suburban areas where blacks and Hispanics are more likely to live offer relatively few high-wage opportunities. For example, in the Atlanta region, predominantly white Gwinnett County accounts for 18 percent of all suburban jobs in the region and 19 percent of high-wage suburban jobs. As was discussed earlier, blacks—including high-wage blacks—are underrepresented in Gwinnett County jobs. Similarly, Fairfax County accounts for 23 percent of the region's high-wage jobs, but only 14 percent of high-wage blacks work there.

A person's residential location may play a role in determining access to employment location, but it certainly is not a perfect predictor. In general, people, regardless of their race or ethnicity, are much more likely to work in the central cities of the metropolitan areas studied here than to live in them. High-wage white workers are especially likely to work in but not live in central cities. However, as illustrated in Table 5.5, the percentage of racial or ethnic groups who live in the outer suburbs corresponds closely to the percentage who work there. Patterns of residential segregation that limit minority access to some suburban communities have the potential to limit access to employment opportunities in these communities as well.

Summary of Findings

To summarize, in six very different metropolitan regions we find minority workers (and especially low-wage black workers) overrepresented in central cities, while jobs (especially low-wage jobs) are situated widely throughout the suburbs. Although many minorities have gained access to suburban residential communities, these are often not the suburban jurisdictions that offer the most promising job opportunities. Correspondingly, black workers in particular are underrepresented in jobs that are located in predominantly white suburban communities. On the other hand, Hispanic workers are generally just as likely as non-Hispanic whites to find employment in the white suburbs. This evidence confirms that patterns of residential segregation and employment location are far more complex—and varied—than envisioned by Kain's original spatial mismatch concept. It also shows that residential segregation continues to put considerable distance between

TABLE 5.5 Ratio of the Share of Employees to the Share of Residents by Race and Ethnicity in Selected Metros

		All Workers			Low-Wage Workers			High-Wage Workers		
		City	Inner Suburbs	Outer Suburbs	City	Inner Suburbs	Outer Suburbs	City	Inner Suburbs	Outer Suburbs
Atlanta	White	2.9	1.1	0.7	2.5	1.1	0.8	2.4	0.9	0.6
	Black	2.0	0.7	0.9	1.4	0.8	1.0	2.1	0.7	0.8
	Hispanic	2.3	0.8	0.9	2.1	0.8	1.0	2.6	1.0	0.6
Boston	White	2.0	1.0	0.8	1.4	1.0	0.9	3.3	0.9	0.7
	Black	1.0	1.2	0.8	0.9	1.2	0.9	1.4	0.9	0.6
	Hispanic	1.0	1.1	0.9	0.8	1.1	1.0	1.7	0.8	0.7
Houston	White	1.8	0.7	0.7	1.5	0.8	0.8	2.0	0.5	0.5
	Black	1.1	0.7	0.8	1.0	0.9	1.0	1.5	0.6	0.5
	Hispanic	1.2	0.8	0.9	1.1	0.9	1.0	1.5	0.7	0.6
Philadelphia	White	1.3	0.9	1.0	1.0	1.0	1.0	2.7	0.8	0.9
	Black	0.9	1.1	1.1	0.8	1.4	1.1	1.2	0.8	1.1
	Hispanic	0.9	1.1	1.0	0.8	1.2	1.0	1.6	0.8	1.0
Seattle	White	1.5	1.0	0.8	1.3	1.1	0.9	1.7	0.9	0.6
	Black	1.3	0.9	0.8	1.2	1.0	0.9	1.5	0.8	0.8
	Hispanic	1.4	0.9	0.8	1.3	0.9	0.9	1.8	0.9	0.7
Washington, DC	White	3.1	1.0	0.7	1.9	1.0	0.9	2.8	0.8	0.7
	Black	1.9	0.8	0.6	1.3	0.9	0.9	2.8	0.7	0.7
	Hispanic	2.2	0.9	0.8	1.5	0.9	1.0	2.8	0.8	0.7

minority workers, especially blacks, and areas of greatest employment opportunity. To understand these patterns more fully, future analyses should dig deeper, exploring differences by gender, industry, and occupation in these and other metropolitan markets.

Job Openings and Neighborhood Composition

An analysis by Stoll *et al.* (2000) provides additional insight on patterns of residential segregation and employment location. This analysis linked census data on the racial composition of subareas within the cities and suburbs of Atlanta, Boston, Chicago, and Los Angeles to a survey of employers that provides information about recently filled job openings and those hired to fill them. The authors focused on low-skill jobs and on less-educated workers, and grouped contiguous census tracts into seven subareas for each metropolitan area: the central business district, black central city, Hispanic central city, white central city, black suburbs, integrated suburbs, and white suburbs.

Overall, the authors find that the ratio of newly filled jobs to population is approximately the same in central-city areas (other than the central business district) as in the suburbs but that the ratio of jobs to population is much higher in white subareas than in minority and integrated subareas. Consistent with the analysis discussed above, the study shows that low-skill jobs are much more decentralized than high-skill jobs, with roughly two-thirds of the low-skill openings located in the white suburbs. In addition, the ratio of low-skill jobs to less-educated people varies dramatically by subarea and is consistently lowest in black and Hispanic central-city areas and highest in the white suburbs. Moreover, nearly half of all low-skill jobs in the white suburbs are inaccessible by public transportation, making it particularly difficult for minority residents of other subareas to reach them. The authors argue that although jobs in the central business district may be physically accessible, these jobs tend to be highly competitive and may require higher skills (Holzer 1996).

The analysis by Stoll *et al.* (2000) also concludes that the race or ethnicity of new hires for low-skill jobs generally matches the racial composition of the area where the jobs are located. This outcome appears to be explained in part by the racial/ethnic composition of applicant pools. However, the minority share of applicants for jobs in the white suburbs is significantly higher than the minority share of population in these areas, suggesting that blacks and Hispanics are trying to get jobs in white suburbs. Racial differences in the probability of success vary considerably across the four metropolitan areas included in the study by Stoll *et al.*, but, in general, blacks appear to be preferred in black central-city areas and black suburbs but disadvantaged in white central-city areas and white and integrated suburbs.

Understanding Why Location Matters

The fact that residential segregation continues to separate the neighborhoods in which most minority workers live from areas of employment opportunity in both cities and suburbs is important, but it does not fully explain the mechanisms through which spatial mismatch contributes to unequal employment outcomes. Certainly, distance and the resultant commuting costs are part of the explanation. Empirical evidence confirms that blacks are less likely than whites to apply for low-skill jobs in the suburbs (Holzer 1996; Stoll *et al.* 2000) because they lack information about specific job openings (Ihlanfeldt and Sjoquist 1998) and also because they are simply unfamiliar with the locations of major suburban job centers (Ihlandfeldt 1997).

Not only are suburban job opportunities distant from minority neighborhoods but they are often distant from transit stations. For example, the study discussed earlier that focused on employment opportunities in Atlanta, Boston, Detroit, and Los Angeles found that only about half of all low-skill jobs in the white suburbs were accessible by public transportation, as compared to almost all low-skill jobs in the central business district, and over 80 percent of those in other parts of the central city (Stoll *et al.* 2000). Proximity to transit stations has been shown to help explain the racial composition of a firm's workforce (Ihlanfeldt and Young 1996).

Location per se is not the only source of employment inequality. Recent research highlights three other major factors that put minority workers at a disadvantage in today's labor markets: (1) differences in skills, experience, and credentials; (2) limited information and references for job search and application; and (3) prejudice and discrimination. I suggest that residential segregation exacerbates all three of these problems, and not just for low-skilled members of minority groups, who are most likely to be concentrated in central city neighborhoods, but also for better-educated minoriy-group members living in the segregated suburbs.

Skills, Experience, and Credentials

Labor market experts generally agree that differences between whites and minorities in educational attainment, skills, and experience are major contributors to unequal employment outcomes. Some argue that these differences explain most of the inequality in employment and wages and, consequently, that policies to narrow the gap between whites and minorities should focus primarily on education (Jencks and Phillips 1998). Even if education and experience only account for part of the problem, they are clearly important.

In today's labor market the importance of key work skills is growing as a determinant of employment success even for low-wage jobs. Historically, manufacturing jobs paid relatively high wages for unskilled labor, but increasingly, even low-skill jobs require higher levels of cognitive skills, including reading and writing ability, computer skills, and the ability to interact effectively with customers and coworkers (Holzer 1996). Analysis of hiring practices indicates that employers increasingly look for candidates with specific skills and certifications. The economic boom of the 1990s made it harder for employers to find qualified workers, and those seeking lower-skilled workers changed their hiring behaviors, becoming more willing to hire minorities, college dropouts, and welfare recipients. Despite the tight labor market, employers continued to impose higher skill requirements, putting more emphasis on the attainment of specific skills (Holzer *et al.* 2003).

Residential segregation clearly contributes to minorities' unequal educational attainment and hence to their disadvantaged position in the evolving labor market. Black high school graduation rates, employment rates, and wages are all negatively affected by the level of black–white segregation in a city. Other things being equal, high levels of segregation have been shown to increase high school dropout rates among blacks, reduce employment among blacks (while increasing the white employment rate), and widen the gap between black and white wages (Cutler and Glaeser 1997). Other analysis indicates that public school desegregation plans of the 1970s reduced high school dropout rates among blacks by between one and three percentage points (half of the total decline achieved during the decade), while having no effect on dropout rates among whites (Guryan 2001).

Racial and ethnic segregation undermines the educational attainment, skills, and qualifications of minorities in several ways, including school quality. The effects are most obvious—and most severe—in distressed central city neighborhoods, where many low-income members of minority groups are concentrated.[4] Many high-poverty neighborhoods are served by failing public schools with high dropout rates, low instructional quality, and poor test scores (O'Regan and Quigley 1996). Black and Hispanic children attending these schools are at a tremendous disadvantage even if they stay in school and work hard.

In addition, other conditions typical of distressed central city neighborhoods further undermine their chances of succeeding academically and attaining the skills necessary to compete effectively in today's labor markets. In particular, peer pressure plays a critical role in shaping the choices of young people. Adolescents spend roughly twice as much time with peers as they do with their parents or other adults (Connell and Halpern-Felsher 1997). Thus, young people can be profoundly influenced by their immediate peer groups (Berndt 1996; Steinberg and Silverberg 1986), which are often composed primarily of neighbors and schoolmates. Youths' peer groups are certainly not determined solely by neighborhood, but neighborhood is likely to have a significant effect on the choice of peer group. If many young people in a community are uninterested in school or are engaging in crime and other dangerous behaviors, teenagers will be more apt to see these activities as acceptable behavior. Indeed, Anderson (1994: 94) reports that in some inner-city communities the "toughening-up one experiences in prison can actually enhance one's reputation on the street."

The literature on adolescent educational attainment provides general support for the notion that neighborhood distress plays an important role (Aaronson 1997; Brooks-Gunn *et al.* 1993; Case and Katz 1991; Clark 1992; Crane 1991; Datcher 1982; Dornbusch *et al.* 1991; Duncan 1994; Duncan *et al.* 1997; Garner and Raudenbush 1991; Haveman and Wolfe 1994). Young people from high-poverty and distressed neighborhoods are less successful in school than their counterparts from more affluent communities; they achieve lower grades, are more likely to drop out, and are less likely to go to college. Kids from poor neighborhoods are also less likely to get jobs during and immediately after high school. Finally, young people who live in high-crime areas have been found to be more likely to commit crimes themselves (Case and Katz 1991).

The effects of residential segregation on educational achievement are not limited to distressed central-city neighborhoods. Growing up in segregated suburbs can also undermine the potential of minority young people, though in more subtle ways. Minority neighborhoods generally have lower house values than comparable white neighborhoods and, consequently, a lower property tax base from which to fund public schools (Oliver and Shapiro 1997). In the inner suburbs of the Washington, DC metropolitan area, the average price for a single-family home in predominantly black Prince George's County was $195,400 in 2003 and in predominantly white Fairfax County was $365,900 (Turner *et al.* 2004). Public school performance in minority suburban communities typically falls considerably short of the standard expected of schools in the white suburbs (Cashin 2004). In fact, a panel study of Texas public school students finds that the achievement of black students declines significantly as the percentage of blacks in their schools rises. The negative effect of segregation appears to be the most severe for children in the upper half of the ability distribution, as students of lower ability are less likely to be affected (Hanushek *et al.* 2005).

Another way in which schools in minority neighborhoods may be disadvantaged stems from teachers' preferences to work close to where they grew up or in areas with similar characteristics to their hometowns. A recent study (Boyd *et al.* 2005) finds that these preferences are widespread and argues that schools in central cities may have access to pools of less qualified teachers than schools in more affluent and predominantly white communities.

Finally, there is some evidence to suggest that community norms and expectations about attending college (or attending an elite college or university) are lower for young people growing up in predominantly minority communities (Cashin 2004), and the lower house values in these communities translate into lower levels of wealth accumulation, which may limit the ability of minority parents to finance an elite college education (Oliver and Shapiro 1997). Even for middle- and upper-income minority families who have escaped the distress of inner-city neighborhoods, residential segregation may restrict young people's educational achievement, perpetuating their disadvantage in today's increasingly demanding labor markets.

Information and References

A second important set of factors that help determine labor market success involves information—not only a job seeker's access to information about possible job openings but also an employer's information about a candidate's likely performance. When job openings are advertised using only community newspapers, bulletin boards, or help-wanted signs, job seekers living in distant neighborhoods may never find out about them (Holzer *et al.* 1994). The spatial separation of employment centers (especially suburban job centers) from minority neighborhoods may prevent a minority job seeker from finding out about potential opportunities.

In addition, however, many employers rely heavily on referrals from their current employees to fill open positions, in part because so many jobs (even low-skilled jobs) require cognitive and social skills. References provide some assurance to an employer that a candidate has the skills necessary to succeed (Holzer 1996; Holzer and Ihlanfeldt 1996). Consequently, social networks may determine the openings a job seeker learns about and whether he or she receives credible references for these positions. Research on the role of networks in the job search process has documented a high and rising reliance on friends, relatives, and acquaintances. Moreover, informal job search methods tend to be effective and increase the likelihood of both finding and keeping a job. In particular, recommendations from in-house workers have been shown to be critical to finding jobs (Kasinitz and Rosenberg 1996; Sullivan 1989; Wial 1991; Ioannides and Loury 2004).

The effectiveness of these informal job search methods is not equal for all racial and ethnic groups. In general, minority job seekers are less successful in using their networks of family and friends than whites (Ioannides and Loury 2004). Again, although residential segregation is not the only reason why minorities have less effective networks, it certainly is a factor, particularly for minorities living in high-poverty central city neighborhoods and also for those in the segregated suburbs.

A substantial body of research indicates that residents of high-poverty central-city neighborhoods are often isolated from networks of people who can provide information about jobs or references to prospective employers (O'Regan 1993; Pastor and Adams, 1996). Not only are employment rates low in these segregated communities, but relatively few neighbors work in the expanding employment centers of the suburbs. Thus, neighbors cannot provide either information or referrals for the full range of job opportunities available in a metropolitan region. Neighbors certainly are not the only information source to which job seekers can turn, but the available evidence suggests that poor people's social ties are more localized than those of middle-class people (Briggs 1997) and are at least partially dependent on networks within the neighborhood (Pastor 2001).

Little research has focused on the issue of job networks for members of minorities living in segregated suburban areas. It seems likely that the problem is less severe than in central-city neighborhoods because a much higher share of residents work. For example, in 2000 the unemployment rate among black men was 7.6 percent in Prince George's County—almost half that of Washington, DC, at 15.7 percent. As was discussed earlier, few blacks in the Washington, DC region work in the high-wage employment centers of suburban Fairfax County. Even a high-wage worker living in predominantly black Prince George's County is likely to have a network of neighbors, family, and friends who work mostly in Washington, DC, and offer little or no access to the expanding employment opportunities of Fairfax County. Indeed, empirical evidence confirms that, even after distance and transportation access have been controlled for, the ability of minorities to get jobs in an area depends significantly on the ethnic composition of that area (Stoll *et al.* 2000).

Prejudice and Discrimination

Although white prejudices about the intelligence, diligence, and reliability of blacks and Hispanics have been waning over the past several decades, negative stereotypes still persist (Pew Research Center 2003). There is strong evidence that prejudiced attitudes on the part of employers result in discrimination against qualified minority job applicants (Turner *et al.* 1991; Ihlanfeldt and Sjoquist 1998). Blacks are particularly unlikely to be hired for jobs that require higher cognitive skills, especially daily computer use, arithmetic, or customer interaction (Holzer 1996). Many analysts have suggested that customer prejudice may also be a factor, since the racial composition of a firm's workforce has been found to be related both to the race of the manager and to the racial composition of the firm's customers (Ihlanfeldt and Young 1996).

Residential segregation helps fuel the persistence of racial and ethnic prejudice and discrimination in a number of ways. One of the most direct links involves the racial composition of a firm's customers. In communities that are racially and ethnically mixed, a firm's customer base is likely to be more diverse, eliminating one of the incentives for managers to discriminate against minority job applicants. Additionally, residents of minority neighborhoods may be disadvantaged by employer stereotypes about these communities. Recent research has shown that people's perception of disorder in a neighborhood is influenced by the neighborhood's racial composition as well as by objective indicators of disorder (Sampson and Raudenbush 2004). Thus, minority neighborhoods are likely to be stigmatized by outsiders who simply assume that residents are less likely to succeed in school, work hard, or obey the law.

Residential segregation also may sustain minorities' misperceptions and fears about whites. Even in the segregated suburbs, where employment, incomes, and education levels are high, young people have only limited experience with whites and may therefore avoid whites and predominantly white neighborhoods (Sjoquist 1996). Indeed, Braddock (1980) argues that patterns of social interactions at a young age may shape a child's patterns of behavior and interactions for the long run. In particular, he argues that minority students who attend racially segregated schools and who have not interacted with students of different races tend to overestimate the degree of hostility that they will experience in interracial situations. As adults, these students tend to make choices that maintain their separation from whites when they become adults, which could limit their access to economic and social opportunities.

Implications for Policy

What can policy makers do to address the multiple ways in which the persistence of residential segregation contributes to employment inequality? The most obvious and direct response has been to reduce the information and transportation barriers created by physical distance through programs that help central-city residents find jobs in suburban areas and provide assistance with the reverse commute.[5] Unfortunately, the most recent effort to rigorously evaluate the effectiveness of programs that help inner-city workers find and commute to suburban jobs found no significant benefits with respect to either employment levels or wages among participants.

Specifically, the Bridges-to-Work (BtW) demonstration was designed and launched in the mid-1990s by Public/Private Ventures with support from the Department of Housing and Urban Development and a consortium of foundation funders to connect the presumed surplus of work-ready applicants in central-city neighborhoods to existing employment opportunities in the suburbs (Roder and Scrivner 2005). The BtW design included three program elements: (1) a suburban job placement mechanism, including the recruitment of suburban employers to hire central-city residents; (2) targeted commuting services for inner-city residents; and (3) limited supportive services intended to directly address the challenges of the suburban commute. This third element, which attempted to help participants sustain their connection to the suburban labor market by addressing problems created or exacerbated by the suburban commute, distinguished BtW from earlier reverse commute experiments.[6]

Four sites—Baltimore, Denver, Milwaukee, and St. Louis—implemented the BtW intervention as controlled experiments, with random assignment of applicants to treatment and control groups. All four sites encountered serious problems with recruitment and retention of eligible participants. Although thousands of people inquired about the BtW program or applied to participate, only about 10 percent were actually enrolled. This drop-off resulted from program managers screening out people who did not meet standards for work readiness and from applicants withdrawing from consideration once they understood what the program offered.

Across the four sites, the BtW interventions produced no statistically significant effects on employment or income overall. Participant retention proved to be a major problem; two-thirds of participants were placed in a BtW job, but most used the program services for only a short time. Focus groups and interviews with program staff suggest that the low retention was due to participants' personal struggles, dissatisfaction with certain aspects of their suburban jobs, and the long commute. Moreover, the economy was booming during the second half of the 1990s, and jobs were opening up throughout the metropolitan areas, making the BtW program less attractive or essential for the targeted work-ready population.

The disappointing findings from the BtW demonstration suggest that trying to solve the spatial mismatch problem through transportation strategies alone may be ineffective; other employment barriers, many of which are caused or exacerbated by residential segregation, must also be addressed. In other words, transportation strategies may play a role, but they are unlikely to be effective unless they are linked to help with training and job retention strategies. Specifically, helping central-city residents find and keep suburban jobs may require substantial investments in job readiness training (to compensate for the poor performance of local schools and the absence of role models in high-poverty neighborhoods), ongoing mentoring (to help minority workers overcome their inexperience and uncertainties about interacting with whites), and more intensive outreach (to inform central-city residents about the availability of job opportunities in unfamiliar suburban locations). Even so, in some metropolitan areas the distance between minority neighborhoods and suburban employment locations may simply make it unfeasible to design reverse commuting strategies that are both effective and affordable (Turner and Rawlings 2005).

This leads to the consideration of strategies for tackling residential segregation more directly and expanding opportunities for minorities to live closer to suburban employment centers. Other chapters in this volume discuss fair housing and inclusionary zoning strategies for opening up suburban jurisdictions to minorities. The evidence and analysis presented in this chapter suggest that these strategies should focus on suburban areas where job opportunities are clustered. In recent decades, black and Hispanic households have begun to gain access to suburban residential communities, but, in many cases, the suburban jurisdictions where they live are distant from the areas of greatest job growth and opportunity. Fair housing and inclusionary zoning initiatives need to be more targeted to jurisdictions like Fairfax County in the Washington, DC region, where jobs are plentiful and schools are high-performing.

In addition to strategies aimed at opening suburban housing markets to greater diversity, housing policies can provide direct assistance to members of minorities who want to move to more opportunity-rich neighborhoods. Evidence from two demonstration initiatives suggest that assisted housing mobility strategies can improve employment outcomes for low-income minority-group members. Long-term research on black families that moved from segregated neighborhoods in Chicago to white or racially mixed suburban neighborhoods as part of the Gautreaux demonstration finds significant increases in employment and reductions in welfare recipiency (Rosenbaum and Deluca 2000). More recent evidence from the Moving to Opportunity (MTO) demonstration has not detected statistically significant employment or earnings effects for participants who received housing vouchers to relocate from high-poverty public and assisted housing developments to low-poverty neighborhoods throughout their metro areas (Orr *et al.* 2004). Analysis of data for individual MTO sites, however, does reveal significant influence on employment and earnings in New York City and Los Angeles; multivariate analysis of differences among MTO movers suggests that those who relocated to stable, predominantly white suburban neighborhoods did experience substantial earnings gains (Cove 2006).

Future policy conversations should look for opportunities to influence employment locations as well as residential locations. Incentives to encourage employers to locate in more central locations (to which residents from a variety of neighborhoods can reasonably commute) near transit hubs (to provide easier access for workers who rely on public transportation), and in racially mixed or minority jurisdictions, could help reduce imbalances between where minorities live and where job opportunities are greatest. These types of strategies are often promoted by smart growth advocates because of their potential to counteract urban sprawl, and, if intelligently implemented, they may also help counteract the employment effects of residential segregation. Moreover, state and regional economic development strategies should focus on attracting more employment opportunities to areas where minorities predominate. For example, in the Washington, DC metropolitan area, the region's Transportation Planning Board is exploring land-use scenarios in which more economic growth occurs in Prince George's County and other eastern suburbs, where blacks are concentrated (Turner *et al.* 2004).

Finally, although most efforts to address the employment barriers created and sustained by residential segregation have focused on low-wage workers and distressed central-city neighbourhoods, the barriers facing middle- and upper-income minorities living in segregated suburbs also warrant attention. Possible strategies include information referrals to help minority professionals learn about and apply for jobs in predominantly white suburban employment centers; in-person or Web-based networks to expand minority job seekers' circle of family, neighbors, and friends; mentoring programs to help minority workers joining a predominantly white workforce for the first time; and car pooling or ride-sharing programs for intersuburban commuters. Residential segregation creates more daunting barriers to employment for low-skilled workers than for more highly educated and qualified workers. Even for skilled professionals, patterns of residential segregation have the potential to limit access to areas of employment opportunity and growth in many metropolitan areas.

Annex Tables

Please refer to page 176–193.

Notes

1. The assignment of names was based on empirical analysis of data from birth certificates of all babies born in Massachusetts over a five-year period. Examples of the names used are Emily Walsh and Lakisha Washington or Brendan Baker and Jamal Jones.
2. This analysis uses data from the 2000 census Transportation Planning Package on the place of residence and place of employment of all workers, where a worker is defined as an individual who was employed for at least one week during 1999. The analysis was conducted by the Urban Institute, with support from the Fannie Mae Foundation, for inclusion in this book. It is intended to explore differential patterns of residential and workplace location as a starting point for further analysis. Future studies might involve multivariate analysis, controlling for gender and other worker attributes, as well as industry and other workplace attributes.
3. The residential patterns of workers reported here correspond very closely to patterns for total population and households.
4. See Massey and Denton (1993) to understand how residential segregation led to the concentration of minority poverty.
5. To date, the policy discussion has focused on the mismatch between minority neighborhoods in the central-city and suburban job centers, not the mismatch discussed earlier between minority neighborhoods in the suburbs and suburban employment centers.
6. Among the services included in the programs' original plans were a guaranteed ride home in an emergency, payment of day-care costs to cover the extra time required to commute to the suburbs, and staff assistance dealing with diversity issues in the workplace.

ANNEX 5.A Percentage of Workers by Wage Level, Race, and Residence Location in the Washington, DC Metropolitan Area, 2000

	All Races	All Workers				
		White	Black	Asian	Hispanic	Other
Total Region		100.0	100.0	100.0	100.0	100.0
District of Columbia		6.7	20.9	4.9	10.8	10.3
Inner Core		8.0	4.1	7.5	13.3	9.8
Arlington County, VA	4.5	5.0	1.6	5.2	8.8	5.1
Alexandria city, VA	3.0	3.1	2.5	2.3	4.5	4.7
Inner Suburbs		48.8	61.1	77.9	61.4	58.1
Montgomery County, MD	17.8	18.2	11.4	30.2	22.9	19.1
Prince George's County, MD	15.6	6.7	42.4	9.3	11.8	14.9
Fairfax County, VA	20.6	23.1	7.2	37.3	25.7	23.5
Fairfax city, VA	0.5	0.5	0.1	0.8	0.7	0.4
Falls Church city, VA	0.2	0.3	0.0	0.3	0.2	0.2
Outer Suburbs		26.0	11.2	8.8	12.6	17.1
Calvert County, MD	1.5	2.1	0.8	0.2	0.2	0.9
Charles County, MD	2.4	2.8	2.5	0.5	0.6	2.5
Frederick County, MD	4.0	6.0	0.9	0.9	1.1	2.0
Loudoun County, VA	3.6	4.9	1.0	2.8	2.4	2.8
Prince William County, VA	5.9	6.6	4.6	3.3	6.0	6.4

Stafford County, VA	1.9	2.6	0.9	0.5	0.7	1.7
Manassas city, VA	0.7	0.8	0.4	0.4	1.1	0.6
Manassas Park city, VA	0.2	0.3	0.1	0.1	0.3	0.3
Far Suburbs		10.5	2.7	0.9	2.0	4.7
Clarke County, VA	0.3	0.4	0.1	0.0	0.0	0.1
Culpeper County, VA	0.6	0.8	0.4	0.1	0.3	0.4
Fauquier County, VA	1.1	1.6	0.4	0.2	0.3	0.6
King George County, VA	0.3	0.4	0.2	0.0	0.1	0.2
Spotsylvania County, VA	1.8	2.4	0.9	0.3	0.6	1.6
Warren County, VA	0.6	0.9	0.1	0.0	0.1	0.2
Fredericksburg city, VA	0.4	0.5	0.3	0.0	0.2	0.4
Berkeley County, WV	1.4	2.2	0.2	0.1	0.2	0.7
Jefferson County, WV	0.8	1.2	0.2	0.1	0.2	0.5

Low-Wage Workers

Total Region		100.0	100.0	100.0	100.0	100.0
District of Columbia		6.2	25.5	6.2	12.4	11.4
Inner Core		5.5	5.2	7.7	14.0	10.5
Arlington County, VA	4.2	3.5	2.2	5.5	9.4	5.3
Alexandria city, VA	2.7	2.0	3.0	2.3	4.6	5.2

ANNEX 5.A *Continued*

		Low-Wage Workers				
	All Races	White	Black	Asian	Hispanic	Other
Inner Suburbs		*43.7*	*54.2*	*75.3*	*61.0*	*55.7*
Montgomery County, MD	16.7	16.0	11.7	27.1	22.1	17.8
Prince George's County, MD	15.7	8.1	35.8	11.7	12.4	13.9
Fairfax County, VA	18.3	18.9	6.5	35.3	25.5	23.3
Fairfax city, VA	0.5	0.5	0.1	1.0	0.8	0.4
Falls Church city, VA	0.2	0.2	0.0	0.2	0.2	0.2
Outer Suburbs		*28.7*	*11.0*	*9.4*	*10.6*	*16.4*
Calvert County, MD	1.5	2.3	1.1	0.2	0.2	0.8
Charles County, MD	2.4	3.2	2.4	0.8	0.4	2.3
Frederick County, MD	4.4	7.4	1.1	1.2	0.7	1.8
Loudoun County, VA	3.0	4.3	0.9	2.0	2.1	2.2
Prince William County, VA	5.9	7.2	4.2	4.1	5.1	6.4
Stafford County, VA	2.1	3.2	0.9	0.7	0.6	1.8
Manassas city, VA	0.8	0.9	0.4	0.4	1.2	0.7
Manassas Park city, VA	0.2	0.3	0.1	0.1	0.3	0.4
Far Suburbs		*15.9*	*4.1*	*1.3*	*2.1*	*6.0*
Clarke County, VA	0.3	0.5	0.1	0.0	0.0	0.1
Culpeper County, VA	0.9	1.3	0.7	0.2	0.4	0.6
Fauquier County, VA	1.2	2.0	0.6	0.2	0.2	0.7

				High-Wage Workers		
King George County, VA	0.4	0.6	0.4	0.0	0.1	0.2
Spotsylvania County, VA	2.1	3.3	1.1	0.4	0.5	2.1
Warren County, VA	0.8	1.5	0.2	0.1	0.1	0.2
Fredericksburg city, VA	0.7	0.9	0.6	0.1	0.3	0.5
Berkeley County, WV	2.0	3.7	0.3	0.1	0.2	0.9
Jefferson County, WV	1.2	2.1	0.3	0.2	0.2	0.8
Total Region		*100.0*	*100.0*	*100.0*	*100.0*	*100.0*
District of Columbia		*8.9*	*16.2*	*5.1*	*12.2*	*11.6*
Inner Core		*10.0*	*3.4*	*5.4*	*11.4*	*7.9*
Arlington County, VA	5.7	6.2	1.6	4.4	6.9	5.4
Alexandria city, VA	3.5	3.8	1.9	1.0	4.5	2.5
Inner Suburbs		*60.2*	*69.0*	*82.5*	*63.1*	*64.9*
Montgomery County, MD	23.7	23.7	16.5	34.7	26.8	21.6
Prince George's County, MD	7.2	3.6	40.0	4.8	5.5	8.7
Fairfax County, VA	30.7	32.0	12.3	42.1	29.9	33.7
Fairfax city, VA	0.4	0.5	0.1	0.6	0.7	0.5
Falls Church city, VA	0.4	0.4	0.0	0.3	0.2	0.4
Outer Suburbs		*17.1*	*10.3*	*6.2*	*11.9*	*13.1*
Calvert County, MD	0.9	1.0	0.4	0.6	0.4	0.2
Charles County, MD	1.3	1.3	1.8	0.4	0.9	1.2

ANNEX 5.A *Continued*

		High-Wage Workers				
	All Races	White	Black	Asian	Hispanic	Other
Frederick County, MD	2.6	3.0	0.6	0.4	1.9	2.3
Loudoun County, VA	4.9	5.5	1.9	3.1	2.9	3.7
Prince William County, VA	4.1	4.3	4.5	1.5	4.1	4.2
Stafford County, VA	1.3	1.4	0.7	0.1	0.8	1.1
Manassas city, VA	0.4	0.5	0.3	0.1	0.7	0.3
Manassas Park city, VA	0.1	0.1	0.1	0.0	0.1	0.2
Far Suburbs		*3.8*	*1.1*	*0.8*	*1.4*	*2.5*
Clarke County, VA	0.1	0.1	0.0	0.0	0.0	0.0
Culpeper County, VA	0.3	0.3	0.0	0.0	0.0	0.0
Fauquier County, VA	1.0	1.1	0.3	0.2	0.5	0.6
King George County, VA	0.2	0.2	0.0	0.0	0.0	0.1
Spotsylvania County, VA	0.8	0.9	0.5	0.0	0.4	0.8
Warren County, VA	0.2	0.2	0.0	0.1	0.0	0.0
Fredericksburg city, VA	0.2	0.2	0.0	0.0	0.2	0.3
Berkeley County, WV	0.3	0.4	0.0	0.3	0.2	0.3
Jefferson County, WV	0.3	0.4	0.1	0.1	0.1	0.5

Source: Census Transportation Planning Package, 2000.

ANNEX 5.B Percentage of Workers by Wage Level, Race, and Workplace Location in the Atlanta Metropolitan Area, 2000

				All Workers			
	All Races	White	Black	Asian	Hispanic	Other
Total Region	100.0	100.0	100.0	100.0	100.0	100.0
Atlanta City	24.7	20.6	35.9	22.5	23.1	24.5
DeKalb (part)	1.2	0.9	1.9	1.1	2.6	1.3
Fulton (part)	23.5	19.8	34.0	21.4	20.4	23.2
Inner Suburbs	44.3	43.1	46.3	49.2	44.7	48.5
Clayton	4.6	4.0	6.2	5.0	3.7	4.9
Cobb	14.1	15.7	9.6	12.3	15.3	15.5
DeKalb (part)	13.6	11.0	19.6	20.0	13.8	15.7
Douglas	1.5	1.9	0.9	1.0	1.1	1.4
Fulton (part)	10.5	10.6	10.0	10.9	10.9	10.9
Outer Suburbs	24.8	28.4	14.5	26.5	28.6	23.3
Cherokee	1.9	2.6	0.3	1.1	2.5	1.7
Coweta	1.4	1.7	1.1	0.4	0.9	0.8
Fayette	1.7	2.0	1.0	1.1	1.1	1.1
Forsyth	2.0	2.6	0.4	1.5	2.9	1.7
Gwinnett	13.4	14.5	8.5	20.0	18.9	14.6
Henry	1.6	1.9	1.2	0.9	0.8	1.4
Newton	0.9	1.1	0.8	0.5	0.4	0.4

ANNEX 5.B *Continued*

| | All Workers | | | | | |
	All Races	White	Black	Asian	Hispanic	Other
Paulding	0.3	0.4	0.1	0.1	0.1	0.3
Rockdale	1.5	1.7	1.1	1.0	1.1	1.3
Far Suburbs	6.2	7.8	3.3	1.9	3.6	3.8
Barrow	0.2	0.2	0.0	0.1	0.1	0.1
Bartow	1.5	2.0	0.6	0.6	1.1	0.8
Butts	0.1	0.1	0.1	0.0	0.0	0.1
Carroll	1.7	2.1	1.0	0.4	0.9	1.1
Dawson	0.0	0.1	0.0	0.0	0.0	0.1
Haralson	0.1	0.1	0.0	0.0	0.0	0.0
Heard	0.0	0.0	0.0	0.0	0.0	0.0
Jackson	0.7	0.9	0.2	0.3	0.8	0.3
Lamar	0.0	0.0	0.1	0.0	0.0	0.0
Meriwether	0.1	0.1	0.0	0.0	0.0	0.1
Pickens	0.4	0.6	0.1	0.0	0.3	0.3
Pike	0.0	0.0	0.0	0.0	0.0	0.0
Spalding	1.1	1.2	1.1	0.4	0.4	0.8
Walton	0.3	0.3	0.1	0.0	0.0	0.2
	Low-Wage Workers					
Total Region	100.0	100.0	100.0	100.0	100.0	100.0

Atlanta City	20.5	13.2	34.0	20.2	22.2	21.8
DeKalb (part)	1.4	0.9	2.0	1.0	3.0	1.4
Fulton (part)	19.1	12.3	32.0	19.3	19.1	20.3
Inner Suburbs	43.4	41.0	46.4	50.9	44.2	49.4
Clayton	5.1	4.2	7.1	6.4	3.7	5.7
Cobb	14.2	16.4	9.4	12.8	15.6	16.0
DeKalb (part)	13.0	8.9	19.3	21.2	13.8	16.3
Douglas	2.1	2.8	1.2	1.5	1.1	1.7
Fulton (part)	9.1	8.7	9.4	8.9	10.0	9.7
Outer Suburbs	27.7	34.4	14.7	27.4	29.6	23.4
Cherokee	2.6	3.8	0.3	1.5	2.9	2.2
Coweta	1.9	2.4	1.5	0.4	1.0	1.2
Fayette	2.1	2.9	1.3	1.2	1.0	1.7
Forsyth	2.2	3.0	0.4	1.3	3.3	1.3
Gwinnett	13.4	14.9	7.4	20.6	19.0	13.6
Henry	2.1	2.7	1.6	1.2	0.8	1.4
Newton	1.2	1.5	1.0	0.6	0.4	0.6
Paulding	0.4	0.7	0.1	0.1	0.1	0.5
Rockdale	1.8	2.3	1.3	0.6	1.1	1.0
Far Suburbs	8.3	11.5	4.9	1.5	4.0	5.4
Barrow	0.2	0.4	0.1	0.2	0.1	0.0
Bartow	1.7	2.5	0.6	0.3	1.2	0.9
Butts	0.1	0.2	0.1	0.0	0.0	0.1

ANNEX 5.B *Continued*

| | All Races | | Low-Wage Workers | | | |
		White	Black	Asian	Hispanic	Other
Dawson	0.0	0.1	0.0	0.0	0.0	0.2
Haralson	0.1	0.2	0.0	0.0	0.0	0.0
Heard	0.0	0.0	0.0	0.0	0.0	0.0
Jackson	1.0	1.5	0.3	0.3	0.9	0.4
Lamar	0.1	0.1	0.1	0.0	0.0	0.1
Meriwether	0.1	0.1	0.1	0.0	0.0	0.2
Pickens	0.6	0.9	0.1	0.0	0.3	0.2
Pike	0.1	0.1	0.0	0.0	0.1	0.0
Spalding	1.5	1.7	1.7	0.2	0.4	1.0
Walton	0.3	0.4	0.2	0.0	0.0	0.0
Total Region	100.0	100.0	100.0	100.0	100.0	100.0
Atlanta City	30.3	29.8	38.1	24.3	25.0	32.6
DeKalb (part)	0.9	0.9	1.2	1.4	0.8	1.4
Fulton (part)	29.4	29.0	36.8	22.9	24.2	31.2
Inner Suburbs	46.0	45.8	45.6	49.2	50.2	48.9
Clayton	2.7	2.4	5.0	2.1	4.2	6.2
Cobb	14.4	15.0	9.0	11.8	16.7	13.6
DeKalb (part)	12.7	11.8	17.7	19.2	14.4	18.4
Douglas	0.7	0.7	0.5	0.0	1.0	1.5
Fulton (part)	15.5	15.8	13.4	16.0	13.9	9.3

	20.7	21.1	14.6	24.5	22.7	17.4
Outer Suburbs						
Cherokee	1.4	1.5	0.4	1.5	2.3	1.1
Coweta	0.7	0.7	0.6	1.1	0.2	0.0
Fayette	1.2	1.2	0.8	0.9	1.4	0.5
Forsyth	2.1	2.3	0.6	1.1	1.4	0.6
Gwinnett	13.0	13.1	10.2	17.8	16.2	13.3
Henry	0.8	0.9	0.6	0.9	0.0	0.9
Newton	0.4	0.5	0.4	0.5	0.0	0.0
Paulding	0.2	0.2	0.1	0.0	0.4	0.2
Rockdale	0.8	0.8	0.8	0.7	0.7	0.8
	3.0	3.2	1.7	2.0	2.2	1.1
Far Suburbs						
Barrow	0.1	0.1	0.0	0.1	0.0	0.0
Bartow	1.0	1.1	0.7	1.2	0.2	0.7
Butts	0.0	0.0	0.1	0.0	0.2	0.0
Carroll	0.6	0.7	0.4	0.2	0.7	0.0
Dawson	0.0	0.1	0.0	0.0	0.0	0.0
Haralson	0.0	0.0	0.0	0.0	0.0	0.0
Heard	0.0	0.0	0.0	0.0	0.0	0.0
Jackson	0.3	0.3	0.1	0.2	0.4	0.0
Lamar	0.0	0.0	0.0	0.0	0.0	0.0
Meriwether	0.0	0.0	0.0	0.0	0.0	0.0
Pickens	0.3	0.3	0.1	0.2	0.2	0.2
Pike	0.0	0.0	0.0	0.0	0.0	0.0
Spalding	0.4	0.4	0.3	0.2	0.4	0.2
Walton	0.1	0.2	0.1	0.0	0.0	0.0

Source: Census Transportation Planning Package, 2000.

ANNEX 5.C Percentage of Workers by Wage Level, Race, and Workplace Location in the Washington, DC Metropolitan Area, 2000

		All Workers				
	All Races	White	Black	Asian	Hispanic	Other
Total Region		100.0	100.0	100.0	100.0	100.0
District of Columbia		20.5	39.4	21.7	23.3	26.0
Inner Core		8.8	8.9	9.8	12.1	9.5
Arlington County, VA	6.1	5.9	5.8	6.9	7.8	6.2
Alexandria city, VA	3.0	2.9	3.0	2.9	4.2	3.3
Inner Suburbs		46.6	43.0	60.0	52.7	49.4
Montgomery County, MD	15.7	15.6	12.8	21.6	20.1	16.6
Prince George's County, MD	11.0	8.8	18.7	9.2	8.5	10.0
Fairfax County, VA	18.9	20.6	10.8	26.9	21.9	20.9
Fairfax city, VA	1.2	1.3	0.5	1.8	1.6	1.4
Falls Church city, VA	0.3	0.3	0.2	0.6	0.6	0.4
Outer Suburbs		16.6	6.5	7.6	9.9	11.4
Calvert County, MD	0.7	1.0	0.5	0.1	0.2	0.6
Charles County, MD	1.4	1.6	1.3	0.5	0.5	1.4
Frederick County, MD	3.2	4.5	0.8	1.1	1.0	1.4
Loudoun County, VA	3.0	3.6	1.1	2.9	3.0	2.6
Prince William County, VA	3.2	3.7	2.0	2.0	3.8	3.7
Stafford County, VA	1.0	1.3	0.5	0.4	0.5	0.9

			All Workers	Low-Wage Workers		
Total Region	100.0	100.0	100.0	100.0	100.0	100.0
District of Columbia	11.7	32.6	16.8	19.2	19.4	10.1
Inner Core		5.6	7.8	8.9	12.6	10.1
Arlington County, VA	4.5	3.3	4.5	5.9	7.8	6.4
Alexandria city, VA	3.0	2.3	3.3	3.1	4.8	3.7
Inner Suburbs		44.2	46.7	63.6	55.3	51.7
Montgomery County, MD	16.3	15.2	14.2	21.3	21.4	16.9
Prince George's County, MD	12.3	9.0	22.4	11.6	8.6	10.9
Fairfax County, VA	17.6	18.0	9.4	28.1	23.0	21.8
Fairfax city, VA	1.4	1.5	0.5	1.9	1.8	1.6
Falls Church city, VA	0.4	0.4	0.2	0.7	0.5	0.5
Manassas city, VA	0.7	0.8	0.3	0.4	0.7	0.7
Manassas Park city, VA	0.1	0.1	0.0	0.1	0.2	0.1
Far Suburbs		7.4	2.2	0.9	2.0	3.8
Clarke County, VA	0.2	0.3	0.1	0.0	0.1	0.1
Culpeper County, VA	0.5	0.6	0.3	0.1	0.3	0.4
Fauquier County, VA	0.7	1.0	0.3	0.2	0.4	0.4
King George County, VA	0.4	0.5	0.2	0.1	0.2	0.3
Spotsylvania County, VA	1.0	1.3	0.5	0.2	0.5	0.9
Warren County, VA	0.4	0.6	0.1	0.1	0.1	0.2
Fredericksburg city, VA	0.7	1.0	0.4	0.2	0.3	0.7
Berkeley County, WV	0.9	1.4	0.2	0.1	0.2	0.4
Jefferson County, WV	0.5	0.8	0.1	0.1	0.1	0.3

ANNEX 5.C *Continued*

| | | | | Low-Wage Workers | | |
	All Races	White	Black	Asian	Hispanic	Other
Outer Suburbs		24.8	9.1	9.3	10.6	13.3
Calvert County, MD	1.1	1.6	0.9	0.2	0.2	0.7
Charles County, MD	2.1	2.7	2.0	0.6	0.5	1.8
Frederick County, MD	4.2	7.0	1.1	1.2	1.0	1.4
Loudoun County, VA	3.3	4.5	1.1	2.8	3.0	2.4
Prince William County, VA	4.7	5.8	3.0	3.2	4.4	4.9
Stafford County, VA	1.5	2.3	0.7	0.6	0.5	1.3
Manassas city, VA	0.7	0.9	0.3	0.4	0.8	0.6
Manassas Park city, VA	0.1	0.1	0.0	0.2	0.2	0.2
Far Suburbs		13.7	3.9	1.5	2.2	5.5
Clarke County, VA	0.3	0.4	0.1	0.0	0.1	0.1
Culpeper County, VA	0.8	1.1	0.5	0.2	0.4	0.8
Fauquier County, VA	1.1	1.7	0.6	0.2	0.3	0.5
King George County, VA	0.3	0.5	0.3	0.1	0.1	0.1
Spotsylvania County, VA	1.7	2.6	0.9	0.4	0.5	1.4
Warren County, VA	0.7	1.1	0.2	0.1	0.1	0.1
Fredericksburg city, VA	1.3	1.8	0.8	0.3	0.4	1.2
Berkeley County, WV	1.5	2.7	0.3	0.1	0.2	0.8
Jefferson County, WV	1.0	1.7	0.2	0.1	0.1	0.4

High-Wage Workers

Total Region	100.0	100.0	100.0	100.0	100.0	
District of Columbia		32.9	46.2	28.0	41.4	37.0
Inner Core		11.7	8.8	9.0	10.4	8.8
Arlington County, VA	8.4	8.7	6.4	7.3	8.0	6.3
Alexandria city, VA	2.8	3.0	2.5	1.7	2.4	2.5
Inner Suburbs		45.8	40.5	57.3	40.7	44.9
Montgomery County, MD	15.1	15.1	12.5	19.6	14.4	14.1
Prince George's County, MD	6.9	6.2	12.8	8.4	7.0	6.6
Fairfax County, VA	22.6	23.3	14.4	28.0	18.3	22.6
Fairfax city, VA	0.9	1.0	0.5	1.0	0.8	1.5
Falls Church city, VA	0.3	0.2	0.3	0.4	0.1	0.2
Outer Suburbs		7.5	3.8	5.0	6.5	7.0
Calvert County, MD	0.3	0.3	0.1	0.2	0.1	0.3
Charles County, MD	0.5	0.5	0.5	0.3	0.5	0.7
Frederick County, MD	1.4	1.6	0.5	0.8	1.6	1.7
Loudoun County, VA	2.4	2.7	1.1	1.8	1.8	1.7
Prince William County, VA	1.4	1.4	1.0	1.1	1.6	1.5
Stafford County, VA	0.4	0.5	0.2	0.2	0.2	0.3
Manassas city, VA	0.5	0.6	0.3	0.5	0.7	0.7
Manassas Park city, VA	0.0	0.0	0.0	0.0	0.0	0.0

		High-Wage Workers				
	All Races	White	Black	Asian	Hispanic	Other
Far Suburbs		*2.1*	*0.6*	*0.7*	*1.0*	*2.4*
Clarke County, VA	0.1	0.1	0.0	0.0	0.0	0.0
Culpeper County, VA	0.2	0.2	0.1	0.0	0.1	0.2
Fauquier County, VA	0.3	0.4	0.1	0.2	0.3	0.2
King George County, VA	0.3	0.3	0.1	0.1	0.0	0.8
Spotsylvania County, VA	0.3	0.3	0.2	0.1	0.1	0.3
Warren County, VA	0.1	0.1	0.1	0.0	0.0	0.0
Fredericksburg city, VA	0.3	0.3	0.1	0.0	0.3	0.5
Berkeley County, WV	0.2	0.3	0.0	0.1	0.1	0.0
Jefferson County, WV	0.1	0.1	0.1	0.1	0.1	0.4

Source: Census Transportation Planning Package, 2000.

ANNEX 5.D Percentage of Workers by Wage Level, Race, and Workplace Location in the Houston Metropolitan Area, 2000

				All Workers		
	All Races	White	Black	Asian	Hispanic	Other
Total Region	100.0	100.0	100.0	100.0	100.0	100.0
Houston City	57.4	51.3	69.3	69.3	61.9	58.1
Fort Bend (part)	0.1	0.1	0.3	0.1	0.1	0.1
Harris (part)	57.3	51.2	68.9	69.2	61.8	58.0
Inner Suburbs	23.4	25.7	17.0	18.3	23.0	23.6
Harris (part)	23.4	25.7	17.0	18.3	23.0	23.6
Outer and Far Suburbs	19.2	23.0	13.7	12.4	15.2	18.3
Austin	0.4	0.5	0.2	0.1	0.3	0.3
Brazoria	3.8	4.6	2.0	1.5	3.3	3.4
Chambers	0.4	0.6	0.2	0.1	0.2	0.4
Fort Bend (part)	4.6	4.5	4.5	6.5	4.6	4.2
Galveston	4.1	4.8	3.8	2.3	3.2	4.7
Liberty	0.8	1.1	0.6	0.1	0.3	0.6
Montgomery	4.5	6.2	1.6	1.6	2.9	4.1
San Jacinto	0.1	0.2	0.1	0.0	0.0	0.1
Waller	0.4	0.5	0.6	0.1	0.3	0.5

ANNEX 5.D *Continued*

				Low-Wage Workers		
	All Races	White	Black	Asian	Hispanic	Other
Total Region	100.0	100.0	100.0	100.0	100.0	100.0
Houston City	53.5	39.3	67.0	66.2	61.5	55.0
Fort Bend (part)	0.1	0.0	0.3	0.2	0.1	0.1
Harris (part)	53.4	39.2	66.6	65.9	61.4	54.9
Inner Suburbs	24.6	29.8	17.0	20.7	22.8	24.0
Harris (part)	24.6	29.8	17.0	20.7	22.8	24.0
Outer and Far Suburbs	21.9	30.9	16.1	13.1	15.7	21.0
Austin	0.5	0.7	0.4	0.1	0.3	0.4
Brazoria	4.0	6.1	2.1	1.5	3.0	3.7
Chambers	0.4	0.7	0.2	0.1	0.2	0.4
Fort Bend (part)	5.1	5.2	4.8	7.3	4.7	5.1
Galveston	4.8	6.2	4.8	2.4	3.4	5.3
Liberty	1.0	1.8	0.8	0.1	0.4	0.8
Montgomery	5.4	9.2	1.9	1.5	3.3	4.5
San Jacinto	0.2	0.4	0.2	0.0	0.1	0.2
Waller	0.5	0.6	0.8	0.1	0.4	0.6

High-Wage Workers

Total Region	100.0	100.0	100.0	100.0	100.0	100.0
Houston City	66.4	66.4	68.0	71.7	62.3	60.3
Fort Bend (part)	0.1	0.0	0.2	0.0	0.1	0.0
Harris (part)	66.3	66.3	67.8	71.7	62.2	60.3
Inner Suburbs	19.7	19.5	18.2	17.7	24.2	27.5
Harris (part)	19.7	19.5	18.2	17.7	24.2	27.5
Outer and Far Suburbs	13.9	14.1	13.8	10.6	13.4	12.2
Austin	0.2	0.2	0.2	0.0	0.2	0.4
Brazoria	2.9	2.9	2.3	1.8	4.0	1.3
Chambers	0.3	0.3	0.3	0.1	0.1	0.2
Fort Bend(part)	4.2	4.2	5.1	5.0	3.8	4.0
Galveston	2.3	2.3	3.4	0.9	2.3	3.8
Liberty	0.3	0.3	0.5	0.2	0.2	0.2
Montgomery	3.4	3.7	1.2	2.5	2.7	1.9
San Jacinto	0.0	0.0	0.0	0.0	0.0	0.2
Waller	0.3	0.3	0.8	0.0	0.1	0.4

Source: Census Transportation Planning Package, 2000.

References

Aaronson, Daniel. 1997. "Sibling Estimates of Neighborhood Effects." In Jeanne Brooks-Gunn, Greg J. Duncan, and J. Lawrence Aber (eds.) *Neighborhood Poverty II: Policy Implications in Studying Neighborhoods.* New York: Russell Sage Foundation Press.

Anderson, Elijah. 1994. "The Code of the Streets." *Atlantic Monthly,* May, pp. 81–94.

Berndt, Thomas J. 1996. "Transitions in Friendship and Friends' Influence." In Julia Graber, Jeanne Brooks-Gunn, and Anne C. Petersen (eds.) *Transitions through Adolescence: Interpersonal Domains and Contexts.* Mahwah, NJ: Erlbaum.

Bertrand, Marianne and Sendhil Mullainathan. 2003. "Are Emily and Brendan More Employable than Lakisha and Jamal? A Field Experiment on Labor Market Discrimination." NBER Working Paper No. 9873. Cambridge, MA: National Bureau of Economic Research.

Boyd, Donald, Hamilton Lankford, Susanna Loeb, and James Wyckoff. 2005. "The Draw of Home: How Teachers' Preferences for Proximity Disadvantage Urban Schools." *Journal of Policy Analysis and Management* 24(1): 113–132.

Braddock, J.H. 1980. "The Perpetuation of Segregation across Levels of Education: A Behavioral Assessment of the Contract-Hypothesis." *Sociology of Education* 53: 178–186.

Briggs, Xavier de Souza. 1997. "Brown Kids in White Suburbs: Housing Mobility and the Multiple Faces of Social Capital." Paper presented at the FannieMae Foundation Annual Housing Conference, Washington, DC.

Brooks-Gunn, Jeanne, Greg J. Duncan, Pamela Kato Klebanov, and Naomi Sealand. 1993. "Do Neighborhoods Influence Child and Adolescent Development?" *American Journal of Sociology* 99(2): 353–395.

Case, Anne and Lawrence Katz. 1991. "The Company You Keep: The Effects of Family and Neighborhood on Disadvantaged Youth." NBER Working Paper No. 3705. Cambridge, MA: National Bureau of Economic Research.

Cashin, Sheryll. 2004. *The Failures of Integration: How Race and Class Are Undermining the American Dream.* New York: Public Affairs.

Clark, Rebecca. 1992. "Neighborhood Effects of Dropping Out of School among Teenage Boys." Working paper. Washington, DC: The Urban Institute.

Connell, James Patrick and Bonnie Halpern-Felsher 1997. "How Neighborhoods Affect Educational Outcomes in Middle Childhhood and Adolescence: Conceptual Issues and an Empirical Example." In Jeanne Brooks-Gunn, Greg J. Duncan, and J. Lawrence Aber (eds.) *Neighborhood Poverty I: Context and Consequences for Children.* New York: Russell Sage Foundation Press.

Conrad, Cecilia A. 2001. "Racial Trends in Labor Market Access and Wages: Women," in Neil J. Smelser, William Julius Wilson, and Faith Mitchell (eds.) *America Becoming: Racial Trends and Their Consequences.* Washington, DC: National Academy Press.

Cove, Elizabeth. 2006. *Moving On Over, Moving On Up: Employment Outcomes for MTO Relocatees.* Washington, DC: The Urban Institute.

Crane, Jonathan. 1991. "The Epidemic Theory of Ghettoes and Neighborhood Effects on Dropping Out and Teenage Childbearing." *American Journal of Sociology* 96(5): 1226–1259.

Cross, Harry *et al.* 1990. *Employer Hiring Practices: Differential Treatment of Hispanic and Anglo Job Seekers.* Washington, DC: Urban Institute Press.

Cutler, David M. and Edward L. Glaeser. 1997. "Are Ghettos Good or Bad?" *Quarterly Journal of Economics* 112(3): 827–872.

Datcher, Linda. 1982. "Effects of Community and Family Background on Achievement." *Review of Economics and Statistics* 64: 32–41.

Dornbusch, Sanford M., Phillip Ritter, and Laurence Steinberg. 1991. "Community Influences on the Relation of Family Statuses to Adolescent School Performance: Differences between African Americans and Non-Hispanic Whites." *American Journal of Education* 99(4): 543–567.

Duncan, Greg J. 1994. "Families and Neighbors as Sources of Disadvantage in the Schooling Decisions of White and Black Adolescents." *American Journal of Education* 103(1): 20–53.

Duncan, Greg J., James Patrick Connell, and Pamela Klebanov. 1997. "Conceptual and Methodological Issues in Estimating Causal Effects of Neighborhoods and Family Conditions on Individual Development." In Jeanne Brooks-Gunn, Greg J. Duncan, and J. Lawrence Aber (eds.) *Neighborhood Poverty I: Context and Consequences for Children.* New York: Russell Sage Foundation Press.

Garner, Catherine and Stephen Raudenbush. 1991. "Neighborhood Effects on Educational Attainment: A Multilevel Analysis." *Sociology of Education* 64: 251–262.

Guryan, Jonathan. 2001. "Desegregation and Black Dropout Rates." NBER Working Paper No. 8345. Available at http://www.nber.org/papers/w8345 (accessed March, 6 2005).

Hanushek, Eric A., John F. Kain, and Steven G. Rivkin. "New Evidence about *Brown v. Board of Education*: The Complex Effects of School Racial Composition on Achievement." NBER Working Paper No. 8741. Available at http://www.nber.org/papers/w8741 (accessed March 6, 2005).

Haveman, Robert H. and Barbara L. Wolfe. 1994. *Succeeding Generations: On the Effects of Investments in Children.* New York: Russell Sage Foundation Press.

Holzer, Harry J. 1996. *What Employers Want: Job Prospects for Less Educated Workers.* New York: Russell Sage Foundation.

Holzer, Harry J. 2001. "Racial Differences in Labor Market Outcomes among Men." In Neil J. Smelser, William Julius Wilson, and Faith Mitchell (eds.) *America Becoming: Racial Trends and Their Consequences.* Washington, DC: National Academy Press.

Holzer, Harry J. and Keith R. Ihlanfedt. 1996. "Spatial Factors and the Employment of Blacks at the Firm Level." *New England Economic Review* May/June Special Issue: 65–82.

Holzer, Harry J., Keith R. Ihlanfeldt, and David L. Sjoquist. 1994. "Work, Search, and Travel among White and Black Youth." *Journal of Urban Economics* 35: 320–345.

Holzer, Harry J., Steven Raphael and Michael A. Stoll. 2003. *Employers in the Boom: How Did the Hiring of Unskilled Workers Change during the 1990s?* Washington, DC: The Urban Institute.

Holzer, Harry, Paul Offner, and Elaine Sorensen. 2004. *Declining Employment among Young Black Less-Educated Men: The Role of Incarceration and Child Support.* Washington, DC: The Urban Institute.

Ihlandfeldt, Keith R. 1997. "Information on the Spatial Distribution of Job Opportunities with Metropolitan Areas." *Journal of Urban Economics* 41: 218–242.

Ihlanfeldt, Keith R. and David L. Sjoquist. 1998. "The Spatial Mismatch Hypothesis: A Review of Recent Studies and Their Implications for Welfare Reform." *Housing Policy Debate* 9(4): 849–892.

Ihlanfeldt, Keith R. and Madelyn V. Young. 1996. "The Spatial Distribution of Black Employment between the Central City and the Suburbs." *Economic Inquiry* 34: 693–707.

Ionnides, Yannis M. and Linda Datcher Loury. 2004. "Job Information Networks, Neighborhood Effects, and Inequality." *Journal of Economic Literature* 42: 1056–1093.

Jargowsky, Paul. 2003. *Stunning Progress, Hidden Problems: The Dramatic Decline of Concentrated Poverty in the 1990s.* Washington, DC: Brookings Institution.

Jencks, Christopher and Meredith Phillips (eds.) 1998. *The Black–White Test Score Gap.* Washington, DC: Brookings Institution Press.

Kain, John F. 1968. "Housing Segregation, Negro Employment, and Metropolitan Decentralization." *Quarterly Journal of Economics* 82(2): 175–192.

Kasinitz, Philip and Jan Rosenberg. 1996. "Missing the Connection: Social Isolation and Employment on the Brooklyn Waterfront." *Social Problems* 43(2): 180–196.

Kingsley, G. Thomas and Kathryn Pettit. 2003. *Concentrated Poverty: A Change in Course.* Washington, DC: The Urban Institute.

Massey, Douglas S. and Nancy Denton. 1993. *American Apartheid: Segregation and the Making of the Underclass.* Cambridge, MA: Harvard University Press.

Oliver, Melvin L. and Thomas M. Shapiro. 1997. *Black Wealth/White Wealth: A New Perspective on Racial Inequality.* New York: Routledge.

O'Regan, Katherine M. 1993. "The Effect of Social Networks and Concentrated Poverty on Black and Hispanic Youth Unemployment." *Annals of Regional Science 2.7* December: 327–342.

O'Regan, Katherine M. and Quigley, John M. 1996. "Spatial Effects upon Employment Outcomes: The Case of New Jersey Teenagers." *New England Economic Review* (May/June): 41–57.

Orr, Larry, Judith D. Feins, Robin Jacob *et al.* 2003. *Moving to Opportunity Interim Impacts Evaluation.* Washington, DC: U.S. Department of Housing and Urban Development.

Pastor, Manuel, Jr. 2001. "Geography and Opportunity." In Neil J. Smelser, William Julius Wilson, and Faith Mitchell (eds.) *America Becoming: Racial Trends and Their Consequences.* Washington, DC: National Academy Press.

Pastor, Manuel, Jr. and Ava R. Adams. 1996. "Keeping Down with the Joneses: Neighbors, Networks, and Wages." *Review of Regional Economics* 26(2): 115–145.

Pew Research Center for the People and the Press. 2003. "The 2004 Political Landscape: Evenly Divided and Increasingly Polarized" (accessed January 28, 2006).

Raphael, Steven and Michael A. Stoll. 2002. *Modest Progress: The Narrowing Spatial Mismatch between Blacks and Jobs in the 1990s.* Washington, DC: The Brookings Institution Living Cities Census Series.

Roder, Anne and Scott Scrivner. 2005. *Seeking a Sustainable Journey to Work: Findings from the National Bridges to Work Demonstration.* Philadelphia: Public/Private Ventures.

Rosenbaum, James E. and Stephanie Deluca. 2000. *Is Housing Mobility the Key to Welfare Reform? Lessons from Chicago's Gautreax Program.* Washington, DC: Brookings Institution.

Sampson, Robert J. and Stephen W. Raudenbush. 2004. "Seeing Disorder: Neighborhood Stigma and the Social Construction of Broken Windows." *Social Psychology Quarterly* 67: 319–342.

Sjoquist, David. 1996. "Spatial Mismatch and Social Acceptability." Working paper. Georgia State University, Policy Research Center.

Smith, James P. 2001. "Race and Ethnicity in the Labor Market: Trends over the Short and Long Term." In Neil J. Smelser, William Julius Wilson, and Faith Mitchell (eds.) *America Becoming: Racial Trends and Their Consequences.* Washington, DC: National Academy Press.

Steinberg, Laurence and Susan B. Silverberg. 1986. "The Vicissitudes of Autonomy in Early Adolescence." *Child Development* 57: 841–851.

Stoll, Michael A., Harry J. Holzer, and Keith R. Ihlanfeldt. 2000. "Within Cities and Suburbs: Racial Residential Concentration and the Spatial Distribution of Employment Opportunities across Sub-Metropolitan Areas." *Journal of Policy Analysis and Management* 19(2): 207–231.

Sullivan, Mercer L. 1989. *Getting Paid: Youth Crime and Work in the Inner City.* Ithaca, NY: Cornell University Press.

Turner, Margery Austin and Lynette Rawlings. 2005. *Overcoming Concentrated Poverty and Isolation: Lessons from Three HUD Demonstrations.* Washington, DC: The Urban Institute.

Turner, Margery Austin, Michael Fix, and Raymond J. Struyk. 1991. *Opportunities Denied, Opportunities Diminished: Racial Discrimination in Hiring.* Washington, DC: Urban Institute Press.

Turner, Margery Austin, Kathryn L.S. Pettit, G. Thomas Kingsley *et al.* 2002. *Discrimination in Metropolitan Housing Markets: Results from Phase I of HDS2000.* Washington, DC: U.S. Department of Housing and Urban Development.

Turner, Margery Austin, Kathryn L.S. Pettit, G. Thomas Kingsley *et al.* 2004. *Housing in the Nation's Capital: 2004.* Washington, DC: The Fannie Mae Foundation.

Wial, Howard. 1991. "Getting a Good Job: Mobility in a Segmented Labor Market." *Industrial Relations* 30(3): 396–416.

Wilson, William Julius. 1987. *The Truly Disadvantaged: The Inner City, the Underclass, and Public Policy.* Chicago: University of Chicago Press.

CHAPTER 6

Impacts of Housing and Neighborhoods on Health: Pathways, Racial/Ethnic Disparities, and Policy Directions

DOLORES ACEVEDO-GARCIA AND THERESA L. OSYPUK

[T]here are big health inequalities within countries. Let's take the United States, for example. If you catch the metro train in down-town Washington, DC, to suburbs in Maryland, life expectancy is 57 years at beginning of the journey. At the end of the journey, it is 77 years. This means that there is a 20-year life expectancy gap in the nation's capital, between the poor and predominantly African American people who live downtown, and the richer and pre-dominantly non-African American people who live in the suburbs.

(Michael Marmot, Chair of the World Health Organization's Commission on Social Determinants of Health, 2005 (Marmot & World Health Organization, 2005))

Sixty-one percent of the black poor in the Washington, DC metropolitan area live inside the District of Columbia; while 85 percent of the region's non-black poor live outside the District in the Maryland and Virginia suburbs. Twenty-six percent of the region's poor blacks live in a high-poverty (poverty rate > 30 percent), inner-city neighborhood, compared with only 2 percent of the nonblack poor (Turner, 1997). Are these racial segregation and poverty concentration patterns related to the twenty-year racial disparity in life expectancy in DC? Public health research increasingly suggests that they are, thus making it imperative to look for solutions to health disparities beyond individual risk factors.

In the United States there are wide and persisting racial/ethnic disparities in mortality and health (Williams *et al.*, 1997; Pamuk *et al.*, 1998). With the exception of suicide, blacks exhibit consistently higher mortality than whites from the major causes of death, namely heart disease, cancer, diabetes, liver disease, pneumonia and influenza, HIV/AIDS, and homicide (Pastor, 2001). Blacks also exhibit higher rates of low birth weight, higher infant mortality, worse elderly mortality rates, higher prevalence of disability, and shorter life expectancy (Kington & Nickens, 2001). For instance, while in 1999 the US infant mortality rate (that is, the rate at which babies die before their first birthday) was 5.8 per 1,000 live births among white babies, it was 14.6—2.5 times higher—among black babies. Mental health is one of the few health areas where blacks are healthier than whites.

To understand possible causes of the large and persistent racial (black–white) disparities in health, it is necessary to focus on factors that either differentially or uniquely affect racial minorities or whites (LaVeist, 2003). Common explanations of health disparities include individual-level factors such as health behaviors (e.g., diet, physical activity, substance use); psycho-social factors (e.g., stress), access to health care, experience of discrimination, genetics, and differential socioeconomic position (i.e., income, education, occupation, wealth). Although most of these explanations likely contribute to racial health disparities, their relative contribution is unclear (Williams, 2001).

Researchers have noted that even after accounting for the individual level factors listed above, substantial racial/ethnic health disparities remain (Williams *et al.*, 1997). For example, even after taking into account maternal age, education, and health behaviors and medical risk factors during pregnancy, black babies are more likely to be of low birth weight (Acevedo-Garcia *et al.*, 2005). Yet this disparity may not be attributable to genetic differences, as black babies born to immigrant mothers are significantly less likely to be of low birth weight than their counterparts born to (presumably genetically similar) U.S.-born black mothers (Acevedo-Garcia *et al.*, 2005). To address the limited explanatory power of individual-level factors, a body of research has also explored contextual factors that influence health and differentially affect racial/ethnic minorities. Such contextual factors include housing, neighborhood, and metropolitan area environments.

This chapter addresses (1) the multidimensional relationship between housing disparities and health disparities, (2) potential policy solutions to tackle health disparities by addressing housing disparities, and (3) directions for strengthening the link between low-income housing policy and health by affirmatively pursuing fair housing principles—that is, proactively promoting relocation of low-income households to low-poverty and racially mixed neighborhoods.

We propose that a fair housing perspective is a useful lens for examining the links between housing and health. First, discrimination in housing markets, limited desegregation and poverty deconcentration incentives in housing assistance programs, and exclusionary zoning have contributed to racial/ethnic disparities in housing and neighborhood environment that underlie health disparities. Second, health disparities may serve as a measure of discriminatory impact when housing policy is being evaluated, specifically whether government agencies administer their housing and urban development programs in a manner that *affirmatively furthers* the purposes of the Fair Housing Act.[1] Undoubtedly, racial/ethnic disparities in housing are a matter of concern in their own right. Their effect on health makes them even more unjustifiable, and the need to address them even more urgent.

Pathways between Housing Disparities and Health Disparities

To the extent that multiple dimensions of housing influence health, housing disparities may be a key social determinant of the large racial/ethnic health disparities that exist in the United States. Discrimination in various housing markets, limited pursuit of fair housing objectives (i.e., poverty deconcentration and desegregation) in assisted housing programs, and exclusionary zoning have patterned racial/ethnic disparities in housing outcomes (Schill & Wachter, 1995; Pendall, 2000; Briggs, 2005a). Therefore, they may also be considered distal social determinants of health disparities.

In our framework, the word "discrimination" is used broadly to denote barriers that affect racial/ethnic minorities regardless of whether discriminatory intent exists or can be demonstrated. Therefore, we include both active and overt discrimination, such as steering by housing market agents, as well as more subtle exclusionary practices such as zoning policies limiting high-density, affordable housing. Both types of forces have contributed to a racially unequal geography of opportunity (Briggs, 2005a). Since most adult diseases develop over a long time and have complex (not singular) etiologies (Bartley *et al.*, 1997; Berkman & Kawachi, 2000a), it is important to note that our conceptual framework is probabilistic, not deterministic.

The general pathways articulated throughout this section are summarized in Table 6.1. For instance, as listed in the first row, one form of racial discrimination in housing sales markets manifests as real estate agents' steering of racial minorities to lower-quality neighborhoods, which leads to lower home values among minority groups, slower wealth accumulation, as well as exposure to disadvantaged physical and social neighborhood environments. The link between worse neighborhoods and health occurs through stress pathways, exposure to environmental hazards, limited health-promoting

TABLE 6.1 Selected Hypothesized Pathways between Effects of Discrimination in Housing and Unfavorable Health Outcomes among US Racial/Ethnic Minorities vis-à-vis Whites

Effects of Discrimination in Housing Sales Markets	Mediating Factors	Mediating Factors	Documented Association between Mediating Factor and Health
Lower homeownership rates among racial/ethnic minorities	Lower wealth accumulation among racial/ethnic minorities	—	Homeownership status associated with health and mortality independent of income/education
			Wealth level associated with health and mortality independent of income/education
Limited access to low-poverty neighborhoods	Lower home values among racial/ethnic minority home-owners ("segregation tax")	Lower wealth	—
Limited access to low-poverty neighborhoods	Disadvantaged physical and social neighborhood environment (e.g., poverty concentration, high exposure to violence)	High stress	Residence in disadvantaged neighborhoods associated with health and mortality independently of individual-level socioeconomic status
		Exposure to environmental hazards	
		Limited health-promoting features (e.g., walkability, access to healthy food)	
		Socioeconomically disadvantaged social networks	Lower socioeconomic status associated with higher morbidity and mortality
		Limited socioeconomic advancement	

Effects of Discrimination in Housing Rental Markets	Mediating Factors	Mediating Factors	Documented Association between Mediating Factor and Health
Higher prevalence of structurally inadequate housing among racial/ethnic minorities	Exposure to dangerous structures (e.g., windows, stairs in disrepair) Exposure to lead Exposure to allergens (e.g., cockroaches, rodents)	–	Health problems associated with inadequate housing (e.g., injuries; toxic lead levels in blood; allergies/asthma)
Limited access to low-poverty neighborhoods	Disadvantaged physical and social neighborhood environment (e.g., poverty concentration, high exposure to violence)	High stress Exposure to environmental factors Limited health-promoting features (e.g., walkability, access to healthy food) Socioeconomically disadvantaged social networks Risk of violent victimization	Residence in disadvantaged neighborhoods associated with health and mortality independently of individual-level socioeconomic status

Effects of Discrimination in Mortgage Markets	Mediating Factors	Mediating Factors	Documented Association between Mediating Factor and Health
Higher probability of obtaining subprime mortgage loans among racial/ethnic minorities	Higher risk of default/foreclosure among racial/ethnic minorities	Lower wealth	Wealth level associated with health and mortality independent of income/education
		High stress	Stress associated with negative health outcomes

TABLE 6.1 *Continued*

Effects of Limited Pursuit of Fair Housing in Low-Income Housing Programs	Mediating Factors	Mediating Factors	Documented Association between Mediating Factor and Health
Low-income homeownership for minorities disproportionately concentrated in segregated, high-poverty neighborhoods	Disadvantaged physical and social neighborhood environment (e.g., poverty concentration, high exposure to violence)	High stress Risk of violent victimization	Residence in disadvantaged neighborhoods associated with health and mortality independently of individual-level socioeconomic status
Rental assistance housing disproportionately concentrated in segregated, high-poverty neighborhoods		Exposure to environmental hazards Limited health promoting features (e.g., walkability, access to healthy food) Socioeconomically disadvantaged social networks Limited socioeconomic development	Lower socioeconomic status associated with higher morbidity and mortality

Effects of Exclusionary Zoning Policies	Mediating Factors	Mediating Factors	Documented Associating between Mediating Factor and Health
Limited availability of affordable housing in suburban jurisdictions, where neighborhoods have lower poverty rates and better public goods	Disproportionate representation of minorities in central-city neighborhoods which tend to have more disadvantaged physical and social environments	High stress Exposure to environmental hazards Limited health-promoting features (e.g., walkability, access to healthy food) Socioeconomically disadvantaged social networks	Residence in disadvantaged neighborhoods associated with health and mortality independently of individual-level socioeconomic status

features, and strained social networks. As another example, the last row of Table 6.1 outlines how by limiting minority access to suburban jurisdictions, where schools tend to be better than in central cities, exclusionary zoning is implicated in the lower educational attainment of minorities, which is associated with worse health over the life course. For five areas (housing sales market, housing rental market, mortgage market, low-income assisted housing policies, and exclusionary zoning) we map out the factors that may link lowering discrimination to health through a chain of events that plays out across time.

The rest of this section discusses pathways through which discrimination in housing has contributed to racial health disparities through the racial patterning of housing variables that influence health. The second section will discuss ways in which, by helping rectify housing disparities, housing policy may help address health disparities. The third section will propose that housing policy for low-income households may help address racial disparities more effectively if infused with fair housing principles.

Wealth, Homeownership, and Health

Unfavorable health outcomes among U.S. minority groups may be influenced by substantial racial/ethnic differences in wealth holdings, which largely reflect disparities in homeownership rates, and in home values among those who are homeowners. As is discussed in other chapters, discrimination in sales and home mortgage markets has contributed to racial/ethnic disparities in wealth by limiting the prevalence of and returns to home-ownership for minorities.

WEALTH DISPARITIES AND HEALTH DISPARITIES

According to the 2004 Survey of Consumer Finances, the median income for minority families was just over $29,800 compared to $49,400 for non-Hispanic white families—a gap of nearly $20,000—while the median wealth for minority families was about $24,800 compared to $140,700 for non-Hispanic white families—a gap of more than $115,000 (Bucks et al., 2006). Across income groups, the wealth level of the average African American is significantly lower than the wealth level of the average white with a comparable income (Conley, 1999; Shapiro, 2004).

Socioeconomic status (SES) is one of the strongest predictors of health and illness (Williams, 2001). Moreover, compelling evidence has demonstrated that not only do those in poverty experience worse health, but there is a *gradient* between SES and health such that every additional higher level of SES confers better health, regardless of which metric of SES or which health outcome is studied (Marmot & Wilkinson, 2001). This suggests that SES patterns the distribution of exposure to health-enhancing resources and health-damaging factors (Lynch & Kaplan, 2000), including adequate (or inadequate) housing and neighborhoods. Social position is associated with onset and progression of disease via biological, psychosocial, and behavioral routes (Berkman & Macintyre, 1997; Adler & Ostrove, 1999). Accumulation of *material* insults such as poor-quality housing or dangerous neighborhoods across the life course nurtures or harms health. Socioeconomic status may also be associated with health or illness through *psychosocial* mechanisms (e.g., control, anxiety, insecurity, social affiliations) (Marmot & Wilkinson, 2001). For instance, the stress one experiences by recognizing one's relative place in a hierarchy induces physiologic changes as one is subjected to conflict or threat (Adler & Ostrove, 1999). A related concept is allostatic load, when the body is adapting to chronic stressors, and as a result the physiologic system becomes taxed over time (McEwen & Wingfield, 2003). Stress from experiences of racial discrimination or lack of control over one's life associated with inability to move away from a poor or unsafe neighborhood may be associated with allostatic load.

Part of the large health disparities between African Americans and whites can be accounted for by similarly patterned racial disparities in income and education (Syme, 1987; Marmot *et al.*, 1997, 1998; Berkman & Kawachi, 2000a; Marmot, 2000). Lower SES measured by income and education is associated with higher overall and cause-specific mortality, as well as a greater probability of detrimental physical and mental health conditions such as cancer, cardiovascular disease, and depression (Pamuk *et al.*, 1998; Cooper *et al.*, 2001; Winkleby & Cubbin, 2003).

However, even after accounting for income and education, African Americans experience worse health than whites (Williams, 2001). This gap may be related to differences in wealth levels between African Americans and whites. Given the large racial disparities in wealth at any income level, social epidemiologists are increasingly questioning the use of income as a solid single indicator of SES (Braveman *et al.*, 2005).

In some studies, wealth has been shown to be a significant variable in explaining racial disparities in adult mortality. Huie *et al.* (2003) hypothesized that wealth may have a stronger effect on health and mortality than income, because (1) while income may show high variability over the life course, wealth is more stable, and thus may help protect individuals during adverse life situations; (2) the cumulative nature of wealth may reflect prior socioeconomic experiences during critical developmental periods, which may have influenced present health status; and (3) US wealth disparities are much greater than income disparities, which may explain the persistence of racial disparities in health after accounting for income disparities. Additionally, wealth disparities have intergenerational effects. For instance, African Americans have less savings and fewer assets they can apply toward financing their children's education and homeownership (Conley, 1999; Simmons, 2001; Boehm & Schlottman, 2002; Shapiro, 2004).

Huie *et al.* (2003) found that in the 1990s, after age, sex, and marital status had been controlled for, African Americans were 67 percent more likely to die than whites during the study follow-up period.[2] Taking wealth differences into account reduced the racial disparity in mortality to 54 percent, while taking income difference into account reduced the disparity to 43 percent. Taking into consideration wealth and income differences simultaneously reduced the disparity to 38 percent.

WEALTH DISPARITIES AND HOMEOWNERSHIP DISPARITIES

Racial wealth disparities reflect substantially lower rates of homeownership among blacks, as well as significantly lower home values among black homeowners. In 2003 the homeownership rate for whites was 75.1 percent, but only 48.4 percent for blacks, 47.4 percent for Hispanics, and 56.5 percent for Asians (Joint Center for Housing Studies, 2004). Race/ethnicity constitutes a more powerful determinant of wealth stratification than immigrant status (Hao, 2004). While low homeownership rates among Hispanics and Asians partly reflect the large proportion of immigrants in these groups, immigration does not account for the low homeownership rate among blacks (Hao, 2004).

Not only are homeownership rates lower for minorities but also the returns to homeownership are considerably lower for blacks and Hispanics than for whites. For instance, in 2001 the average net worth of white home-owners was $207,000, while the average net worth of black homeowners was $72,000 and that for Hispanics $73,000 (Joint Center for Housing Studies, 2004). Importantly, racial/ethnic disparities in home values likely reflect locational disparities—that is, minority homeownership is more likely to occur in lower-income neighborhoods. Rusk (2001) showed that in 1990, as a result of residential segregation, given equivalent income levels, African Americans received 18 percent less value for their homes than did whites.

DISPARITIES IN HOMEOWNERSHIP AND HEALTH

Robert and House (1996) showed that homeownership has a positive effect on health status, independent of income and education. Although there is evidence that homeownership is associated with improved health outcomes, we know very little about whether this effect is a function of homeownership itself, increased wealth, unmeasured (residual) socioeconomic status, better housing, and/or neighborhood quality (Macintyre *et al.*, 1998; Dunn, 2000; Dunn & Hayes, 2000; Macintyre *et al.*, 2002; Cummins *et al.*, 2005). Since homeownership is the main asset holding for most Americans (Simmons, 2001; Orzechowski & Sepielli, 2003), it may have an independent effect on health because it captures some of the effect of wealth. Additionally, it has been hypothesized that homeownership may confer additional protective effects through its positive psychological effects, and through housing and neighborhood quality.

However, onerous homeownership terms such as high debt may have a detrimental effect on health (Nettleton & Burrows, 1998; Rohe *et al.*, 2001; Retsinas & Belsky, 2002). Minorities are more likely to obtain subprime (i.e., predatory) loans than whites (U.S. Department of Housing and Urban Development, 2000). Neighborhood racial/ethnic composition—that is, a high proportion of black residents—appears to increase the likelihood of obtaining a subprime mortgage loan (Calem *et al.*, 2004).

Housing Quality and Health

Housing, as we have seen, confers fewer returns for members of racial/ethnic minorities than for whites in economic terms—that is, housing values—but also in terms of housing quality, which in turn influences health. Housing discrimination may indirectly contribute to disparities in housing quality because it constrains minorities to searching for housing in neighborhoods where inadequate housing is more common.

Studies based on data from the American Housing Survey found that after age, income, education, and location had been controlled for, blacks were more likely than whites to live in inadequate housing. Additionally, over time housing units occupied by black households were less likely to be repaired than those occupied by white households. Inadequate units occupied by black households had proportionally more deficient conditions and more severe conditions than inadequate units occupied by white households (Dozier, 1999; Kutty, 1999).

Racial/ethnic differences in the quality of housing units (e.g., lead and allergen prevalence) may influence the disproportionate prevalence of serious health conditions (e.g., lead poisoning, asthma) among racial/ethnic minorities. Some of these conditions affect minority children but also play out over the life course. Therefore, they may have implications for adult health and socioeconomic outcomes.

For example, indoor household allergen levels are related to degree of household disrepair (measured by the presence and number of physical housing problems, such as holes in the ceilings and walls, water damage), after adjusting for individual family attributes (Rauh *et al.*, 2002). Chronic exposure to allergens in the indoor environment from mold, pets, mice and rats, cockroaches, and dust mites is associated with asthma (Breysse *et al.*, 2004). Asthma status and severity increase the likelihood of children missing school days (Moonie *et al.*, 2006), and thus may affect not only educational success (e.g., school dropout rate) but also parental work attendance (Diette *et al.*, 2000).

The literature is well developed on the pathological effects of various housing attributes such as high-rise housing, crowding, dampness, and cold (Dunn, 2000). Indeed, most of the literature on housing and health has focused on the effect of these material aspects of housing on specific illnesses, examining various physical, chemical, and biological exposures in housing units (Allen, 2000; Dunn, 2000). For instance, as discussed in a review of the literature, lead exposure affects neurodevelopmental functioning in children; lack of safe drinking water, ineffective waste disposal, and overcrowding have long been identified as routes for infectious disease transmission; and poorly designed (or maintained) housing is a cause of injuries such as burns and falls (Krieger & Higgins, 2002).

Housing inadequacy may also affect behavioral and mental health outcomes. Evans *et al.* (2001) reported that housing quality (structural quality, privacy, indoor climate, hazards, cleanliness/clutter, and children's resources) was significantly related to psychological distress and a behavioral index of learned helplessness.

Neighborhoods and Health

Evidence presented in other chapters indicates that housing discrimination has influenced patterns of racial/ethnic residential segregation and thus has increased the likelihood that the minority poor live in concentrated-poverty neighborhoods. Discrimination has also prevented minorities of all SES levels from achieving neighborhood environments that are consistent with their socioeconomic status. Different forms of discrimination have limited minority access to suburban, low-poverty neighborhoods. These forms include discrimination in housing sales and rental markets on the basis of race, family size, and receipt of housing assistance, as well as exclusionary policies that limit the availability of multi-family and affordable housing in many suburban jurisdictions (Schill & Wachter, 1995; Briggs, 2005b).

Since the physical and social environment of neighborhoods may influence health status *above and beyond* individual-level SES, racial/ethnic disparities in neighborhood quality may be a factor in health disparities. As was discussed earlier, health is positively associated with wealth levels, homeownership, and housing quality, which are all strongly patterned along racial lines. Additionally, health is influenced by neighborhood physical and socioeconomic environment, social environment (e.g., violent crime), infrastructure, amenities, and services. Even after taking into account individuals' SES, better neighborhood environments may have a positive influence on health. For example, poor individuals may experience better health in low-poverty than in high-poverty neighborhoods.

DISPARITIES IN NEIGHBORHOOD ENVIRONMENT

U.S. blacks and Hispanics are more likely to live in high-poverty neighborhoods than whites (Logan & Lewis Mumford Center for Comparative Urban and Regional Research, 2002). Disparities in neighborhood environment are only partially accounted for by racial/ethnic disparities in individual-level SES. Racial/ethnic minorities are more likely to live in disadvantaged neighborhoods than whites with comparable incomes. As reported by the Lewis Mumford Center, in many metro areas blacks with incomes over $60,000 live in neighborhoods with a lower median household income than whites earning under $30,000 (Logan et al., 2003). On average in 1999, blacks lived in neighborhoods where the median income was $35,306, whereas whites lived in neighborhoods where the median income was $51,459—a disparity of $16,153. Even affluent blacks (i.e., households earning over $60,000) lived in neighborhoods that were not consistent with their own income level. On average, affluent blacks lived in neighborhoods where the median income was $44,668, whereas affluent whites lived in neighborhoods with a median income of $60,363—a disparity of $15,695 (Logan & Lewis Mumford Center for Comparative Urban and Regional Research, 2002). Racial differences in wealth (including parental wealth) as well as housing discrimination may contribute to racial disparities in neighborhood environment.

NEIGHBORHOOD ENVIRONMENT AND HEALTH

Health outcomes, health behaviors, and the location of services and amenities that are conducive to healthy living are patterned according to neighborhood SES and racial/ethnic composition. There is empirical evidence that after taking into account individual-level factors, disadvantaged neighborhood environments (e.g., poverty concentration) have a detrimental effect on health outcomes, including mortality, child and adult physical and mental health, and health behaviors (Macintyre & Ellaway, 2000; Ellen et al. 2001; Pickett & Pearl, 2001; Macintyre et al., 2002; Ellen & Turner, 2003; Kawachi & Berkman, 2003; Macintyre & Ellaway, 2003). For instance, a study of the association between neighborhood disadvantage and the availability of illegal drugs found, after controlling for age, gender, and race, that the odds of being approached by someone selling drugs were ten times higher among individuals living in the most disadvantaged neighborhoods (highest quartile) than among individuals living in the least disadvantaged neighborhoods (lowest quartile) (Storr et al., 2004).

Furthermore, some empirical evidence suggests that in metropolitan areas where racial residential segregation is higher, adult and infant mortality rates, and low birthweight rates, among African Americans are higher. Residential segregation negatively affects the health of African Americans, possibly through its detrimental effects on individual (e.g., employment, education) and neighborhood-level (e.g., concentrated poverty) factors (Williams & Collins, 2001; Acevedo-Garcia & Lochner, 2003; Acevedo-Garcia *et al.*, 2003). As was shown by Ellen (2000) and Osypuk *et al.*, under review), after taking into account individual-level risk factors such as low education and single motherhood, African American women are more likely to have low-birth-weight or pre-term birth babies in metropolitan areas where segregation is higher.

How Strong Is the Evidence of Neighborhood Effects on Health?

Several research reviews have noted that despite compelling empirical results, the evidence on neighborhood effects on health is not conclusive, owing to important methodological limitations (Macintyre & Ellaway, 2000, 2003; Ellen *et al.*, 2001; Macintyre *et al.*, 2002; Ellen & Turner, 2003; Kawachi & Berkman, 2003). Since the vast majority of studies have used nonexperimental, cross-sectional research designs, it is not possible to rule out selection bias as a possible explanation for neighborhood effects (Oakes, 2004). Unmeasured factors that affect both neighborhood choice and health outcomes could potentially account for the association between, say, neighborhood poverty level and health. A high incidence of health problems in high-poverty, distressed neighborhoods does not necessarily mean that the neighborhood environment actually *caused* those problems. It may mean instead that many families with problems end up living in the same neighborhood, perhaps because housing was more affordable there or discrimination closed the door to other neighborhoods. Nonexperimental studies have tried to minimize selection bias by utilizing multilevel statistical analysis to distinguish the effect of individual and family characteristics from the independent effect of neighborhood conditions on health outcomes.[3]

The Moving to Opportunity (MTO) policy demonstration constitutes a notable exception, owing to its experimental longitudinal design. Since this experimental study assigned families to receive vouchers for moving to poor and nonpoor neighborhoods randomly (i.e., independently of family and individual characteristics), reported effects on health can be attributed to differences in neighborhood environment (Leventhal & Brooks-Gunn, 2001, 2003a; Goering *et al.*, 2002; Goering, 2003; Goering & Feins, 2003; Acevedo-Garcia *et al.*, 2004).

Sponsored by the Department of Housing and Urban Development and begun in 1994, MTO was conceived as a housing mobility policy experiment. Eligible participants from central-city public housing located in high-poverty neighborhoods (i.e., poverty rate ≥ 40 percent) in five metropolitan areas[4] were randomly assigned to one of three groups:

1. The treatment group (also referred to as the experimental or MTO group) was offered both a Section 8 housing voucher that could be redeemed only in a low-poverty neighborhood (i.e., poverty rate ≤ 10 percent) and housing search counseling.
2. The Section 8 group was offered a geographically unrestricted Section 8 housing voucher.
3. The in-place control group did not receive a voucher, but remained eligible for public housing.

All of the participants consisted of low-income families, and most were racial/ethnic minorities (Goering, 2003; Goering & Feins, 2003).

To date, the MTO demonstration has shown better health in the MTO group, and in some instances also in the health of the regular Section 8 voucher group vis-à-vis the control group of public housing families.[5] The most recent follow-up study indicated a lower rate of adult obesity (body mass index[6] (BMI) ≥ 30) in the MTO group (U.S. Department of Housing and Urban Development et al., 2003). In the MTO demonstration, lower obesity rates in adults may be partly due to healthier diets, as the MTO group showed increased consumption of fruits and vegetables (U.S. Department of Housing and Urban Development et al., 2003).

This effect is noteworthy because the prevention of obesity has emerged as a national public health priority. The United States is facing an epidemic of overweight and obesity that disproportionately affects African Americans and Hispanics, as well as those of lower SES. The prevalence of obesity among US adults is 30.5 percent (1999–2002) and has increased markedly over the past decade—from 23 percent in 1988–1994 (National Center for Health Statistics & Centers for Disease Control and Prevention, 2004). Obesity increases the risk of illness from many serious medical conditions, results in approximately 300,000 premature deaths each year, and is associated with $117 billion in costs. Most of the cost associated with obesity is due to type 2 diabetes, coronary heart disease, and hypertension (U.S. Department of Health and Human Services, 2001).

MTO adults also showed significant improvements in mental health, including reductions in psychological distress and depression, and increasing feelings of calm and peacefulness. Improved mental health was also shown in the first MTO follow-up study in two of the five sites, New York (Leventhal & Brooks-Gunn, 2003; 2003a, b) and Boston (Katz et al., 2001), as well as in the Yonkers study of scattered-site public housing (Briggs & Yonkers Family and Community Project, 1997). The consistency of these results across different studies is encouraging.

Improvements in mental health are not surprising, given that fear of crime was the main reason why MTO participants wanted to move out of their neighborhoods. Adults and children moving to low-poverty neighborhoods reported increases in their perception of safety and reductions in the likelihood of observing and being victims of crime (US Department of Housing and Urban Development *et al.*, 2003). Considerable stress in the neighborhoods of origin may have also resulted from chronic exposure to poor-quality housing and schools, two additional reasons why participants looked forward to moving out of those neighborhoods (US Department of Housing and Urban Development *et al.*, 2003). In addition to improvements in adult mental health, girls in the MTO group, and in some instances also girls in the Section 8 voucher group, reported improvements in their mental health, including reductions in psychological distress, depression, and generalized anxiety disorder (US Department of Housing and Urban Development *et al.*, 2003). Girls aged 15–19 in the MTO group also had better health behaviors than their counterparts in public housing, for example, lower rates of smoking and marijuana use (US Department of Housing and Urban Development *et al.*, 2003).

Nonexperimental studies also indicate that residents of higher-SES neighborhoods show a lower prevalence of mental health problems. The Yonkers Scattered-Site Public Housing evaluation team documented recent violent victimization, depression and anxiety symptoms, and substance use among mothers (Briggs & Yonkers Family and Community Project, 1997; Briggs *et al.*, 1999). The group that moved to neighborhoods with new scattered-site public housing reported lower prevalence of depression symptoms, problem drinking, marijuana use, and experience of violent or traumatic events compared with those who stayed in the segregated Yonkers public housing neighborhoods (Briggs & Yonkers Family and Community Project, 1997). Similarly, evidence from the Project on Human Development in Chicago Neighborhoods suggests that poor mental health in children—that is, clinical levels of internalizing behavior problems (depression, anxiety, withdrawal, and somatic problems)—is associated with concentrated disadvantage, independent of family demographic characteristics, maternal depression, and earlier child mental health scores (Xue *et al.*, 2005). In the Chicago study, "concentrated disadvantage" comprised the poverty rate, the percentage of residents receiving public assistance, the percentage of female-headed families, the unemployment ratio, and the percentage of African American residents.

Ironically, although health improvements were not among the stated goals of MTO, they are currently among the most apparent gains realized by participating families. MTO has provided some of the most compelling and methodologically sound evidence to date that neighborhoods matter for health.[7] In the long run, the positive effects of housing mobility on health may lead to improvements in other areas over the life course. For instance, healthier children may do better in school, and healthier adults may be able to hold better and more stable jobs.

Although the reductions in obesity and mental health problems are promising, we should also note that at the latest follow-up, the MTO demonstration did not find significant improvements in other health outcomes such as those relating to asthma, blood pressure, and alcohol use, all of which could also be influenced by neighborhood conditions.[8]

WHY DO NEIGHBORHOODS MATTER FOR HEALTH?

Possible mechanisms through which neighborhoods influence health may range from direct physical influences such as exposure to toxic waste to the cumulative stress associated with living in unsafe neighborhoods with limited resources. Additionally, since disadvantaged neighborhoods may limit opportunities for upward social mobility, neighborhoods may also influence health status by shaping socioeconomic attainment throughout the life course. In turn, the distribution of good health in society is strongly related to socioeconomic position, with those at the top of the socioeconomic ladder having better health than those at the middle and those at the bottom (Berkman & Kawachi, 2000a).

In an annotated bibliography on neighborhoods and health, Flournoy and Yen (2004) found that most of the conceptual frameworks focused on (1) neighborhood social relationships and norms; (2) community institutions and services; (3) direct environmental factors (e.g., pollution) and indirect environmental factors that may influence health behaviors (e.g., access to healthy food); and (4) broader structural issues that affect neighborhoods (e.g., residential segregation at the metropolitan area level).

Neighborhoods provide inputs that may improve or hinder health. For example, neighborhoods may enhance the possibility of maintaining a healthy diet and/or an adequate level of physical activity. For example, neighborhoods may have a low (high) density of fast food outlets and/or have adequate (limited) walkability.

SELECTED PATHWAYS BETWEEN NEIGHBORHOOD ENVIRONMENT AND MENTAL HEALTH

Disadvantaged neighborhoods may expose individuals to living conditions that induce high levels of stress, for instance, crime and violence, unemployment, idle youth, abandoned houses, drug dealing, and unresponsive or abusive police.

Better mental health among adults and girls living in low-poverty neighborhoods (compared to their counterparts living in public housing in high-poverty neighborhoods) is the clearest and most consistent finding of MTO in relation to health outcomes (Leventhal & Brooks-Gunn, 2001, 2003b; US

Department of Housing and Urban Development *et al.*, 2003; Acevedo-Garcia *et al.*, 2004). The lower prevalence of depression and anxiety may be due to reduced exposure to crime and violence in low-poverty neighborhoods, and to having been able to address concerns about neighborhood safety.

Other sources of environmental stress highly prevalent in disadvantaged neighborhoods may include street traffic (and the associated noise and risk of traffic-related accidents), unsafe common spaces such as playgrounds, and inadequate facilities and public services such as structurally deficient school buildings (Evans, 2004). As Evans (2004) noted, in addition to being psychosocial stressors, all the above features are stark evidence of physical environmental hazards in poor neighborhoods.

SELECTED PATHWAYS BETWEEN NEIGHBORHOOD ENVIRONMENT AND PHYSICAL HEALTH

Improvements in mental health associated with moving from high- to low-poverty neighborhoods may have important implications for physical health, as well as nonhealth outcomes such as education and employment. Environmental stressors in segregated neighborhoods may induce physiological responses to cope with stress that for some individuals may eventually result in low birth weight, early mortality, and impaired cognitive development (Massey, 2004). Improved mental health may translate into improved economic outcomes, as individuals with major depression (compared to individuals without the disorder) may be more likely to experience poor health status, bed days, limitations in physical or job functioning, and high levels of financial strain (Judd *et al.*, 1996).

Self-reported mental health status may be correlated with physiological responses to stress, as measured by biomarkers such as cortisol and catecholamines.[9] Therefore, worse mental health may be a marker for increased risk of physiological disregulation, which in turn may be associated with a higher risk of health problems.

Neighborhood conditions may interact with individual-level factors such as susceptibility to disease. Higher cardiovascular reactivity—that is, the physiologic response from a resting state to psychological or physical stressors—may be associated with a higher risk of hypertension or coronary heart disease. Individuals with high cardiovascular reactivity who live in high-stress neighborhood environments would have more frequent and greater physiological stress responses than individuals who either are not highly reactive or live in low-stress neighborhoods. In other words, there may be an interaction between cardiovascular reactivity and exposure to neighborhood stressors. Healthwise, the individuals at higher risk of cardiovascular disease would be those with high cardiovascular reactivity who live in high-stress neighborhoods. Additionally, chronic exposure to high-stress neighborhood environments may lead to higher cardiovascular reactivity, even among individuals who initially have low cardiovascular reactivity.[10]

In sum, living in disadvantaged neighborhoods may increase stress, which is associated with health problems such as cardiovascular disease. Stress may result, for example, from high exposure to violence, and have long-lasting effects over the life course. Arline Geronimus (1992, 1996) suggested that cumulative stress may result in "weathering" or premature health deterioration. For example, the risk of hypertension and the risk of having a low-birthweight baby may increase more rapidly with age among African American women than among white women, because the former are more likely to be systematically and chronically exposed to stressors such as poor neighborhoods.

The link between stress induced by disadvantaged neighborhood environments and physiological responses to stress may contribute to explaining the high prevalence of physical health problems in such neighborhoods. However, there are also neighborhood factors that may influence physical health directly (i.e., not mediated by stress). Various studies have shown that the proportion of racial/ethnic minorities and low-SES households at the neighborhood level is positively associated with exposure to environmentally hazardous sites and industrial facilities, and air toxics (Brown, 1995; Faber & Krieg, 2002; Morello-Frosch *et al.*, 2002). For example, Apelberg *et al.* (2005) evaluated disparities in cancer risk from exposure to air toxics in Maryland. Neighborhoods (i.e., census tracts) with high proportions of African American residents (highest quartile) were three times more likely to be high risk (>90th percentile of risk) than those with low proportions of African Americans (the lowest quartile). Neighborhoods in the lowest quartile of socioeconomic position were also more likely to be high risk than those in the highest quartile. Air toxics may also contribute to the disproportionate burden of asthma in disadvantaged neighborhoods (Larsen *et al.*, 2002). Therefore, although biosocial models have focused largely on the physiological pathways between chronic stress and illness (Massey, 2004), exposure to multiple hazards in segregated neighborhoods may also have more direct implications for physical health (Evans, 2004).

SELECTED PATHWAYS BETWEEN NEIGHBORHOOD ENVIRONMENT AND HEALTH BEHAVIORS

Neighborhood conditions also influence health behaviors such as diet, physical activity, smoking, and alcohol consumption. Studies have shown that low-income and minority neighborhoods tend to have a higher density of venues not conducive to positive health outcomes. For example, there tend to be more supermarkets in predominantly white neighborhoods than in predominantly black neighborhoods (Morland *et al.*, 2002), but more fast food restaurants in black neighborhoods. In a study of New Orleans, Block *et al.* (2004) showed that predominantly black neighborhoods had 2.4 fast food restaurants per square mile compared to 1.5 restaurants in predominantly white neighborhoods. Thus, poor and minority communities may not have equal access to the variety of healthy food choices available to wealthy and nonminority communities (Morland *et al.*, 2002). Such racial disparities in neighborhood environment may contribute to the disparities we observe in health conditions, such as obesity, that are largely dependent on health behaviors, such as those relating to diet and physical activity. Moreover, not only is the actual presence of health-promoting venues limited in low-income and minority areas, but also the marketing of unhealthy products is more aggressive in those neighborhoods (Ammerman & Nolden, 1995; Stoddard *et al.*, 1997; Luke *et al.*, 2000).

Public health research is increasingly paying attention to the relationship between the built environment and health. For instance, concern about the national increase in obesity rates has motivated an examination of the role of the built environment. Investigators have used various indicators to assess whether the built environment is conducive to physical activity. Some indicators describe the built environment at the metropolitan area level, for example, sprawl, while others address the neighborhood level, for example, walkability. Residents of high-walkability neighborhoods report higher levels of neighborhood aesthetics, and safety. These perceptions may contribute to higher levels of physical activity and thus lower obesity (Saelens *et al.*, 2003). Studies have shown that the built environment may be less conducive to physical activity in low SES and minority communities. In Boston the safety of playgrounds at the neighborhood level is lower in areas with a higher proportion of African American residents (Cradock *et al.*, 2005). Additional public health research is needed to document and address other racial/ethnic disparities in the built environment and their influence on health (behaviors).

Health behaviors are also influenced by (perceived) neighborhood social environment—that is, safety. For example, parental perceptions of the neighborhood as unsafe were independently associated with an increased risk of being overweight in 7-year-old children (Lumeng *et al.*, 2006). Possibly, neighborhood safety has an effect on children's lifestyle, such as time spent on physical activity.

NEIGHBORHOODS AND HEALTH IN A LIFE COURSE PERSPECTIVE
Neighborhood conditions may influence health outcomes in all age groups (Pickett & Pearl, 2001). However, exposure to neighborhood disadvantage during childhood may be particularly harmful as the effects of this exposure may continue into adolescence and adulthood. Children growing up in

disadvantaged neighborhoods may face difficult challenges, including a hazardous physical environment, low-quality schools, and lack of public safety. Research shows that poor neighborhood conditions may put children at risk for developmental delays, teen parenthood, and academic failure (Brooks-Gunn *et al.*, 1997; Leventhal & Brooks-Gunn, 2000).

In addition to affecting quality of life during childhood, these effects may also have serious and possibly irreversible consequences over the life course, and intergenerationally. Evidence from the Gautreaux study showed that for children the beneficial effects of moving to suburban neighborhoods continued over adolescence and adulthood (Rosenbaum & Popkin, 1990, 1991; Rosenbaum, 1994, 1995).

Important issues remain for researchers in terms of identifying not only *what* neighborhood exposures matter, but also *when* in the life course the exposure matters most. For instance, an exposure might be very influential during a "critical period," which is "when an exposure acting during a specific period has lasting or lifetime effects on the structure or function of organs, tissues, and body systems which are not modified in any dramatic way by later experience" (Ben-Shlomo & Kuh, 2002: 286). For example, Barker and coworkers propose the fetal origins hypothesis, purporting that adult chronic disease (such as cardiovascular disease or non-insulin-dependent diabetes) originates from poor growth *in utero* (Barker & Martyn, 1992; Barker *et al.*, 1993). Moreover, some investigators have argued that social policy might be most effective at protecting health if focused during critical or sensitive biological periods (Bartley *et al.*, 1997).

Applying the critical periods framework to housing and health, if adverse housing or neighborhood conditions exert a detrimental effect on a child, and if certain periods in childhood are particularly sensitive to this exposure, then the exposure may exert long-term effects—or effects that may lie latent or dormant for many years. Hence, present disparities in housing conditions, and inadequate housing and neighborhood conditions, should be expected to contribute to future disparities in health. Therefore, even if thirty years from now discrimination in housing were to disappear entirely, minority adults who were raised in inferior housing and neighborhoods (compared to whites) would still face worse health conditions—even in the hypothetical absence of any current discrimination. Past housing may matter considerably for current and future health, although the empirical work probing how and when specific aspects of housing matter is not as well developed for socio-economic and neighborhood exposures as it has been for, say, chemical exposures such as exposure to lead.

The Role of Housing Policies in Reducing Health Disparities

There is evidence on the health effects of interventions that address physical and biological exposures at the level of the housing unit (e.g., lead abatement) (Krieger & Higgins, 2002). However, we know considerably less about the health effects of interventions and policies that address the socio-economic (e.g., homeownership promotion, affordability) and spatial (e.g., poverty deconcentration and desegregation) aspects of housing. In a review of seventy-two articles on U.S. interventions to improve health by modifying housing, Saegert *et al.* (2003) found that most interventions (92 percent) addressed only one health problem (e.g., lead poisoning, injuries, or asthma). The authors concluded that current interventions reflect a narrow view of the relationships between housing and health.

Given the pathways between housing and health discussed in the previous section, here we discuss the evidence that housing policy may help reduce health disparities by addressing racial disparities in housing. We address first housing policies that primarily target the socioeconomic aspects of housing, and then housing policies aimed at deconcentrating poverty and ameliorating racial residential segregation. We do not discuss policies to address the physical adequacy and quality of housing units because these topics have been extensively reviewed in the literature—see, for instance, Krieger and Higgins (2002) and Saegert *et al.* (2003).

In the United States, minorities disproportionately bear the burden of housing problems, including low rates of homeownership, inadequate housing, and residence in disadvantaged neighborhoods. Several areas of U.S. housing policy address such housing problems (Orlebecke, 2000; Quigley, 2000), and thus have the potential to improve the health status of low-income and minority households.

As is documented in this book, historically and presently, housing discrimination has been a fundamental reason why minorities disproportionately face multiple housing problems. Hence, fighting housing discrimination is at the root of addressing racial disparities in housing and thus housing disparities in health. However, as discussed below, in addition to housing antidiscrimination policy, other housing policy areas may be considered as tools for addressing racial/ethnic disparities in health, especially if infused with fair housing principles.

In order for housing policies to enhance minorities' opportunities to achieve better health, they need to affirmatively pursue fair housing objectives. As stated by Briggs, "housing is unavoidably about *where*" (2005a: 5). As reviewed earlier, public health research suggests that health is also about *where*. Housing policies for low-income households may have positive effects on health by improving individual socioeconomic status. They may potentially have greater impact on health if they affirmatively pursue minorities' access to neighborhoods with physical and social environments conducive to good health.

Powerful racial/ethnic stratification barriers may limit the effectiveness of housing policies. For example, fragmentation of metropolitan areas into multiple local jurisdictions that enact exclusionary zoning regulations restricts access to suburban neighborhoods for minority and low-income families (Altshuler *et al.*, 1999; Downs, 2000; Pendall, 2000; Katz, 2004). Housing discrimination is another impediment to minority and low-income homeownership and access to better neighborhoods (Turner, 1998; Turner *et al.*, 2002). Therefore, housing advocates and policy researchers believe that housing programs for low-income and minority households should work in collaboration with fair housing and regional equity advocates (Turner, 1998, 2005; Goering *et al.*, 2003; Briggs, 2005; Poverty and Race Research Action Council, 2005a, b; Tegeler *et al.*, 2005).

Housing Affordability and Health

Among both homeowners and renters, housing affordability problems disproportionately affect minorities. In the United States, housing is considered affordable if a household devotes 30 percent or less of its monthly income to housing. In the 1990s, 14.3 percent of blacks and 12.5 percent of Hispanic homeowners living in the twenty-five largest cities spent at least half of their incomes on housing (Simmons & Fannie Mae Foundation, 2004).

A central goal of rental assistance (i.e., rental subsidy) programs for low-income households is to address housing affordability. Excessive housing expenditures are likely to have an impact on health by reducing households' disposable income and thus crowding out health-related expenditures such as spending on food and health care. However, there is little research on the health effects of policies to address housing affordability. As an exception, a health impact assessment of the affordability aspects of the rental assistance Section 8 program on children's health in Massachusetts indicated that reducing housing assistance (by instituting time limits for housing subsidies) would put children's health at risk, owing to family budget trade-offs between housing expenses and other basic needs, such as food, and through exposure to substandard housing. These budget trade-offs could result in a 50 percent increase in food insecurity, which is related to malnutrition, poor growth, and increased risk of illness (Child Health Impact Working Group *et al.*, 2005).

Low-Income Homeownership and Health

Given the disproportionate representation of minorities among low-income homeowners and the less favorable neighborhood outcomes among black and Hispanic homeowners (Belsky & Duda, 2002), low-income homeownership programs should be supplemented with segregation and poverty deconcentration objectives. Homeownership accompanied by improved neighborhood choice would address both the pathway between household wealth and health, and the pathway between neighborhood environment and health. However, to date, U.S. low-income and minority homeownership programs have not addressed locational issues proactively (Belsky & Duda, 2002).

More efforts are needed to close the homeownership gaps further, to make sure that minority and low-income families are not overburdened by the financial commitments that accompany homeownership, and to lower discriminatory and other barriers that prevent them from realizing homeownership in low-poverty neighborhoods with access to quality public goods (Belsky & Duda, 2002; Retsinas & Belsky, 2002).

To our knowledge, no research studies have evaluated the health effects of low-income and minority homeownership programs. In the absence of improved access to better neighborhoods, homeownership may be detrimental if it limits a household's mobility and thus ability to escape an unsafe neighborhood or a deficient school system. However, there is very limited research on the benefits of low-income homeownership by location—for instance, the health benefits of owning a home in a low-poverty neighborhood vis-à-vis a high-poverty neighborhood. Nor has there been research on the health effects of the excessive financial burden of homeownership (Nettleton & Burrows, 1998) endured disproportionately by U.S. minority households.

Mixed-Income Housing and Health

A 2003 review in the *American Journal of Preventive Medicine* examined research on the health effects of mixed-income housing (Anderson *et al.*, 2003). According to the authors' conceptual framework, mixed-income housing might have a beneficial effect on health, because it would lead to an increase in social capital by reducing the isolation experienced in high-poverty neighborhoods, help to raise expectations of community norms, and increase the quality of public services, as well as improving access to private goods and safety. However, this research review found insufficient empirical evidence that mixed-income housing programs have improved health outcomes.

A Statistics Canada analysis based on self-rated health data from the 1996–1997 National Population Health Survey, in combination with neighborhood-level data, found that self-rated health status was higher among disadvantaged individuals who shared neighborhoods with more affluent residents compared to their counterparts living in more socio-economically segregated neighborhoods (Hou & Myles, 2004).[11] According to the authors, the causal mechanism could be "material" (i.e., better neighborhood services, amenities, less exposure to environmental risk factors) and/or social (e.g., "learning effects" from being exposed to people with presumably healthier lifestyles).[12] Hou and Myles (2004) concluded that "these results suggest that populations may benefit from housing and zoning strategies that encourage economically 'mixed' neighborhoods and discourage high levels of residential segregation by income level."

In the United States, one of the premises of the public housing revitalization HOPE VI program is that by deconcentrating poverty and creating mixed-income communities, low-income families will form social networks with neighbors in their new communities (Popkin *et al.*, 2002, 2004). These networks are hypothesized to offer a range of benefits for former public housing residents, including positive role models and peer groups, and access to information about economic opportunities. As was discussed earlier, similarly, public health researchers have hypothesized that poor individuals residing in mixed-income neighborhoods may have access to social networks with healthier behaviors, and better health information. However, research on mixed-income communities has provided little evidence that social mixing has any direct positive impacts through social interaction and/or social networks (Varady & Walker, 2003). HOPE VI families presumed to have relocated to mixed-income neighborhoods have reported low levels of social interaction with their neighbors (Buron *et al.*, 2002).

Poverty Deconcentration in Housing Rental Assistance and Health

Increasingly there is consensus that, in addition to addressing affordability, housing rental assistance should improve access to better neighborhoods. Again this approach is consistent with tackling both household socio-economic and neighborhood environment factors that contribute to health disparities.

Since the mid-1970s the United States has pursued housing vouchers, instead of public housing, as the primary means of providing housing assistance to low-income families, as it became clear that public housing had promoted racial residential segregation and poverty concentration (Schill & Wachter, 1995).

PUBLIC HOUSING PROJECTS AND HEALTH

There is evidence that the health of public housing residents, who are disproportionately members of racial/ethnic minorities,[13] is considerably worse than the health of the average American. The HOPE VI Panel Study conducted by the Urban Institute examined the living conditions of residents of severely distressed public housing at five sites, both at baseline and after housing redevelopment. At baseline, HOPE VI adults reported dramatically lower overall physical and mental health status than national averages

(Popkin *et al.*, 2002). The proportion of adults who reported "excellent" or "very good" physical health was much lower (38 percent) than the overall national average (68 percent) and than the minority national average (60 percent) in the 2001 National Health Interview Survey. Similarly, 29 percent reported poor mental health, compared to 20 percent in the 1999 National Survey of American Families. Furthermore, 39 percent reported having a chronic health condition such as high blood pressure, diabetes, or arthritis; and 22 percent reported having been diagnosed with asthma (versus 10 percent nationally).

HOPE VI children faced substandard housing (e.g., lead paint, mold, inadequate heat, and pest infestations) and extremely dangerous neighborhood conditions (e.g., shootings and drug-related crime) (Popkin *et al.*, 2002). Accordingly, they had higher rates of health problems than those of low-income children in national surveys. HOPE VI parents reported substantially lower health ratings for their children than those reported for children in national samples. Twenty-five percent of children aged 0–5 had been diagnosed with asthma, more than three times the national average (Popkin *et al.*, 2002).

Thus, from the HOPE VI research it appears that the poor health of public housing residents is influenced both by inadequate housing units (e.g., physical, chemical, and biological exposures) and by poor neighborhood environments (e.g., exposure to violence).

HOUSING VOUCHERS AND HEALTH

Because of the ills associated with public housing, rental assistance is increasingly given primarily through housing subsidies, i.e., Section 8 vouchers. In theory, vouchers allow households to find housing in any neighborhood of their metropolitan area where affordable units exist, instead of having to reside in deprived, racially segregated neighborhoods where many public housing projects are located. Data from the Department of Housing and Urban Development show that, indeed, while on average public housing residents live in neighborhoods that are 59 percent minority, households receiving Section 8 vouchers live in neighborhoods that are 39 percent minority (U.S. Department of Housing and Urban Development, 1997). Similarly, individuals receiving Section 8 vouchers are less likely to live in high-poverty neighborhoods than individuals in public housing. In the late 1990s, 14.8 percent of voucher recipients lived in high-poverty neighborhoods (poverty rate > 30 percent), compared with 53.6 percent of public housing residents (Turner, 1998).

The evidence that, in addition to addressing housing affordability, Section 8 may contribute to improving access to low-poverty neighborhoods suggests that it may result in better health outcomes through these two pathways.

However, although a few studies have assessed the health effects of the affordability component of Section 8 (Child Health Impact Working Group *et al.*, 2005), there has not been a study of the health effects of its locational component, apart from the inclusion of a Section 8 group in the Moving to Opportunity study.

HOUSING MOBILITY PROGRAMS AND HEALTH

Housing policy experts recognize that although, in principle, housing vouchers offer more neighborhood choices, improved neighborhood outcomes are constrained, especially for some groups, such as racial/ethnic minorities and central-city residents (Turner, 1998).[14] Black (25 percent) and Hispanic (28 percent) families on Section 8 are more likely than white (8 percent) families to live in neighborhoods where poverty is concentrated (poverty rate ≥ 30 percent) (Devine *et al.*, 2003).[15]

Because of the racial disparities in neighborhood outcomes within the Section 8 voucher program, housing policy experts have recommended coupling Section 8 with fair housing efforts, as well as developing housing mobility initiatives (Turner, 1998). Since the mid-1990s the Department of Housing and Urban Development has introduced mobility policies and programs to encourage voucher holders to move from high-poverty to low-poverty neighborhoods by providing housing search assistance and connecting voucher holders with landlords in low-poverty neighborhoods (Cunningham & Sawyer, 2005).

As was discussed earlier, the Moving to Opportunity demonstration evaluated both the regular Section 8 program and a mobility-enhanced version of Section 8 (i.e., MTO) for their impact on health—compared to housing assistance through public housing projects. To date, the results of the MTO demonstration suggest that a mobility-enhanced Section 8 program may improve the health (and quality of life) of low-income families by helping them move out of high-poverty neighborhoods. In this policy demonstration the two treatment groups (Section 8 and MTO) and the control group (public housing) were all receiving housing assistance. Since housing affordability was addressed for all three groups, the differences in health outcomes across groups may be attributed to location (i.e., differences in neighborhood environment). Thus, MTO does not provide estimates of the health benefits associated with addressing housing affordability—that is, MTO provides a conservative estimate of the overall health effects of housing assistance, which comprise both affordability and neighborhood effects.

ENHANCING MOBILITY PROGRAMS TO IMPROVE HEALTH

Housing mobility is not a panacea. Even within mobility programs, the legacy of housing discrimination may be hard to overcome. An examination of the

Chicago Housing Opportunity Program (Cunningham & Sawyer, 2005) showed that among those who received mobility services, larger families, those receiving welfare assistance, and those relocating from public housing were less likely to move to low-poverty neighborhoods. Also, black households were less likely to move to "opportunity neighborhoods" (poverty rate < 23.5 percent) than comparable white and Hispanic households, as well as more likely to initially live in racially segregated neighborhoods and to continue to live in such neighborhoods (Cunningham & Sawyer, 2005). These findings highlight that although mobility programs may offer promising results, highly vulnerable families may not be able to benefit from them, and that housing discrimination issues should be addressed concurrently (Popkin et al., 2004; Cunningham & Sawyer, 2005). Also, as minorities move to the suburbs and low-poverty areas, they are likely to encounter discrimination. Therefore, an increased need exists for those moving into such areas for advocacy services and dissemination of information addressing discrimination issues.

There is considerable room to improve housing mobility. Therefore, it is encouraging that even a limited mobility program such as MTO has had some positive effects on health. Housing policy experts have suggested that housing mobility can be strengthened if supplemented with efforts to help the distressed neighborhoods of origin, as well as with assistance for families during and after relocation (Katz, 2004; Popkin et al., 2004). Enhanced housing mobility programs should address concerns about leaving the neighborhood of origin, which may include not having access to a known healthcare provider, leaving a familiar public school (system), and losing a supportive social network. Severing links with the neighborhood of origin should be followed up by information, counseling, and support to help residents adapt to their new neighborhood. These services should be comprehensive—that is, addressing the housing search process, though important, is not sufficient. Additionally, services should be offered for several months or years after the move, until residents feel comfortable in their new neighborhood.

Given the high prevalence of health problems among public housing residents, mobility programs should take into account disease management issues. For example, if relocation results in severing ties with neighborhood healthcare providers, it may worsen health outcomes. Additionally, evidence from the Gautreaux mobility program indicated that those moving to the suburbs may be less satisfied with medical care, possibly because in those neighborhoods there are fewer healthcare providers serving low-income families, or former residents of public housing may be less familiar with them. In MTO, among those eligible to move, some did not want to because they were afraid of losing access to health care in their neighborhood.

Also, families with a disabled member were less successful in moving to low-poverty neighborhoods. This suggests that although more prosperous neighborhoods may offer some better opportunities to maintain good health, residents' attachment to healthcare providers in disadvantaged neighborhoods may be a barrier to their moving. Therefore, comprehensive mobility initiatives should assist individuals in finding alternative sources of health care in their new neighborhoods, and ensuring continuity of treatment (Acevedo-Garcia *et al.*, 2004).

Using Fair Housing Principles to Strengthen the Links between Housing Policy and Health

Socioeconomic differences at the individual level and differences in neighborhood environment partly account for racial/ethnic disparities in health. Although the improvement of neighborhood outcomes has not been a central component of U.S. low-income housing policy, the literature on neighborhoods and health suggests that access to better neighborhoods would multiply the socioeconomic benefits of housing policy. Both higher socioeconomic status and better neighborhoods have been found to have positive, independent, and, in some instances, multiplicative effects on health status.

U.S. rental assistance policy not only addresses housing affordability, but also has increasingly tried to tackle access to better neighborhoods. In this regard, the principles that have guided rental assistance in the past three decades are consistent with a view of health as the product of family socioeconomic status and neighborhood physical and social environment. However, there is ample room for a more aggressive pursuit of fair housing objectives in the delivery of rental assistance, as access to low-poverty neighborhoods is strongly patterned along racial lines. There is even more room for pursuit of fair housing principles in the delivery of low-income homeownership, since these programs have addressed locational issues only marginally.

Desegregation and poverty deconcentration goals should be pursued explicitly, and progress toward them evaluated rigorously in housing programs for low-income families, namely homeownership and rental assistance. Federal legislation requires that housing programs are administered in a manner that "affirmatively furthers" fair housing (§ 3608 of the Fair Housing Act). Numerous court decisions resulting from litigation against housing authorities have confirmed that housing authorities should promote racial desegregation and poverty deconcentration.[16] However, some housing assistance programs (e.g., the Low Income Housing Tax Credit) do not include explicit poverty deconcentration or racial desegregation objectives, and do not require that state agencies collect data appropriate for assessing compliance with fair housing goals (Tegeler, 2005a). Even within programs that have had as a goal enhancing neighborhood choice, e.g., Section 8, racial minorities have had more limited access to better neighborhoods than white families (Turner, 1998; Devine *et al.*, 2003).

Thus, improving neighborhood outcomes calls for strengthening the links between housing assistance and fair housing policy. Antidiscrimination litigation has contributed to furthering the desegregation and deconcentration objectives of rental assistance programs in some metropolitan areas, and is also on the agenda of housing policy advocates, makers, and researchers (Goering *et al.*, 2003). However, in addition to litigation, by statute, fair housing principles should be embedded in the regular practice and evaluation of housing assistance programs. Social epidemiology research on racial/ethnic health disparities and neighborhood effects can inform both civil rights litigation and a broader agenda of access to opportunity neighborhoods.

Evaluating housing assistance policies with a fair housing lens may contribute to reducing racial/ethnic segregation and poverty concentration patterns in assisted housing. A fair housing perspective requires addressing whether the housing policies in question have had a discriminatory impact (even if discrimination was not intentional). Discriminatory impact occurs if a behavior or practice that does not necessarily involve intentional discrimination has an adverse effect on members of a disadvantaged racial group. The courts have recognized two kinds of discriminatory effect: (1) greater adverse impact on one group than another, or (2) harm to the community by the perpetuation of segregation.[17] Although discriminatory impact that cumulates across domains may not be unlawful, it may have important social implications. For instance, discrimination by housing agencies may confine tenants from racial/ethnic minority groups to highly disadvantaged neighborhoods, which in turn may negatively impact the health of these groups.[18] Even if discriminatory housing agencies can be found liable for housing discrimination, there may not be a legal mechanism to allocate blame for health disparities that such discrimination might induce (Blank *et al.*, 2004). Yet from a social perspective we would want to identify and measure these cross-domain effects, as they might help strengthen an antidiscrimination agenda.

Documenting disparities in health outcomes between families receiving housing assistance in high-poverty neighborhoods and families receiving housing assistance in low-poverty neighborhoods may help to provide evidence of discriminatory impact. Failure to affirmatively promote desegregation and deconcentration may have a disproportionate negative impact on the health of minority families.

We need to better track locational outcomes under various housing assistance policies to assess whether they are contributing to the remedying of poverty concentration and racial segregation. The links between housing and health discussed here suggest that it would be valuable to measure health outcomes in housing policy demonstrations using experimental research designs, as well as quasi- or nonexperimental designs, such as those involving pre- and postintervention measurement of health outcomes without a control group. More comprehensive (preferably experimental) evaluations should measure health outcomes before and after relocation in neighborhoods with different poverty levels. Experimental designs will allow us to determine which forms of housing assistance (e.g., mixed-income public housing developments, housing vouchers accompanied by mobility counseling, low-income homeownership) result in access to better neighborhood environments, as well as health and other outcomes under different neighborhood conditions. For instance, what are the health benefits of being a renter in a low-poverty neighborhood versus owning a home in a higher-poverty neighborhood?

Health outcomes may serve as evidence of discriminatory impact if the health of otherwise comparable families is better under housing assistance programs that do affirmatively further fair housing (i.e., proactively promote relocation to low-poverty and racially mixed neighborhoods) than under programs that do not. MTO and HOPE VI have clearly documented that health problems are highly prevalent in the public housing population. Housing assistance policy cannot ignore this reality. Some housing revitalization and mobility programs may improve health outcomes, but for us to learn whether they do, changes in health status should be a standard benchmark in the evaluation of housing assistance programs.

Linking administrative databases of public housing assistance to health insurance and healthcare administrative databases (e.g., Medicare, Medicaid, and SCHIP) could also contribute to making explicit the links between fair housing (e.g., desegregation and deconcentration goals) and health. The suggestion to link housing assistance and health data is consistent with the 2004 recommendations of the National Research Council on measurement and data needs toward eliminating health disparities, specifically that "DHHS should develop a culture of sharing data both within the department *and with other federal agencies*, toward understanding and reducing disparities in health and health care" (National Research Council *et al.*, 2004: 7; emphasis added).

The United States is trying to address racial disparities in health (U.S. Department of Health and Human Services, 2003). Sharp racial disparities also exist in housing at multiple levels, including access to safe homes and neighborhoods. Given the effects of housing, neighborhood quality, and segregation on health, the public health field is embarking upon a more systematic understanding of how addressing housing disparities at multiple levels may contribute to correcting health disparities. Fair housing principles constitute a logical framework for understanding and addressing the links between housing and health disparities.

Acknowledgments

We gratefully acknowledge support from the W.K. Kellogg Foundation (*Diversity Data*, Dolores Acevedo-Garcia, co-PI), the Russell Sage Foundation (*Social Inequality and Health*, 83-01-03, Lisa F. Berkman, PI), and the Robert Wood Johnson Foundation Health and Society Scholars Program (for Theresa Osypuk, Cohort 3 Scholar at University of Michigan), as well as feedback from Lindsay Rosenfeld, Philip Tegeler, and participants at the 2004 National Housing Conference (Fannie Mae Foundation, Washington, DC, November 2004), and the Third National Conference on Housing Mobility (Poverty and Race Research Action Council, Washington, DC, December 2004).

Notes

1. Section 808(d) of the *Fair Housing Act* (Title VII of the *Civil Rights Act* of 1968, as amended) establishes that "all executive departments and agencies shall administer their programs and activities relating to housing and urban development (including any Federal agency having regulatory or supervisory authority over financial institutions) in a manner affirmatively to further the purposes of this subchapter and shall cooperate with the Secretary to further such purposes."
2. Survival rates were calculated over the period 1992–1998.
3. Some studies have also used propensity scores. The propensity score is used primarily in observational studies for reducing bias and increasing precision. The propensity score is a summary from all observed background covariates, which seeks to balance observed covariates across the two (theoretical) treatment groups, to simulate the balanced distribution of confounders achieved through experimental design (D'Agostino, 1998).
4. The five metropolitan areas are Baltimore, Boston, Chicago, Los Angeles, and New York.
5. Findings from the Gautreaux study suggest that enhancing minority access to suburban neighborhoods may improve outcomes (Rosenbaum & Popkin, 1990, 1991; Rosenbaum *et al.*, 1991; Rosenbaum, 1994, 1995). Although the Gautreaux study did not measure health outcomes, we may hypothesize that the improvement in social determinants of health such as education, employment, and earnings could have led to an improvement in health outcomes. Also, improvements in health, for instance, mental health, could have contributed to improvements in employment status.
6. The BMI evaluates an individual's weight status in relation to height. BMI is generally used as the first indicator in assessing body fat and has been the most common method of tracking weight problems and obesity among adults. BMI is a mathematical formula in which a person's body weight in kilograms is divided by the square of his or her height in meters. The BMI is highly correlated with body fat. The criterion for obesity is the same for men and women (National Center for Health Statistics & Centers for Disease Control and Prevention, 2004).
7. While the Moving to Opportunity experimental design eliminates selection—one of the most serious threats to internal validity in observational neighborhood studies—some threats to validity remain, including the Hawthorne effect, compensatory rivalry, and compensatory equalization (Orr, 1999). For a methodological discussion of validity threats with respect to MTO and other housing mobility research, see Acevedo-Garcia *et al.* (2004).
8. For a complete review of the MTO health effects, see Acevedo-Garcia *et al.* (2004).

9. The subjective experience of stress does not always correlate with physiological mediators of stress (McEwen *et al.*, 1999).
10. The discussion in this paragraph was adapted from the MacArthur Research Network on Socioeconomic Status and Health, Psychosocial Notebook, Cardiovascular Reactivity Summary (Allen & Psychosocial Working Group, 2000).
11. The study sample included more than 34,000 people living in 3,044 census tracts in Canada's twenty-five largest metropolitan areas.
12. Alternatively, as with most research on neighborhood effects, the statistical association between health status and neighborhood income and education levels may reflect selection bias or unmeasured differences in individual characteristics.
13. According to the 1997 *Picture of Subsidized Housing* data (HUD), 58 percent of Section 8, 68 percent of public housing, 37 percent of new and rehabilitated Section 8, and 53 percent of Section 236 households belonged to racial/ethnic minority groups. The respective average proportion minority at the neighborhood level for these four types of assisted housing was 39 percent, 59 percent, 34 percent, and 40 percent (U.S. Department of Housing and Urban Development, 1997).
14. Section 8 has been successful in facilitating moves to low-poverty neighborhoods in some areas, e.g. Alameda County, California, but success has been limited in other areas, e.g. Chicago (Varady & Walker, 2003).
15. Encouragingly, though, more than 20 percent of both black and Hispanic families live in neighborhoods where the poverty rate is less than 10 percent, and more than 50 percent of both groups live in neighborhoods where the poverty rate is below 20 percent.
16. Most recently (January 2005), a new federal court ruling in *Thompson v. HUD* (the Baltimore public housing desegregation class action filed by the Maryland American Civil Liberties Union in 1994) places the responsibility on the Department of Housing and Urban Development (HUD) for its failure to actively promote regional housing opportunities for the Baltimore region's low-income families living in federally assisted housing (Tegeler, 2005b).
17. *Arlington Heights II*, 558 F.2d at 1290, and *Huntington*, 844 F.2d at 937 cited by Roisman (2000).
18. As another example, discrimination by real estate agents may result in housing segregation, which in turn affects educational quality (because of the local tax financing of schools) and long-term educational and labor market outcomes (Blank *et al.*, 2004).

References

Acevedo-Garcia, D. and K. A. Lochner (2003). Residential Segregation and Health. In I. Kawachi and L. F. Berkman (eds.) *Neighborhoods and Health* (pp. 265–287). New York, Oxford University Press.

Acevedo-Garcia, D., K. A. Lochner, T. L. Osypuk, and S. Subramanian (2003). Future Directions in Residential Segregation and Health Research: A Multilevel Approach. *American Journal of Public Health* 93(2): 215–221.

Acevedo-Garcia, D., T. L. Osypuk, R. E. Werbel, E. R. Meara, D. M. Cutler, and L. F. Berkman (2004). Does Housing Mobility Policy Improve Health? *Housing Policy Debate* 15(1): 49–98.

Acevedo-Garcia, D., M.-J. Soobader, and L. F. Berkman (2005). The differential effect of foreign-born status on low-birthweight by race/ethnicity and education. *Pediatrics* 115: e20–e30.

Adler, N. E. and J. M. Ostrove (1999). Socioeconomic Status and Health: What We Know and What We Don't. *Socioeconomic Status and Health in Industrial Nations: Social, Psychological, and Biological Pathways* 896: 3–15.

Allen, C. (2000). On the "Physiological Dope" Problematic in Housing and Illness Research: Towards a Critical Realism of Home and Health. *Housing, Theory and Society* 17: 49–67.

Allen, M. T. and Psychosocial Working Group (2000). Cardiovascular Reactivity Summary, Psychosocial Notebook, Cardiovascular Reactivity, MacArthur Research Network on Socioeconomic Status and Health. 2005. Available at http://www.macses.ucsf.edu/Research/Psychosocial/notebook/reactivity.html.

Altshuler, A., W. Morrill, H. Wolman, F. Mitchell and Committee on Improving the Future of U.S.

Cities through Improved Metropolitan Area Governance, eds. (1999). *Governance and Opportunity in Metropolitan America*. Washington, DC, National Academy Press.

Ammerman, S. D. and M. Nolden (1995). Neighborhood-based tobacco advertising targeting adolescents. *Western Journal of Medicine* 162(6): 514–518.

Anderson, L. M., J. S. Charles, M. T. Fullilove, S. C. Scrimshaw, J. E. Fielding, J. Normand *et al.* (2003). Providing Affordable Family Housing and Reducing Residential Segregation by Income: A Systematic Review. *American Journal of Preventive Medicine* 24(3–Supplement 1): 47–67.

Apelberg, B., T. Buckley, and R. White (2005). Socioeconomic and Racial Disparities in Cancer Risk from Air Toxics in Maryland. *Environmental Health Perspectives* 113(6): 693–699.

Barker, D. J. and C. N. Martyn (1992). The Maternal and Fetal Origins of Cardiovascular Disease. *Journal of Epidemiology and Community Health* 46: 8–11.

Barker, D. J., P. D. Gluckman, K. M. Godfrey, J. E. Harding, J. A. Owens, and J. S. Robinson (1993). Fetal Nutrition and Cardiovascular Disease in Adult Life. *Lancet* 341: 938–941.

Bartley, M., D. Blane, and S. Montgomery (1997). Health and the Lifecourse: Why Safety Nets Matter. *British Medical Journal* 314: 1194–1196.

Belsky, E. S. and M. Duda (2002). Anatomy of the Low-Income Homeownership Boom in the 1990s. In N. P. Retsinas and E. S. Belsky (eds.) *Low-income Homeownership: Examining the Unexamined Goal* (pp. 15–63). Cambridge, MA, and Washington, DC, Joint Center for Housing Studies, Brookings Institution Press.

Ben-Shlomo, Y. and D. Kuh (2002). A Life Course Approach to Chronic Disease Epidemiology: Conceptual Models, Empirical Challenges, and interdisciplinary perspectives. *International Journal of Epidemiology* 31: 285–293.

Berkman, L. and I. Kawachi, eds. (2000a). *Social Epidemiology*. New York, Oxford University Press.

Berkman, L. F. and I. Kawachi (2000b). A Historical Framework for Social Epidemiology. In L. F. Berkman and I. Kawachi (eds.) *Social Epidemiology* (pp. 3–12). New York, Oxford University Press.

Berkman, L. F. and S. Macintyre (1997). The Measurement of Social Class in Health Studies: Old Measures and New Formulations. *IARC Scientific Publications (Lyon)* (138): 51–64.

Blank, R. M., M. Dabady, C. F. Citro, and Committee on National Statistics and National Research Council, eds. (2004). *Measuring Racial Discrimination*. Washington, DC, National Academy Press.

Block, J., R. Scribner, and K. DeSalvo (2004). Fast Food, Race/Ethnicity, and Income: A Geographic Analysis. *American Journal of Preventive Medicine* 27(3): 211–217.

Boehm, T. P. and A. M. Schlottman (2002). Housing and Wealth Accumulation: Intergenerational Impacts. In N. P. Retsinas and E. S. Belsky (eds.) *Low-Income Homeownership: Examining the Unexamined Goal* (pp. 407–426). Cambridge, MA, and Washington, DC, Joint Center for Housing Studies, Brookings Institution Press.

Braveman, P. A., C. Cubbin, S. Egerter, S. Chideya, K. S. Marchi, M. R. Metzler *et al.* (2005). Socioeconomic Status in Health Research: One Size Does Not Fit All. *Journal of the American Medical Association* 294(22): 2879–2888.

Breysse, P., N. Farr, W. Galke, B. Lanphear, R. Morley, and L. Bergofsky (2004). The Relationship between Housing and Health: Children at Risk. *Environmental Health Perspectives* 112(15): 1583–1588.

Briggs, X. d. S. (2005a). Introduction. In X. d. S. Briggs (ed.) *The Geography of Opportunity: Race and Housing Choice in Metropolitan America* (pp. 1–16). Washington, DC, Brookings Institution Press.

Briggs, X. d. S. (2005b). Politics and Policy: Changing the Geography of Opportunity. In X. d. S. Briggs (ed.) *The Geography of Opportunity: Race and Housing Choice in Metropolitan America* (pp. 310–341). Washington, DC, Brookings Institution Press.

Briggs, X. S. and Yonkers Family and Community Project (1997). *Yonkers Revisited: The Early Impacts of Scattered-Site Public Housing on Families and Neighborhoods*. A Report to the Ford Foundation. New York, Columbia University Teachers College, Harvard University, and Michigan State University.

Briggs, X. S., J. T. Darden, and A. Aidala (1999). In the Wake of Desegregation: Early Impacts of Scattered-Site Public Housing on Neighborhoods in Yonkers, New York. *Journal of the American Planning Association* 65: 27–49.

Brooks-Gunn, J., G. J. Duncan, and J. L. Aber (1997). *Neighborhood Poverty*. New York, Russell Sage Foundation.

Brown, P. (1995). Race, Class, and Environmental Health: A Review and Systematization of the Literature. *Environmental Research* 69(1): 15–30.

Bucks, B. K., A. B. Kennickell, and K. B. Moore (2006). *Recent Changes in U.S. Family Finances: Evidence from the 2001 and 2004 Survey of Consumer Finances*. Washington, DC, Federal Reserve Board, Division of Research and Statistics.

Buron, L., S. J. Popkin, D. Levy, L. E. Harris, and J. Khadduri (2002). *The HOPE VI Resident Tracking Study: A Snapshot of the Current Living Situation of Original Residents from Eight Sites*. Washington, DC, The Urban Institute.

Calem, P. S., J. E. Hershaff and S. M. Wachter (2004). Neighborhood Patterns of Subprime Lending: Evidence from Disparate Cities. *Housing Policy Debate* 15(3): 603–622.

Child Health Impact Working Group, L. Smith, E. W. Brown, J. Cook, and L. Rosenfeld (2005). *Affordable Housing and Child Health: A Child Health Impact Assessment of the Massachusetts Rental Voucher Program*. Boston, MA, Boston University.

Conley, D. (1999). *Being Black, Living in the Red: Race, Wealth and Social Policy in America*. Berkeley, CA, University of California Press.

Cooper, R. S., J. F. Kennelly, R. Durazo-Arvizu, H.-J. Oh, G. Kaplan, and J. Lynch (2001). Relationship between Premature Mortality and Socioeconomic Factors in Black and White Populations of US Metropolitan Areas. *Public Health Reports* 116: 464–473.

Cradock, A., I. Kawachi, G. Colditz, C. Hannon, S. Melly, J. Wiecha *et al.* (2005). Playground Safety and Access in Boston Neighborhoods. *American Journal of Preventive Medicine* 28(4): 357–363.

Cummins, S., S. Macintyre, S. Davidson, and A. Ellaway (2005). Measuring Neighbourhood Social and Material Context: Generation and Interpretation of Ecological Data from Routine and Non-routine Sources. *Health and Place* 11: 249–260.

Cunningham, M. K. and N. Sawyer (2005). *Moving to Better Neighborhoods with Mobility Counseling*. Washington, DC, The Urban Institute.

D'Agostino, R. B. (1998). Tutorial in Biostatistics: Propensity Score Methods for Bias Reduction in the Comparison of a Treatment to a Non-randomized Control Group. *Statistics in Medicine* 17: 2265–2281.

Devine, D. J., R. W. Gray, L. Rubin, and L. B. Taghavi (2003). *Housing Choice Voucher Location Patterns: Implications for Participant and Neighborhood Welfare*. Washington, DC, U.S. Department of Housing and Urban Development, Office of Policy Development and Research Division of Program Monitoring and Research.

Diette, G., L. Markson, E. Skinner, T. Nguyen, P. Algatt-Bergstrom, and A. Wu (2000). Nocturnal Asthma in Children Affects School Attendance, School Performance, and Parents' Work Attendance. *Archives of Pediatric and Adolescent Medicine* 154: 923–928.

Downs, A. (2000). *Housing Policies in the New Millennium*. Housing Policy in the New Millennium, Washington, DC, U.S. Department of Housing and Urban Development.

Dozier, W. H. (1999). *Minorities. Housing Characteristics. Housing Rehabilitation. Housing Quality*. Western Michigan University.

Dunn, J. R. (2000). Housing and Health Inequalities: Review and Prospects for Research. *Housing Studies* 15(3): 341–366.

Dunn, J. R. and M. V. Hayes (2000). Social Inequality, Population Health and Housing: A Study of Two Vancouver Neighborhoods. *Social Science and Medicine* 51: 563–587.

Ellen, I. G. (2000). Is Segregation Bad for Your Health? The Case of Low Birth Weight. In W. G. Gale and J. R. Pack (ed.) *Papers on Urban Affairs* (pp. 203–238). Washington, DC, Brookings Institution Press.

Ellen, I. G. and M. A. Turner (2003). Do Neighborhoods Matter and Why? In J. Goering and J. D. Feins (eds.) *Choosing a Better Life? Evaluating the Moving to Opportunity Social Experiment* (pp. 313–338). Washington, DC, Urban Institute Press.

Ellen, I. G., T. Mijanovich, and K.-N. Dillman (2001). Neighborhood Effects on Health: Exploring the Links and Assessing the Evidence. *Journal of Urban Affairs* 23(3–4): 391–408.

Evans, G. W. (2004). The Environment of Childhood Poverty. *American Psychologist* 59(2): 77–92.

Evans, G. W., H. Saltzman, and J. L. Cooperman (2001). Housing Quality and Children's Socioemotional Health. *Environment and Behavior* 33(3): 389–399.

Faber, D. and E. Krieg (2002). Unequal Exposure to Ecological Hazards: Environmental Injustices in the Commonwealth of Massachusetts. *Environmental Health Perspectives* 110(Suppl. 2): 277–288.

Flournoy, R. and Yen, I. (2004). *The Influence of Community Factors on Health: An Annotated Bibiography*. Oakland, CA, PolicyLink and The California Endowment.

Geronimus, A. T. (1992). The Weathering Hypothesis and the Health of African-American Women and Infants: Evidence and Speculations. *Ethnicity and Disease* 2(3): 207–221.

Geronimus, A. T. (1996). Black/White Differences in the Relationship of Maternal Age to Birthweight: A Population-Based Test of the Weathering Hypothesis. *Social Science and Medicine* 42(4): 589–597.

Goering, J. (2003). The Impacts of New Neighborhoods on Poor Families: Evaluating the Policy Implications of the Moving to Opportunity Demonstration. *FRBNY Economic Policy Review* June: 113–140.

Goering, J. and J. D. Feins, eds. (2003). *Choosing a Better Life? Evaluating the Moving to Opportunity Social Experiment*. Washington, DC, Urban Institute Press.

Goering, J., J. D. Feins, and T. M. Richardson (2002). A Cross-Site Analysis of Initial Moving to Opportunity Demonstration Results. *Journal of Housing Research* 13(1): 1–30.

Goering, J., J. D. Feins, and T. M. Richardson (2003). What Have We Learned about Housing Mobility and Poverty Deconcentration? In J. Goering and J. D. Feins (eds.) *Choosing a Better Life? Evaluating the Moving to Opportunity Social Experiment* (pp. 3–36). Washington, DC, Urban Institute Press.

Hao, L. (2004). Wealth of Immigrant and Native-Born Americans. *International Migration Review* 38(2): 518–546.

Hou, F. and J. Myles (2004). *Neighbourhood Inequality, Relative Deprivation and Self-Perceived Health Status*. Ottawa, Statistics Canada.

Huie, S. A. B., P. M. Krueger, R. G. Rogers, and R. A. Hummer (2003). Wealth, Race, and Mortality. *Social Science Quarterly* 84(3): 667–684.

Joint Center for Housing Studies (2004). *The State of the Nation's Housing: 2004*. Cambridge, MA, Harvard University, Graduate School of Design and John F. Kennedy School of Government.

Judd, L., M. Paulus, K. Wells, and M. Rapaport (1996). Socioeconomic Burden of Subsyndromal Depressive Symptoms and Major Depression in a Sample of the General Population. *American Journal of Psychiatry* 153(11): 1411–1417.

Katz, B. (2004). *Neighborhoods of Choice and Connection: The Evolution of American Neighborhood Policy and What It Means for the United Kingdom*. Washington, DC, The Brookings Institution, Metropolitan Policy Program.

Katz, L. F., J. R. Kling, and J. B. Liebman (2001). Moving to Opportunity in Boston: Early Results of a Randomized Mobility Experiment. *Quarterly Journal of Economics* 116(2): 607–654.

Kawachi, I. and L. F. Berkman, eds. (2003). *Neighborhoods and Health*. New York, Oxford University Press.

Kington, R. S. and H. W. Nickens (2001). Racial and Ethnic Differences in Health: Recent Trends, Current Patterns, Future Directions. In N. J. Smelser, W. J. Wilson, F. Mitchell, and National Research Council (eds.) *America Becoming: Racial Trends and Their Consequences*, vol 2. Washington, DC, National Academy Press.

Krieger, J. and D. L. Higgins (2002). Housing and Health: Time Again for Public Health Action. *American Journal of Public Health* 92(5): 758–768.

Kutty, N. K. (1999). Determinants of Structural Adequacy of Dwellings. *Journal of Housing Research* 10(1): 27–43.

Larsen, G., C. Beskid, and L. Shirname-More (2002). Environmental Air Toxics: Role in Asthma Occurrence? *Environmental Health Perspectives* 110(Suppl. 4): 501–504.

LaVeist, T. A. (2003). Racial Segregation and Longevity among African Americans: An Individual-Level Analysis. *Health Services Research* 38(6): 1719–1733.

Leventhal, T. and J. Brooks-Gunn (2000). The Neighborhoods They Live In: The Effects of Neighborhood Residence on Child and Adolescent Outcomes. *Psychological Bulletin* 126(2): 309–337.

Leventhal, T. and J. Brooks-Gunn (2001). Moving to Better Neighborhoods Improves Health and Family Life among New York Families. *Poverty Research News*. New York, NY, Joint Center for Poverty Research: 5.

Leventhal, T. and J. Brooks-Gunn (2003a). The Early Impacts of Moving to Opportunity on Children and Youth in New York City. In J. Goering and J. Feins (eds.) *Choosing a Better Life: Evaluating the Moving to Opportunity Social Experiment* (pp. 213–244). Washington, DC, Urban Institute Press.

Leventhal, T. and J. Brooks-Gunn (2003b). Moving to Opportunity: An Experimental Study of Neighborhood Effects on Mental Health. *American Journal of Public Health* 93(9): 1576–1582.

Logan, J. R. and Lewis Mumford Center for Comparative Urban and Regional Research (2002). *Separate and Unequal: The Neighborhood Gap for Blacks and Hispanics in Metropolitan America.* Albany, NY, Lewis Mumford Center for Comparative Urban and Regional Research.

Logan, J. R., D. Oakley, and J. Stowell (2003). *Segregation in Neighborhoods and Schools: Impacts on Minority Children in the Boston Region.* Albany, NY, Lewis Mumford Center for Comparative Urban and Regional Research.

Luke, D., E. Esmundo, and Y. Bloom (2000). Smoke Signs: Patterns of Tobacco Billboard Advertising in a Metropolitan Region. *Tobacco Control* 9(1): 16–23.

Lumeng, J., D. Appugliese, and H. Cabral (2006). Neighborhood Safety and Overweight Status in Children. *Archives of Pediatrics and Adolescent Medicine* 160(1): 25–31.

Lynch, J. and G. Kaplan (2000). Socioeconomic Position. In L. F. Berkman and I. Kawachi (eds) *Social Epidemiology* (pp. 13–35). New York, Oxford University Press.

Macintyre, S. and A. Ellaway (2000). Ecological Approaches: Rediscovering the Role of the Physical and Social Environment. In L. F. Berkman and I. Kawachi (eds.) *Social Epidemiology* (pp. 332–348). New York, Oxford University Press.

Macintyre, S. and A. Ellaway (2003). Neighborhoods and Health: An Overview. In I. Kawachi and L. F. Berkman (eds.) *Neighborhoods and Health* (pp. 20–42). New York, Oxford University Press.

Macintyre, S., A. Ellaway, G. Der, G. Ford, and K. Hunt (1998). Do Housing Tenure and Car Access Predict Health Because They Are Simply Markers of Income or Self Esteem? A Scottish Study. *Journal of Epidemiology and Community Health* 52(10): 657–664.

Macintyre, S., A. Ellaway, and S. Cummins (2002). Place Effects on Health: How Can We Conceptualise, Operationalise and Measure Them? *Social Science and Medicine* 55: 125–139.

Marmot, M. (2000). Multilevel Approaches to Understanding Social Determinants. In L. Berkman and I. Kawachi (eds.) *Social Epidemiology* (pp. 349–367). New York, Oxford University Press.

Marmot, M. and R. G. Wilkinson (2001). Psychosocial and Material Pathways in the Relation between Income and Health: A Response to Lynch *et al. British Medical Journal* 322: 1233–1236.

Marmot, M. and World Health Organization (2005). Interview with Professor Sir Michael Marmot, World Health Organization. 2005. Available at http://www.who.int/social_determinants/advocacy/interview_marmot/en/.

Marmot, M., C. D. Ryff, L. L. Bumpass, M. Shipley, and N. F. Marks (1997). Social Inequalities in Health: Next Questions and Converging Evidence. *Social Science and Medicine* 44(6): 901–910.

Marmot, M. G., R. Fuhrer, S. L. Ettner, N. F. Marks, L. L. Bumpass, and C. D. Ryff (1998). Contribution of Psychosocial Factors to Socioeconomic Differences in Health. *Milbank Quarterly* 76(3): 403–448.

Massey, D. S. (2004). Segregation and Stratification: A Biosocial Perspective. *Du Bois Review* 1(1): 1–19.

McEwen, B. S. and J. C. Wingfield (2003). The Concept of Allostasis in Biology and Biomedicine. *Hormones and Behavior* 43: 2–15.

McEwen, B., T. Seeman, and Allostatic Load Working Group (1999). *Allostatic Load and Allostasis, Allostatic Load and Allostasis Notebook,* MacArthur Research Network on Socioeconomic Status and Health. 2005. Available at http://www.macses.ucsf.edu/Research/Allostatic/notebook/allostatic.html.

Moonie, S., D. Sterling, L. Figgs, and M. Castro (2006). Asthma Status and Severity Affects Missed School Days. *Journal of School Health* 76(1): 18–24.

Morello-Frosch, R., M. Pastor, C. Porras, and J. Sadd (2002). Environmental Justice and Regional Inequality in Southern California: Implications for Future Research. *Environmental Health Perspectives* 110(Suppl. 2): 149–154.

Morland, K., S. Wing, A. Diez-Roux, and C. Poole (2002). Neighborhood Characteristics Associated with the Location of Food Stores and Food Service Places. *American Journal of Preventive Medicine* 22(1): 23–29.

National Center for Health Statistics and Centers for Disease Control and Prevention (2004). *Prevalence of Overweight and Obesity among Adults: United States, 1999–2002,* National Center for Health Statistics, Centers for Disease Control and Prevention. 2005. Available at http://www.cdc.gov/nchs/products/pubs/pubd/hestats/obese/obse99.htm.

National Research Council, M. V. Ploeg, and E. Perrin, eds. (2004). *Eliminating Health Disparities: Measurement and Data Needs.* Washington, DC, National Research Council, Committee on National Statistics, Division of Behavioral and Social Sciences and Education. Panel on DHHS Collection of Race and Ethnicity Data.

Nettleton, S. and R. Burrows (1998). Mortgage Debt, Insecure Homeownership and Health: An Exploratory Analysis. *Sociology of Health and Illness* 20(5): 731–753.

Oakes, J. M. (2004). The (Mis)Estimation of Neighborhood Effects: Causal Inference in a Practicable Social Epidemiology. *Social Science and Medicine* 58(10): 1929–1952.

Orlebecke, C. J. (2000). The Evolution of Low-Income Housing Policy, 1949 to 1999. *Housing Policy Debate* 11(2): 489–519.

Orr, L. L. (1999). *Social Experiments: Evaluating Public Programs with Experimental Methods.* Thousand Oaks, CA, Sage Publications.

Orzechowski, S. and P. Sepielli (2003). *Net Worth and Asset Ownership of Households: 1998 and 2000.* Washington, DC, US Census Bureau.

Osypuk, T. L. and D. Acevedo-Garcia. Are preterem birth racial disparities higher in hypersegregated areas? (under review).

Pamuk, E., D. Makuc, K. Heck, C. Reuben, and K. Lochner (1998). *Socioeconomic Status and Health Chartbook. Health, United States, 1998.* Hyattsville, MD, National Center for Health Statistics.

Pastor, M. (2001). Geography and Opportunity. In N. J. Smelser, W. J. Wilson, F. Mitchell, and National Research Council (eds.) *America Becoming: Racial Trends and Their Consequences* (pp. 435–468). Washington, DC, National Academy Press.

Pendall, R. (2000). Local Land Use Regulation and the Chain of Exclusion. *Journal of the American Planning Association* 66(2): 125–142.

Pickett, K. E. and M. Pearl (2001). Multilevel Analyses of Neighbourhood Socioeconomic Context and Health Outcomes: A Critical Review. *Journal of Epidemiology and Community Health* 55(2): 111–122.

Popkin, S. J., D. Levy, L. E. Harris, J. Comey, M. K. Cunningham, and L. Buron (2002). *HOPE VI Panel Study: Baseline Report.* Washington, DC, Urban Institute (submitted to the Annie E. Casey Foundation, the John D. and Catherine T. MacArthur Foundation, the Rockefeller Foundation, and the U.S. Department of Housing and Urban Development).

Popkin, S. J., B. Katz, M. K. Cunningham, K. D. Brown, J. Gustafson, and M. A. Turner (2004). *A Decade of HOPE VI: Research Findings and Policy Challenges.* Washington, DC, Urban Institute (prepared for U.S. Department of Housing and Urban Development, Office of Policy Development and Research, under a subcontract with Abt Associates Inc.).

Poverty and Race Research Action Council (2005a). *Civil Rights Implications of the 2005 "Flexible Voucher" Proposal.* Washington, DC, Poverty and Race Research Action Council.

Poverty and Race Research Action Council (2005b). *Protecting Housing Mobility in the Section 8 Program.* Washington, DC, Poverty and Race Research Action Council.

Quigley, J. M. (2000). A Decent Home: Housing Policy in Perspective. In W. G. Gale and J. R. Pack (eds.) *Papers on Urban Affairs* (pp. 53–99). Washington, DC, Brookings Institution Press.

Rauh, V., G. Chew, and R. Garfinkel (2002). Deteriorated Housing Contributes to High Cockroach Allergen Levels in Inner-City Households. *Environmental Health Perspectives* 110(Suppl 2): 323–327.

Retsinas, N. P. and E. S. Belsky (2002). Examining the Unexamined Goal. In N. P. Retsinas and E. S. Belsky (eds.) *Low-Income Homeownership. Examining the Unexamined Goal* (pp. 1–12). Washington, DC, Joint Center for Housing Studies, Harvard University, and Brookings Institution Press.

Robert, S. and J. S. House (1996). SES Differentials in Health by Age and Alternative Indicators of SES. *Journal of Aging and Health* 8(3): 359–388.

Rohe, W. M., S. V. Zandt, and G. McCarthy (2001). *The Social Benefits and Costs of Homeownership: A Critical Assessment of the Research.* Cambridge, MA, Harvard University Joint Center for Housing Studies.

Roisman, F. W. (2000). *An Outline of Principles, Authorities, and Resources Regarding Housing Discrimination and Segregation.* Oakland, CA, and Washington, DC, National Housing Law Project.

Rosenbaum, J. E. (1994). Housing Mobility Strategies for Changing the Geography of Opportunity. Working Paper, Institute for Policy Research, Northwestern University, Evanston, IL.

Rosenbaum, J. E. (1995). Changing the Geography of Opportunity by Expanding Residential Choice: Lessons from the Gautreaux Program. *Housing Policy Debate* 6(1): 231–269.

Rosenbaum, J. E. and S. J. Popkin (1990). *Economic and Social Impacts of Housing Integration.* Evanston, IL, Center for Urban Affairs and Policy Research.

Rosenbaum, J. E. and S. J. Popkin (1991). Employment and Earnings of Low-Income Blacks Who Move to Middle-Class Suburbs. In C. Jencks and P. E. Peterson (eds.) *The Urban Underclass* (pp. 342–56). Washington, DC, Brookings Institution.

Rosenbaum, J. E., Popkin, S. J., Kaufman, J. F., and Rusin, J. (1991). Social Integration of Low-Income Black Adults in Middle-Class White Suburbs. *Social Problems* 38(4): 448–461.

Rusk, D. (2001). *The "Segregation Tax": The Cost of Racial Segregation to Black Homeowners.* Washington, DC, Brookings Institution, Center on Urban and Metropolitan Policy: 14.

Saegert, S. C., S. Klitzman, N. Freudenberg, J. Cooperman-Mroczek, and S. Nassar (2003). Healthy Housing: A Structured Review of Published Evaluations of US Interventions to Improve Health by Modifying Housing in the United States, 1990–2001. *American Journal of Public Health* 93(9): 1471–1477.

Saelens, B. E., J. F. Sallis, J. B. Black, and D. Chen (2003). Neighborhood-Based Differences in Physical Activity: An Environment Scale Evaluation. *American Journal of Public Health* 93(9): 1552–1558.

Schill, M. H. and S. M. Wachter (1995). Housing Market Constraints and Spatial Stratification by Income and Race. *Housing Policy Debate* 6(1): 141–167.

Shapiro, T. M. (2004). *The Hidden Cost of Being African American: How Wealth Perpetuates Inequality.* New York, Oxford University Press.

Simmons, P. A. (2001). Changes in Minority Homeownership during the 1990s. *Fannie Mae Foundation Census Notes* 7(September 2001): 16.

Simmons, P. A. and Fannie Mae Foundation (2004). *A Tale of Two Cities: Growing Affordability Problems amidst Rising Homeownership for Urban Minorities.* Washington, DC, Fannie Mae Foundation.

Stoddard, J. L., C. Johnson, T. Boley-Cruz, and S. Sussman (1997). Targeted Tobacco Markets: Outdoor Advertising in Los Angeles Minority Neighborhoods. *American Journal of Public Health* 87(7): 1232–1233.

Storr, C. L., C.-Y. Chen and J. C. Anthony (2004). "Unequal Opportunity": Neighbourhood Disadvantage and the Chance to Buy Illegal Drugs. *Journal of Epidemiology and Community Health* 58: 231–237.

Syme, S. L. (1987). Social Determinants of Disease. *Annals of Clinical Research* 19(2): 44–52.

Tegeler, P. (2005a). Back to Court: The Federal Role in Metropolitan Housing Segregation. *Shelterforce Online* 140(March–April).

Tegeler, P. D. (2005b). The Persistence of Segregation in Government Housing Programs. In X. d. S. Briggs (ed.) *The Geography of Opportunity: Race and Housing Choice in Metropolitan America* (pp. 197–216). Washington, DC, Brookings Institution Press.

Tegeler, P., M. Cunningham, and M. A. Turner, eds. (2005). *Keeping the Promise: Preserving and Enhancing Housing Mobility in the Section 8 Housing Choice Voucher Program.* Conference Report of theThird National Conference on Housing Mobility. Washington, DC, Poverty and Race Research Action Council.

Turner, M. A. (1997). Segregation by the Numbers. *Washington Post.*

Turner, M. A. (1998). Moving Out of Poverty: Expanding Mobility and Choice through Tenant-Based Housing Assistance. *Housing Policy Debate* 9(2): 373–394.

Turner, M. A. (2005). Preserving the Strengths of the Housing Choice Voucher Program, Statement of Margery Austin Turner before the Subcommittee on Housing and Community Opportunity, Committee on Financial Services, United States House of Representatives. Washington, DC, Urban Institute.

Turner, M. A., S. L. Ross, G. C. Galster, J. Yinger, and The Urban Institute (2002). Discrimination in Metropolitan Housing Markets: Phase 1. Washington, DC, Urban Institute.

U.S. Department of Health and Human Services (2001). *The Surgeon General's Call to Action to Prevent and Decrease Overweight and Obesity.* Rockville, MD, US Department of Health and Human Services, Public Health Service, Office of the Surgeon General.

U.S. Department of Health and Human Services (2003). *Healthy People 2010,* volume 1 (second edition), U.S. Department of Health and Human Services. 2004. Available at http://www. healthypeople.gov/Document/tableofcontents.htm#volume1.

U.S. Department of Housing and Urban Development (1997). *1997 Picture of Subsidized Households Quick Facts*, US Department of Housing and Urban Development. 2005. Available at http://www.huduser.org/datasets/assthsg/picqwik.html.

U.S. Department of Housing and Urban Development (2000). *Unequal Burden: Income and Racial Disparities in Subprime Lending in America*. Washington, DC, U.S. Department of Housing and Urban Development.

U.S. Department of Housing and Urban Development, Office of Policy Development and Research, L. Orr, J. D. Feins, R. Jacob, E. Beecroft *et al.* (2003). *Moving to Opportunity for Fair Housing Demonstration Program: Interim Impacts Evaluation*. Washington, DC, U.S. Department of Housing and Urban Development.

Varady, D. P. and C. C. Walker (2003). Housing Vouchers and Residential Mobility. *Journal of Planning Literature* 18(1): 17–30.

Williams, D. R. (2001). Racial Variations in Adult Health Status: Patterns, Paradoxes, and Prospects. In N. J. Smelser, W. J. Wilson, F. Mitchell and National Research Council (eds.) *America Becoming: Racial Trends and Their Consequences* (pp. 371–410). Washington, DC, National Academy Press.

Williams, D. R. and C. Collins (2001). Racial Residential Segregation: A Fundamental Cause of Racial Disparities in Health. *Public Health Reports* 116(September–October): 404–416.

Williams, D. R., Y. Yu, J. S. Jackson, and N. B. Anderson (1997). Racial Differences in Physical and Mental Health: Socioeconomic Status, Stress, and Discrimination. *Journal of Health Psychology* 2(3): 335–351.

Winkleby, M. and C. Cubbin (2003). Influence of Individual and Neighbourhood Socioeconomic Status on Mortality among Black, Mexican-American, and White Women and Men in the United States. *Journal of Epidemiology and Community Health* 57(6): 444–452.

Xue, Y., T. Leventhal, J. Brooks-Gunn, and F. Earls (2005). Neighborhood Residence and Mental Health Problems of 5- to 11-year-olds. *Archives of General Psychiatry* 62(5): 554–563.

CHAPTER 7

Neighborhood Segregation, Personal Networks, and Access to Social Resources

RACHEL GARSHICK KLEIT

Introduction

How does the relative racial and economic segregation of a neighborhood influence social networks? Concerns about the role of social ties and the influence of segregation arise from both John Kain's (1968) work on spatial disconnects in urban regions and William Julius Wilson's (1987) work suggesting that living in neighborhoods of extreme segregation causes the social and economic isolation of the underclass. The causal mechanisms for the social and economic deficits could be spatial or social structural. Neighborhood location or composition may have an effect on economic isolation (for a review, see Kleit 2001b). Kain's work inspired decades of research on the regional spatial mismatch between the urban housing location of blacks and the suburban location of better jobs (for reviews, see Glaeser *et al.* 2004; Ihlanfeldt and Sjoquist 1998).

Alternatively, social structure could be responsible for isolation. Poor residents could lack connections to job opportunities within their own communities (Kasinitz and Rosenberg 1996), or they could lack ties that reach out of poor neighborhoods to opportunities in stable middle-income areas (Hurlbert *et al.* 1998). Furthermore, these ties may shape not only access to resources but also perceptions of opportunities (Hurlbert *et al.* 1998; Galster and Killen 1995). Job search methods also may vary with neighborhood poverty, and those in high-poverty neighborhoods may make more use of informal contacts with those having lower levels of education, which could lead to having lower annual earnings compared to those in neighborhoods with lower rates of poverty (Elliott 1999). One proposed solution for both spatial and structural social and economic isolation has been to encourage poverty dispersal policies (for a review of dispersal policies, see Goetz 2003).

At the same time, residential economic and racial segregation imposes a variety of influences on social networks that may or may not be related to the story of restricted access to social and economic opportunity. While social networks can influence how we are socialized, our expectations in life, and our ability to find good jobs, they can also influence our ability to obtain social support and our perspectives on people from backgrounds other than our own. In a neighborhood context we are also concerned simply with relationships among neighbors—the community that arises in segregated and desegregated settings.

In this chapter I evaluate the nature and depth of social networks in both segregated and desegregated neighborhoods, linking observed variation by race or ethnicity and nativity status. The chapter is divided into five subsections. The first describes the theoretical background of the role of social networks as social capital in providing access to social and economic opportunity. It outlines the general propensity of social networks for homogeneity, and the limiting implications of social homogeneity and class status for economic information and action. The second section explores the social capital within social networks that can act as social support, especially through neighboring relationships in both segregated and diverse neighborhoods, with special emphasis on the implications for women and ethnic and racial minorities. The third section examines the potential for neighborhood economic and racial desegregation to create relationships among disparate groups of people, which increase community tolerance, racial understanding, and access to opportunity. The fourth section overlays geography on these general social-structural issues, addressing how neighborhoods influence social relationships and the effects of living in areas of concentrated poverty that are segregated by both race and income. It also assesses empirical findings on racial and economic desegregation for access to social and economic opportunity through social networks and looks especially to experiences with public housing dispersal programs. The fifth section summarizes the negative economic and social effects of segregated neighborhoods on social networks, delineates what works in creating positive social network outcomes in desegregated areas, and hypothesizes on the role of neighborhood choice in the creation of beneficial relationships.

Social Networks and Access to Social and Economic Opportunity

While the concern of this chapter is the relationship between social networks and segregation—a spatially bound consideration of neighborhoods—

people's involvement in social networks can be nonspatial. People are embedded in social networks that act as vital links to larger social systems (Wellman 1988). Networks affect the flow of resources and information to and from the individual (Lin 2001).

Social Networks as Social Capital

Some consider this flow of resources and information across people to be a form of social capital in that relationships with others may facilitate action, provide information, or make connections between the micro level and the macro level (Coleman 1988). James Coleman (1988) outlines three types of social capital. First, he describes the social capital based on people "doing things for each other" (Coleman 1988: S102). These relations are based on "trustworthiness of the social environment, which means that obligations will be repaid, and the actual extent of obligations held" (Coleman 1988: S102). This type of social capital is a web of mutual obligations that maintain helpful relations among people who trust each other to fulfill their obligations to each other. People who habitually help others have more social capital on which to draw. Second, he discusses social capital as the "potential for information inherent in social relations" (Coleman 1988: S104). People use their social relations to gather information about things with which they themselves have no contact, but that information later shapes their actions. Therefore, social capital can be social relations "that provide information that facilitates action" (Coleman 1988: S104). Third, Coleman comments, "When a norm exists and is effective, it constitutes a powerful, though sometimes fragile form of social capital" (1988: S104). This type of social capital, unlike the previous two, both facilitates and restricts action.

In considering how social capital might function, Briggs (1998) suggests that social capital can act horizontally as social support and vertically as social leverage. Lin conceptualizes an overarching theory of network social capital, defining social capital as the "social resources embedded in a social structure which are accessed and/or mobilized in purposive actions" (2001: 29). Furthermore, he outlines a social network approach to social capital that emphasizes "investment in social relations by individuals through which they gain access to embedded resources to enhance expected returns of instrumental or expressive actions" (Lin *et al.* 2001: 18–19). Instrumental returns include wealth, power, and reputation, while expressive returns include physical and mental health and life satisfaction. Yet, as Portes (1998) notes, ties that provide social support may facilitate social control but may not be the same ties that provide help finding a job. Furthermore, ties that provide social support clash with those that enable social leverage, if local norms must be overturned to facilitate economic action.

Social Networks and Economic Action

Generally, the more diverse the types of people to whom an individual has access, the wider the range of information available to that person and the more likely it is that he or she will experience better outcomes when looking for a job. Yet the capacity for varied and valuable information differs among social networks, and the ability to use such information also differs across demographic groups. Generally, greater diversity in an individual's social network affords access to different societal circles (Burt 1983; Campbell *et al.* 1986; Marsden 1987; Wellman and Potter 1999). Such breadth of contact with different social spheres is helpful for gathering information (Marsden 1987).

Additionally, Granovetter's (1973, 1982, 1995b) concept of the strength of weak ties posits that weak ties—those that are of short duration, not emotionally close, not mutually confiding, with infrequent contact, and not necessarily engaged in reciprocal services—reach out of homogeneous cliques to allow for diversity of information and contact. Furthermore, the more close knit a group of people is, the less access there is to diverse resources. We can think about group closeness in terms of a network's density and in terms of its level of diversity. Density is a measure of closeness in a group. If all of one's friends know each other, that would be a close-knit group. If the social network is less dense, then the group is loosely knit and weaker. Furthermore, people who have many overlapping ties in a network—that is, one individual fulfills multiple roles—tend to have similar behaviors and attitudes (Erickson 1988). Multistranded ties are also more durable and intimate than specialized ties (Wellman *et al.* 1988).

Typically, social networks tend toward homogeneity, which works against the availability of high-quality, varied job information (McPherson *et al.* 2001). Furthermore, as Lin and Dumin (1986) argue, even if diverse resources are available, not everyone can make use of them because people need the social resources to employ them, and those who are poor may lack social resources.

The Job Search, Information, and Poverty

Lower-income people may have limited access to information about good jobs because of the tendency of their social networks to be homogeneous and their lack of social resources to make use of more diverse sources of information. People usually find jobs through personal contacts, formal methods, or direct application (Corcoran *et al.* 1980; Campbell and Rosenfeld 1985; Granovetter 1995a). However, some workers find jobs without searching, depending on some sort of social resource (see the review by Granovetter 1995a). In the past twenty-five years, theorizing among both economists and sociologists about modeling the labor market has sought to consider the nature and role of social resources in the job-matching process (Granovetter 1981; Montgomery 1991; Fernandez and Castilla 2001; Marsden 2001). One key aspect of this literature has been a theorized connection between better jobs and better social resources (see the review by Granovetter 1995a; Lin 2001; Erickson 2001; and Lin et al. 1981).

Yet, as Granovetter summarizes, in some social groups, finding jobs through contacts may be the best option, but the jobs "may still be of poor quality by general standards if this is all the group can provide" (1995a: 151). Working-class ties may lead to jobs, but such contacts may lead to jobs that are no better than anyone else's in the group (see, for example, Kasinitz and Rosenberg 1996; Wial 1988). Poverty is perpetuated by an individual's lack of weak ties and limited network range, which decrease access to instrumental resources (Hurlbert et al. 2001).[1]

Network Limitations for Minorities and Women

While ethnic relations may facilitate and support job searching and identifying job opportunities (Fawcett 1989; Light et al. 1999), they also may be limiting if the ethnic ties are not connected to relations with useful job information (Waldinger 1995; Braddock and McPartland 1987). For blacks, the amount of racial diversity within their networks may be an important factor in finding a good job (Braddock and McPartland 1987). While personal contacts may facilitate job attachment (Holzer 1988; Korenman and Turner 1996), blacks whose networks are composed of individuals fulfilling multiple roles—that is, coworker and neighbor—are more likely to have job options that are low-paying when relying on personal contacts (Holzer 1988; Korenman and Turner 1996; Campbell and Rosenfeld 1985). For blacks, the greater the degree to which people in an individual's network fulfill multiple roles—such as being neighbor, coworker, and kin—the greater the likelihood of finding lower-paying jobs than those of other blacks. The opposite was true for whites. It is the information available within a network that is important, not the structure (Green et al. 1999; Coverdill 1998). The racial diversity of the network is an indication of the quality of the information available. The mere presence of quality information in a network does not guarantee that it will improve a network member's job search; positive social capital, such as trust, mutual obligations, and social norms, must also be present in a network for social ties to aid a job search (Smith 2003). In the absence of such social capital, individuals have no motivation to help one another.

For women, spatial and social limitations converge somewhat differently. When job hunting, women tend to use personal contacts less frequently (Rosenfeld et al. 1975; Ensel 1979; Campbell 1985; Campbell and Rosenfeld

1985; Sheppard and Belitsky 1966; Sanders 1995) and formal methods more often than men (Campbell and Rosenfeld 1985; Hanson and Pratt 1991; Sanders 1995); this may be necessary to overcome information deficits in their networks (Campbell 1985). For women, effective job contacts are likely to be men (Ensel 1979), but women's networks contain fewer men (Campbell and Rosenfeld 1985; Hanson and Pratt 1991; Drentea 1998). Gender-homophilous contacts can have a significantly negative effect on the socioeconomic status of the job sought (Beggs and Hurlbert 1997; Hurlbert *et al.* 2001). Women who have diverse and large networks are more likely to hold paid positions and have network bridges to those of better education; knowing people outside the neighborhood may enable women to use their social networks more effectively to find a job (Stoloff *et al.* 1999). These effects also must be considered in concert with space and time limitations because of household responsibilities; women face a limitation on the range of employment opportunities open to them as compared to those available to men (Hanson and Pratt 1991). Very low-income women may be much more likely to experience a spatial limitation in a job search because of their dependence on social ties, direct application, and falling into opportunities without a search (Chapple 2001). Black women and their social networks may be more spatially bound (Gilbert 1998). The spatial limitations of poor women may lead to increased opportunities for social support while reinforcing economic limitations.

Social Networks and Social Support

While diverse networks can provide diverse information, the tendency of social networks toward homogeneity is associated with the ability to obtain social support. Social support is associated with dense, strong, and homophilous ties rather than weak and heterophilous ties (for a review, see Hurlbert *et al.* 2001; Wellman and Frank 2001). Informal support arises from core, homogeneous networks. Increased network density, strong ties, and homogeneity combined with a sense of belonging and a high degree of normative consensus associated with these high levels of social integration help to facilitate a routinization of support among people in the core network (Hurlbert *et al.* 2001).

While weaker ties may provide information, a relatively small number of emotionally strong ties probably provide broader support in terms of emotional aid, services, and companionship (Wellman and Wortley 1990). While proximity can promote both large and small services among people, proximity is not related to receiving social support in the form of companionship, emotional aid, and financial aid, because these can actually be offered over long distances. Interactions in group settings do not foster social support, and the involvement of kin in a social support system is based on the aid of a relatively small number of immediate kin. Women tend to provide more emotional support than men.

A network is more than the sum of one-on-one relationships, because as an entity it can exert group pressure to provide support (Wellman and Frank 2001). Network capital functions on many different levels that are based on an individual's social status, the size of the network, the similarity of network members, the availability and delivery of resources within the network, the history of support and reciprocity, the composition of the network, the way information flows through the network, and indirect ties. Different levels of a network are nested within others.

Willmott's (1987) study of suburban Londoners points to the role of kin in providing social support. He suggests that in the absence of kin, friends can provide particular types of aid, but creating local friendships on which one can depend instead of kin is not always easily done. Those in the working class did not fare well when they did not live in proximity to family members, and the absence of accessible transportation made it difficult to receive support from familial relationships.

The importance of neighbors in providing social support depends on the type of aid needed (Wireman 1984). People tend to use friends when they need to agree about tastes or if long-term support is needed. Neighbors are best at everyday contact that does not require a long-term commitment. In research conducted in Nashville, Tennessee, Campbell and Lee (1992) found that those who are economically advantaged have larger networks because they are more integrated into the larger society. These individuals do not need strong links to neighbors for day-to-day support. However, those of lower socioeconomic status need nearby support and cultivate it within their neighborhoods because of a relative lack of social integration and more tenuous financial status.

In short, those who are poor, more tied to their neighborhoods, and less mobile tend to be more tied to their neighborhoods for their day-to-day social support needs.

Social Networks, Intergroup Contact, and Tolerance

The literature discussed above focuses on social networks as the embedded location of social capital, whether for social support or social leverage, to borrow Briggs's (1998) phrasing. Social networks in a neighborhood situation may also bring together people who might not otherwise meet each other. Contact theory suggests that people of different backgrounds will be more likely to interact if the groups have equal status when interacting within a given situation, are able to work toward common goals, have intergroup cooperation, and have support from authority for positive contacts (Allport 1979; Pettigrew 1998).

Studies of contact theory date from the early 1950s and present varied evidence (Ford 1986), usually, as Pettigrew (1998) delineates, because researchers have not noted that when optimal conditions are violated, negative effects occur. While the settings in which contact theory has been studied focus most frequently on school (Ford 1986; Moody 2001) and housing situations (Deutsch and Collins 1968; Wilner *et al.* 1952, 1955; Ford 1986), the theory has been tested in a variety of contexts that include not only black and white contacts but contacts among diverse ethnicities, the elderly, the disabled, and AIDs patients (Pettigrew 1998). Equal-status contact is not limited to notions of social class but can be created through being of equal status within a situation, such as a committee or sports team, where people work together toward a common goal.

It is those contact-theory studies in housing that are of concern here, as they most clearly suggest that, under certain conditions, social network contact will foster more positive sentiments among people of different racial backgrounds or ethnicities. Proximity is insufficient to engender positive perceptions; equal-status, supported, and goal-oriented contacts are vital to positive changes in attitudes. Pettigrew (1998) also suggests that the contact situation must allow the participants the opportunity to become friends. In integrated neighborhoods it is vital that contacts occur in particular types of situations that are facilitated by community-building activities, including attending a block party, collaborating on a community issue, or cleaning up common areas.

In their extension of contact theory, Emerson *et al.* (2002) argue that the conditions of contact theory facilitate the creation of diverse ties that can be important for broadening the economic and social opportunities of individuals. The conditions of contact theory not only may encourage positive interracial contact and the creation of positive attitudes toward other groups but also may facilitate diversity of social ties. Perhaps these positive conditions can facilitate the use of these more diverse ties by people who would not usually have the social resources to employ them.

Social Networks and Place

This chapter builds an argument based primarily on a nonspatial understanding of the importance of social ties that are not based on proximity for social leverage and support. Situations of equal-status contact may be important not only for nurturing positive attitudes between different social groups but also for enhancing the diversity of social networks, which is key in the nonspatial view of access to opportunity through social networks.

Before addressing how segregation and integration might influence social networks, we must understand whether and how place influences social relationships. This section examines the influence of place—urban versus suburban places, as well as density, proximity, and commonality—on social networks.

How Do Neighborhoods Influence Social Relations?
Community of residence influences the type of nonkin with whom people associate but not the number, and those who are involved with neighbors generally have few sources for relationships outside the neighborhood. When Fischer (1982) comments, "Those who are most involved with neighbors tended to be those with few sources of extraneighborhood (nonkin) ties elsewhere," he means those not working or working part time, those new to the city, and those committed to home by marriage or homeownership.

During the last twenty-five years of the twentieth century, socializing in neighborhoods generally declined slowly while extraneighborhood socializing increased even more slowly (Guest and Wierzbicki 1999). However, for certain population groups, the neighborhood is still an important locale; neighborhood socializing by the elderly and the unemployed did not decline.

Urban Neighborhoods, Suburban Neighborhoods, and Community
The fear is that some groups in urban neighborhoods are isolated. While socializing with neighbors may be declining generally, urban sociology has spent much time showing that those who live in urban neighborhoods are not unusually isolated. With trends of urbanization in the late nineteenth century, Tönnies ([1887] cited in Flanagan 1993) characterized the differences between relationships in urban areas and suburban areas as *gemeinschaft* and *gesellschaft*—between rural areas characterized by strong interdependent relations and urban areas where ties to others are more distant. The notion was that people in urban areas were isolated from kin, and ties were attenuated. Urban sociologists Wirth (1938) and Simmel (1950) suggest that there are fundamental differences in urban relationships that make them more distant, alienating, and instrumental than those in rural settings. Yet the community studies of the mid-twentieth century demonstrated that the neighborhood was the locale for social ties, especially in working-class and poor areas (e.g., Suttles 1968, 1972; Kornblum 1974). For lower-income residents in urban areas, survival may depend on interactions with a core network that often comprises kin and friends who find themselves in similar situations (Stack 1974).

Wellman's (Wellman and Leighton 1979; Wellman 1979) work delineates three perspectives on urban neighborhoods: the community-lost perspective of early urban sociologists, the community-saved perspective presented in community studies, and a community-liberated perspective, which Wellman suggests views kinship ties as important but not primary. People create personal community networks that are a set of active community ties that are socially diverse, spatially dispersed, and sparsely knit. These relationships are not necessarily bound by neighborhoods. As Fischer (1982) discusses, residents of urban areas are less involved with their neighbors than are residents of small towns. People in cities turn to neighbors only if they find them compatible in some way. Urban areas are more likely to produce networks with higher levels of racial and ethnic heterogeneity (Marsden 1987).

Living in urban areas may have a differential effect on blacks and whites. While whites in urban environments may tend to become more involved with subcultures of interest, blacks do not appear to be involved in minority subcultures (Deng and Bonacich 1991). Urban blacks have social networks that are more racially diverse and less dense than those of rural blacks.

In suburban environments in the United States, scholars have commented on the attenuation of community at the neighborhood level (for a review, see Schwartz 1980). In particular, the writers of the third quarter of the twentieth century viewed low-density suburbs as the negation of community and communal relationships. Sprawl has been viewed as weakening household connections to immediate neighbors because it reduces spontaneous social interactions (for a review, see Freeman 2001). While those with lower incomes have more ties within their neighborhoods, those who live in car-dependent neighborhoods tend to have fewer ties to neighbors (Freeman 2001).

The Role of Proximity and Social Homogeneity

Factors that may influence the interaction of larger-level social structure and neighborhood composition are physical density, proximity to others, and social homogeneity. While neighboring has been declining, it is not a thing of the past. People do establish and maintain social ties with neighbors (Festinger et al. 1950; Wellman and Potter 1999; McPherson et al. 2001), but the conditions have to be right. Michelson (1976) suggests that proximity is only effective in encouraging interaction when there are conditions of real or perceived homogeneity and where there is a need of mutual aid, such as performing small home repairs. Homogeneity—as regards stage of life, homeownership (and thus proprietary interests), lifestyle, and values—is the basis for social relationships and may be more important than propinquity (Gans 1967, 1968; Michelson 1976). McPherson et al. (2001) comment that the most basic source of homophily is space; we are more likely to have contact with those who are closer to us geographically than those who are distant.

The dependence of interaction on real or perceived homogeneity is supported by a number of studies. It was apparent in suburban Levittown, Pennsylvania (Gans 1967). While close ties made before the move to the new suburb were maintained, communal ties developed when people were open to interactions with strangers, and everyone was perceived to be fairly homogeneous with regard to social class. As Michelson (1976) points out, this was one of the main selling points for the development.

Similarly, peer relationships were the center of adult life in Boston's West End before its redevelopment (Gans 1962). Membership in a peer group is rooted in familial relationships, and becoming part of a peer group (like making someone a godparent) was a way to maintain relationships. Neighbors were included in this group if they were friends. Social relations in the neighborhood were based on a homogeneous trait: the common social status of the residents.

Suttles (1968, 1972) also points out that homogeneity of traits is the basis for social relations. He suggests that people do make choices about their associations within a given territory. Again, people associate with others of the same social standing. Religion, ethnic background, race, and income group are just a few examples of common traits upon which residents might base their concept of social standing.

Fischer's (1982) subcultural theory of urbanism encompasses these ideas and suggests that people form social ties based upon many attributes other than kin and locality. Relationships are formed on the basis of ethnicity, occupation, lifestyle, and other common traits. Within these communities, people find "fellowship, guidance, and meaning" (Fischer 1982: 194).

Social Networks in Economically and Racially Segregated Neighborhoods
If proximity and perceived homogeneity are important for the creation of relationships in neighborhoods, what are the social network implications for economically and racially segregated neighborhoods and integrated neighborhoods?

POOR PEOPLE IN ECONOMICALLY SEGREGATED NEIGHBORHOODS
Social network structures tend to vary by socioeconomic status, and the social networks of those with lower incomes may tend to be more tied to place and to homogeneously low income, contain more close relationships, and contain more overlapping relations (Fischer 1982; Marsden 1987; Oliver 1988; Campbell and Lee 1992). Oliver's (1988) research demonstrates that when socioeconomic groups live in separate neighborhoods, their neighborhood networks can reflect those differences.

Furthermore, Campbell and Lee (1992), in their study of eighty-one Nashville, Tennessee, neighborhoods, find that people with lower socioeconomic status tend to have smaller, more intense neighborhood networks than those with higher socioeconomic status. They conclude that general social integration affects neighborhood networks. Those of higher socio-economic status have larger neighborhood networks because of their better integration into society in general, but they do not require strong links to neighbors for daily support. Individuals of lower socioeconomic status have more need for support from neighbors because of their relative lack of social integration and more uncertain financial situation. These findings control for the income stratum of the individual's census tract. Therefore, the networks of low-income people are more intense and locally based.

Several studies contradict these findings. Hurlbert *et al.* (1998, 2001) explored the networks of poor people in an underclass neighborhood and found that rather than being involved in more intense and strong rela-tionships, these people tended to have more weak relationships than those in middle-income areas. They also found that those living in underclass areas were more likely to find jobs through contacts and that the social networks of the poor were not more geographically concentrated than those of the nonpoor. Kadushin and Jones's (1992) research also contradicts the notion that low-income people in urban neighborhoods possess strong ties that compensate for the disadvantages of living in their neighborhoods. In their 1988 survey of New York City residents, Kadushin and Jones found that New Yorkers with high levels of education are more likely to benefit from neighborhood-based ties than those with lower levels of education.

Even if low-income people have ties that may be more intense and locally based, they may also forge ties to different groups of people. Susan Greenbaum (1982) showed that both strong and weak ties occur among neighbors, with weak ties being more numerous. Moreover, both types of ties can have a bridging function. As an alternative to Granovetter, Greenbaum suggests that urban ties are more often weak among those who live on the same block, and the ties that bridge the blocks are often strong or multiplex. She concludes, "Multiplex ties make more effective bridges than do weak ties of acquaintanceship and that the presence of strong ties among neighbors generally enhances overall integration of neighborhoods" (Greenbaum 1982: 379). However, Greenbaum's research concerns neighborhood mobilization, not access to opportunity.

RACIAL SEGREGATION

The stereotype of urban black neighborhoods is one of social disorganiza-tion (Myrdal 1964). Research does not support this view. Early work by Feagin (1970) highlights the frequent friendship ties within an urban black neighborhood and notes that they occur within relatively smaller social networks. Oliver (1988) examines the social networks within three black neighborhoods in Los Angeles, illustrating that the residents of these neighborhoods have ties to complex and large social networks that vary with their neighborhood economic status. He argues against the stereotype of social disorganization in urban black neighborhoods. People living in the low-income area are more likely to have strong kin- and neighborhood-based ties than people in the two middle-class areas, where networks are more likely to contain friends. In all three communities, ties reached beyond the local area, and people in the low-income community were more likely to have multistranded ties that involved more than one setting. Indeed, neighborhood organization membership was higher in the low-income area.

Tigges *et al.* (1998) found that living in neighborhoods of higher poverty has negative effects on urban blacks' social networks. Those living in higher-poverty areas tend to be more isolated within their households, living alone or with only school-aged children. They also have fewer close ties outside the household, fewer employed ties, and fewer ties to college-educated individuals than do poor blacks living in less poor areas. Their findings do not closely compare the social networks of poor blacks and whites, but it is likely that poor whites also experience at the very least internal household isolation.

Those living in higher-poverty neighborhoods may have more spatially bound social networks, and this limitation may be intensified for poor urban blacks and restrict their information about access to opportunity.

Social Networks in Desegregated Neighborhoods

The research summarized above suggests that the social ties of the urban poor can be spatially bound, and spatial restrictions can be more intense for blacks. If neighborhood relationships are based on proximity, real or perceived homogeneity, and a need for mutual aid, how does living in an economically or racially desegregated neighborhood influence social networks? What effect does freely choosing to live in a neighborhood have on social networks? Does a lack of choice matter in the eventual creation of social networks that might lead to better social and economic opportunity?

INTEGRATION, SOCIAL NETWORKS, AND ACCESS TO OPPORTUNITY

The research on the effect of desegregation and access to opportunity has been conducted primarily in the context of public housing dispersal programs that have focused on the economic desegregation of the residents, with one notable exception (Elliott 1999).

Elliott (1999) found that most job seekers in both low- and high-poverty neighborhoods employ a combination of formal and informal strategies. Residents of high-poverty neighborhoods were more likely than job seekers from low-poverty neighborhoods to use informal strategies to look for work, which leads to lower annual earnings than does the use of formal channels.

Less educated workers in high-poverty neighborhoods were twice as likely to acquire jobs through neighbors as less-educated workers in low-poverty neighborhoods and therefore had disappointing job outcomes.

In evidence from a housing dispersal program, Briggs (1998) examined access to opportunity through social networks for youth living in the small clusters of public housing that resulted from the remedy to the Yonkers housing desegregation lawsuit. Briggs surveyed 132 youths; half lived in public housing located in poor minority-dominated southwest Yonkers and half moved to small public housing developments in affluent white east Yonkers. He concluded that those who moved experienced social support from living in their small developments; they had ties that helped them cope with everyday life. Those who moved were not able to obtain the benefits that might come from living in less poor areas, such as better access to job information, a recommendation for a scholarship or a loan, or other factors that might lead to opportunities. These youths tended to live in *ethnic fishbowls* (Briggs 1998: 208) and were only partially integrated into their surrounding neighborhoods. Therefore, they did not have the expected increases in social opportunities that relocation to less poor areas was supposed to provide. The youths had been living in their communities for three years or less, and it may be that over time they would develop ties to the larger community. Thus far, the clusters of low-income minorities in middle-income areas have done little to encourage contact between residents and the wider community.

My work (Kleit 2001b, 2002) considers whether a more scattered pattern of development may be more successful in creating ties to the larger community and to better job information. I compare the quality of the job search networks of public housing residents living in small clusters versus those living in a more scattered pattern in the same affluent suburb of Washington, DC. The findings indicate that having public housing residents living in a more scattered pattern is associated with more diversity in job search networks and with more frequent use of formal search methods to find a job. Those living in the more clustered housing tended to use social resources and informal search methods to find a job. Dispersed residents tended to look for jobs of higher prestige, but the use of formal methods was not associated with obtaining a better-quality job. Those who used informal methods, if they were offered a job, were seeking a job of higher prestige than if they were not offered a job. Those who used direct application and were offered jobs had jobs that were not as high quality.

Programs that disperse the poor more broadly may enable individuals to increase the different types of information to which they have access. Alternatively, these programs may also force dispersed residents to depend on more formal methods of search that yield better-quality jobs. It may be that the level of dispersal matters, and simply building clusters of low-income housing in nonpoor areas may not ensure increased access to opportunity. From a social capital perspective, it may be that clustered residents need go no further than their local neighborhood to find job information; however, dispersed residents must obtain job information through nonlocal ties. Dispersed residents are forced to reach beyond their local neighborhood to find new social resources—inherent in social relations—that provide them with increased access to a broader array of opportunities.

However, better information and a propensity to use formal methods of searching do not guarantee better outcomes. Instead, something about living in a more dispersed situation may cause the observed effects. Living in an environment that is not associated with other poor people and that is relatively safe may allow people to get ahead.

Furthermore, the positive effects of living in dispersed housing may be an artifact of the research. If dispersed and clustered residents choose to live in scattered or clustered housing, then the effects we see for dispersed housing could be overstated. These differences might also be associated with omitted variables, such as the type of job held previously or the number of years in the workforce—factors that may influence job search methods and job quality. Dispersed and clustered residents might also value different types of social networks, and those preferences could skew the findings regarding social ties.

Neighboring Relationships, Social Support, and Neighborhood Racial and Economic Integration

There is more research on social support in neighborhoods that are racially and economically integrated, including studies comparing social networks in communities that happen to be integrated to those in neighborhoods that are not integrated (Lee *et al.* 1991), to those in neighborhoods that are purposely integrated (Wireman 1984), and to those in neighborhoods that are undergoing gentrification (Anderson 1992; Caulfield 1994). Other studies examine programs that purposely desegregate poor public housing residents through public housing desegregation lawsuits (Briggs 1998; Popkin *et al.* 2000), through the siting of public housing (Kleit 2001b), and through the HOPE VI program (Kleit 2005).

Lee *et al.* (1991) examined neighboring relationships in white, mixed, and black neighborhoods, and neighborhoods that were poor, middle-income, and wealthy. They found that the black neighborhoods had higher levels of neighboring than did the white neighborhoods, and while the levels in integrated sites fell between the black and white levels, all engaged frequently in neighboring. The effect of race on neighboring is greater, however, as a personal rather than a contextual attribute, and blacks neighbor more than whites. Blacks and whites differ in the style of their neighboring as well. Blacks are more often engaged in instrumental relations, characterized by exchanges of information, support, and assistance, rather than casual ones. Whites more frequently engage in short conversations.

In examining the effect of integration on social networks in neighborhoods that were purposely integrated, Wireman (1984) discussed the new communities of Columbia, Maryland, and Reston, Virginia. Wireman found that integrated communities will not necessarily recreate an "idealized gemeinschaft." In both communities, there was limited social interaction between the races and an extensive system of all-black social organizations. Wireman (1984: 112) provided guidelines to evaluate success:

> A community that is integrated successfully will be characterized by the following: integrated housing; access for both races to facilities and services; opportunities for members of different racial groups and economic status to associate in civic affairs and voluntary associations and to form friendships; some recognition by all residents of the unique experiences and contributions of all groups; and not more interracial or class conflict or discomfort than exist elsewhere in the society. This definition does not require that blacks and whites become friends, merely that they have the opportunity to do so. Nor does it require that all conflicts cease.

How do residents deal with conflict? At the time of Wireman's analysis, residents felt uncomfortable noticing racial differences. Color was held to be irrelevant, and residents felt that to "connect any behavioral patterns with color would be an admission of unconscious racism . . . they ignore the fact of racial differences and do not confront problems directly, an approach that can create further mutual misunderstandings" (Wireman 1984: 102).

Elijah Anderson's *Streetwise: Race, Class, and Change in an Urban Community* (1992) documents the gentrification of Village and Northton, two adjacent communities in a northeastern U.S. city. The Village was a racially and economically diverse community that had a history of racial tolerance because of its large Quaker population, present since the 1950s. Blacks and whites, each with a separate social network, comprised the Village's middle class. Northton was traditionally poorer. As the population of the Village grew, the two communities became more blatantly communities of haves and have-nots. Because the majority of whites were middle to upper income and blacks, poor to working class, class and color distinctions blurred. Anderson commented that the only real opportunity for primary relations to be formed between blacks and whites is when class is equal. Some of the black middle class in the area saw all whites as racist;

others were more cosmopolitan and have some white friends, although most close friends are black. Older, homeowning, churchgoing black families served as a buffer, maintaining polite but superficial relations with white neighbors.

The resolutions of public housing desegregation lawsuits have often involved either construction of housing in white areas or vouchers to enable minority residents to move to predominantly white areas. These resolutions encourage residents to move, although residents can self-select to take part in the remedy. Focus group results from the *Baseline Assessment on Public Housing Desegregation Cases: Cross-Site Report* (vol. 1–2, April 2000) indicate a variety of experiences integrating into their new neighborhoods (Popkin *et al.* 2000). A substantial proportion of those who moved felt accepted in their new neighborhoods, receiving aid or an especially warm welcome from neighbors. Many liked their new neighborhoods but were troubled by gossip and racial stereotyping. Those who moved to areas with relatively few members of minority groups isolated themselves and did not socialize with their neighbors; their experience was similar to that of individuals with language barriers or who moved from ethnically separate communities, such as the Hmong refugees.

Briggs (1998) found that those youths who moved from minority areas to white areas had social relationships with people in the microneighborhood of their housing complex, but not with white neighbors outside the complex or with individuals from their old neighborhood. This lack of relationships outside the complex might be a result of the youths' recent arrival in the neighborhood at the time of the study. It also may be that they would rather have stayed in their original neighborhood where their social ties were. Kleit (2001b) speculates that the lack of relationships with the external community has to do with the degree of dispersal of the housing.

To examine the role of dispersal, I (Kleit 2001a) compared the neighboring relationships of residents living in dispersed and small clusters of public housing developments throughout a Washington, DC suburb. Both groups tended to know their neighbors and depended on them for aid to similar degrees. While those in the more scattered patterns do know their nonpoor neighbors, they tend to feel less emotionally close to them. Assignment to public housing was not subject to resident choice.

In the case of a new mixed-income HOPE VI site, public housing residents have less choice than do market-rate residents about living in the neighborhood (Kleit 2005). In this new neighborhood, people of different social status did not necessarily know each other. Given previous research on the role of unequal social status in preventing the formation of positive ties among neighbors, we might ask what would enable positive social relations to arise. Systematic differences among housing tenures by language, family composition, and patterns of local facility use and community involvement curtailed social interactions in this new neighborhood. Because the homeowners and renters were so different demographically (for example, homeowners did not have children and tended to speak English, while renters had children and might not speak English), the barriers to finding things in common were high. The role of proximity was key. Residents, especially homeowners, tended to neighbor with people nearby. This implies that the proximity of the various housing tenures and income groups in a mixed-income development has implications for their social interactions. Everyone, whether living in market-rate or subsidized housing, was positive about living in the development and finds the diversity enriching, making the choice of living there key in making it a good place to live—although social relationships may be more limited than one might suspect.

In sum, those who choose to move to neighborhoods undergoing gentrification are often seeking the diversity of urban areas. Those who lived in the neighborhood before the new arrivals are limited in their choices and may seek to create relationships based on perceived homogeneity. In programs that purposely mix races, ethnicities, and those of widely different incomes, those who choose to move to more diverse neighborhoods may have more motivation to develop social network relations with others unlike them. While proximity aids the creation of relationships, perceived and real demographic differences can be barriers to forming more than superficial relationships across groups.

Neighborhoods, Integration, and Positive Social Network Outcomes

This chapter has explored the implications of neighborhood segregation and integration on social networks. Areas that may be affected include an individual social-capital perspective in which social networks are the locale for embedded social and economic resources and social support within social relations. The creation of positive relationships across groups of people, including those from different racial groups, different economic status, and different ethnicities, may also be affected. These social-network relationships do not necessarily take place in a geographically defined neighborhood. For most people, neighborhood influences generally shape social networks only a little.

In the past twenty-five years, overall neighborhood socializing has declined, but for the elderly, the unemployed, the poor, and those who lack mobility neighborhoods, it is a vital source of social relations. Blacks tend to depend more on neighbors for instrumental aid, while whites appear more casual in their neighboring. The social relations of poor black women especially are based on proximity. The composition of the neighborhood can have important implications for these groups.

For those in areas of extreme poverty, quality economic information can be extremely limited because poor residents are tied to the neighborhood, and others in the neighborhood are not good sources of information on high-quality and varied economic opportunities. In terms of social network effects, living in areas of extreme poverty limits the quality of economic information available in social networks, even if the homogeneity of the relationships makes these social relations a rich source of social support. In racially segregated neighborhoods, blacks tend to be involved in multi-stranded relationships that overlap different organizations.

For those who are more dependent on their neighborhood social relations, desegregation alone will not remedy the limited economic information available in social networks. It is likely that certain conditions must be present for lower-income people to use neighborhood relationships to their instrumental advantage or for people of different races or ethnicities to interact in a positive way. The social resources to use these ties must be present. Whether one thinks about those social resources as the social norms aspect of social capital, friendships, or the necessary conditions of contact theory, equal-status, supported, goal-oriented contacts are essential for positive changes in attitudes and the willingness of those with more locally bound social networks to use more diverse ties for their own instrumental advantage. Fostering these types of relations through community-building activities can help create the perceived homogeneity that is important to the creation of relationships in neighborhoods. Only planned communities can actually facilitate proximity in proactive ways through site planning and design. Given the lack of attention paid to this idea in the literature, we can only hypothesize about the role of choice in the creation of positive social relations and whether those who find themselves in desegregated neighborhoods by choice are more inclined to create relationships that lead to better social ties with neighbors.

Social networks formed in neighborhoods can be important for social and economic advancement, for increasing tolerance, and for building community. For those living in economically and racially segregated neighborhoods, the extent to which individuals are bound to the neighborhood may be reflected in their social networks. Even in integrated neighborhoods, unless a level of trust or commonality is built, these individuals will not necessarily use those social relations. Under the right conditions—those that enable relationships based on commonality among those who might not otherwise have much in common—such relationships can be vital in people's lives.

Note

1.   While Granovetter's (1973) hypothesis on the nature of helpful social resources (the strength of weak ties hypothesis) provoked a generation of research on job matching, unmeasured social and human capital (Bridges and Villemez 1986), and the information available to the searcher (Marsden and Hurlbert 1988), may be more important than weak ties. More recently, both Coverdill (1998) and Mouw (2000) have argued that personal contacts are not only the result of network structure but also part of the matching process that influences posthire outcomes. Others (Montgomery 1992) argue that network structure alone, not the type used, is important. Social resources exercised through personal ties are likely important for job matching because of the structure of social ties and/or the content available through those ties.

While the literature as a whole has argued for social network effects on job finding, a later article by Mouw (2003) suggests that the relationship between social network characteristics and better jobs (defined by either higher wages or higher job prestige) is spurious and the result of everyone in the network being alike. He found that there is little consistent evidence that using contacts affects wages or occupational prestige, and that such searches do not result in better outcomes than when formal job search methods are used.

The question remains, do good contacts lead to good jobs? Erickson (2001) argues that social networks that contain high levels of social capital are associated with finding better jobs. This may support Mouw's assertion that social capital effects are the result of homophily, not a causal effect of social networks on wages or prestige.

References

Allport, Gordon J. 1979. *The Nature of Prejudice*. Reading, MA: Addison-Wesley.

Anderson, Elijah. 1992. *Streetwise: Race, Class, and Change in an Urban Community*. Chicago: University of Chicago Press.

Beggs, John J., and Jeanne S. Hurlbert. 1997. The Social Context of Men's and Women's Job Search Ties: Membership in Voluntary Organizations, Social Resources, and Job Search Outcomes. *Sociological Perspectives* 40 (4): 601–622.

Braddock, Jomills M. II, and James M. McPartland. 1987. How Minorities Continue to be Excluded from Equal Employment Opportunities: Research on Labor Market and Institutional Barriers. *Journal of Social Issues* 43: 5–39.

Bridges, William, and Wayne J. Villemez. 1986. Informal Hiring and Income in the Labor Market. *American Sociological Review* 51 (4): 574–582.

Briggs, Xavier de Souza. 1998. Brown Kids in White Suburbs: Housing Mobility and the Many Faces of Social Capital. *Housing Policy Debate* 9 (1): 177–221.

Burt, Ronald S. 1983. Range. In Ronald S. Burt and Michael J. Minor (eds.) *Applied Network Analysis: A Methodological Introduction*. Beverly Hills, CA: Sage, pp. 176–194.

Campbell, Karen E. 1985. Women's and Men's Job Searches, Job Changes, and Social Resources. PhD dissertation, University of North Carolina.

Campbell, Karen E., and Barrett A. Lee. 1992. Sources of Personal Neighbor Networks: Social Integration, Need, or Time? *Social Forces* 70 (4): 1077–1100.

Campbell, Karen E., and Rachel Rosenfeld. 1985. Job Search and Job Mobility: Sex and Race Differences. In Richard L. Simpson and Ida H. Simpson (eds.) *Research in the Sociology of Work*, Vol. 3. Greenwich, CT: JAI Press, pp. 147–174.

Campbell, Karen E., Peter V. Marsden, and Jeanne S. Hurlbert. 1986. Social Resources and Socioeconomic Status. *Social Networks* 8: 97–117.

Caulfield, Jon. 1994. *City Form and Everyday Life: Toronto's Gentrification and Critical Social Practice*. Toronto: University of Toronto Press.

Chapple, Karen. 2001. Out of Touch, Out of Bounds: How Social Networks Shape the Labor Market Radii of Women on Welfare in San Francisco. *Urban Geography* 22 (7): 617–640.

Coleman, James S. 1988. Social Capital in the Creation of Human Capital. *American Journal of Sociology* 94 (Supplement): S95–S120.

Corcoran, Mary, Linda Datcher, and Greg J. Duncan. 1980. Information and Influence Networks in Labor Markets. In Greg J. Duncan and James N. Morgan (eds.) *Five Thousand American Families. Patterns of Economic Progress*, Vol. 8. Ann Arbor: University of Michigan, pp. 1–37.

Coverdill, James E. 1998. Personal Contacts and Post-Hire Job Outcomes: Theoretical and Empirical Notes on the Significance of Matching Methods. In Kevin T. Leicht (ed.) *Research in Social Stratification and Mobility*, Vol. 16. Stamford, CT: JAI Press, pp. 247–269.

Deng, Zhong, and Philip Bonacich. 1991. Some Effects of Urbanism on Black Social Networks. *Social Networks* 13: 35–50.

Deutsch, Morton, and Mary Evans Collins. 1968. *Interracial Housing: A Psychological Evaluation of a Social Experiment.* New York: Russell and Russell.

Drentea, Patricia. 1998. Consequences of Women's Formal and Informal Job Search Methods for Employment in Female-Dominated Jobs. *Gender and Society* 12 (3): 321–338.

Elliott, James R. 1999. Social Isolation and Labor Market Insulation: Network and Neighborhood Effects on Less-Educated Urban Workers. *Sociological Quarterly* 40 (2): 199–216.

Emerson, M. O., R. T. Kimbro, and G. Yancey. 2002. Contact Theory Extended: The Effects of Prior Racial Contact on Current Social Ties. *Social Science Quarterly* 83 (3): 745–761.

Ensel, Walter M. 1979. Sex, Social Ties, and Status Attainment. Doctoral dissertation, State University of New York.

Erickson, Bonnie H. 1988. The Relational Basis of Attitudes. In Berry Wallman and S.D. Berkowitz (eds.) *Social Structures: A Network Approach.* Cambridge: Cambridge University Press, pp. 99–121.

Erickson, Bonnie H. 2001. Good Networks and Good Jobs: The Value of Social Capital to Employers and Employees.In Nan Lin, Karen Cook, and Ronald S. Burt (eds.) *Social Capital: Theory and Research.* New York: Aldine de Gruyter, pp. 127–58.

Fawcett, James T. 1989. Networks, Linkages, and Migration Systems. *International Migration Review* 13 (3): 671–680.

Feagin, Joe R. 1970. A Note on the Friendship Ties of Black Urbanites. *Social Forces* 49: 303–308.

Fernandez, Roberto M., and Emilio J. Castilla. 2001. How Much Is That Network Worth? Social Capital In Employee Referral Networks. In Nan Lin, Karen Cook, and Ronald S. Burt (eds.) *Social Capital: Theory and Research.* New York: Aldine de Gruyter, pp. 85–104.

Festinger, Leon, Stanley Schachter, and Kurt Back. 1950. *Social Pressures in Informal Groups: A Study of Human Factors in Housing.* New York: Harper.

Fischer, Claude S. 1982. *To Dwell among Friends.* Chicago: University of Chicago Press.

Flanagan, William G. 1993. *Contemporary Urban Sociology.* Cambridge: Cambridge University Press.

Ford, W. Scott. 1986. Favorable Intergroup Contact May Not Reduce Prejudice: Inconclusive Journal Evidence. *Social Science Research* 70 (4): 256–258.

Freeman, Lance. 2001. The Effects of Sprawl on Neighborhood Social Ties: An Explanatory Analysis. *Journal of the American Planning Association* 67 (1): 69.

Galster, George C., and Sean P. Killen. 1995. The Geography of Metropolitan Opportunity: A Reconnaissance and Conceptual Framework. *Housing Policy Debate* 6 (1): 7–43.

Gans, Herbert J. 1962. *The Urban Villagers.* New York: The Free Press.

Gans, Herbert J. 1967. *The Levittowners: Ways of Life and Politics in a New Suburban Community.* New York: Random House.

Gans, Herbert J. 1968. Planning as Social Life: Friendship and Neighbor Relations in Suburban Communities. In Herbert J. Gans (ed.) *People and Plans: Essays on Urban Problems and Solutions.* New York: Basic Books, pp. 152–165.

Gilbert, Melissa R. 1998. "Race," Space, and Power: The Survival Strategies of Working Poor Women. *Annals of the Association of American Geographers* 88 (4): 595–621.

Glaeser, Edward L., Eric A. Hanushek, and John M. Quigley. 2004. Opportunities, Race, and Urban Location: The Influence of John Kain. *Journal of Urban Economics* 56 (1): 70–79.

Goetz, Edward G. 2003. Housing Dispersal Programs. *Journal of Planning Literature* 18 (1): 3–16.

Granovetter, Mark S. 1973. The Strength of Weak Ties. *American Journal of Sociology* 78: 1360–1380.

Granovetter, Mark S. 1981. Toward a Sociological Theory of Income Differences. In Ivar Berg (ed.) *Sociological Perspectives on Labor Markets.* New York: Academic Press, pp. 11–47.

Granovetter, Mark S. 1982. The Strength of Weak Ties: A Network Theory Revisited. In Peter V. Marsden and Nan Lin (eds.) *Social Structure and Network Analysis.* Beverly Hills, CA: Sage, pp. 105–130.

Granovetter, Mark S. 1995a. Afterward 1994: Reconsiderations and a New Agenda. In Mark S. Granovetter (ed.) *Getting a Job: A Study of Contacts and Careers.* Chicago: University of Chicago Press.

Granovetter, Mark S. 1995b. *Getting a Job: A Study of Contacts and Careers*. Chicago: University Of Chicago Press.

Green, Gary Paul, Leann M. Tigges, and Daniel Diaz. 1999. Racial and Ethnic Differences in Job-Search Strategies in Atlanta, Boston, and Los Angeles. *Social Science Quarterly* 80 (2): 263–278.

Greenbaum, Susan. 1982. Bridging Ties at the Neighborhood Level. *Social Networks* 4: 367–384.

Guest, Avery M., and Susan K. Wierzbicki. 1999. Social Ties at the Neighborhood Level: Two Decades of GSS Evidence. *Urban Affairs Review* 35 (1): 92–111.

Hanson, Susan, and Geraldine Pratt. 1991. Job Search and the Occupational Segregation of Women. *Annals of the American Association of Geographers* 81 (2): 229–253.

Holzer, Harry J. 1988. Search Method Use by Unemployed Youth. *Journal of Labor Economics* 6: 1–20.

Hurlbert, Jeanne S., John J. Beggs, and Valerie A. Haines. 1998. Exploring the Relationship between the Network Structure and Network Resource Dimensions of Social Isolation: What Kinds of Networks Allocate Resources in the Underclass? Unpublished manuscript.

Hurlbert, Jeanne S., John J. Beggs, and Valerie A. Haines. 2001. Social Networks and Social Capital in Extreme Environments. In Nan Lin, Karen Cook, and Ronald S. Burt (eds.) *Social Capital: Theory and Research*. New York: Aldine de Gruyter, pp. 209–231.

Ihlanfeldt, Keith R., and David L. Sjoquist. 1998. The Spatial Mismatch Hypothesis: A Review of Recent Studies and Their Implications for Welfare Reform. *Housing Policy Debate* 9 (4): 849–892.

Kadushin, Charles, and Delmos J. Jones. 1992. Social Networks and Urban Neighborhoods in New York City. *City and Society* 6 (1): 58–75.

Kain, John F. 1968. Housing Segregation, Negro Employment and Metropolitan Decentralization. *Quarterly Journal of Economics* 82: 175–197.

Kasinitz, Philip, and Jan Rosenberg. 1996. Missing the Connection: Social Isolation and Employment on the Brooklyn Waterfront. *Social Problems* 43 (2): 180–196.

Kleit, Rachel Garshick. 2001a. Neighborhood Relations in Scattered-Site and Clustered Public Housing. *Journal of Urban Affairs* 23 (4–5): 409–30.

Kleit, Rachel Garshick. 2001b. The Role of Neighborhood Social Networks in Scattered-Site Public Housing Residents' Search for Jobs. *Housing Policy Debate* 12 (3): 541–574.

Kleit, Rachel Garshick. 2002. Job Search Networks and Strategies in Scattered-Site Public Housing. *Housing Studies* 17 (1): 83–100.

Kleit, Rachel Garshick. 2005. HOPE VI New Communities: Neighborhood Relations in Mixed-Income Housing. *Environment and Planning A* 37 (8): 1413–1441.

Korenman, Sanders, and Susan C. Turner. 1996. Employment Contacts: the Minority–White Wage Differences. *Industrial Relations* 35 (1): 106–122.

Kornblum, William. 1974. *Blue Collar Community*. Chicago: University of Chicago Press.

Lee, Barrett A., Karen E. Campbell, and Oscar Miller. 1991. Racial Differences in Urban Neighboring. *Sociological Forum* 6 (3): 525–550.

Light, Ivan, Richard B. Bernard, and Rebecca Kim. 1999. Immigrant Incorporation in the Garment Industry of Los Angeles. *International Migration Review* 33 (1): 5–25.

Lin, Nan. 2001. *Social Capital: A Theory of Social Structure and Action*. Cambridge: Cambridge University Press.

Lin, Nan, and Mary Dumin. 1986. Access to Occupations through Social Ties. *Social Networks* 8: 365–385.

Lin, Nan, John C. Vaughn, and Walter M. Ensel. 1981. Social Resources and Occupation Status Attainment. *Social Forces* 59 (4): 1163–1181.

Lin, Nan, Karen Cook, and Ronald S. Burt (eds.) 2001. *Social Capital Theory and Research*. New York: Walter de Gruyter.

Marsden, Peter V. 1987. Core Discussion Networks of Americans. *American Sociological Review* 52: 122–131.

Marsden, Peter V. 2001. Interpersonal Ties, Social Capital, and Employer Staffing Practices. In Nan Lin, Karen Cook, and Ronald S. Burt (eds.) *Social Capital Theory and Research*. New York: Aldine de Gruyter, pp. 105–126.

Marsden, Peter V., and Jeanne S. Hurlbert. 1988. Social Resources and Mobility Outcomes: A Replication and Extension. *Social Forces* 66: 1038–1059.

McPherson, Miller, Lynn Smith-Lovin, and James M. Cook. 2001. Birds of a Feather: Homophily in Social Networks. *Annual Review of Sociology* 27: 415–444.

Michelson, William. 1976. *Man and His Urban Environment: A Sociological Approach, with Revisions.* Reading, MA: Addison-Wesley.

Montgomery, James. 1991. Social Networks and Labor-Market Outcomes: Toward an Economic Analysis. *American Economic Review* 81 (5): 1408–1418.

Montgomery, James. 1992. Job Search and Network Composition: Implications of the Strength-of-Weak-Ties Hypothesis. *American Sociological Review* 57 (5): 586–596.

Moody, James. 2001. Race, School Integration, and Friendship Segregation in America. *American Journal of Sociology* 107 (3): 679–716.

Mouw, Ted. 2000. Social Networks and Job Search: Do Contacts Matter? Unpublished manuscript.

Mouw, Ted. 2003. Social Capital and Finding a Job: Do Contacts Matter? *American Sociological Review* 68: 868–898.

Myrdal, Gunnar. 1964. *An American Dilemma.* New York: Harper.

Oliver, Melvin L. 1988. The Urban Black Community as Network: Toward a Social Network Perspective. *Sociological Quarterly* 29: 623–645.

Pettigrew, Thomas F. 1998. Intergroup Contact Theory. *Annual Review of Psychology* 49: 65–85.

Popkin, Susan J., George C. Galster, Kenneth Temkin, Carla Herbig, Diane K. Levy, and Elise Richer. 2000. *Baseline Assessment of Public Housing Desegregation Cases: Cross-Site Draft Report*, vol. 1. Washington, DC: The Urban Institute, US Department of Housing and Urban Development.

Portes, Alejandro. 1998. Social Capital: Its Origins and Applications in Contemporary Sociology. *Annual Review of Sociology* 24: 1–23.

Rosenfeld, Carl, Kopp Michelotti, and William V. Deuterman. 1975. Jobseeking Methods Used by American Workers. U.S. Department of Labor, Bureau of Labor Statistics, Bulletin N. 1886. Government Printing Office, Washington, DC.

Sanders, Karin. 1995. The "Gift" and "Request" Network: Differences between Women and Men in the Receipt and the Effect of Information concerning the Labor Market. *European Journal of Women's Studies* 2: 205–218.

Schwartz, Barry. 1980. The Suburban Landscape: New Variation on an Old Theme. *Contemporary Sociology* 9 (5): 640–650.

Sheppard, Harold L., and A. Harvey Belitsky. 1966. *The Job Hunt: Job-Seeking Behavior of Unemployed Workers in a Local Economy.* Baltimore, MD: Johns Hopkins Press.

Simmel, Georg. 1950. The Metropolis and Mental Life. In Kurt Wolff (ed.) *The Sociology of Georg Simmel*, pp. 409–424.

Smith, Sandra Susan. 2003. Exploring the Efficacy of African-Americans' Job Referral Networks: A Study of the Obligations of Exchange around Job Information and Influence. *Ethnic and Racial Studies* 26 (6): 1029–1045.

Stack, Carol. 1974. *All Our Kin: Strategies for Survival in a Black Community.* New York: Harper and Row.

Stoloff, Jennifer A., Jennifer L. Glanville, and Elisa Jane Bienenstock. 1999. Women's Participation in the Labor Force: The Role of Social Networks. *Social Networks* 21: 91–108.

Suttles, Gerald. 1968. *The Social Order of the Slum.* Chicago: University of Chicago Press.

Suttles, Gerald. 1972. *The Social Construction of Communities.* Chicago: University of Chicago Press.

Tigges, L. M., I. Browne, and G. P. Green. 1998. Social Isolation of the Urban Poor: Race, Class, and Neighborhood Effects on Social Resources. *Sociological Quarterly* 39 (1): 53–77.

Waldinger, Roger. 1995. The "Other Side" of Embeddedness: A Case-Study of the Interplay of Economy and Ethnicity. *Ethnic and Racial Studies* 18 (3): 555–580.

Wellman, Barry. 1979. The Community Question: The Intimate Networks of East Yorkers. *American Journal of Sociology* 85 (5): 1201–1231.

Wellman, Barry. 1988. Structural Analysis: From Method and Metaphor to Theory and Substance. In Barry Wellman and S.D. Berkowitz (eds.) *Social Structures: A Network Approach.* Cambridge: Cambridge University Press, pp. 19–61.

Wellman, Barry, and Kenneth A. Frank. 2001. Network Capital in a Multilevel World: Getting Support from Personal Communities. In Nan Lin, Karen Cook, and Ronald S. Burt (eds.) *Social Capital: Theory and Research.* New York: Aldine de Gruyter, pp. 233–273.

Wellman, Barry, and Barry Leighton. 1979. Networks, Neighborhoods and Communities. *Urban Affairs Quarterly* 14: 363–390.

Wellman, Barry, and Stephanie Potter. 1999. The Elements of Personal Communities. In Barry Wellman (ed.) *Networks in the Global Village.* Boulder, CO: Westview Press, pp. 49–92.

Wellman, Barry, and Scot Wortley. 1990. Different Strokes from Different Folks: Community Ties and Social Support. *American Journal of Sociology* 96 (3): 558.

Wellman, Barry, Peter J. Carrington, and Alan Hall. 1988. Networks as Personal Communities. In Barry Wellman and S.D. Berkowitz (eds.) *Social Structures: A Network Approach.* Cambridge: Cambridge University Press, pp. 130–184.

Wial, Howard J. 1988. The Transition from Secondary to Primary Employment: Jobs and Workers in Ethnic Neighborhood Labor Markets. Doctoral dissertation, Massachusetts Institute of Technology.

Willmott, Peter. 1987. *Friendship Networks and Social Support.* London: Policy Studies Institute.

Wilner, Daniel, Rosabelle Price Walkley, and Stuart W. Cook. 1952. Residential Proximity and Intergroup Relations in Public Housing Projects. *Journal of Social Issues* 8 (1): 45–69.

Wilner, Daniel, Rosabelle Price Walkley, and Stuart W. Cook. 1955. *Human Relations in Interracial Housing.* Minneapolis: University of Minnesota Press.

Wilson, William Julius. 1987. *The Truly Disadvantaged.* Chicago: University of Chicago Press.

Wireman, Peggy. 1984. *Urban Neighborhods, Networks, and Families: New Forms for Old Values.* Lexington, MA: Heath.

Wirth, Louis. 1938. Urbanism as a Way of Life. *American Journal of Sociology* 44 (July): 3–24.

CHAPTER **8**

Continuing Isolation: Segregation in America Today

INGRID GOULD ELLEN

Racial segregation remains a stubborn reality in U.S. metropolitan areas. While residential segregation between blacks and whites has declined over the past few decades, it has changed only slowly, and levels of segregation remain extremely high, especially in the northeastern and midwestern regions of the country. Less segregated than blacks, Hispanics and Asians have experienced levels of segregation that are undiminished since 1980 (in fact, Asians have become slightly more segregated).

The goal of this chapter is to summarize what we know about the possible causes of racial and ethnic segregation in the present-day United States. While focusing largely on black–white segregation, this chapter also explores how the bundle of causes of segregation may differ for other racial and ethnic groups.

The chapter concludes that there is no single explanation for the persistence of segregation. Patterns of settlement tend to change slowly, and thus the legacy of blockbusting, redlining, and the many other blatant acts of discrimination that occurred before the passage of the Fair Housing Act lives on. Yet contemporary segregation is not simply a relic of the past; it is also the result of ongoing, present-day residential moves that are restricted by ongoing discrimination and racial tensions. Perhaps most central are the everyday decisions of white households to avoid moving to racially integrated and largely minority communities.

The chapter is organized as follows: the first section provides an overview of trends in segregation over the past century. The second section outlines the various possible causes of segregation. The third section summarizes the evidence of the relative importance of these factors in explaining the contemporary segregation of blacks, and the fourth section considers the roots of segregation for Asians and Hispanics. The final section explores policy implications.

Background on Segregation

Some historical perspective on segregation is useful, since segregation levels have changed considerably over the course of the twentieth century. In the early decades of the century, large numbers of blacks migrated from the rural South to the industrial cities of the North. As black households moved into northern cities, segregation in those cities rose dramatically (Cutler *et al.* 1999; Taueber and Taueber 1965). Segregation in southern cities increased as well, as the patterns of residence that developed during slavery continued to break down (Taueber and Taueber 1965). After World War II, a second wave of black migration to northern cities occurred, and again it was accompanied by an increase in segregation. The increases were particularly large in the industrial cities of the Northeast and Midwest. By 1970, nearly 80 percent of the black population in the average metropolitan area would have had to move to a different census tract to achieve racial integration (Cutler *et al.* 1999).

Since 1970, black–white segregation has steadily declined (Lewis Mumford Center 2001; Glaeser and Vigdor 2001; Iceland *et al.* 2002), and, as Table 8.1 shows, the number of racially integrated neighborhoods in U.S. metropolitan areas has grown. Table 8.1 also makes it clear that much of the increase in integration has been driven by the decline in all-white neighborhoods—a shift of census tracts from all-white to moderately integrated. While more than half of all metropolitan census tracts were less than 1 percent black in 1970, just one in five were less than 1 percent black in 2000. Meanwhile, the proportion of census tracts that had a majority of black residents actually increased during this time period. In other words, the declines in segregation between 1970 and 2000 were achieved largely through the integration of predominantly white neighborhoods, not through the integration of predominantly black communities.

While they have not experienced the same declines in segregation (Iceland *et al.* 2002; Lewis Mumford Center 2002), Hispanic and especially Asian households remain considerably less segregated than blacks. Black–white segregation levels remain uniquely high, especially in large cities and in northeastern and midwestern metropolitan areas.

TABLE 8.1 Distribution of Census Tracts by Percentage Black, 1970–2000 (universe: all metropolitan areas, as defined in 2000)

Racial Composition	1970	1980	1990	2000
<1% black	55.1	41.3	31.8	20.7
1–10% black	22.3	32.5	38.6	46.1
10–50% black	12.4	15.2	17.9	21.8
>50% Black	10.1	11.0	11.7	11.4
Number of census tracts	34,128	42,524	44,159	50,956

Source: Ellen (2007).

Potential Causes of Segregation

Students of segregation generally divide the explanations for segregation into those that suggest market failures in the housing market and those that imply the housing market is operating just as markets should—sorting people according to their preferences and ability to pay.

Typically, two sorts of market failures are offered. The first is an information failure: households fail to learn about housing opportunities in neighborhoods and jurisdictions in which they are racially underrepresented. For example, white households tend to learn almost exclusively about housing opportunities in white communities, while minority households mostly get information about opportunities in minority neighborhoods. These information failures may be rooted in differences in housing search patterns or in racially segmented information networks.

The second and more disturbing failure is housing market discrimination—the specific acts of sellers, landlords, realtors, and lenders to restrict the choices of minority households and keep them out of white neighborhoods. Also included are more subtle acts of steering, by which realtors steer households to consider homes and apartments in neighborhoods that match their race and ethnicity. These explanations clearly call for policies, such as increased enforcement of fair housing laws, to address the market failures.

The other categories of explanations for segregation, which are typically viewed as more benign, are differences in income and preferences. The argument regarding income differences is obvious: housing tends to be distributed across different neighborhoods according to price and rent levels. Since minority households on average have lower incomes than white households, the two groups end up in different neighborhoods. While such differences in income between racial groups are troubling in themselves, they suggest nothing particularly troubling about the operation of housing markets.

The role of preferences demands more discussion. While researchers tend to group preferences into a single category, there are at least four distinct types of preferences that might explain the observed patterns and that call for distinct responses. First, minority and white households may simply have different preferences for the nonracial attributes of communities, such as the characteristics of the local housing stock and the nature of local public services. These preferences lead them to choose different neighborhoods and jurisdictions. Second, households may desire to live among others of the same race who share the same customs and way of life. Third, households may not care so much about living with others just like them, but they may dislike living among particular racial groups because of individually based racial prejudice. Finally, race-based neighborhood stereotyping may explain the reluctance of whites to share neighborhoods with blacks (Ellen 2000a). Specifically, whites avoid integrated neighborhoods because they assume that such neighborhoods will inevitably become all-black and experience the decline in public services and neighborhood conditions that they associate with largely black areas.

Evidence on Causes of Black–White Segregation

Over the past few decades, many researchers have studied the high levels of residential segregation between blacks and whites and have hotly debated the underlying causes. This section reviews this literature to assess the relative importance of each of the factors outlined above in explaining present-day black–white segregation.

Information Gaps: Evidence

There is surprisingly little research examining the role of information in sustaining segregation. The few studies that have examined and compared how homes in largely minority and largely white neighborhoods are marketed find significant differences (Galster *et al.* 1987; Newburger 1981; Turner and Wienk 1993). For instance, Turner and Wienk (1993) provide intriguing evidence from Washington, DC, that homes for sale in pre-dominantly black or integrated neighborhoods are marketed quite differently than similar homes in predominantly white neighborhoods. In particular, they find that homes in black or integrated neighborhoods are much less likely to be advertised in citywide newspapers and much less likely to be marketed through open houses. These differences in marketing could lead to significant disparities in the housing information available to different racial groups. More recent research investigating whether these patterns hold true today would be welcome.

Researchers also tend to find that blacks and whites rely on somewhat distinctive methods to search for housing, but these differences appear to be modest and the results are not consistent across studies (Turner and Wienk 1993; Farley 1996; Newburger 1999). For example, using 1992 data from Detroit, Farley (1996) finds that black households are less likely to rely on real estate brokers and more likely to rely on informal methods of housing search that include word of mouth and driving through neighborhoods, methods that suggest a more geographically restricted search. Turner and Wienk (1993) find that blacks are more likely to rely on real estate agents in the Washington, DC metropolitan area, while Newburger (1999) reports that low-income black homebuyers in Philadelphia search a wider set of neighborhoods than do their white counterparts. Clearly, more research is needed to understand the role of search practices in explaining segregation.

Discrimination

It is undeniable that housing market discrimination played a forceful role in restricting the mobility of black households in the past. In the public sector, public housing was explicitly segregated by race, and the Federal Housing Administration recommended the use of private, restrictive covenants that prohibited black occupancy and taught its underwriters to avoid integrated areas. Evidence exists that until the passage of the Fair Housing Act, discrimination in the private housing market was widespread, with realtors and lenders commonly refusing to serve blacks moving into white neighborhoods (Massey and Denton 1993).

It is also undeniable that discrimination by sales and rental agents persists (Turner and Ross 2004; Yinger 1995). The best evidence on housing discrimination comes from three national audit studies conducted by the Urban Institute in 1977, 1989, and 2000 (Turner et al. 2002). The most recent national audit study of paired testers reveals that while the blatant block-busting techniques and outright door-slamming behavior that were pervasive in the 1950s and 1960s have faded away, housing market discrimination persists in more subtle forms and continues to be a barrier for black and Hispanic households in both rental and sales markets (Turner and Ross 2004). For example, the study also reports strong evidence that black homebuyers are steered away from white neighborhoods. These forms of housing discrimination are illegal, but they persist nonetheless, which suggests that enforcement of fair housing laws is inadequate.

The most recent national audit study also provides some evidence of a decline in discrimination. The study's authors compared the incidence of discrimination in 1989 and 2000, and reported significant declines in most areas (Turner et al. 2002). One exception was discrimination against Hispanic renters, for whom there was little change evident during the 1990s. In addition, the incidence of steering black homebuyers appears to have increased over the decade. Other, less direct evidence of a decline in discrimination comes from Cutler *et al.* (1999), who analyze racial differentials in house prices to examine the roots of segregation. In particular, they argue that if segregation is largely due to discriminatory barriers keeping black households in predominantly black areas or choices by black households to live in such areas, we would observe blacks paying more than whites for housing in more segregated cities. If segregation is primarily due to the desires of whites to live among other whites, then we would observe whites paying more than blacks for housing in more segregated cities. Using this price differential approach, they find evidence that in 1940 segregation was largely caused by housing market discrimination, restrictive covenants, and other practices that kept blacks out of largely white neighborhoods. However, they conclude that by 1990 the balance had shifted and that segregation had become more a function of the decentralized decisions of whites to avoid black neighborhoods.

The dramatic decline shown in Table 8.1 in the number of neighborhoods with little or no black presence offers some additional, albeit suggestive, evidence that black households attempting to move to all-white areas face fewer barriers today than they have in the past. Table 8.2 provides further support, suggesting that between 1990 and 2000, homogeneous white neighborhoods were ten times more likely to become integrated than were homogeneous black neighborhoods. To the extent that neighborhoods become integrated, they become integrated through the entry of minority households into predominantly white neighborhoods. It is far less likely that neighborhoods become integrated through the entry of white households into predominantly minority areas. Indeed, more than 97 percent of the neighborhoods that became newly integrated in 2000 (i.e., neighborhoods that were integrated in 2000 but not in 1990) were predominantly white in 1990. Strikingly, across all metropolitan areas in the United States, there were only 67 census tracts (out of a total of nearly 50,000) that were predominantly black in 1990 and became integrated in 2000.

It is worth underscoring that none of these studies or stylized facts suggests that discrimination does not exist; rather, they suggest that the nature of discrimination has shifted and that the discriminatory barriers blocking black households from moving into predominantly white neighborhoods have declined in recent decades. Given sufficient effort, black households are now able to find rental and ownership housing in communities that were previously closed to them. Yet discrimination persists, and its continued presence may shape residential patterns. Indeed, the mere presence of discrimination may lead many black households to avoid even seeking homes in predominantly white areas.

TABLE 8.2 Proportion of Census Tracts that Became Integrated in 2000, by 1990 Neighborhood Type

Neighborhood Type in 1990	Percentage Integrated in 2000
Homogeneous white	22.8
Homogeneous black	2.0
Homogeneous Hispanic	2.1
Homogeneous other	2.4

Source: Adapted from Ellen (2007).

Income Differences

Significant differences remain between the economic status of minority and white households. Table 8.3 shows that in 1999 the median income among non-Hispanic whites was nearly 60 percent higher than that for blacks and 44 percent higher than that for Hispanics. On average, Asian households actually had incomes that were 15 percent higher than those of non-Hispanic whites. Large differences in poverty are evident as well, with poverty rates among black and Hispanic households roughly triple the rate for whites and double the rate for Asians. In addition, studies typically find that on average the asset holdings of black households are only about one-fourth or one-fifth of those of white households (Altonji *et al.* 2000; Altonji and Doraszelski 2001). Several studies find that these differences in wealth persist, even after differences in income and other factors have been controlled for (Altonji and Doraszelski 2001).

Despite these significant differences, virtually every study that has examined the role of income differences in driving segregation has found that income differences between blacks and whites account for only a modest share of segregation patterns (Farley 1986; Kain 1986; Gabriel and Rosenthal 1989; Ihlanfeldt and Scafidi 2002). An analysis focused on the San Francisco metropolitan area (Bayer *et al.* 2004) included a broad set of sociodemographic variables—income, education, occupation, household composition, immigration status, years in the United States, and language spoken at home—and found that they play a somewhat greater role in segregation. Even so, this broad set of factors collectively explains only 30 percent of black segregation. (Income, education, occupation, and household composition together account for just 20 percent of black segregation.) Moreover, it is important to stress that this study analyzed residential patterns in a single western metropolitan area, with moderate levels of segregation. Sociodemographic characteristics might explain a smaller fraction of black segregation in more highly segregated areas.

TABLE 8.3 Median Household Income and Poverty Rates by Race/Ethnicity, 1999

Race of Household Head	Median Household Income	Poverty Rate
Non-Hispanic white	$44,157	8.1%
Black	$27,910	24.9%
Hispanic	$30,746	22.6%
Asian	$50,960	12.6%

Source: Poverty rates from Bishaw and Iceland (2003). Income figures from Historical Income Tables, U.S. Census Bureau.

None of these studies considers differences in wealth, and it seems likely that a greater share of segregation could be explained if differences in wealth were also taken into account. Yet one recent study found that racial differences in asset holdings explain very little of the lower rate of black entry into predominantly white areas (South *et al.* 2004).

Preferences

As was noted earlier, it is possible that racial differences in preferences for housing types and local public services help explain black–white segregation levels. There are very few systematic studies that explore the extent of these differences. Galster (1979) finds only minor variations in tastes between blacks and whites, once income and other household characteristics are taken into account. Bajari and Kahn (2005) report that white households have a greater demand for large, single-family detached dwellings, but the authors have limited controls for socioeconomic status. Thus, while the authors control for income and education of the household head, race may still capture differences in permanent income and wealth in their models. In the end, there is too little evidence to conclude that there are meaningful differences in taste for housing and local public services across racial groups.

Several authors have suggested that a key factor driving segregation is a desire for self-segregation or ethnic clustering on the part of blacks (Clark 1986; Patterson 1997). While it is certainly plausible that affirmative desires for clustering on the part of blacks plays a role in segregation, surveys of residential preferences provide little support for the self-segregation hypothesis. Such surveys generally find that black households prefer not to live in largely black neighborhoods and suggest that black households are willing to move into neighborhoods of almost any racial mix, as long as they are not the very first black household in the community (Farley *et al.* 1978, 1993; Bobo and Zubrinsky 1996; Charles 2000). Meanwhile, studies examining housing prices find no evidence that black households pay a premium to live in more segregated areas (Galster 1982; Cutler *et al.* 1999). Cutler *et al.* (1999) also find no relationship between stated desires for segregation among blacks living in a metropolitan area and the actual level of segregation in that area. Moreover, as John Kain (1976) pointed out, given that segregation levels of blacks are so much higher than those of other ethnic groups, we would have to assume that blacks have an unusually strong desire for segregation, far beyond that even of recent immigrants, whose foreign language and customs would seem to make such clustering natural.

This is not to say that black preferences do not contribute to some degree to current segregation. Ihlanfeldt and Scafidi (2002) find that while most blacks prefer integrated neighborhoods, a sizable minority identify all or mostly black neighborhoods as their preferred location. Blacks with stronger tastes for black neighbors tend to live in neighborhoods with a higher percentage of black residents, suggesting that they are acting on those preferences in making their residential choices. Still, the effects are small, and the authors acknowledge that continuing housing segregation cannot be attributed solely to these preferences.

Moreover, the authors ultimately cannot divorce a desire for living among black families from a fear of the hostility one might encounter when entering white areas. Consider that roughly 90 percent of the black respondents to the 1992 Detroit Area Survey who said they would not move into an all-white area reported that their reason was that the whites living there would be hostile and unfriendly (Farley *et al.* 1994). Similarly, analyzing data from Atlanta, Boston, Detroit, and Los Angeles in the mid-1990s, Krysan and Farley (2002) find that a large majority of the black respondents who said that they would not move into an all-white area gave discomfort and fear of hostility from whites as their reason. Only 4 percent of blacks avoiding all-white neighborhoods said they were doing so for cultural reasons. The expressed reluctance among many blacks to move into predominantly white neighborhoods appears to be driven less by benign desires on the part of blacks for self-segregation than by a fear of white hostility.

The residential preferences of white households appear to play a more significant role in maintaining segregation. For one thing, survey evidence consistently shows that whites simply care a great deal more about neighborhood racial composition than blacks (Farley *et al.* 1993; Bobo and Zubrinsky 1996). For another, evidence shown in Table 8.2 suggests that neighborhoods are far more likely to become integrated through blacks moving into predominantly white neighborhoods than through whites moving into predominantly black neighborhoods. Recall that just sixty-seven neighborhoods in the entire United States shifted from being predominantly black to being racially integrated between 1990 and 2000. White avoidance of predominantly black neighborhoods appears to be a more significant barrier to integration than the hesitancy of blacks to move into pre-dominantly white areas.

Cutler *et al.* (1999) also find evidence to suggest that white preferences are more critical. As has been noted already, they find that whites pay more than blacks for equivalent housing in more segregated cities, suggesting that whites are willing to pay a premium to live in segregated white neighbor-hoods. In sum, there is considerable evidence that white household decisions, particularly the decision not to move into predominantly black and integrated neighborhoods, contribute to segregation.

The next question is the dominant motivation underlying this avoidance. There is little evidence to suggest that this white avoidance is motivated by a benign desire on the part of whites to live among other whites. For one thing, surveys of residential preferences suggest that whites are far less resistant to living among nonblack minority groups, such as Asians, than to living among blacks (Emerson *et al.* 2001; Bobo and Zubrinsky 1996; Charles 2000). More fundamentally, it is hard to understand why whites, as the dominant group in U.S. society, would feel any need to cluster in order to enjoy special traditions and customs (Ellen 2000a).

A more plausible explanation for white avoidance is that it is motivated by racial prejudice against blacks; whites avoid mixed neighborhoods because they simply do not want to live near black households. While surely some white households harbor such views, evidence from surveys of racial preference suggests a decline in such prejudice over time (Schuman *et al.* 1997). Of course, since this evidence comes from self-reported surveys, the observed decline may simply be due to greater social stigma attached to expressions of racial prejudice.

A third possibility is that white avoidance behavior is explained by race-based neighborhood stereotyping—the negative views that white house-holds, as well as some black households, hold on the social, economic, and physical characteristics of largely black neighborhoods. White households may not dislike living next to a black household per se; rather, many white households may associate predominantly black neighborhoods with diminished neighborhood quality and resilience. With this viewpoint, race clearly matters but chiefly as a signal of the structural strength of a com-munity. White households, and some minority households too, assume that racially integrated neighborhoods will inevitably become all black and that neighborhood quality will deteriorate (Ellen 2000a).

It is naturally difficult to distinguish empirically between individually based racial animus and race-based neighborhood stereotyping, but past research provides considerable support for the notion of race-based neighborhood stereotyping. (Certainly there is no evidence that race-based neighborhood stereotyping is declining, as there is for racial prejudice.)

Sampson and Raudenbush (2004) find strong evidence that households use racial composition, particularly percentage black, as a signal of a neighborhood's quality and social cohesion. In addition, several studies find that residents who are more invested in a community's quality and therefore have more to lose from the changes that they believe to be correlated with minority population growth (e.g., homeowners, and households with children) are more resistant to black neighbors than other households, even after differences in socioeconomic status have been controlled for (Charles 2000; Ellen 2000a).

Further support for race-based neighborhood stereotyping comes from the fact that racial composition factors in the decisions of white households to move into a neighborhood to a greater degree than it does in the decision as to whether or not to leave. People already living in a community are likely to have considerable information about its quality and future prospects, and thus will tend to be less concerned about racial composition. By contrast, when choosing among many alternative communities, outsiders may find it easier to rely simply on racial composition as a presumed signal of neighborhood quality and conditions.

Finally, Ellen (2000a) finds that integrated neighborhoods are more likely to remain stable over time if residents and outsiders have reason to believe that they will remain racially stable over time and/or if neighborhood conditions and housing demand are believed to be particularly secure. This may be because of the presence of a stabilizing institutional presence such as a university.

Evidence on Causes of Segregation for Asian and Hispanic Households

There is far less research investigating the bundle of factors responsible for the segregation of Asian and Hispanic households. However, the evidence that exists suggests that the causes differ from those driving black–white segregation and that white avoidance generally plays a lesser role.

First, differences in socioeconomic status appear to explain a much greater share of the segregation experienced by Asians and Hispanics. In their 2004 study of segregation in the San Francisco metropolitan area, Bayer *et al.* find that income, education, occupation, and household composition collectively explained over 60 percent of Hispanic segregation as compared to just 20 percent of black segregation. Earlier studies relying on 1970, 1980, and 1990 census data report similar results: class differences consistently explain a greater share of Hispanic segregation than of black segregation (Massey 1979; Denton and Massey 1988; Alba and Logan 1993; Alba *et al.* 2000). Fewer studies investigate the roots of Asian segregation, but those that do generally find that class differences make a significant contribution; Asians who are college educated, own their homes, and have higher incomes live in communities with much higher proportions of whites (Alba and Logan 1993; Alba *et al.* 2000).

There is also evidence that desire for ethnic clustering on the part of minorities plays a greater role in the segregation of nonblack minorities, especially Asians. To some extent, this clustering is driven by the fact that so many Asians and Latinos are immigrants. In 2000, 69 percent of the Asian population and 40 percent of the Hispanic population in the United States were foreign born (Malone *et al.* 2003). Not surprisingly, immigrant groups tend to cluster when they first arrive in the United States; by settling in communities populated by other immigrants who share their language and customs, immigrants ease the transition to their new environment.

As their time in the United States increases, both Asian and Hispanic households appear to become less segregated (Alba *et al.* 2000). Similarly, in their study of residential patterns in the San Francisco Bay area published in 2004, Bayer *et al.* find that Asians and Hispanics who have stronger English language skills and who are U.S. citizens are less segregated. Specifically, they find that the language spoken at home, English language ability, citizenship status, and years in the United States together account for 40 percent of Asian segregation and 30 percent of Hispanic segregation. Segregated neighborhoods appear to be a stepping stone for foreign-born Latinos and, especially, foreign-born Asians when they arrive in the United States.

Research also suggests that white avoidance generally plays a lesser role in the segregation of Asians and Latinos than it does in the segregation of blacks. Surveys of racial preferences, for example, consistently show that white households are far more comfortable living in neighborhoods with high percentages of Asians and Hispanics than they are in areas with high percentages of blacks (Charles 2000; Bobo and Zubrinsky 1996). Furthermore, Ellen (2000b) finds that the ethnic change that occurs in Hispanic–white and Asian–white areas is driven more by minority demand and demographic realities than by white avoidance behavior. This is in contrast to the change occurring in black–white areas. Class differences between minorities and whites appear to be especially relevant in predicting racial transition in the case of Asian–white communities; Asian–white neighborhoods with poorer Asians are far more likely to lose whites than those with wealthier Asians. By contrast, class differences appear largely irrelevant to subsequent ethnic change in neighborhoods shared by whites and Hispanics, and those shared by whites and blacks.

In sum, the causes of segregation appear to vary across minority groups. Although the research is limited, the evidence generally suggests that causes are more benign and transitory in the case of Asians. As their incomes and educations rise, their English skills improve, and their time in the United

States increases, their segregation levels tend to diminish. For Hispanic segregation, the evidence is somewhat more mixed, but again the causes appear more benign and the segregation itself more transitory as compared to the segregation of blacks.

This is not to say that Hispanics and Asians do not face discrimination and prejudice. Indeed, the latest national audit study of discrimination suggests that Hispanic renters continue to face discrimination from rental agents at levels comparable to blacks (Turner and Ross 2004), and that Asians and Pacific Islanders face discrimination in the market for owner-occupied housing (Turner and Ross 2003). The point is simply that, on average, discrimination and white avoidance may not be as central in driving segregation for Asians and Hispanics as they are in the case of blacks.

It is worth underscoring that considering Asians and Hispanics as single, monolithic groups is overly simplistic. Research that explores the segregation levels of different Asian and Hispanic subpopulations typically finds significant variation (Massey and Bitterman 1985; Ellen 2000b; Alba *et al.* 2000). For instance, researchers have typically found that the residential patterns of Puerto Ricans more closely resemble those of blacks than those of other Hispanics (Denton and Massey 1989; Massey and Denton 1993; Massey and Bitterman 1985).

There are good reasons to suspect that the explanations for segregation vary across subgroups as well. For certain subgroups, recent immigrants or groups from particular regions, discrimination and white avoidance may be more central in explaining segregation. Massey and Bitterman (1985) argue that the higher levels of segregation among Puerto Ricans result from their African ancestry and the fact that whites are more likely to perceive them as black. Unfortunately, the national audit studies did not have sufficient sample sizes to explore such subgroups. However, the results do suggest significant discrimination against Hispanic renters but not against Hispanic home-buyers. Turner and Ross (2003) posit that this may be because of the differences between Hispanic renters and homebuyers—that is, renters are far more likely to be lower-income, first-generation immigrants. Native-born white households may be quite open to sharing neighborhoods with higher-income, assimilated Hispanic households but not with more recent, lower-income arrivals. This is consistent with the above-noted evidence suggesting that higher-income, native-born Hispanics experience very low levels of segregation.

Conclusion and Policy Implications

This chapter strives to demonstrate that a multiplicity of factors help to explain the persistence of segregation in U.S. metropolitan areas. In the past, much work on segregation has debated the extent to which discrimination was the key cause of the segregation of blacks. This argument took on a fair degree of urgency because the implication seemed to be that if, and only if, segregation was caused by discrimination, then segregation was something to worry about. If discrimination was not the key cause, then the assumption seemed to be that segregation was driven by benign individual preferences, and we should remain largely unconcerned. Such a dichotomy is false.

The race-based preferences that undergird segregation are simply not so benign. Much of current black–white segregation is caused by the ongoing refusal of whites to move into integrated and largely black neighborhoods because of negative racial attitudes—particularly race-based stereotypes about the quality of life in these communities. While these decisions may not be legally actionable, they are surely more troubling than decisions to cluster voluntarily with other members of one's own ethnic group. Moreover, these decisions are driven by negative attitudes and stereotypes that are themselves shaped by segregation and encourage the continuing discrimination by landlords, real estate agents, and lenders.

Finally, whatever the precise mix of causes, there is a growing body of evidence that suggests that segregation imposes significant social costs. Segregation may fuel prejudice, and there is increasing evidence to suggest that it can have detrimental effects on the life chances of blacks (Cutler and Glaeser 1997; Ellen 2000c; O'Regan and Quigley 1996).

White avoidance appears to play a lesser role in the segregation of Hispanics and Asians than it does in the segregation of blacks. Segregation is driven to a greater extent by differences in socioeconomic status, levels of proficiency with the English language, and minority preferences for ethnic clustering. This is not to say that discrimination and white avoidance do not play a role, but that these factors play a less dominant role than they do in the case of blacks. Put simply, Hispanic households and, particularly, Asian households are better able to translate gains in education and income into greater residential choices.

It is important to reiterate that although they have remained relatively steady over the past few decades, the segregation levels of Hispanics and especially Asians are far less severe than those of blacks. Moreover, in contrast to the growing body of work suggesting that segregation undermines the life chances of blacks, there has been little research on the effects of segregation on Hispanics and Asians. For all these reasons, it remains unclear whether we should think about segregation of these groups in the same light as we think about the segregation of blacks. More research is needed to understand the underlying causes and consequences, and how they vary for particular subgroups.

Finally, what kinds of policies are advisable in light of the findings in this chapter? First and foremost, continued efforts to combat discrimination in housing and mortgage markets are critical. Discrimination continues to restrict housing choices of minority households and discourages them from seeking out housing opportunities in largely white areas. In addition, racial steering by real estate agents preserves existing patterns of segregation and artificially limits demand in largely minority and integrated communities. Finally, housing market discrimination helps to maintain predominantly white areas as an option to which whites can escape, and in this way fuels white avoidance (Yinger 1995).

Fair housing policies should not end with antidiscrimination efforts, however. First, the findings here suggest that government at all levels should be encouraged to provide information that can expose what is false or exaggerated in the stereotypes many households hold about minority groups and their communities. Second, government should ensure that information about available housing opportunities reaches a broad and diverse set of groups. It should consider affirmative efforts to encourage white households to look at homes in minority neighborhoods and to encourage minority households to consider homes in predominantly white areas. Finally, efforts to bolster the quality of schools, neighborhood safety, and the general physical appearance of integrated and changing neighborhoods are also likely to promote the stability of integration (in addition to their obvious direct benefits); visible signs of decline and worries about public services can significantly undermine faith in a neighborhood's strength.

References

Alba, Richard, and John R. Logan. 1993. "Minority Proximity to Whites in Suburbs: An Individual-Level Analysis of Segregation." *American Journal of Sociology* 98: 1388–1427.

Alba, Richard, John R. Logan, and Brian Stults. 2000. "The Changing Neighborhood Contexts of the Immigrant Metropolis." *Social Forces* 79: 587–621.

Altonji, Joseph, and Ulrich Doraszelski. 2001. "The Role of Permanent Income and Demographics in Black–White Differences in Wealth." NBER Working Paper 8473.

Altonji, Joseph, Ulrich Doraszelski, and Lewis Segal. 2000. "Black/White Differences in Wealth." *Economic Perspectives* 4(1): 38–50.

Bajari, Patrick, and Matthew E. Kahn. 2005. "Estimating Housing Demand with an Application to Explaining Racial Segregation in Cities." *Journal of Business and Economic Statistics* 23: 20–33.

Bayer, Patrick, Robert McMillan, and Kim Rueben. 2004. "What Drives Racial Segregation? New Evidence Using Census Microdata." *Journal of Urban Economics* 56(3): 514–535.

Bishaw, Ale, and John Iceland. 2003. *Poverty: 1999*. U.S. Census Bureau, Census 2000 Brief Series, C2KBR-19.

Bobo, Lawrence, and Camille Zubrinsky. 1996. "Attitudes on Residential Integration: Perceived Status Differences, Mere In-Group Preference, or Racial Prejudice?" *Social Forces* 74(3): 883–909.

Charles, Camille Zubrinsky. 2000. "Neighborhood Racial Composition Preferences: Evidence from a Multiethnic Metropolis." *Social Problems* 47: 379–407.

Clark, William A. V. 1986. "Residential Segregation in American Cities: A Review and Interpretation." *Population Research and Policy Review* 5(2): 95–127.

276 • Ingrid Gould Ellen

Cutler, David M., and Edward L. Glaeser. 1997. "Are Ghettos Good or Bad?" *Quarterly Journal of Economics* 112(3): 827.

Cutler, David, Edward Glaeser, and Jacob Vigdor. 1999. "The Rise and Decline of the American Ghetto," *Journal of Political Economy* 107: 455–506.

Denton, Nancy, and Douglas Massey. 1988. "The Dimensions of Residential Segregation." *Social Forces* 67: 281–315.

Denton, Nancy, and Douglas Massey. 1989. "Racial Identity among Caribbean Hispanics: The Effect of Double Minority Status on Residential Segregation." *American Sociological Review* 54: 790–808.

Ellen, Ingrid Gould. 2000a. "A New White Flight? The Dynamics of Neighborhood Change in the 1980s." In Nancy Foner, Ruben G. Rumbaut, and Steven J. Gold, eds., *Immigration Research for a New Century: Multidisciplinary Perspectives.* New York City: Russell Sage Foundation, pp. 423–441.

Ellen, Ingrid Gould. 2000b. *Sharing America's Neighborhoods: The Prospects for Stable Racial Integration.* Cambridge, MA: Harvard University Press.

Ellen, Ingrid Gould. 2000c. "Is Segregation Bad for Your Health? The Case of Low Birthweight." *Brookings–Wharton Papers on Urban Affairs:* 203–238.

Ellen, Ingrid Gould. 2007. "How Integrated Did We Become during the 1990s?" In John M. Goering, ed., *Fragile Rights in Cities.* Lanham, MD: Rowman and Littlefield, pp. 123–142.

Emerson, Michael O., Karen J. Chai, and George Yancey. 2001. "Does Race Matter in Racial Segregation? Exploring the Preferences of White Americans." *American Sociological Review* 66: 922–935.

Farley, John E. 1986. "Segregated City, Segregated Suburbs: To What Extent Are They Products of Black–White Socioeconomic Differentials?" *Urban Geography* 2: 180–187.

Farley, Reynolds. 1996. "Racial Differences in the Search for Housing: Do Whites and Blacks Use the Same Techniques to Find Housing?" *Housing Policy Debate* 7(2): 367–385.

Farley, Reynolds, Howard Schuman, Suzanne Bianchi, Diane Colasanto, and Shirley Hatchett. 1978. "Chocolate Cities, Vanilla Suburbs: Will the Trend toward Racially Separate Communities Continue?" *Social Science Research* 7: 319–344.

Farley, Reynolds, Charlotte Steeh, Tara Jackson, Maria Krysan, and Keith Reeves. 1993. "Continued Residential Segregation in Detroit: 'Chocolate City, Vanilla Suburbs' Revisited." *Journal of Housing Research* 4 (1993).

Farley, Reynolds, Charlotte Steeh, Tara Jackson, Maria Krysan, and Keith Reeves. 1994. "Stereotypes and Segregation: Neighborhoods in the Detroit Area." *American Journal of Sociology* 100: 750–780.

Gabriel, Stuart A., and Stuart S. Rosenthal. 1989. "Household Location and Race: Estimates of a Multinomial Logit Model." *Review of Economics and Statistics* 71: 240–249.

Galster, George. 1979. "Interracial Differences in Housing Preferences." *Regional Science Perspectives* 9(1): 1–17.

Galster, George. 1982. "Black and White Preferences for Neighborhood Racial Composition." *AREUEA Journal* 10: 39–66.

Galster, George. 1988. "Residential Segregation in American Cities: A Contrary Review." *Population Research and Policy Review* 7: 93–112.

Galster, George, Fred Freiberg, and Diane Houk. 1987. "Racial Differences in Real Estate Advertising Practices: An Exploratory Case Study." *Journal of Urban Affairs* 9: 199–215.

Glaeser, Edward, and Jacob Vigdor. 2001. *Racial Segregation in the 2000 Census: Promising News.* Washington, DC: Brookings Institution Center on Urban and Metropolitan Policy.

Iceland, John, and Daniel Weinberg with Erica Steinmetz. 2002. *Racial and Ethnic Residential Segregation in the United States: 1980–2000.* U.S. Census Bureau Special Reports, Washington, DC.

Ihlanfeldt, Keith, and Benjamin Scafidi. 2002. "Black Self-Segregation as a Cause of Housing Segregation: Evidence from the Multi-City Study of Urban Inequality." *Journal of Urban Economics* 51: 366–390.

Kain, John F. 1976. "Race, Ethnicity, and Residential Location." In Ronald Grieson, ed., *Public and Urban Economics,* Lexington, MA: Lexington Books, pp. 267–292.

Kain, John F. 1986. "The Influence of Race and Income on Racial Segregation and Housing Policy."

In John M. Goering, ed., *Housing Desegregation and Federal Policy*. Chapel Hill, NC: University of North Carolina Press, pp. 99–118.

Kain, John F., and John M. Quigley. 1975. *Housing Markets and Racial Discrimination: A Microeconomic Analysis*. New York: Columbia University Press.

Krysan, Maria, and Reynolds Farley. 2002. "The Residential Preferences of Blacks: Do They Explain Persistent Segregation?" *Social Forces* 80(3): 937–980.

Lewis Mumford Center. 2001. "Ethnic Diversity Grows, Neighborhood Integration Lags Behind." Available at http://mumford.albany.edu/census/report.html.

Malone, Nolan, Kaari F. Baluja, Joseph M. Costanzo, and Cynthia J. Davis. 2003. "The Foreign-Born Population: 2000." U.S. Census Bureau: Census 2000 Brief.

Massey, Douglas S. 1979. "Effects of Socioeconomic Factors on the Residential Segregation of Blacks and Spanish Americans in United States Urbanized Areas." *American Sociological Review* 44: 1015–1022.

Massey, Douglas S., and B. Bitterman. 1985. "Explaining the Paradox of Puerto Rican Segregation." *Social Forces* 64(2): 306–331.

Massey, Douglas S., and Nancy Denton. 1993. *American Apartheid*. Cambridge, MA: Harvard University Press.

Newburger, Harriet. 1981. "The Nature and Extent of Racial Steering Practices in U.S. Housing Markets." Unpublished manuscript.

Newburger, Harriet. 1999. "Mobility Patterns of Lower Income First-Time Homebuyers in Philadelphia." *Cityscape* 4: 201–220.

O'Regan, Katherine, and John Quigley. 1996. "Teenage Employment and the Spatial Isolation of Minority and Poverty Households." *Journal of Human Resources* 31: 692–702.

Patterson, Orlando. 1997. *The Ordeal of Integration: Progress and Resentment in America's "Racial" Crisis*. Cambridge, MA: Harvard University Press.

Sampson, Robert, and Stephen W. Raudenbush. 2004. "Seeing Disorder: Neighborhood Stigma and the Social Construction of 'Broken Windows.'" *Social Pyschology Quarterly* 67(4): 319–342.

Schuman, Howard, Charlotte Steeh, Lawrence Bobo, and Maria Krysan. 1997. *Racial Attitudes in America: Trends and Interpretations*. Cambridge, MA: Harvard University Press.

South, Scott, Kyle Crowder, and Erick Chavez. 2006. "Wealth, Race, and Inter-Neighbourhood Migration." *American Sociological Review* 71 (February): 72–94.

Taeuber, Karl E., and Alma F. Taeuber. 1965. *Negroes in Cities: Residential Segregation and Neighborhood Change*. New York: Atheneum.

Turner, Margery Austin, and Stephen L. Ross. 2003. *Discrimination in Metropolitan Housing Markets: Phase 2—Asians and Pacific Islanders*. Final Report Submitted to U.S. Department of Housing and Urban Development, Washington, DC.

Turner, Margery Austin, and Stephen L. Ross. 2004. "Housing Discrimination in Metropolitan America: Findings from the Latest National Paired Testing Study." University of Connecticut Working Paper.

Turner, Margery Austin, and Ron Wienk. 1993. "The Persistence of Segregation in Urban Areas: Contributing Causes." In G. Thomas Kingsley and Margery Austin Turner, eds., *Housing Markets and Residential Mobility*. Washington, DC: Urban Institute Press, pp. 193–216.

Turner, Margery Austin, Stephen L. Ross, George C. Galster, and John Yinger. 2002. *Discrimination in Metropolitan Housing Markets: National Results from Phase 1 HDS 2000*. Final Report Submitted to U.S. Department of Housing and Urban Development, Washington, DC.

Yinger, John. 1995. *Closed Doors, Opportunities Lost: The Continuing Cost of Housing Discrimination*. New York: Russell Sage Foundation Press.

CHAPTER 9

Trends in the U.S. Economy: The Evolving Role of Minorities

DEAN BAKER AND HEATHER BOUSHEY

Executive Summary

This chapter examines a number of recent trends in the U.S. economy and society, and projects the implications of their continuation over the next two decades. Most importantly, this chapter notes that the past two decades have been marked by a sharp growth in wage inequality. This has meant that the bulk of the population, which gets most of its income from working, has received little benefit from the economy's growth over the past quarter-century. This is a sharp contrast with the thirty years following the end of World War II, when most of the country shared in the gains from economic growth.

This chapter notes that if current trends in the labor market continue, wage inequality is likely to increase further in the years ahead. The growth in inequality is likely to be more a function of institutional relationships, which tend to protect high-end workers such as doctors and lawyers, than an intrinsic feature of the economy. The institutions that protected workers at the middle and the bottom of income distribution, such as, most importantly, unions, are being rapidly eroded. The growth in inequality in total compensation is probably even greater than the growth in wage inequality since many workers at the middle and bottom of the wage distribution are losing employer-provided health insurance and pensions. The vast majority of workers at the top of the distribution still enjoy these benefits.

Projections of employment growth by industry and occupation show no clear trend toward increasing or decreasing demand for skilled workers.

While many highly skilled occupations will see rapid job growth, this is also true for many occupations requiring little skill.

The United States is doing a poor job educating its children relative to other rich countries and even compared to some developing countries. In math, science, and literacy tests, students in the United States rank near the bottom among students from rich countries. While the United States led the world in training students in science and engineering thirty years ago, it has been surpassed by the European Union (EU) and will soon be passed by China as well.

Black and Hispanic students have performed worse than the student population as a whole on standardized exams. While black and Hispanic students had been making substantial progress in closing the gap with white students in the United States, this largely stopped during the past fifteen years. If the achievement levels of these students do not improve, it will imply declining performance for the country as a whole, since they will be a growing share of the student population in the decades ahead.

In addition, poor educational outcomes are likely to lead to poor labor market outcomes. If black and Hispanic students do not get good education, then their prospects for secure employment, with decent wages and health insurance, will be badly diminished. The ability to extend homeownership among these populations will be very limited if they do not have the skills they need to secure decent jobs.

The number of people incarcerated in the United States and the cost of the corrections system have both increased rapidly over the past quarter-century. If the trend of the past few years continues (a slowdown from the growth rate in the 1980s and early 1990s), more than 3.5 million people will be incarcerated in 2025. The corrections system will cost the country 2.7 percent of GDP, an amount equal to $340 billion in 2005.

Blacks and Hispanics enter the criminal justice system in grossly disproportionate numbers. Close to 40 percent of the incarcerated population is black. While the total number of advanced degrees in mathematics, engineering, and science awarded during 2002–2003 (the most recent year for which data is available) was 97,200, more than 2 million people are now in prison or jail.[1] Young blacks are far more likely to be incarcerated than to secure an advance degree in a technical field or even graduate college.

Healthcare costs are already putting the United States at an enormous disadvantage relative to other countries. The United States currently spends more than twice as much per person as the average for other rich countries, even though it ranks near the bottom in health outcomes. However, this handicap is projected to grow rapidly in the years ahead. By 2025, healthcare costs are projected to increase by 5 percentage points of GDP, an amount equivalent to $630 billion in 2005, or $2,100 per person. The projected difference in healthcare costs between the United States and other rich countries in 2025 amounts to the equivalent of draining $1.2 trillion from the economy (in 2005) to pay for the waste in the healthcare system.

In the past decade, house prices have also vastly outpaced the overall rate of inflation. While this run-up in house prices will likely be reversed in the years ahead, at the moment it creates a situation in which the typical worker is finding it ever more difficult to become a homeowner.

As is shown in Figure 9.1, the growth in average hourly wages over the past decade has lagged substantially behind the growth in education costs, house prices, and health care. If recent trends continue, middle- and lower-income families will find it increasingly difficult to pay for their children's education, to buy a house, and to pay for their health insurance.

These trends present a picture of a country that will face very serious problems in the decades ahead. The gaps between rich and poor will be considerably larger than they are at present. In addition, the United States is in danger of falling far behind much of the world in maintaining the quality of its workforce. Furthermore, the inefficiency of its healthcare system means both that many people will likely lack access to health care and that it will be very costly to those who do maintain access. If the employer-provided system of health care manages to survive the next two decades, firms that pay for their workers' health care will be at a serious competitive disadvantage relative to firms in countries with more efficient healthcare systems. Finally, the

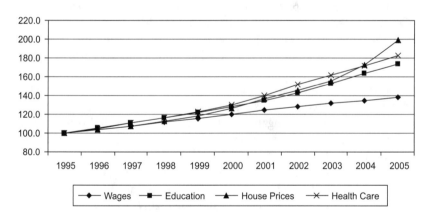

Figure 9.1 Inflation, 1995–2005: wages, education, house prices, and health care.

Source: Bureau of Labor Statistics, Office Federal Housing Enterprise Oversight and Center for Medicare and Medicaid Services. The wage index is based on the Bureau of Labor Statistics average hourly wage series. The education index uses the education component of the Bureau of Labor Statistics consumer price index. The housing index is taken from the Office of Federal Housing Enterprise Oversight House Price Index (the fourth quarter 2005 data extrapolate the growth rate over the first three quarters). The healthcare index shows the Center for Medicare and Medicaid Services estimates for healthcare expenditures per capita. The data for 2004 and 2005 are projections.

cost of the U.S. corrections system will impose a large tax on the economy, acting as another drag on international competitiveness.

While there are no easy solutions to the problems the country currently faces, it does seem clear that these problems will worsen over the next two decades if they are not addressed.

Introduction

In the past quarter-century the gap in wages between higher-paying and lower-paying jobs has increased substantially. Unlike in the first three decades following World War II, the bulk of the gains from productivity growth in the years since 1980 have gone to those at the top end of the income distribution—either in profits or in the form of rising wages and benefits. The bottom half of wage earners have seen little or no gain in wages during this period and are less likely to have healthcare coverage than they were a quarter-century earlier. The loss of healthcare coverage has been especially large among dependants, as employers are far less likely to provide healthcare coverage for their workers' dependants in 2005 than was the case in 1980.[2]

This trend toward growing inequality and less security for the bulk of the population seems likely to continue over the next two decades. To a large extent, the trends over the past quarter-century have been driven by conscious government policy. For example, trade agreements were structured in ways that put tens of millions of less educated workers in direct competition with low-paid workers in developing countries, while protecting highly educated workers in the United States (such as doctors and lawyers) from the same sort of competition. Similarly, the U.S. healthcare system has been structured in a way that allows per-person healthcare costs to rise to levels that are two or three times higher than costs in other wealthy countries; yet despite their lower costs, these other countries achieve better health outcomes. Unless recent trends are reversed, most of the country's workforce is likely to fare poorly during the next two decades. There will also be negative effects on the economy, which will be dragged down by the problems confronting the less well off.

Since blacks and Hispanics are disproportionately in the bottom three-quarters of the wealth and income distribution, they are disproportionately harmed by trends that lead to greater inequality. As the share of the minorities in the population rises over the next two decades, they are likely to be even more disproportionately represented among the poor and disadvantaged than is the case at present. (The Census Bureau projects that the country's population will grow by 81,460,000 people from 2000 to 2030. It projects that non-Hispanic whites will account for just 16.5 percent of this growth.[3])

This chapter reviews several recent trends and discusses their potential effect if they continue over the next two decades. Specifically, it examines (1) trends in wage inequality and job quality; (2) patterns in educational attainment—specifically, how U.S. students perform compared to students in other countries; (3) trends in awarding advanced degrees in high-tech fields such as engineering and computer science; (4) trends in incarceration rates in the United States; and (5) trends in healthcare costs in the United States compared with other countries. Based on an analysis of these recent trends and the likelihood that they will continue in the future, this chapter will speculate on the future prospects of the U.S. economy.

Trends in Wage Inequality since 1980

In the thirty years before 1980, most workers shared in the country's prosperity. Wages moved largely in step with productivity growth, and workers all along the income distribution received roughly the same percentage pay increase year by year. In other words, as the economy prospered, most people could count on their situation improving as well. The real wage of a typical worker increased by 95.8 percent from 1947 to 1973 (productivity grew by 103.5 percent), when the first oil price shock threw the economy into a recession.[4]

This pattern changed in the 1980s. Since 1979, most of the gains from higher productivity growth have gone to workers at the top end of the wage distribution.[5] In the years from 1979 to 2003, productivity increased by a total of 34.9 percent; however, most workers gained little from this growth.[6] Table 9.1 shows the average hourly wage for workers at the 10th wage percentile, 50th percentile, 90th percentile, and 95th percentile over the period from 1979 to 2003.[7]

The data show that workers in the middle of the wage distribution, at the 50th percentile, saw very weak wage growth, less than 0.5 percent annually, over the period from 1979 to 2003. Wages for workers at the bottom, the 10th percentile, barely moved over this period. However, wages for workers at the top of the distribution continued to rise roughly in step with productivity growth over this period. It is worth noting that in the years from 1995 to 2000, wages grew rapidly at all points along the wage distribution, including the middle and bottom. Part of this more rapid growth in wages is attributable to the pickup in productivity growth in the middle of the 1990s, after two decades of slow growth. However, it is also likely that low rates of unemployment—the lowest since the 1960s—created a tight labor market in which most workers were situated to get their share of productivity growth.

The low rate of unemployment achieved at the end of the 1990s was in part the result of a policy decision by the Federal Reserve Board (the Fed).

284 • Dean Baker and Heather Boushey

TABLE 9.1 Trends in Wage Inequality in the United States

Years	Percentage Change in Real Wage			
	10th Percentile	50th Percentile	90th Percentile	98th Percentile
1979–1989	−14.1	0.0	7.4	8.1
1989–1995	1.8	−1.8	3.3	5.4
1995–2000	11.1	7.7	8.7	10.6
2000–2003	3.8	4.2	5.4	4.0
1979–2003	0.9	10.2	27.2	31.1

Source: Mishel *et al.* (2005, table 2.6).

In 1994–1995, the unemployment rate fell into the 5.5 percent to 6.0 percent range that most economists had come to view as full employment. Many economists, including some of the governors of the Fed, argued that the Fed should raise interest rates and slow the economy in order to keep the unemployment rate from falling further. The Fed, led by its chairman, Alan Greenspan, ignored these views and allowed the unemployment rate to continue to fall until it reached 4.0 percent in 2000.

As the unemployment rate rose in the years following 2000, wage growth for those at the middle and bottom gradually ground to a halt. Since 2003 the average hourly wage for a nonsupervisory worker has been stagnant or declining, in spite of the continuation of strong productivity growth. This experience suggests that a commitment to sustaining low rates of unemployment will be very important to ensuring that all workers share the benefits of productivity growth in the future.

There is also an important racial/ethnic dimension to these trends in inequality. Over the past fifteen years there has been virtually no progress in diminishing the gaps between white workers and black and Hispanic workers. Table 9.2a shows the median 9-hourly wage for male workers by race and Hispanic origin over the past fifteen years. Table 9.2b shows the same information for women workers.

As can be seen, the ratio of the median hourly wage for black men to the median wage for white men has been virtually constant over the past fourteen years. The ratio of median hourly wages for black women to white women actually declined by 3 percentage points during this period. Both Hispanic men and Hispanic women saw a decline of 4 percentage points in the ratio of their median hourly wages to the median hourly wage of white men and white women. Asian men, an exception to this pattern, start with a median wage that is 7 percentage points less than the white median and end the

TABLE 9.2a Median Hourly Wage—Men, 1989–2003 (Percentage of White Median)

	1989	1995	2000	2003
African American	72.3	73.1	73.1	72.7
Hispanic	67.3	63.7	64.1	63.4
Asian	93.4	96.3	99.4	104.3

Source: Mishel *et al.* (2005, table 2.24).

TABLE 9.2b Median Hourly Wage—Women, 1989–2003 (Percentage of White Median)

	1989	1995	2000	2003
African American	89.1	86.0	87.5	86.1
Hispanic	79.4	76.1	73.9	75.3
Asian	103.5	102.9	106.6	103.0

Source: Mishel *et al.* (2005, table 2.25).

period with a median wage that is 3 percentage points higher. Asian women had a median hourly wage that was somewhat above the median for white women throughout the period.

The lack of progress in reducing the pay gap between blacks and Hispanics and whites is also reflected in the performance of immigrant workers. Male immigrants who arrived in the United States before 1980 could expect their wages to have fully caught up with their native-born counterparts in less than twenty years, after adjusting for education and experience. Male immigrants coming after 1980 can expect to still see a wage gap compared with comparable native-born workers even after thirty years (Schmitt, 2005).[8]

Urban Demographics

During the period from 1979 to 1999 the populations of central cities became progressively poorer and less white relative to the nation as a whole. While it is difficult to determine whether this trend will continue—not all cities had the same experience over this period—if it does, the prospects for the poor living in inner cities could be bleak because cities will increasingly lack the resources necessary to provide adequate levels of services.

The percentage of inner-city households that fall into the bottom income quintile nationally rose from 24.2 percent in 1979 to 24.9 percent in 1999.[9] The percentage in the next lowest income quintile also rose slightly over this period, going from 21.3 percent to 21.5 percent. By contrast, the percentage of households in the top quintile fell from 17.4 percent to 16.4 percent. This shift indicates that cities are seeing a substantial increase in low-income households but have a dwindling tax base to pay for the services that these families require.

However, it is important to note that many cities did not follow this pattern, experiencing instead disproportionate growth in the percentage of households in the top income quintile during this period. These cities were disproportionately located in the Sunbelt region (see Berube and Tiffany, 2004, table 4). This suggests a disparate pattern of growth in cities, with some containing large and growing pockets of poverty (disproportionately cities in the Rustbelt), while others continue to attract a wide mix of households.

In addition to getting poorer, the urban population is also becoming less white. In 1990 the population of the nation's 100 largest cities was 52.4 percent white, 24.6 percent black, and 17.2 percent Hispanic. In 2000, only 43.8 percent of the urban population was white, with the black share remaining roughly the same at 24.1 percent and the Hispanic share rising to 22.5 percent (Brookings Institution Center on Urban and Metropolitan Policy, 2001). For the country as a whole, 80.8 percent of the population is white, 12.7 black, and 13.4 percent Hispanic.

The trends of the recent past suggest an ominous picture. Many cities may lose more affluent families from their tax base and possibly also suffer politically because suburban whites may care less about cities dominated by blacks and Hispanics. However, it is far from certain that these trends will continue. Energy prices have risen sharply over the past two years, and most projections are that gas prices will remain considerably higher than in the past. This could lead many families to place a premium on living close to their workplace, which would have the effect of pushing people back toward cities. Whether energy prices stay high and how large an effect this has on living patterns remains to be seen.

The Jobs of the Future

Any forecast concerning the nature of the jobs of the future requires a large amount of speculation. The Bureau of Labor Statistics (BLS) provides some basis for this speculation in its annual employment projections. Table 9.3 shows the shares of employment in each of the major industry groups as of 2002, the industry shares of the change in employment during the period 1992 to 2002, and the projected shares in the change in employment from 2002 to 2012. It also shows the average hourly wage in each industry from the most recent available data (July 2004). The industries are ranked by the projected shares of the change in employment for the years 2002 to 2012.

TABLE 9.3 Share of 2002 Employment and Projected Change by Industry

	Employment Shares			
	2002	Change 1992–2002	Projected Change 2002–2012	Average Hourly Wage (2004)
Total non-farm wage and salary (in thousands)	131,063	21,537	21,627	$15.70
Education and health services	12.3%	19.9%	23.8%	$16.17
Professional and business services	12.2	23.4	22.5	$17.44
State and local government	14.3	14.1	11.6	NA
Leisure and hospitality	9.1	11.8	9.9	$8.88
Retail trade	11.5	10.3	9.6	$12.12
Construction	5.1	9.9	9.6	$19.22
Other services	4.7	4.6	4.4	$13.87
Financial activities	6.0	6.1	4.5	$17.55
Transportation and warehousing	3.2	3.5	4.2	$16.86
Wholesale trade	4.3	2.5	3.0	$17.72
Information	2.6	3.6	2.9	$21.38
Federal government	2.1	−1.6	0.1	NA
Utilities	0.5	−0.6	−0.2	$25.53
Mining	0.4	−0.5	−0.3	$18.21
Manufacturing	11.7	−6.9	−0.7	$16.14

Source: Bureau of Labor Statistics (2004).

At the top of the list are the industry groupings education and health services, and professional and business services. Both have average wages above the average for the economy as a whole. It is important to note that these are extremely large groupings that include both high-wage occupations, such as doctors and school principals, and low-wage occupations, such as nurse's aids and custodians. The average hourly wages for the next two most rapidly growing industry groups—the leisure and hospitality sector and retail trade—are the lowest for all industry groups. These two sectors are projected to account for 19.5 percent of the new jobs created over this period, which is approximately equal to their current share of employment.

Perhaps the most interesting aspect of this table is the three industry groupings that are projected to actually lose jobs over the next decade—

utilities, mining, and manufacturing. These three groups, which accounted for approximately 12.5 percent of employment in 2002, all pay considerably more than the average hourly wage. All three groups also experienced substantial declines in employment in the prior decade (a total loss of 1,716,000 jobs), leading to a considerable reduction in their percentage of total employment. The relative decline in employment in these sectors was almost certainly one of the factors contributing to the growth of wage inequality because these sectors have traditionally been a source of relatively high-paying employment for workers without college degrees.

The pattern of benefit provisions tends to mirror the wage distribution. While 74 percent of workers in manufacturing receive healthcare benefits through their employers and 68 percent receive pension benefits, the comparable percentages for workers in the retail sector are 31 percent and 30 percent, respectively (Mishel *et al.*, 2003, table 3.13). The projected pattern of job growth by industry suggests that a growing segment of the workforce will not receive healthcare insurance or a pension through an employer.

Both trade and technology have driven the trends in employment industry over the past decade. In the second quarter of 2005 the United States ran a trade deficit of $680 billion, or 5.5 percent of GDP. This is primarily the result of a deficit in manufactured goods, most of which would be produced domestically if they were not imported. Other things being equal, manufacturing employment would be approximately 21 percent higher (the equivalent of almost 3 million manufacturing jobs) if the United States had balanced trade instead of its current deficit.[10] At least in absolute terms, the manufacturing sector clearly has been the hardest hit by the outsourcing of jobs. Since this sector has been and continues to be a source of relatively high-paying jobs for workers without college degrees, the loss of manufacturing jobs has undoubtedly played a large role in the growth of inequality over the past quarter-century.

However, this trade deficit is not sustainable indefinitely and will likely be partially or completely eliminated in the next decade (Weisbrot and Baker, 2004). The reversal in the trade deficit will increase manufacturing employment in the next decade compared to the projections shown in Table 9.3. The elimination of the trade deficit, or a substantial reduction in its size, will be a force leading to greater wage equality in the decades ahead.

Of course, trade is not the only factor leading to a loss of manufacturing jobs. Productivity growth has also reduced the demand for workers in manufacturing. The manufacturing sector has consistently enjoyed more rapid productivity growth than the economy as a whole. Over the past seventeen years (the period for which data are available), productivity growth in the manufacturing sector has averaged 3.7 percent annually, compared to 2.3 percent in the nonfarm business sector as a whole.[11] Other things being equal, the more rapid pace of productivity growth in manufacturing will reduce the portion of the labor force employed in manufacturing. If productivity growth in manufacturing had been no faster than in the rest of the economy over the past seventeen years, and the economy produced the same quantity of manufacturing goods as it does presently, manufacturing employment would be 26 percent higher.

In short, both the trade deficit and technology have contributed to the loss of manufacturing jobs, with the magnitudes of the two effects being roughly comparable. It is worth noting that trade would have led to a loss of manufacturing jobs in the United States even if the country had not run a trade deficit, because imports of manufactured goods would be paid for with exports of services. This is not nearly as large as the effect of the trade deficit because the surplus on service imports has never been anywhere near as large as the size of the current trade deficit. Furthermore, there has been a sharp rise in service imports in the past three years, so the direction of the long-term balance on service trade is no longer clear.[12]

Jobs by Occupation

The BLS also makes projections of job growth by occupation, which provides some basis for analyzing the skills that will be needed for the jobs of the future. Table 9.4 shows the current employment levels and the projected rate of increase in the twenty most rapidly growing occupations. These twenty occupations are projected to account for 7,840,000 new jobs over the next decade, which is more than 36 percent of projected employment growth.

The projections in the table support the view that the bulk of job creation will be at either the top or the bottom of the labor market. In fact, sixteen of the top twenty most rapidly growing occupations require only short- or medium-term on-the-job training. While high-paying occupations like registered nurses and postsecondary teachers are also projected to grow rapidly, the middle category of jobs is missing from this list. The high-paying occupations in this grouping typically provide workers with health care, pensions, and relatively stable employment. However, the occupational categories that dominate this list tend to offer relatively few benefits and insecure employment. Of the sixteen occupations that require only short- or medium-term on-the-job training only one, teacher assistants, is ranked as being in the more stable half of occupations by security of employment.

In short, there is no clear trend in the educational requirements in the occupations that are projected to grow most rapidly in the next decade. While there will be growth in some occupations requiring high skills, there will also be rapid growth in occupations requiring relatively little skill. It is entirely

TABLE 9.4 Employment Levels and Changes by Occupation

	Total Employment (in thousands)		2002 Median Annual Earnings	2002 Earnings Quartile	Education and Training Level[a]
	2002	Change 2002–2012 (thousands)			
Registered nurses	2,284	623	48,090	Very high	4
Postsecondary teachers	1,581	603	49,090	Very high	7
Retail salespersons	4,076	596	17,710	Very low	1
Customer service representatives	1,894	460	26,240	Low	2
Combined food preparation and serving workers	1,990	454	14,500	Very low	1
Cashiers, except gaming	3,432	454	15,420	Very low	1
Janitors and cleaners	2,267	414	18,250	Very low	1
General and operations managers	2,049	376	68,210	Very high	5
Waiters and waitresses	2,097	367	14,150	Very low	1
Nursing aides, orderlies, and attendants	1,375	343	19,960	Low	1
Truck drivers, heavy and tractor-trailer	1,767	337	33,210	High	2
Receptionists and information clerks	1,100	325	21,150	Low	1
Security guards	995	317	19,140	Very low	1
Office clerks, general	2,991	310	22,280	Low	1
Teacher assistants	1,277	294	18,660	Very low	1
All other business operations specialists	1,056	290	50,680	Very high	5
Sales reps, wholesale and manufacturing	1,459	279	42,730	Very high	2
Home health aides	580	279	18,090	Very low	1
Personal and home care aides	608	246	16,250	Very low	1
Truck drivers, light or delivery services	1,022	237	23,870	Low	1
Landscaping and groundskeeping workers	1,074	237	19,770	Low	1

Source: Bureau of Labor Statistics, Employment Projections by Occupation, 2002–2012.

Note: [a] The numbering for education and training is as follows:

1 – short-term on-the-job training; 2 – moderate-term on-the-job training; 3 – postsecondary vocational award; 4 – associate degree; 5 – bachelor's degree; 6 – master's degree; 7 – doctoral degree.

possible that the occupational mix of 2020 will require fewer skills on average than the occupational mix of 2005.

Educational Attainment

While the United States consistently is at or near the top in international comparisons of per capita GDP, the most basic measure of national wealth, it consistently ranks near the bottom of wealthy nations in educational attainment. While there is some evidence of progress in lower grades in recent years, it is not clear that this progress will be sustained; there has been no corresponding improvement in performance among secondary school students. Furthermore, large gaps remain in the educational performance of black or Hispanic students compared with white students. Since these minority groups represent a rapidly growing share of school-age children, the failure to raise their performance will mean a deterioration in overall educational standards and a less well-educated workforce in the years ahead.[13]

The first set of columns in Table 9.5 shows the ranking among wealthy countries of 15-year-old students on overall mathematical literacy. The second set shows the ranking of eighth-graders on a science achievement test. As can be seen, the performance of students in the United States ranks well below the performance of students in most other wealthy countries in both subjects. It even ranks below the performance of some of the former Soviet bloc countries, such as the Slovak Republic, Poland, and Hungary, all of which are far poorer than the United States. If students in the United States consistently underperform students in other developed and even developing countries, this will impede their ability to compete for higher-paying jobs in the future.

Part of the relatively poor performance of students in the United States is attributable to the continuing gap in educational achievement between white students and black and Hispanic students. Table 9.6 shows average trends in reading scores for white, black, and Hispanic students over the past three decades at age. (The pattern in math scores is similar.)

As can be seen, there were small gains for 17-year-olds as a group from 1971 to 1990, but this progress was reversed more recently. Black students showed substantial gains from 1971 to 1990, but in the past fourteen years their scores have declined slightly. There is a similar pattern among Hispanic students. If this pattern of stagnant or declining test scores continues, especially among racial and ethnic minorities, then U.S. students will fare even more poorly compared with students in other countries. It is worth noting that the situation is somewhat more positive at lower grade levels, where recent test results indicate considerable progress in both math and reading skills among black and Hispanic students at ages 9 and 13. It remains

TABLE 9.5 International Comparisons of Math and Science Literacy

	Math Literacy		Science Literacy
Finland	544	Hungary	552
Korea	542	Japan	550
Netherlands	538	Korea	549
Japan	534	Netherlands	545
Canada	532	Australia	540
Belgium	529	Czech Republic	539
Switzerland	527	England	538
New Zealand	525	Finland	535
Australia	524	Belgium	535
Czech Republic	516	Slovak Republic	535
Iceland	515	Canada	533
Denmark	514	Russian Federation	529
France	511	Bulgaria	518
Sweden	509	**United States**	**515**
Austria	506	New Zealand	510
Germany	503	Italy	493
Ireland	503		
Slovak Republic	498		
Norway	495		
Poland	490		
Hungary	490		
Spain	485		
United States	483		
Russian Federation	468		
Portugal	466		
Italy	466		
Greece	445		

Source: Program for International Student Assessment. These data can be found in the National Center for Education Statistics, Program for International Student Assessment, http://nces.ed.gov/surveys/international/IntlIndicators/index.asp?SectionNumber=3&SubSectionNumber=4&IndicatorNumber=40.

to be seen whether this progress will carry through at higher grade levels. If the gap between the educational achievement of black and Hispanic children and the achievement of white children is not closed substantially in the next two decades, the United States will fall much further back in its relative international standing in education.

TABLE 9.6 Average Reading Scores: 17-Year-olds, 1971–2004

	1971	1980	1990	1999	2004
Total	285	285	290	288	285
White	291	293	297	295	293
Black	239	243	267	264	264
Hispanic	–	261	275	271	264

Source: National Center for Education Statistics. These data are taken from the National Center for Education Statistics (NCES), Long-Term Trends on the National Assessment of Educational Progress exams. The table shows reading scores for 17-year-olds, but the NCES Web site includes results for both math and reading for 9-year-olds, 13-year-olds, and 17-year-olds (http://nces.ed.gov/nations reportcard/ltt/results2004/2004_sdts.asp).

Trends in Engineering and Science Degrees

In 1975 the United States was the clear leader in science and engineering education, producing far more college graduates in these fields than any of its competitors, in addition to a much larger number of PhDs. This is no longer the case; the European Union (EU) now produces a much larger number of PhDs in these fields, and China is projected to pass the United States in this category by the end of the decade. Furthermore, a large and growing percentage of the degree recipients at U.S. universities are not native-born Americans, which presumably means that they have less inherent affinity for the United States. While many foreign-born graduates in these fields will opt to spend most of their careers in the United States, many may choose to return to their home country, leaving the United States at a greater disadvantage in the supply of highly skilled workers in these areas.

Table 9.7 shows the ratio of PhDs granted in foreign universities to PhDs granted in the United States in selected years since 1975 and projections for 2010. In 1975 the United States was by far the world leader in the number of PhDs granted in these fields, granting somewhat more degrees than the EU countries, combined, and nearly ten times as many as Japan. By 2001 the EU was producing 54 percent more PhDs in science and engineering, and Japan and China were both producing close to one-third as many. If we project recent trends, China will be producing 26 percent more PhDs in these fields than the United States by 2010, and the EU will be producing nearly twice as many. In 2002, 35.4 percent of the PhDs awarded in the physical sciences at U.S. universities went to foreign-born students. In engineering, the share going to foreign-born students was 58.7 percent (Freeman, 2005, table 2).

TABLE 9.7 Ratio of Science and Engineering PhDs Granted by Foreign Universities to Those Granted by U.S. Universities

	1975	1989	2001	2003	2010
Major Asian countries	0.22	0.48	0.96		
China	NA	0.05	0.32	0.49	1.26
Japan	0.11	0.16	0.29		
European Union	0.93	1.22	1.54	1.62	1.92

Source: Freeman (2005).

The same pattern can be found in the share of foreign-born workers in the science and engineering fields. Table 9.8 shows the foreign-born share of workers in science and engineering occupations in the years from 1990 to 2004. The table shows that a large and growing share of the people working in the United States in these fields are foreign born, especially at more advanced levels. This suggests that the United States is not educating enough of its own students to fill these positions. It also indicates that the United States may have difficulty sustaining an adequate workforce in the technical fields if the foreign-born workers increasingly decided to return to their home countries.

In short, the United States is already far behind much of the world in the quality of education it provides its children. In particular, students in most European countries do far better on average on standardized achievement tests. As a result, the United States is already heavily dependent on immigrant workers in many technical areas. However, the United States' standing in international educational performance is likely to drop considerably in the near future because of the rapid growth in science and technical training in China and India. Within a decade, China is likely to far exceed the United

TABLE 9.8 Foreign-Born Share of Science and Engineering Employment

	1990 (%)	2000 (%)	2004 (%)
Bachelors	11	17	17
Masters	19	29	32
All PhDs	24	38	37
PhDs under age 45	27	52	—
Post-doc.	49	57	—

Source: Freeman (2005).

States in the number of students it graduates each year in science and engineering. If current trends in educational achievement continue, the United States will be ever more dependent on attracting foreign workers to fill highly skilled jobs in the U.S. economy.

Trends in Incarceration Rates and Spending on Criminal Justice

Since 1980 there has been a rapid increase in the number of people in prisons or jail. (In general, a jail is a county or local facility where prisoners are sent for terms of less than one year. Prisons are state or federal facilities that house people serving longer sentences.) The number of people incarcerated more than quadrupled between 1980 and 2003, from 504,000 in 1980 to 2,086,000 in 2003. The growing incarceration rate is largely attributable to longer sentences and more stringent parole guidelines. There has been a slower rate of growth in the prison and jail population in the past few years, and it is reasonable to believe that the extraordinary growth rate of the 1980s and early 1990s will not return, but this possibility cannot be ruled out. Figure 9.2 projects the growth path for the combined prison and jail population over the next two decades, assuming that the slower growth rate from 1999 to 2003 is maintained.

The annual growth rate of the incarcerated population during this four-year period was 2.5 percent, down from a 6.4 percent growth rate for the period from 1980 to 2003. If this lower growth rate is maintained during the next 20 years, 3.6 million people will be incarcerated in the United States in 2025. If we project from the 1999 to 2003 growth rate, 6.5 million people will be on probation and 1.5 million will be on parole. Spending on the criminal

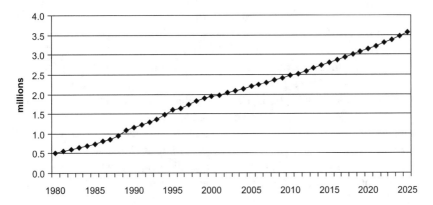

Figure 9.2 The U.S. prison and jail population.

Source: Bureau of Justice statistics and authors' calculations.

justice system will have risen to 2.7 percent of GDP, which is the equivalent of $340 billion a year, given the size of the economy in 2005.

If incarceration rates follow this pattern, it will place both an enormous burden on the economy and a situation in which a large segment of the population is under the control of the criminal justice system. The effect of these patterns is felt disproportionately by blacks, and black men in particular. In 2003, 44 percent of the people who were in prison or jail were black. More than 12 percent of black men between the ages of 25 and 29 were either in prison or in jail in 2004.[14] This percentage will increase substantially over the next two decades if current trends continue.

In 2001, the last year for which full data are available, the country spent almost $170 billion on law enforcement, including the costs of running the courts and the jails.[15] By comparison, public expenditure on education in the 2000–2001 school year was $560 billion (*Economic Report of the President, 2005*, table 1386). With the cost of law enforcement approaching one-third the amount the government spends educating children, improved education could improve life prospects and reduce crime and incarceration rates. This would mean substantial savings to the government in a relatively short period of time, plus the obvious societal benefits from a lower crime rate.

Trends in Healthcare Costs

The United States already spends a far larger share of its GDR on health care than other wealthy countries. In 2005 the United States spent 15.6 percent of its GDR on health care—nearly twice the average for wealthy countries. Remarkably, the country has very little to show in the way of outcomes for this spending. It ranks near the bottom of the industrialized world in both life expectancy and infant mortality rates. Table 9.9 shows spending per capita on health care among OECD countries, along with life expectancies. As can be seen, the United States ranks second from the bottom in terms of life expectancy (Denmark is slightly lower), but its healthcare expenditures per capita are more than twice the average for other wealthy countries.

While Table 9.9 presents a bleak picture of the U.S. healthcare system, it is likely to look even worse in the future. Healthcare costs have been rising rapidly, and they are projected to continue to rise at a rapid pace in the foreseeable future. Figure 9.3 shows the Centers for Medicare and Medicaid Services (CMS) projections for the increase in healthcare spending over the next two decades. By 2025, healthcare spending is projected to increase by an amount that is nearly equal to 5 full percentage points of GDR. This would be $630 billion in 2005, or more than $2,100 per person.

If the growth of healthcare costs in the United States follows this pattern, the gap in healthcare spending between the United States and other countries

TABLE 9.9 International Comparisons of Life Expectancy and Healthcare Costs

	Life Expectancy at Birth (1999)	Cost Per Capita PPP (2001)
Australia	79.0	$2,513
Austria	78.1	$2,191
Belgium	77.6	$2,490
Canada	79.0	$2,792
Denmark	76.6	$2,503
Finland	77.4	$1,841
France	78.8	$2,561
Germany	77.7	$2,808
Greece	78.1	$1,511
Iceland	79.6	$2,643
Italy	79.0	$2,212
Japan	80.6	$2,131
Netherlands	77.9	$2,626
New Zealand	78.3	$1,710
Norway	78.4	$2,920
Spain	78.6	$1,600
Sweden	79.5	$2,270
United Kingdom	77.4	$1,992
Non-U.S. average	**78.4**	**$2,295**
United States	**76.7**	**$4,887**

Source: OECD Health Care Statistics, 2004.
Note: PPP stands for purchasing power parity.

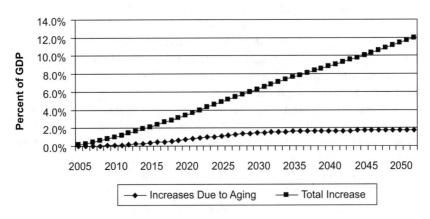

Figure 9.3 The growth in healthcare spending as a share of GDP.

will be more than 10 percentage points of GDR by 2025. This would amount to $1.2 trillion a year, given the current size of the U.S. economy, or $16,000 for an average family of four. In terms of U.S. competitiveness, if the additional expenditures do not add anything to the quality of health care in the United States, the unnecessary expense of the U.S. healthcare system is equivalent to imposing a tax of this magnitude on the U.S. economy. While the health care of people at the top of the income spectrum in the United States is comparable to the care received by high-income people in other countries, the health care of the bottom 60 percent in the United States is notably worse than in other wealthy countries, in spite of the much higher spending in the United States (see Keating and Hertzman, 2000).

Prospects for the Future

The Near Term: Getting Trade on a Sustainable Path

Current trends in the U.S. economy and society suggest that the country may face very serious problems in the decades ahead. The economy is already on a path that virtually all economists recognize is unsustainable for any substantial period of time. It is running a current account deficit of almost $800 billion a year, or almost 7 percent of GDR. This is the amount of money that the United States must borrow from abroad each year to cover its trade deficit, which is mostly attributable to manufactured goods that can be bought more cheaply elsewhere than in the United States. On its current path of borrowing, the net debt of the United States will exceed the total value of the stock market in little more than a decade. The net debt of the United States will exceed the combined value of both the stock market and national stock of housing in little more than two decades if the trade deficit remains constant relative to the size of the economy.

Until the 1980s the United States was actually building up financial assets from other countries. In fact, in 1980 the United States was the world's largest international creditor. During the 1980s and 1990s the United States began to borrow heavily from other nations; first it ran down its net asset position, eventually becoming a net debtor in the mid-1990s.

At the moment, the United States is able to borrow enough money to cover its trade deficit primarily because foreign central banks (most importantly the Japanese and Chinese central banks) are buying vast amounts of U.S. dollars in order to sustain the dollar's value. This point is important, because it means that the U.S. trade deficit is not being sustained by investors who think they will get a good return on their investments in the United States—there are not enough investors who believe that they can get a good return on their U.S. investments to support the current value of the dollar.

Rather, the dollar is being supported by foreign governments that think that keeping a high dollar is good for their own economies.

By keeping the value of the dollar high against their own currencies, these foreign central banks are able to ensure that the price of their exports is low for consumers in the United States. (In other words, Japan's central bank uses yen to buy dollars to keep the dollar high against the Japanese yen.) This sustains the demand for the foreign countries' exports, helping to boost their economies. Effectively, these foreign central banks are paying consumers in the United States to buy their products by buying up vast amounts of dollars every year.

However, there is no reason that these foreign central banks have to pay people in the United States to buy their exports. They can pay consumers in Argentina, Germany, Mozambique, or anywhere else to buy their exports. They can also pay their own consumers to buy their products. In other words, being able to buy things is not a unique attribute of consumers in the United States. At the moment it may be convenient for Japan, China, and other countries with large amounts of exports to the United States to keep current trading patterns in place, but there is no reason to believe that they will be interested in maintaining this pattern over time. At some point the central banks that are presently propping up the dollar will look to other foreign markets, or more likely simply look to have domestic demand to replace the demand currently being filled by exports to the United States.

When foreign central banks stop propping up the dollar, the dollar will fall to a level that will lead to more balanced trade flows. This decline in the dollar will have both positive and negative effects. The main positive effect will be that U.S. goods and services will suddenly become far more competitive in the international economy. If the dollar declines by 30–40 percent (the likely range needed to bring the trade deficit down to a sustainable level), American goods and services will be 30–40 percent cheaper to foreign consumers, while foreign goods and services will be 30–40 percent more expensive for American consumers.[16] This change in relative prices will allow the United States to compete in many sectors where it is not currently competitive.

However, a sharp fall in the dollar will also have large effects on living standards in the United States. Imports currently account for approximately 16 percent of domestic consumption. If the price of imports were to rise by 30 percent on average, a decline of 4.8 percent in living standards (16 percent multiplied by 30 percent) would result. This would be a sharp decline in living standards that would be especially painful if it occurred rapidly.

Furthermore, the process implied by this decline could make the effect even worse. Most immediately, the decline in the dollar and the resulting rise in import prices would manifest themselves in the form of higher inflation.

Typically, the Fed responds to higher inflation by raising interest rates, which slows the economy and raises the unemployment rate. Eventually, a high unemployment rate puts enough downward pressure on wages to squeeze inflation out of the system. However, this process can be fairly long and painful. It may require four or five years of unemployment that is 2–3 percentage points above current levels in order to offset the inflation that results from higher import prices.

The exact timing and nature of this adjustment process are impossible to predict, but the fact that the U.S. economy will require some adjustment of this sort is indisputable. There is no way that it can continue to borrow money from abroad at anywhere near its current pace. Just as it was necessary for the Japanese stock and real estate bubble of the 1980s to burst before Japan's economy could expand again on a stable path, it will be necessary for the U.S. dollar bubble to burst before the United States can move forward again on a sustainable path. The adjustment process to this bursting will inevitably be painful, and it can be made worse by poor policy responses. In the case of Japan, the economy has still not fully recovered from the collapse of its bubbles after fifteen years.

The Longer Term: After the Adjustment

It is difficult to project with confidence what the longer-term path of the U.S. economy will be after the adjustment to a large decline in the dollar is completed. This section speculates on some of the factors that will play an important role in shaping the economy over the next two decades.

MANUFACTURING

Part of the problem is that some of the current trends, most notably the sharp decline in the manufacturing sector, are a direct result of the overvalued dollar. When the dollar falls to a sustainable level, this trend will be at least in part reversed, as the United States will move closer to a balance in its trade of manufactured goods.

While a fall in the dollar is unlikely to restore manufacturing employment to anywhere near its share of employment of the 1970s or even the 1980s, there is likely to be a substantial rise in manufacturing jobs for a period of several years, as the country produces items domestically that it currently imports.

Currently, manufacturing employment is just over 10 percent of total employment; the increase in domestic production needed to address the trade deficit could increase manufacturing employment by as much as 40 percent, or by an amount equal to 4 percent of total employment. Given current wage patterns, specifically the premium that manufacturing workers typically enjoy in wages and benefits over nonmanufacturing workers with the same education and skill level, this rise in manufacturing employment is likely to provide a substantial boost to the situation of many workers without college degrees.

However, the rise in manufacturing employment associated with the elimination of the trade deficit is likely to be only a temporary respite when measured against a longer-term trend. It is likely that productivity in manufacturing will continue to outpace overall productivity growth, as it has for as long as it has been measured. This means that any rise in the manufacturing share of total employment because of the elimination of the trade deficit will gradually be reduced over the following decades because of differential trends in productivity growth.

If the prospect of a one-time jump in manufacturing employment is a potential positive for many workers, the rest of the picture is much less so. The most important economic issue is likely to be the continuing rise in healthcare costs projected by the CMS and others. This will make health care ever less affordable with time in both the public and the private sector. In the public sector, rising healthcare costs will impose an ever greater strain on budgets at all levels of government. This will force either major cutbacks in programs such as Medicare and Medicaid, large cuts in other areas of government spending, or substantial tax increases. Any of these outcomes will be extremely unpopular politically.

Health Care

Rising healthcare costs in the private sector will lead more employers to roll back healthcare coverage and require larger copayments from workers; in many cases, employers may eliminate coverage altogether. In either case, workers' access to adequate health care will become more tenuous. In addition, rising healthcare costs will impose a large burden on employers that continue to provide coverage. While they will attempt to cover some of their healthcare costs by limiting workers' pay increases, inevitably a portion of the increase in healthcare costs will be absorbed by firms (at least in the short term), forcing them to raise prices and/or accept lower profit margins.

The projections show that in twenty years' time the United States will be paying approximately 10 percentage points *more* of its GDR to pay for health care than its competitors. This is an enormous drain that will put U.S. firms at a serious disadvantage internationally. It would be comparable to creating a department of government waste that taxed the country $1.2 trillion a year in 2005 to do absolutely nothing. If the country does nothing to reform its healthcare system and bring its costs more in line with those of its international competitors, it will pay a very large price in future decades in terms of both the health of its citizens and the economy.

THE PRISON SYSTEM

The situation with the country's large and growing prison population presents a comparable problem, if on a somewhat smaller scale. While the growth of the prison population has slowed somewhat from its rate in the 1980s and early 1990s, even the slower growth rate of the past five years still implies that 3.6 million people will be incarcerated in twenty years. In addition to the human tragedy associated with such a large population of prisoners, the projected economic costs are enormous. The direct cost of keeping a person incarcerated for one year was more than $30,000 in 2001, an amount that is higher than one year's tuition at all but the most expensive colleges.[17]

This is an enormous loss of potential human resources, as millions of people who would otherwise be productive members of society are instead held behind bars. Of course, this loss is even greater than is indicated by the numbers who are incarcerated at a moment of time. Millions more people will have their lives, their careers, and their families disrupted by spending time in prison. Often it will be difficult for them to pick up where they had left off, after spending two or three years in jail or prison.

The projected growth path for the prison population also implies substantial growth in public expenditures on corrections. Assuming that the slower growth path of the past four years is sustained, by 2025 the country will be spending an amount equal to 2.7 percent of its GDR (approximately $340 billion a year at the 2005 level of GDR) on its corrections system. This expenditure will be another source of competitive drag relative to other wealthy countries. The correction system in most European countries costs just 0.1–0.2 percent of their GDR.

There is no simple answer to crime and the factors leading to a growing prison population. However, it is important to note that the United States is the only wealthy country that seems to have this sort of problem. Rates of incarceration in other wealthy countries are less than a quarter (in some cases less than one-tenth) the rate in the United States. There are many important differences between the United States and other wealthy countries, but it is worth noting that no other wealthy country has the same degree of inequality as the United States or the lack of social protections in the form of health insurance and other public services to assist the poor. It is also worth noting that the huge gap in incarceration rates between the United States and the rest of the world is a relatively recent phenomenon, as the number of people incarcerated in the United States quadrupled in the past quarter-century. It is reasonable to believe that an alternative set of public policies in the United States could lead to a substantial reduction in the size of the prison and jail population.

EDUCATION

The United States is facing a situation in which it is rapidly losing whatever advantage it had in the quality of the education of its workforce. Most European countries already had workforces that were educated comparable to, if not better than, the workforce in the United States. This was true both at the level of skills of a typical worker, and also in terms of the percentage of the workforce with advance training in science and education. The levels of performance of schoolchildren on standardized exams suggests that the workers currently coming out of European school systems may already have more skills on average than their U.S. counterparts.

However, the biggest change on the horizon is the rapid educational upgrading that is occurring in Asia—especially in China and India. On recent trends, China will soon far exceed the United States in the numbers of students it graduates each year with advanced degrees in science and engineering. India is probably not too far behind on this trajectory. While the United States was by far the world leader in these areas forty years ago, it will soon be trailing not only the EU but also China and India. Already the United States relies on foreign-born workers to fill a large and rapidly growing share of its jobs requiring advanced training in science and engineering. Whether it will continue to attract such workers, as the economies in their home countries continue to achieve rapid growth, is an open question.

With Europe already ahead of the United States by many measures of educational achievement, and China and India rapidly gaining, the ability of the United States to maintain any important edge over its competitors in the quality of its workforce is very much in doubt. It is troubling that students in the United States have failed to achieve substantial gains in most areas over the past two decades. This is especially troubling in the case of black and Hispanic children. The gap between the performance of black and white students, and Hispanic and white students, has not been narrowed over the past fifteen years. White students are rapidly diminishing as a share of the total student population. If the performance of these minority groups does not substantially improve, it will lead to a reduction in overall performance because of a change in composition.

In this sense, improving the educational attainments of blacks and Hispanics is not simply a question of social justice. Given their growing share of the student population and the future workforce, improving the educational performance of these groups is necessary if the United States is going to maintain a highly skilled workforce in future decades. If nothing is done to address current gaps in educational performance, the U.S. economy is likely to suffer from having a less skilled workforce, and blacks and Hispanics will suffer as a result from having fewer opportunities for well-paid jobs.

Conclusion

The U.S. economy has gone through a quarter-century in which the bulk of the gains from economic growth have gone to those at the top of the income distribution. Most workers have seen only a small portion of these gains. This is in sharp contrast to the experience of the thirty years immediately following the end of World War II, during which the economy grew rapidly and the gains were widely shared. Much of this shift was due to conscious policy, as the country pursued trade and regulatory policies that had the effect of putting downward pressure on the wages of most of the workforce and leaving those at the top protected.

The current path has several features that make it unsustainable. Most importantly, the large trade deficit is clearly not sustainable. As soon as foreign central banks stop supporting the dollar by massive purchases of U.S. financial assets, the dollar will plummet and bring the trade deficit down to a manageable level. In addition, the United States also has a path of spending on health care that will not be sustainable indefinitely. If it continues on its current course, the gap between the United States and its competitors on expenditures for health care will be approximately 10 percentage points of GDP—the equivalent of $1.2 trillion in 2005. It is difficult to see how businesses in the United States can absorb this sort of extra expense and still remain competitive internationally.

The growth trend in the prison population poses a similar if smaller problem. On its current path, the size of the incarcerated population will increase to 3.6 million by 2025. Spending on corrections will rise to 2.7 percent of GDR, the equivalent of $340 billion in 2005. If the country continues on this path, it will incur an enormous economic cost that is attributable to the loss of many potentially productive workers and the expenses associated with a corrections system of this size.

Finally, the United States has been seriously lagging in the educational attainment of its students. This shows up as scores on international achievement tests that are well below the scores of students in other countries. It also shows up in the rapid decline in the portion of advanced degrees in science and engineering that go to students from the United States. The United States is already heavily dependent on immigrant workers to fill jobs in science and engineering. It is likely to become substantially more dependent on immigrant workers in these areas if it does not substantially improve the quality of the education its students are receiving.

This is an especially serious problem in the case of black and Hispanic students, whose performances continue to lag substantially behind those of white students. The failure to reduce or eliminate the gaps between the black and Hispanic population and the white population along a wide variety of measures will have increasing consequences as the share of these groups in the nation's population grows over the next few decades. As has been noted in this discussion, in addition to the gap in educational outcomes there is also a large gap in income. There is an even larger gap in wealth, with the average wealth of black and Hispanic families nearing retirement being just over 40 percent of the average wealth of whites in the same age group (Wolff, 2002, table 10).

In short, the United States will face many serious challenges in the next two decades. Its current path does not look very promising for large segments of the population, or for its overall economic prospects. However, it will not be easy to shift it to a more viable long-term path.

Notes

1. These data are taken from the Department of Education 2005, *The Digest of Educational Statistics 2004*, tables 280, 282, 283, 288, 289, 290 (http://nces.ed.gov/programs/digest/d04/lt3.asp#c3a_5).
2. Data on the declining percentage of the workforce receiving employer-provided health insurance can be found in Mishel *et al.* (2005, table 2.14). Data on the diminishing rate of dependent coverage can be found in Boushey and Wright (2004).
3. These data are taken from the Census Department, "Projected Population Change in the United States by Race and Hispanic Origin: 2000–2050," available at http://www.census.gov/ipc/www/usinterimproj/natprojtab01b.pdf.
4. This is the increase in real hourly compensation for workers in nonfarm business sectors shown in the Bureau of Labor Statistics productivity data, available at the "Get Detailed Statistics" portion of its website (http://data.bls.gov/cgi-bin/dsrv).
5. The year 1979 is used as the base for these comparisons because it was the peak year of a business cycle.
6. This measure of productivity growth uses the consumer price index (CPI) as a deflator, rather than the GDP deflator, which is the standard method. The CPI is used as a deflator in order to measure productivity and wage growth against a common denominator; insofar as the CPI measure of inflation differs from the GDP deflator, it would be reasonable to expect a gap between wage and productivity growth. Using a common denominator eliminates this effect.
7. A worker at the 10th percentile earns more than 10 percent of all workers, and less than 90 percent, a worker at the 50th percentile earns more than 50 percent of all workers and less than 50 percent, etc.
8. There is a deterioration in the situation for immigrant women as well, although the falloff is not as large. Issues about sample size, labor force participation, and composition also make it more difficult to assess the situation of immigrant women.
9. These data are based on census data on income, adjusted for differences in living expenses (Berube and Tiffany, 2004).
10. This calculation assumes that half of the trade deficit is completely made up by higher levels of domestic manufacturing output; the other half would correspond to either reduced domestic consumption or increased production of nonmanufactured items. For purposes of the calculation it is assumed that the value of manufacturing output in 2004 is equal to $1,593.2 billion. This is derived by adjusting the nominal value of manufacturing output in 2002 of $1,448.4 billion (*Economic Report of the President, 2004*, table B-12) upward by 10 percent to approximate growth and inflation.
11. These data can be found in the detailed statistics section of the Bureau of Labor Statistics website (www.bls.gov).
12. In the first quarter of 2000 the United States was running a surplus in its service trade at an annual rate of $81.4 billion, or 0.8 percent of GDP. In the second quarter of 2005 (the most recent quarter for which data are available), this surplus had fallen to a $70.3 billion annual rate, or 0.6 percent of GDP (Bureau of Economic Analysis, 2004, *National Income and Product Accounts*, table 4.2.5).

While the outsourcing of some relatively high-paying service-sector jobs, such as computer software designers, has received considerable attention recently, it is not clear exactly what is at issue. In many cases, the import of the service and the import of a finished product are substitutes; the software or the computer that uses the software can be imported if the services of the computer engineer are not imported. The United States has been importing large volumes of high-tech equipment for more than a decade, so it is not clear that there is anything qualitatively different about the recent pattern of foreign outsourcing of many high-tech service jobs.

13. The Census Bureau projects that the black share of the school-age population will be 15.5 percent by 2020, while the Hispanic share will reach 22.9 percent (Projections of the Population by Age, Sex, Race, and Hispanic Origin for the United States: 1999–2100, Middle Series), http://www.census.gov/population/projections/nation/detail/d2011_20.pdf. While this projection implies a near-constant share for blacks, the Hispanic share of the school-age population was just 14.7 percent in 2000.

14. These data are taken from "Facts About Prisons and Prisoners," The Sentencing Project 2005, http//www.sentencingproject.org/pdfs/1035pdf.

15. Justice Department, Bureau of Justice Statistics, 2004. "Justice Expenditure and Employment, 2001," http://www.ojp.usdoj.gov/bjs/pub/pdf/jeeus01.pdf.

16. This is somewhat of a simplification. Changes in currency prices will not be passed on one to one in export and import prices; part of the change in currency prices will be absorbed in lower profit margins.

17. Justice Department, Bureau of Justice Statistics 2004, "Justice Expenditure and Employment 2001," http://www.ojp.usdoj.gov/bjs/abstract/jeeus01.htm. This number only includes the cost of actually keeping a person incarcerated. It does not include the cost of operating the criminal justice system.

References

Berube, A. and T. Tiffany, 2004. *The Shape of the Curve: Household Income Distribution in U.S. Cities 1979–99*. Washington, DC: Brookings Institution.

Boushey, H. and J. Wright, 2004. "Access to Employer Provided Health Insurance as a Dependent on a Family Member's Plan." Washington, DC: Center for Economic and Policy Research. Available at http://www.cepr.net/publications/hi_4_2004_04.html.

Brookings Institution Center on Urban and Metropolitan Policy, 2001. *Census 2000 Matters: Racial Change in the Nation's Largest Cities: Evidence from the 2000 Census*. Washington, DC: Brookings Institution.

Bureau of Labor Statistics, 2004. "Employment Projections by Major Industry," table 1. Available at http://www.bls.gov/news.release/ecopro.t01.htm. Wage data are for July, 2004, from the Bureau of Labor Statistics, 2004, *The Employment Situation: July 2004*.

Economic Report of the President, 2004. Washington, DC: U.S. Government Printing Office.

Economic Report of the President, 2005. Washington, DC: U.S. Government Printing Office.

Freeman, R. 2005. "Does Globalization of the Scientific/Engineering Workforce Threaten U.S. Economic Leadership?" Cambridge, MA: National Bureau of Economic Research Working Paper 11457.

Keating, D. and C. Hertzman (eds.), 2000. *Developmental Health and the Wealth of Nations: Social, Biological, and Educational Dynamics*. New York: Guilford Press.

Mishel, L., J. Bernstein, and H. Boushey, 2003. *The State of Working America, 2002–2003*. Ithaca, NY: Cornell University Press.

Mishel, L., J. Bernstein, and S. Allegretto, 2005. *The State of Working America, 2004–2005*. Ithaca, NY: Cornell University Press.

Weisbrot, M. and D. Baker, 2004. "Fool's Gold: Projections of the U.S. Import Market." Washington, DC: Center for Economic and Policy Research. Available at http://www.cepr.net/Import_Projections.htm.

Wolff, E. 2002. *Retirement Insecurity: The Income Shortfalls Awaiting the Soon-to-Retire*. Washington, DC: Economic Policy Institute.

CHAPTER 10

Prospects and Pitfalls of
Fair Housing Enforcement Efforts

GREGORY D. SQUIRES

> The housing market and discrimination sort people into different
> neighborhoods, which in turn shape residents' lives—and deaths.
> Bluntly put, some neighborhoods are likely to kill you.
>
> (Logan 2003: 33)

Whites and nonwhites continue to live in separate neighborhoods almost
forty years after the Fair Housing Act (the Act) was signed into law. There
may be contentious debate over why it persists, but the fact of segregation
cannot be denied. Equally contentious is the debate over what, if anything,
should be done. Do whites and nonwhites live in separate communities by
choice? If so, perhaps current demographic patterns are of little consequence.
Do these patterns merely reflect economic differences across racial and ethnic
groups? Then the answer might be simply to employ different economic
policies—in particular, better education and training opportunities for racial
and ethnic minorities. Or do they reflect the values of an underclass that
chooses not to be part of mainstream America? In that case, prison might be
the appropriate response.

But virtually all observers agree (at least publicly) that there is no room
for racial and ethnic discrimination in housing markets and that antidiscrimination laws should be enforced. If this is not the top priority, most
agree this is at least one of the tools that belong in the toolbox. But in the
court of public opinion it is not clear that residential segregation remains a
critical problem or that much should be done. Efforts to do so are often

labeled social engineering that accomplishes little more than interfering with the freedom of individuals to choose housing within the limits of their financial resources. Yet social science evidence demonstrates clearly that current housing patterns do not simply reflect individual choice or differing economic capacity and that there are serious consequences of continued racial and ethnic segregation. These consequences affect not only those minority families who are steered to minority neighborhoods but all residents of a region.

Ironically, some recent directions in fair housing enforcement—that is, initiatives intended to bring justice to and provide security for marginalized groups—may have inadvertently undermined efforts to meet the initial goal of the Act to combat discrimination against blacks, who clearly continue to be the most disfavored group protected by the Act. The opportunity costs of new enforcement efforts raise questions that fair housing advocates may choose to ignore, but those costs (including the continuing costs of segregation) do not go away just because they are not subject to scrutiny. The following pages summarize the key lessons that previous chapters have spelled out and offer caveats for future law enforcement efforts.

Causes and Consequences of Segregation

As the contributions to this book demonstrate, there are many costs of housing discrimination and segregation. Denial of access to the home or neighborhood of one's choice adversely affects subsequent generations' educational opportunities, which creates barriers to mobility early in life. As McKoy and Vincent argue in Chapter 4, housing policy is, in many respects, education policy. Segregated housing contributes to employment inequality, particularly for blacks, as Turner delineates in Chapter 5. In Chapter 6, Acevedo-Garcia and Osypuk demonstrate how access to housing and access to health care are intricately linked. Denying housing or neighborhood choice, or permitting homeownership only on predatory terms (as Engel and McCoy demonstrate in Chapter 3 is increasingly the case in minority communities), severely limits the ability to accumulate wealth, because homeownership is a primary vehicle for wealth accumulation. Access to a wide range of amenities through participation in social networks and the accumulation of social capital is severely restricted by segregation, as Kleit reveals in Chapter 7.

But it is not just minority households or central city residents who pay. The persistence of ghettos and barrios in the nation's metropolitan areas, whether in central cities or inner-ring suburbs, undercuts the economic growth, political stability, and social development of entire regions. Cities with large poor populations and high levels of concentrated poverty pay more for a range of public services, including education, police, health care, and fire protection, which increases taxes and reduces their ability to attract middle-class families. High levels of racial segregation reduce the economic productivity of regional economies and increase the cost of policing and providing other services to marginalized groups. Suburbs of depressed cities see less appreciation in housing prices and incomes because of the interdependence of regional economies. Metropolitan areas that exhibit particularly high levels of income inequality grow more slowly than those where income is distributed more equally (Katz 2006; Dreier *et al.* 2004; Bollens 2002). In turn, the competitiveness of the nation's economy generally is undercut, as Baker and Boushey establish in Chapter 9. Uneven development is costly to all parts of many metropolitan areas and to the United States overall in an increasingly global economy.

Racial segregation (if not hypersegregation) coupled with concentrated poverty and urban sprawl reflect and reinforce broader patterns of inequality that have framed the development of the U.S. economy and society generally for at least the past thirty years (Squires and Kubrin 2006; Rusk 1999; Orfield 2007). It is common knowledge and widely accepted by all ends of the political spectrum from the *Wall Street Journal* to *The Nation* that income and wealth have become much more unequally distributed in recent decades. If some central city neighborhoods are making a comeback, it is also the case that economic inequality across metropolitan neighborhoods has increased in recent years (Booza *et al.* 2006). While nationwide measures of segregation have declined for blacks in recent years, black segregation has stubbornly persisted at very high levels in those communities (e.g., New York, Chicago, Detroit) where the black population is concentrated (as Ellen shows in Chapter 8) and segregation of Hispanics and Asians has increased (Dreier *et al.* 2004; Iceland *et al.* 2002). But, as the contributors to this book have demonstrated, these patterns cannot be accounted for by voluntary choices made by individuals in freely competitive markets. They are not primarily the result of economic inequality or a growing underclass that rejects education and work as the keys to moving up and out. Rather, these demographic patterns reflect a range of intentional public policy decisions and private-sector actions that have created many schisms associated with race, class, and other nonmeritocratic markers in American society.

Examples include Federal Housing Administration policies that virtually excluded blacks from federally insured mortgage loans for the first thirty years of that program's operation. Enforcement of racially restrictive covenants helped create the segregated housing patterns that persist. Concentration of public housing in central cities, urban renewal, and federally subsidized highways to facilitate the commute of white suburbanites to their downtown jobs also put the federal stamp of approval on segregation.

Exclusionary zoning laws by virtually all suburbs continue to reinforce the traditional racial demography of the nation's cities and suburbs.

But government has not acted alone. The private sector also contributed, and continues to do so. Blockbusting by unscrupulous real estate agents and their allies among mortgage lending institutions dramatically turned white neighborhoods into black communities in the 1950s and 1960s. Redlining by mortgage lenders and property insurers, along with various predatory practices by financial institutions, perpetuate segregation while stripping equity and wealth from unwary homebuyers along the way. Racial steering by real estate agents, which continues to be documented by fair housing groups on a seemingly daily basis, continues to reinforce segregated patterns established by many powerful institutional actors. In Chapter 2, Massey traces the effect of these practices on the racial and ethnic demography of metropolitan America (see Massey and Denton 1993; Jackson 1985; Gotham 2002; National Fair Housing Alliance 2006a).

The good news is that if intentional policy and practice got us where we are today, other policies and practices can move us in a different direction. And there is some evidence that this is already taking place. Enactment of the earned income tax credit has reduced poverty among working families (Holt 2006). Living wage ordinances in more than 100 communities have lifted the income of many workers well above the minimum wage (Pollin 2005; Pollin and Luce 2002). More than 100 communities have also passed inclusionary zoning laws to increase the supply of affordable housing in previously unaffordable neighborhoods (Rusk 1999). The Gautreaux program in Chicago and the Moving to Opportunity program in five major metropolitan areas have enabled some poor families to move to healthier and safer neighborhoods (Rubinowitz and Rosenbaum 2000; Polikoff 2006; Goering and Feins 2003). The Community Reinvestment Act has generated more than $4 trillion for investment in traditionally underserved neighborhoods (National Community Reinvestment Coalition 2005). The National Fair Housing Alliance (NFHA) and its members have generated $225 million for plaintiffs in their efforts to enforce the Act (National Fair Housing Alliance 2006b).

If progress has been made, much remains to be done. There are no magic bullets. But one essential step to achieving a just and secure economy is equal housing opportunity, unfettered by many long-standing, explicit (and, in recent years, subtle) forms of racial and ethnic discrimination. And one essential tool is effective fair housing law enforcement. Fair housing activities have taken on many new directions in recent years. Additional protected groups (e.g., families with children, handicapped people) and new issues (e.g., immigrant rights) have emerged as part of the fair housing movement. A question that emerged is whether the initial objectives of the Act are being sacrificed in the process.

The Opportunity Costs of Fair Housing Enforcement

In the real world, where the scarcity of resources is all too real, investments we choose to make utilize resources that become unavailable for other uses. Such investment alternatives are what economists refer to as opportunity costs (Rhoads 1994: 11–24). The pursuit of selected fair housing goals utilizes resources and limits the capacity of law enforcement agents to pursue others. The opportunity costs of fair housing enforcement are quite real.

Some current trends and proposed directions in fair housing enforcement may inadvertently undercut efforts to achieve essential fair housing objectives. These developments include the expansion of protected classes, the emergence of new and the seeming disappearance of old unresolved issues, and proposed tools for realizing fair housing objectives. The opportunity costs of such developments are often hidden by the attention paid to the problems that current and proposed activities are designed to ameliorate. It is difficult to argue against virtually any action designed to remedy an inequity—unless there are other severe or long-standing inequities that persist as a result of that action. For example, if the Department of Housing and Urban Development (HUD) were to prosecute the landlord of a six-unit apartment building who refused to rent to families with children, the action would normally be applauded by the fair housing community—unless it were undertaken instead of a secretary-initiated systemic complaint investigation of a rental agency that managed several hundred units and refused to rent to racial minorities. These costs (i.e., the failure to prosecute the systemic investigation) may not have been taken into consideration by proponents when the initial action (e.g., prosecution of the family case) was proposed. This suggests a need for more open policy debate so that these costs do not remain hidden.

However, there may be unintended costs to such open debate. An already fragile fair housing movement could be further splintered and weakened by such a discussion. So, the primary policy objective for fair housing advocates should be to organize for substantially more public and private funding for enforcement, including funds for the creation of more nonprofit fair housing organizations to address new issues and the emergent needs of multiple protected class members (Bowdler and Kamasaki 2007).

Failure to generate more resources will mean that investment in the growing number of protected groups with legitimate grievances or in new issues that arise will threaten resources for traditional fair housing constituencies and concerns. This could lead to increasing alienation from a system of rights that fails to provide any realistic chance of obtaining justice in a fair and timely manner. The political and policy bottom line is that unless more resources are obtained, the currently scarce enforcement dollars will be insufficient for ongoing and emerging claims, and the fledgling interethnic coalitions that have begun to create a more effective fair housing movement could be permanently destabilized and undercut.

Diversity and the Growth of Protected Classes: Bane or Blessing for Fair Housing Enforcement?

That race relations in the United States are no longer a black/white issue is a truism today. Academic and policy representatives of the right, left, and center acknowledge and acclaim the growing diversity of the U.S. population (Thernstrom and Thernstrom 1997; Brown *et al.* 2003; Iceland *et al.* 2002). Diversity is not just a matter of race but extends to ethnicity, religion, gender, disability status, culture, sexual preference, and other lifestyle features (Krysan and Lewis 2004).

When the Act was amended in 1988, two new protected groups were included: the disabled and families with children. A question that arises is whether such changes may compromise efforts to combat housing discrimination against blacks, the original focus of the law and still perceived and treated as the most disadvantaged protected group. Levels of segregation have long been, and continue to be, higher for blacks than for other minority groups, as Massey explains in Chapter 2 (see also Iceland *et al.* 2002). Blacks are less able to translate income and other measures of socioeconomic status into better neighborhoods (e.g., areas where housing values are greater) or more integrated settings (Alba *et al.* 2000; Logan 2002). Black households are also identified by others as the least desirable neighbors when asked to describe their ideal neighborhoods. When asked to describe their neighborhood preferences, one-fifth of whites opted for a neighborhood without blacks, as did one-third of Hispanics and more than 40 percent of Asians. The share of respondents opting for neighborhoods with no whites, Hispanics, or Asians was smaller for each group (Charles 2005). There is also research evidence that whites deliberately avoid blacks and black areas and that this avoidance results from a clear election to avoid blacks as a racial group and not from those factors often associated with black neighborhoods (e.g., high crime, poor schools). No similar aversion has been found in reference to Asians or Hispanics. In one survey, white respondents indicated they would not purchase a home in a neighborhood that had all the features they claimed they wanted, including safe streets and good schools, if there was a substantial presence of black residents. The presence of Asians or Hispanics exerted no similar adverse effect on whites' stated willingness to purchase such homes (Emerson *et al.* 2001). Other groups, particularly Hispanics, confront persistent and sometimes rising levels of discrimination in U.S. housing markets. That dark-skinned Hispanics face far more discrimination than light-skinned Hispanics suggests that at least some of the barriers they encounter reflect racial rather than ethnic discrimination (Bowdler and Kamasaki 2007; Massey 2001). Blacks remain by far the most disadvantaged of all groups protected by the Act and other civil rights laws.

A question for policy and research discussion is whether the addition of new protected groups by 1988 amendments to the Act, coupled with restricted enforcement resources, adversely affects blacks. The declining number and share of complaints that are investigated alleging racial discrimination against blacks suggest this could be the case. Since the amendments took effect, the share of fair housing complaints filed with state and local Fair Housing Assistance Program (FHAP) agencies that allege racial discrimination dropped from 72 percent in 1990, to 44 percent in 1997, and then to 39 percent in 2003. Correspondingly, between 1990 and 1997 the share of complaints alleging discrimination on the basis of disability grew from 0 percent to 26 percent while familial status complaints increased from 0 percent to 24 percent (Schill and Friedman 1999: 62–63). Among complaints received by members of the NFHA, the share alleging they experienced racial discrimination declined from 39 percent in 1996 to 28 percent in 2002 (National Fair Housing Alliance 2003). Among all complaints filed with both HUD and FHAP agencies between 1990 and 2003, the share alleging discrimination on the basis of race declined from 50 percent to 39 percent and the share alleging discrimination against blacks dropped from 45.0 percent to 33.9 percent. These trends also reflect an absolute drop in the number of race complaints from 3,729 to 3,198 and a drop in the number of black complaints from 3,367 to 2,756 (Sheehy 2003). In 2004, for the first time the number of disability complaints exceeded the number of race complaints (U.S. Department of Housing and Urban Development 2006: 2). During 1996–2000, 26 percent of fair housing complaints referred to the Department of Justice by HUD alleged discrimination on the basis of disability and 33 percent alleged racial discrimination. During 2001–2005, complaints alleging disability constituted 43 percent of fair housing complaints referred to Justice by HUD, while complaints alleging discrimination based on race constituted 25 percent (Rosenbaum 2006).

That the absolute number of race complaints would decline, even just modestly, along with the share of all complaints that they represent, suggests that recent enforcement initiatives may have been less supportive for this particular protected group in recent years. Even assuming a decline in the level of discrimination, the minute share of all such incidents that are formally investigated reveals the limitations of current enforcement efforts. Given that the number of violations of the Act that occur each year is conservatively estimated to be approximately 3.7 million, any reduction in current enforcement efforts constitutes costly steps backward for blacks and racial minorities generally, as well as for other protected groups (National Fair Housing Alliance 2004).

These findings raise several questions. Does the declining share of complaints addressing racial discrimination in general and discrimination against blacks in particular represent the appropriate reallocation of fair housing enforcement priorities and resources? If not, what changes in the law, regulations, enforcement resource allocations, or other enforcement-related activities should be made in the future if the goal is to redress the most serious forms of housing discrimination? Does the new evidence on changing patterns of housing discrimination that have emerged from the Housing Discrimination Study 2000, particularly the increase in steering of blacks, suggest new enforcement emphases (Turner *et al.* 2002b; Ross and Turner 2005)? Again, blacks are not the only protected group experiencing widespread unlawful discrimination. But the question arises as to whether the interests of the most disadvantaged group are being further compromised by recent enforcement efforts. And given the small number of violations that are actually investigated, it is evident that more resources are necessary in any case.

Immigration: The Future of both Fair Housing Enforcement and the American City?

Analogous questions arise as a result of the growing immigrant population in the United States. The population of U.S. cities grew significantly during the 1990s, with one-third of that growth nationwide being attributable to immigrants, particularly Hispanics and Asians (Katz 2003). These groups are expected to contribute even more to future urban population growth. Housing providers, including developers, rental agents, mortgage lenders, and insurers, will necessarily look to the housing needs of immigrants as a key to the maintenance and development of their markets despite problems often associated with these groups, including language barriers, mistrust of traditional financial institutions, and legal complications related to citizenship (Joint Center for Housing Studies of Harvard University 2002; Lipman 2003). In many ways, the growing racial and ethnic diversity of the nation, fueled by recent patterns of immigration, is celebrated as one of the nation's many strengths. But there may be a troubling dimension to this emerging diversity. As Stephen Steinberg has argued, that celebration "has deflected attention away from the unique and unresolved problems of race qua blacks. The result is that the nation congratulates itself on its 'diversity' and celebrates its 'multiculturalism,' while the problems of blacks continue to fester from neglect" (2005: 51). Has the fair housing movement unwittingly deflected attention from the problems of blacks?

This prompts the question whether attention paid to new immigrants by housing providers and fair housing law enforcement agencies detracts from attention that still needs to be paid to the housing needs and problems of racial minorities, most particularly blacks. Added to this is the existence of potentially serious conflicts among blacks and between blacks and newly arriving immigrant families that have been chronicled in movies, television shows, the media, and scholarly literature (Lee 2002). The point is not that immigrants do not confront substantial discriminatory barriers or that enforcement agencies should ignore these needs. The question is whether or not, in the absence of more enforcement resources, the interests of blacks and immigrants will suffer. The 2000 Housing Discrimination Study findings (Turner *et al.* 2002a; Ross and Turner 2005) indicate that levels of discrimination against Hispanics may be reaching those found for blacks. But, as was noted above, levels of segregation for blacks remain much higher than those for other groups. Research shows that blacks are least able to translate their income and other measures of individual socioeconomic status into more valuable homes and better neighborhoods, and are named as the least desirable neighbors by other racial and ethnic groups.

It is important to note the many examples of interracial coalitions in which ethnically and racially diverse groups have successfully organized for housing and related services in neighborhoods previously underserved by public and private entities alike. National coalitions like ACORN, the Center for Community Change, Industrial Areas Foundation, the National Community Reinvestment Coalition, the NFHA, and their individual member organizations have joined together in cities across all regions of the country. They have successfully utilized a variety of tactics and pursued initiatives that include Community Reinvestment Act challenges to increase access to mortgage loans, litigation to provide relief for victims of housing discrimination, creation of community land trusts and passage of inclusionary zoning ordinances to create more affordable housing opportunities, advocacy for living wage ordinances, and other steps to improve related municipal services and nurture private action to expand housing availability on more equitable terms (Alperovitz 2005; Gecan 2002; Pollin 2005; Pollin and Luce 2000; Schuman 1998; Sidney 2003; Warren 2001; Wilson 1999; Williamson *et al.* 2002). The way in which scarce fair housing enforcement resources are allocated could undercut such coalitions and fuel long-standing conflicts in the future.

Predatory Lending: Emerging Issue in Consumer Finance

The emergence of new protected groups and their legitimate claims may constitute one challenge to the unfinished business of the nation's long-standing civil rights movement. The emergence of new issues constitutes another.

Presently, predatory lending is by far the most widely debated issue in the financial services industry. While exploitative practices by financial institutions have a long history (e.g., usurious interest rates, pawn shops, land contracts), there are some new twists to long-standing abusive relationships between financial service providers and at least some segments of their market. Consumer and fair housing advocacy groups, regulators, elected officials, industry trade associations, and lenders themselves have called for reforms to reduce the widely recognized, but not very precisely defined, practice of predatory lending. At the end of 2004, at least thirty-six states, the District of Columbia, three counties, and nine municipalities had enacted laws or regulations to restrict predatory practices. At least five bills regarding predatory lending have been introduced in Congress (Engel and McCoy 2004). Several state and federal regulatory agencies have adopted or proposed rules to preempt local or state rules. Such proposals include new legislation as well as proposed revisions of the Community Reinvestment Act, the Home Ownership Equity Protection Act, and others (ACORN 2003; Squires 2004).

Given all the press, policy, and social science attention to this issue, what happened to statutorily driven concerns about traditional, long-standing issues like redlining and discrimination in the delivery of conventional financial services as forces that restrict fair access to homeownership for protected class members? Attention directed to predatory lending can represent time, energy, and resources not devoted to examining the distribution of conventional mortgage loans by mainstream banks, the opening and closing of branch bank offices, the marketing of conventional loan products, the level of counseling provided to various protected class members under the Act, and a range of other practices that were the subject of significant discrimination complaints up through the mid-1990s (Lee 1999: 39; Goering and Wienk 1996; Turner et al. 2002a).

Predatory lending is undoubtedly a significant problem. The rise of subprime lending, along with its concentration in low-income and minority neighborhoods, and its adverse effect on foreclosure rates, property values, and, consequently, property tax revenues, has been documented (Avery et al. 2005; Squires 2004; Calem et al. 2004; Immergluck and Smith 2005). While the tragic consequences that have befallen victims of predatory lenders have been reported around the nation, and the broader community costs are being documented, the pervasiveness of such practices remains unclear.

It is difficult to determine what level of the public's attention and, more importantly, the public's fair housing enforcement resources should be allocated to this issue. Is traditional fair housing enforcement being shortchanged? Should there be a better basis in policy and program enforcement to balance enthusiasm for current hot topics against persistent patterns of exclusion and differential treatment that may have comparable effects on families' housing options?

Will Insurance Redlining Persist?

As new issues arise, old but unresolved issues persist. An issue that seems to have disappeared from current civil rights enforcement policy debates, perhaps particularly to the detriment of blacks, is insurance redlining. Just a few years ago, this issue was at the heart of many debates throughout the industry, among neighborhood organizations, and within the law enforcement community (Berenbaum 1995; Friedman 1995; Karr 1994; Treaster 1996). In the mid-1990s the president issued an executive order calling for HUD to develop regulations clarifying the application of the Act to the property insurance industry (Executive Order No. 12,892, 59, Fed. Reg. 2939 (1994)), and the House passed a bill that would have called for disclosure for the property insurance industry similar to that required by the Home Mortgage Disclosure Act (H.R. 1188, 103rd Congress, 2nd Session, July 20, 1994). Fair housing groups resolved fair housing complaints with the nation's leading property insurers, including State Farm, Allstate, Nationwide, and American Family (Smith and Cloud 1997). But the insurance redlining practices that were the focus of so much attention in the 1990s are barely on the radar screen of state departments of insurance, which are the primary law enforcement officials for the insurance industry. Interest among most fair housing authorities also appears to have diminished in recent years.

The fair housing settlements and subsequent voluntary initiatives by the insurance industry indicate real progress, but has the insurance redlining problem been solved? Debates over the disparate effect of credit scoring suggest that the nature of the problem may have been changed rather than overcome (Birnbaum 2003; Squires 2003; Texas Department of Insurance 2004). At least forty states have enacted or debated legislation to limit the use of credit scores in insurance underwriting (Tuckey 2003). Should more or less attention be paid to insurance redlining today? In the absence of a Home Mortgage Disclosure Act (HMDA)-like disclosure requirement for the property insurance industry (something that has been repeatedly called for by many fair housing and community reinvestment advocacy groups), it may be difficult to make a rational decision for the allocation of scarce resources to this issue (Luquetta and Goldberg 2001; Squires *et al.* 2001). Such disclosure can provide essential transparency leading to greater efficiency in insurance markets and assist fair housing enforcement efforts, just as the HMDA has done in the area of mortgage lending (Olson 2005).

Education: Some Minds May Not be a Terrible Thing to Waste

As new groups make legitimate claims for fair housing protection and the structure of housing and related financial services evolves, various remedial tools are proposed. One tool that is often cited as critical for the realization of fair housing is education. Education has traditionally been regarded as a key mechanism for solving many of the nation's social problems. For more than a decade, HUD and other enforcement agencies have invested millions of dollars annually in a variety of educational efforts designed to inform consumers of their equal housing rights under the law and to warn providers of those practices that violate the law. There are reasons to question the wisdom of such investment.

Research by Abravenal (2002, 2006) suggests that those who are more informed about fair housing law are more likely to take action when they encounter discrimination. Because enforcement of fair housing rules, and particularly the Act, has come to rely almost exclusively on complaints filed by individual consumers, further education is viewed by many agencies as a critical part of future efforts to improve enforcement. But the fact that the current fair housing enforcement system relies so heavily on *individuals* to file formal complaints has been noted as a critical flaw in that system for years (Massey and Denton 1993; Tisdale 1999).

There is also evidence that many housing providers who understand the law may not comply with it because they believe that they are unlikely to be caught, or that if caught, the consequences will be minimal (Bowdler and Kamasaki 2007). If some who are knowledgeable about the law remain undeterred from practicing discrimination, then at least some educational resources are being wasted.

A wiser strategy would rely less heavily on the education of individual consumers, though first-time homebuyers or immigrants who may be new to the concept of civil rights and fair housing arguably would benefit. A more effective strategy would shift the burden from individual complainants to those public and private *institutions* charged with enforcing and complying with the law. This could take the form of more proactive systemic investigations and paired testing by HUD, the U.S. Department of Justice, financial regulatory agencies, state insurance commissioners, and others (Squires 2002; Schill 2007).

Several nongovernmental entities currently have resources that have been and can continue to be used for fair housing education of housing providers and citizens. University extension services, industry trade associations (including the National Association of Realtors and the Mortgage Bankers Association), advocacy groups (e.g., the National Community Reinvestment Coalition, the NFHA, and the Consumer Federation of America), and public schools can provide education on financial literacy, credit counseling, and people's rights under various fair housing, equal credit, and related consumer protection laws.

Only a small number of entities (primarily HUD under the Act, the U.S. Department of Justice, federal financial regulatory agencies, the Federal Trade Commission, along with state and local enforcement agencies) have enforcement authority and ongoing public funding for enforcement activity. They also allocate funding on a regular basis for education campaigns, the effectiveness of which has rarely been evaluated. Those entities should focus on their fair housing enforcement obligations. This is the area where the opportunity costs of fair housing enforcement are the most explicit: every dollar spent on education is a dollar that is unavailable to pay for more fair housing investigators, attorneys, and support nonprofit fair housing organizations or FHAP agencies. Most importantly, there are fewer resources to launch secretary-initiated complaints, or take other industry- or market-wide enforcement actions.

What Should Fair Housing Advocates Support?

The fair housing infrastructure, fragile as it may be, warrants further investment rather than the current practice of disinvestment. When resources are tight, heavy costs are incurred when dollars invested in one set of activities are not available for other purposes. "Opportunity costs do not go away just because people stop thinking of them" (Rhoads 1994: 23). This suggests the need among fair housing advocates to debate more explicitly and publicly how scarce resources are to be allocated by which agencies and for what goals. But such a debate could splinter what is already a relatively fragile coalition for fair housing enforcement. New groups continually make legitimate claims on the fair housing enforcement apparatus, and new issues as well as remedial strategies will appear as the structure of housing and housing-related industries and behavior adapt and change.

The resources for traditional groups and issues have diminished over time. For example, Fair Housing Initiatives Program (FHIP) funding peaked at $26 million in 1995 and, after fluctuating for a few years, has steadily declined to $17.5 million in 2005 (National Fair Housing Alliance 2005). Existing resources are palpably insufficient, and new demands can be seen clearly on the horizon. Debating the appropriate allocation of declining resources relative to emerging and persistent needs might be self-defeating. Perhaps the appropriate response from the fair housing movement is what Samuel Gompers, the first president of the American Federation of Labor, replied when he was asked what labor wanted; he simply said, "More" (Greider 2003: 10).

Concretely, this means more systemic investigations, expanded use of paired testing, and greater numbers of selected but visible secretary-initiated complaints by HUD. A critical starting point would be restoration of the FHIP budget at least to the 1995 funding level of $26 million and more funds for the operating budgets of fair housing enforcement agencies and nonprofit groups. Reliance on individual complaints depends on the least informed and least financially able participants in housing markets for enforcement (Massey and Denton 1993; Tisdale 1999). Paired testing has been proven to be a particularly effective investigative tool for enforcement in housing, mortgage lending, and property insurance (Fix and Turner 1999). FHIP agencies have been effective in investigating complaints, litigating, and pressuring enforcement agencies to act (National Fair Housing Alliance 2005).

As the nation's population continues to diversify, legitimate new claims for fair housing protection will emerge. As housing and related financial industries continue to evolve, new issues will have to be addressed. And as new enforcement tools are developed, they will have to be evaluated on both substantive and political grounds. For new demands to be met while efforts continue to resolve the remaining unfinished business of the civil rights movement, more resources will be essential.

Opportunity costs are real. A public discussion that focuses on how to develop additional needed resources and then to allocate what will inevitably remain scarce resources need not cripple nascent fair housing coalitions that are developing. *More* remains a critical part of the rallying cry for the fair housing movement and for achieving the broader goals of justice and economic security for all.

References

Abravanel, Martin C. 2002. "Public Knowledge of Fair Housing Law: Does It Protect against Housing Discrimination?" *Housing Policy Debate* 13(3): 469–504.

—— 2006. *Do We Know More Now: Trends in Public Knowledge, Support and Use of Fair Housing Law.* Washington, DC: U.S. Department of Housing and Urban Development, Office of Policy Development and Research.

ACORN. 2003. http://www.acorn.org/campaigns/events.php?c=6 (last accessed on October 2, 2003).

Alba, Richard D., John R. Logan, and Brian J. Stults. 2000. "How Segregated Are Middle Class African Americans?" *Social Problems* 47(4): 543–558.

Alperovitz, Gar. 2005. *America beyond Capitalism: Reclaiming Our Wealth, Our Liberty, and Our Democracy.* Hoboken, NJ: John Wiley.

Avery, Robert B., Glenn B. Canner, and Robert Cook. 2005. "New Information Reported under HMDA and Its Application in Fair Lending Enforcement," *Federal Reserve Bulletin* 91 (summer): 143–172.

Berenbaum, David. 1995. "The Unfair Housing Provision," *Washington Post* (August 16): A19.

Birnbaum, Birny. 2003. "Insurer's Use of Credit Scoring for Homeowners Insurance in Ohio," report to the Ohio Civil Rights Commission (January).

Bollens, Scott A. 2002. "In through the Back Door: Social Equity and Regional Governance," *Housing Policy Debate* 13(4): 631–657.

Booza, Jason C., Jackie Cutsinger, and George Galster. 2006. "Where Did They Go? The Decline of Middle-Income Neighborhoods in Metropolitan America." Washington, DC: Brookings Institution, Metropolitan Policy Program.

Bowdler, Janis and Charles Kamasaki. 2007. "Creating a Fair Housing System That Works for Latinos," in John Goering (ed.) *Fragile Rights within Cities: Government, Housing, and Fairness.* New York: Rowman & Littlefield.

Brown, Michael K., Martin Carnoy, Elliott Currie, Troy Duster, David B. Oppenheimer, Marjorie M. Shultz, and David Wellman. 2003. *White-Washing Race: The Myth of a Color-Blind Society.* Berkeley: University of California Press.

Calem, Paul S., Jonathan E. Hershaff, and Susan M. Wachter. 2004. "Neighborhood Patterns of Subprime Lending: Evidence from Disparate Cities," *Housing Policy Debate* 15(3): 603–622.

Charles, Camille Zubrinsky. 2005. "Can We Live Together?: Racial Preferences and Neighborhood Outcomes," in Xavier de Souza Briggs (ed.) *The Geography of Opportunity: Race and Housing Choice in Metropolitan America.* Washington, DC: Brookings Institution Press.

Dreier, Peter, John Mollenkopf, and Todd Swanstrom. 2004. *Place Matters: Metropolitics for the Twenty-first Century,* 2nd edn. Lawrence: University Press of Kansas.

Emerson, Michael O., Karen J. Chai, and George Yancey. 2001. "Does Race Matter in Residential Segregation? Exploring the Preferences of White Americans," *American Sociological Review* 66(6): 922–935.

Engel, Kathleen C. and Patricia A. McCoy. 2004. "Predatory Lending and Community Development at Loggerheads," paper presented at the Community Development Finance Research Conference, Federal Reserve Bank of New York, New York (December 10).

Fix, Michael and Margery Austin Turner (eds.) 1999. *A National Report Card on Discrimination in America: The Role of Testing.* Washington, DC: The Urban Institute.

Friedman, Sam. 1995. "HUD Will Stay in Your Face on Redlining," *National Underwriter* (April 24): 223.

Gecan, Michael. 2002. *Going Public: An Inside Story of Disrupting Politics as Usual.* Boston: Beacon Press.

Goering, John, and Judith D. Feins. 2003. *Choosing a Better Life: Evaluating the Moving to Opportunity Social Experiment.* Washington, DC: The Urban Institute Press.

Goering, John and Ron Wienk (eds.). 1996. *Mortgage Lending, Racial Discrimination, and Federal Policy.* Washington, DC: The Urban Institute.

Gotham, Kevin Fox. 2002. *Race, Real Estate, and Uneven Development: The Kansas City Experience, 1900–2000.* Albany: State University of New York Press.

Greider, William. 2003. *The Soul of Capitalism: Opening Paths to Moral Economy.* New York: Simon & Schuster.

Holt, Steve. 2006. *The Earned Income Tax Credit at Age 30: What We Know.* Washington, DC: Brookings Institution, Metropolitan Policy Program.

Iceland, John, Daniel H. Weinberg, and Erika Steinmetz. 2002. *Racial and Ethnic Residential Segregation in the United States: 1980–2000.* U.S. Census Bureau, Series CENSR-3. Washington, DC: U. S. Government Printing Office.

Immergluck, Dan and Geoff Smith. 2005. *There Goes the Neighborhood: The Effect of Single-Family Mortgage Foreclosures on Property Values.* Chicago: Woodstock Institute.

Jackson, Kenneth T. 1985. *Crabgrass Frontier: The Suburbanization of the United States.* New York: Oxford University Press.

Joint Center for Housing Studies of Harvard University. 2002. *The State of the Nation's Housing 2002.* Cambridge, MA: Joint Center for Housing Studies of Harvard University.

Karr, Albert R. 1994. "Complaints That Some Insurers Are Redlining Minority Homeowners Get U.S., State Attention," *Wall Street Journal* (April 19): A 22.

Katz, Bruce. 2003. "The New Urban Demographics," presentation at the "Housing in the New Marketplace" Conference Federal Reserve Bank of New York (March 20).

—— 2006. "Concentrated Poverty in New Orleans and Other American Cities," *Chronicle of Higher Education* 52(48): B15.

Krysan, Maria and Amanda E. Lewis. 2004. *The Changing Terrain of Race and Ethnicity.* New York: Russell Sage Foundation.

Lee, Bill Lann. 1999. "An Issue of Public Importance: The Justice Department's Enforcement of the Fair Housing Act," *Cityscape* 4(3): 57–78.

Lee, Jennifer. 2002. *Civility in the City: Blacks, Jews, and Koreans in Urban America*. Cambridge, MA: Harvard University Press.

Lipman, Barbara J. 2003. "America's Newest Working Families: Cost, Crowding and Conditions for Immigrants," *New Century Housing* 4 (3): 1–40.

Logan, John R. 2002. *Separate and Unequal: The Neighborhood Gap for Blacks and Hispanics in Metropolitan America*. Albany: Lewis Mumford Center for Comparative Urban and Regional Research, University at Albany.

—— 2003. "Life and Death in the City: Neighborhoods in Context," *Contexts* 2(2): 33–40.

Luquetta, Andrea and Deborah Goldberg. 2001. "Insuring Investment," *Shelterforce* 23(6): 12–15.

Massey, Douglas S. 2001. "Residential Segregation and Neighborhood Conditions in U.S. Metropolitan Areas," in Neil J. Smelser, William Julius Wilson, and Faith Mitchell (eds.) *America Becoming: Racial Trends and Their Consequences*. Washington, DC: National Academy Press.

Massey, Douglas S. and Nancy Denton. 1993. *American Apartheid: Segregation and the Making of the Underclass*. Cambridge, MA: Harvard University Press.

National Community Reinvestment Coalition. 2005. *CRA Commitments*. Washington, D.C.: National Community Reinvestment Coalition.

National Fair Housing Alliance. 2003. Unpublished data provided by staff of the National Fair Housing Alliance.

—— 2004. *2004 Fair Housing Trends Report*. Washington, DC: National Fair Housing Alliance.

—— 2005. *2005 Fair Housing Trends Report*. Washington, DC: National Fair Housing Alliance.

—— 2006a. *Unequal Opportunity: Perpetuating Housing Segregation in America*. Washington, DC: National Fair Housing Alliance.

—— 2006b. *$225,000,000 and Counting*. Washington, DC: National Fair Housing Alliance.

Olson, Mark W. 2005. "Remarks by Governor Mark W. Olson," Community Development Policy Summit: Exploring the Benefits and Challenges of an Ownership Society, Federal Reserve Bank of Cleveland, Cleveland, OH (July 23).

Orfield, Myron. 1997. *Metropolitics: A Regional Agenda for Community and Stability*. Washington, DC and Cambridge, MA: Brookings Institution Press and the Lincoln Institute of Land Policy.

Polikoff, Alexander. 2006. *Waiting for Gautreaux: A Story of Segregation, Housing, and the Black Ghetto*. Evanston, IL: Northwestern University Press.

Pollin, Robert. 2005. "Evaluating Living Wage Laws in the United States: Good Intentions and Economic Reality in Conflict?" *Economic Development Quarterly* 19(1): 3–24.

Pollin, Robert and Stephanie Luce. 2000. *The Living Wage: Building a Fair Economy*. New York: New Press.

Rhoads, Steven E. 1994. *The Economist's View of the World: Government, Markets, and Public Policy*. New York: Cambridge University Press.

Rosenbaum, Steven H. 2006. Address, "What King Wrought? The Impact of the Summer of 1996 on Housing Rights," conference, Chicago, September 8.

Ross, Stephen L. and Margery Turner. 2005. "Housing Discrimination in Metropolitan America: Explaining Changes between 1989 and 2000," *Social Problems* 52(2): 152–180.

Rubinowitz, Leonard S. and James E. Rosenbaum. 2000. *Crossing the Class and Color Lines: From Public Housing to White Suburbia*. Chicago: University of Chicago Press.

Rusk, David. 1999. *Inside Game Outside Game: Winning Strategies for Saving Urban America*. Washington, DC: Brookings Institution Press.

Schill, Michael. 2007. "Implementing the Federal Fair Housing Act: The Adjudication of Complaints," in John Goering (ed.) *Fragile Rights within Cities: Government, Housing, and Fairness*. New York: Rowman & Littlefield.

Schill, Michael H. and Samantha Friedman. 1999. The Fair Housing Amendments Act of 1988: The First Decade," *Cityscape* 4(3): 57–78.

Schuman, Michael H. 1998. *Going Local: Creating Self-Reliant Communities in a Global Age*. New York: The Free Press.

Sheehy, John. 2003. Personal communication from John Sheehy, Office for Fair Housing and Equal Opportunity, U.S. Department of Housing and Urban Development (November 18).

Sidney, Mara S. 2003. *Unfair Housing: How National Policy Shapes Community Action*. Lawrence: University Press of Kansas.

Smith, Shanna L. and Cathy Cloud. 1997. "Documenting Discrimination by Homeowners Insurance Companies through Testing," in Gregory D. Squires (ed.) *Insurance Redlining: Disinvestment,*

Reinvestment, and the Evolving Role of Financial Institutions. Washington, DC: Urban Institute Press.

Squires, Gregory D. 2002. "Organize! The Limits of Public Awareness in Ensuring Fair Housing," *Housing Policy Debate* 13(3): 505–513.

—— 2003. Racial Profiling, Insurance Style: Insurance Redlining and the Uneven Development of Metropolitan Areas," *Journal of Urban Affairs* 25(4): 391–410.

—— 2004. "The New Redlining," in Gregory D. Squires (ed.) *Why the Poor Pay More: How to Stop Predatory Lending.* Westport, CT: Praeger.

Squires, Gregory D. and Charis E. Kubrin. 2006. *Privileged Places: Race, Residence, and the Structure of Opportunity.* Boulder, CO: Lynne Rienner Publishers.

Squires, Gregory D., Sally O'Connor, and Josh Silver. 2001. "The Unavailability of Information on Insurance Unavailability: Insurance Redlining and the Absence of Geocoded Disclosure Data," *Housing Policy Debates* 12(2): 347–372.

Steinberg, Stephen. 2005. "Immigration, African Americans, and Race Discourse," *New Politics* 39 (summer): 42–54.

Texas Department of Insurance. 2004. *Use of Credit Information by Insurers in Texas.* Austin: Texas Department of Insurance.

Thernstrom, Stephan and Abigail Thernstrom. 1997. *America in Black and White: One Nation, Indivisible.* New York: Simon & Schuster.

Tisdale, William R. 1999. Fair Housing Strategies for the Future: A Balanced Approach," *Cityscape* 4(3): 147–160.

Treaster, Joseph B. 1996. "Writing Policies in Cities Once Written Off," *New York Times* (October 30): C1, C6.

Tuckey, Steve. 2003. "Industry Blasts NAIC Proposed Credit Score Disparate Impact Study as 'Biased,'" *American Banker* (September 8).

Turner, Margery Austin, Fred Frieberg, Erin Godfrey, Carla Herbig, Dianne K. Levy, and Robin R. Smith. 2002a. *All Other Things Being Equal: A Paired Testing Study of Mortgage Lending Institutions.* Washington, DC: The Urban Institute, prepared for the U.S. Department of Housing and Urban Development.

Turner, Margery Austin, Stephen L. Ross, George C. Galster, and John Yinger. 2002b. *Discrimination in Metropolitan Housing Markets: National Results from Phase I HDS 2000.* Washington, DC: The Urban Institute.

U.S. Department of Housing and Urban Development. 2006. The State of Fair Housing. Washington, DC: U.S. Department of Housing and Urban Development.

Warren, Mark R. 2001. *Dry Bones Rattling: Community Building to Revitalize American Democracy.* Princeton, NJ: Princeton University Press.

Williamson, Thad, David Imbroscio, and Gar Alperovitz. 2002. *Making a Place for Community: Local Democracy in a Global Era.* New York: Routledge.

Wilson, William J. 1999. *The Bridge over the Racial Divide: Rising Inequality and Coalition Politics.* Berkeley: University of California Press.

CHAPTER 11

Attaining a Just (and Economically Secure) Society

JAMES H. CARR AND NANDINEE K. KUTTY

This book has focused attention on the relationship between housing and access to opportunities. As was discussed in earlier chapters, housing is the central determinant of access to good jobs, quality schools, vibrant and safe communities, and healthy, appreciating property values. As a result, enforcing fair housing and fair lending laws is one of the most direct means to improve access to opportunities and, by extension, economic and social mobility in America. In the introduction to this book we argue that the first step to improve enforcement of fair housing-related mandates is to convince policy makers and the public of the value of this pursuit.

Most often, conversations related to redressing discriminatory practices focus solely on the potential benefits to the injured parties, rather than to society at large. But as African American and Latino households become a growing share of the U.S. population, economic mobility and wealth accumulation for those households will increasingly reflect America's aggregate economic and social vitality. At the same time, many of the challenges facing America's lower-income and minority households are now similar to those impacting middle-income families. Each day, more families find themselves with diminished employer-provided healthcare coverage or no employer healthcare plan at all. Every day, a growing number of workers are encouraged to contribute to their own retirement plans in lieu of employer-funded retirement programs. And each day, more employees find their jobs have been eliminated or have left the country. When these challenges are combined with stagnant wages, diminished savings, increasing debt, and rapidly rising housing, health, and transportation costs, a growing number of middle-class families now worry about their futures and the futures of their children.

Polls by the Pew Charitable Trust, the *New York Times*, CBS News, and some labor organizations show that rising shares of Americans feel that they and their children will experience a lower quality of life in the coming years, and that there is more insecurity and stress in working life today compared to a generation ago (poll results described in Leonhardt, 2006; Greenhouse, 2006; and Yeager, 2006). According to recent Gallup polls, 50 percent to 60 percent of American adults fear that they are not prepared for retirement (Gallup Poll, 2003).

Focus group research by Jared Bernstein and Sylvia Allegretto of the Economic Policy Institute on middle-class persons (all of whom were home-owners and were well connected to the job market) found that members of this group feel their economic lives are riskier than those of the middle-class cohorts that came before them. Many feel that they experience far more economic insecurity than their parents' generation and worry that their children will be even more economically insecure. These middle-class homeowners report that their economic insecurity has increased as jobs have become less secure, wages rise less quickly, healthcare coverage has become less certain, college tuitions have soared, and housing prices are volatile. The focus groups also expressed concern about job instability; many had lost jobs or had spouses who lost jobs. They found that after losing a job, unemployment benefits made up only a small portion of the lost income, and obtaining health insurance privately was very, if not prohibitively, expensive. Many of the middle-class focus group participants said that they face the risk of being unable to support themselves in retirement. Several of them felt they will never have the luxury of retiring (Bernstein and Allegretto, 2006).

Interestingly, policies to shore up the growing instability of America's middle class, such as improved access to quality education, good jobs, adequate health care, and reasonable retirement savings, are also essential for the upward mobility of lower-income and minority households. As we note in Chapter 1, an enduring American myth is the idea that the broad American middle class is a reflection solely of individual hard work and perseverance. While individual effort is important to success, the federal government has played a major role in the extraordinary economic success of America. Failure to recognize or acknowledge this reality may be a leading reason why the public has failed to hold policy makers accountable for many of their anxieties related to economic well-being.

This environment may be about to change. Concern for the future of America's middle class is spreading across research institutions. Institutions such as the Insight Center for Community Economic Development (formerly National Economic Development and Law Center), the New America

Foundation, the Center for Economic Progress, the Center for Budget and Policy Priorities, One Economy, the Corporation for Enterprise Development (CFED), the Manhattan Institute, and the National Conference of Mayors, to name a few, are supporting programs or have produced policy papers that point to the need for improved management of public policy as a way to improve economic opportunity in America. Moreover, in his book *War on the Middle Class*, CNN commentator Lou Dobbs (2006) joins the increasing chorus of voices highlighting a range of concerns facing the middle class. Loss of employer-provided pensions, inadequate health-care coverage, stagnant wages, employment insecurity, outsourcing of jobs, mounting debts, and, increasingly, economic threats from foreign competition are among the core issues he highlights. He notes, accurately, that public policy is an important part of this discussion. A variety of recent statistics on the well-being of the American family reinforce these rising concerns, as well as the imperative that they be taken more seriously by policy makers.

Challenges to the Middle Class

Wealth and Income Disparities

Wealth inequality in the United States has risen sharply since 1977. Currently, the top 1 percent of wealthy households own 34 percent of the nation's wealth. By comparison, in the United Kingdom and in Sweden, the top 1 percent own 20 percent of the wealth. In the U.S., the top 5 percent control more than 50 percent of national wealth while the bottom 50 percent control only 2.8 percent (Collins *et al.*, 2004). It does not take long to see how precarious the nation's middle-class wealth status has already become; today, the bottom 85 percent of households control only 16 percent of total net wealth (Collins *et al.*, 2004).

The period of two and a half decades after World War II was a time of great prosperity and widening of opportunities for Americans. During that time, which epitomized the American dream of upward economic mobility in America, income *growth* was quite evenly distributed: the poorest quintile (20 percent) of the population saw roughly as much increase in income as the next quintile, and so on. However, in the past 30 years or so, the richest groups have seen the greatest income growth. As a result, the income share of the richest quintile increased from 41 percent in 1970 to nearly 48 percent in 2004, while the share of the poorest quintile fell from about 5 percent to 4 percent during the same time (Economic Policy Institute, 2006). Figure 11.1 shows the growth in income and wealth over the past decade, accruing overwhelmingly to the very wealthiest 25 percent of households.

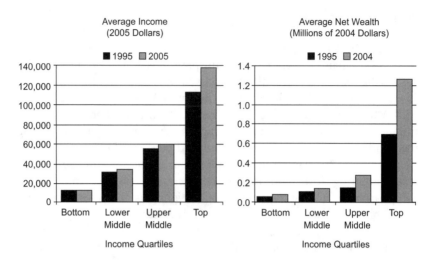

Figure 11.1 Household incomes and wealth are growing strongly only at the top.

Source: Joint Center for Housing Studies tabulations of the 1995 and 2005 Current Population Surveys, and the 1995 and 2004 Surveys of Consumer Finances.

Note: Income quartiles are equal fourths of all households sorted by pre-tax income. Income values are adjusted for inflation using the CPI-UX for All Items. Wealth values are adjusted for inflation using Survey of Consumer Finances methods.

Most of the gains in the top quintile have gone to households at the very top. In 2005 the income share of the richest 1 percent was nearly 22 percent, the highest since 1928. Between 1980 and 2004 the top 0.01 percent saw a quadrupling of income share, the top 0.1 percent saw a tripling, and the top 1.0 percent had to be content with a mere doubling of their income share (Piketty and Saez, 2006). During this same period, the U.S. federal tax system (consisting of individual income tax, corporate income tax, estate tax, and payroll tax) became less progressive. Payroll taxes, which fall hard on middle-class Americans, increased from 6 percent in the early 1960s to over 15 percent by the 1990s and remain that way today (Piketty and Saez, 2007).

Income inequality translates into consumption disparities. The top 20 percent of Americans now account for nearly 60 percent of U.S. consumption while the bottom 40 percent account for merely 10 percent of purchases (Kapur *et al.*, 2006). This has lessened sensitivity within the markets and among policy makers about high oil, housing, and healthcare costs, global imbalances, and an anemic U.S. savings rate, as markets look increasingly to the consumption of the top group to support economic growth (Kapur *et al.*, 2006).

Diminished Economic Mobility

America is known as the Land of Opportunity. "The American Dream" is a catchphrase used all over the world. It remains a popular belief that anyone can achieve the American Dream through hard work, motivation, and perseverance. We take pride in the idea that "only in America" can we see people rising from the lowest rungs of society to the highest within one generation. It is widely held that the United States has open channels of mobility and, as a result, greater economic mobility than anywhere else in the world. But a long-term study at the University of Michigan, led by Gary Solon, found that economic mobility in the United States is lower than in Canada and some Scandinavian countries, and is roughly even with that in the United Kingdom and France (Scott and Leonhardt, 2005).

Although studies measuring economic mobility are difficult to conduct and routinely generate controversy within the research community, many reputable research institutions are reaching the same conclusion: economic mobility in the United States is worsening. A study by Katharine Bradbury and Jane Katz (2002), of the Federal Reserve Bank of Boston, found that fewer families moved from one quintile (or 20 percent bracket) of the income ladder to another during the 1980s than during the 1970s; and that still fewer moved in the 1990s than in the 1980s. A study by the U.S. Bureau of Labor Statistics confirms the finding that economic mobility in America declined from the 1980s to the 1990s (Scott and Leonhardt, 2005).

Sharing Less of the Economic Pie

American workers have received little benefit from the productivity growth of recent times. The productivity of U.S. workers increased by over 30 percent between 1995 and 2005, but real wages of workers in the middle of the distribution increased at a much slower pace. Real wages of the median worker increased by slightly over 6 percent between 1995 and 2000; and by less than 1 percent from 2000 to 2005 (*The Economist*, 2006). Non-supervisory employees (who make up about 80 percent of U.S. workers) saw their real compensation increase by only 4 percent between 1980 and 2005, a period in which U.S. productivity increased by about 70 percent (Faux, 2007). The share of national income going to wages and salaries currently remains at the lowest level on record, with data going back to 1929. In contrast, the share of national income accounted for by corporate profits is at its highest level since 1950 (Aron-Dine and Shapiro, 2007). In the 1980s the earnings gap between the middle and the bottom of the economic distribution became markedly wider, as did the skills gap. Downsizing, outsourcing, other redefinitions at the workplace, and holes in the social safety net are impacting higher rungs of the income ladder than in the past. In contemporary America, while the top income group has soared ahead to unprecedented levels of earnings growth and consumption, the middle group is sliding down closer to the lowest group in terms of earnings and living standards (Yellen, 2006).

Job Insecurity

Despite low official unemployment rates, Americans are pessimistic about job security. It is believed that a large number of people without jobs are not being counted as unemployed because, after repeated failures, they have become discouraged from actively seeking work. The labor force participation rate of men aged 25–64 years actually declined in the last generation. After rising sharply in the 1970s and 1980s, the labor force participation rate of women has leveled off and recently fallen to a level substantially below that of men (Hacker, 2006).

Americans who have experienced unemployment quickly find out the inadequacies of the safety net. Compared to unemployment benefits in most advanced industrial nations, unemployment insurance in the United States replaces a smaller share of income and offers payments for a shorter duration (Yellen, 2006). Unemployment insurance in the United States was never designed to cope with long-term earnings losses, nor does it attempt to compensate for lost benefits. Furthermore, the current system fails to cover millions of even temporarily unemployed workers. In 1995 only about 18 percent of unemployed low-wage workers were collecting unemployment insurance (Hacker, 2006).

Diminishing Health Insurance Coverage, Rising Healthcare Costs

Between 2000 and 2005, health coverage through employer-based programs decreased by about 4 percent; this represents a loss of health insurance for several million Americans (Buchmueller and Valletta, 2006). The number of Americans without health insurance rose steadily over the past thirty years, and has reached a record high of 45 million. According to Jacob Hacker, political scientist at Yale University, healthcare insecurity remains "an inconvenient blot on the heralded success story of the American economy" (2006: 138). Yet just having health insurance, per se, does not necessarily provide the comfort it once offered. Most insurance policies increasingly require substantial out-of-pocket expenditures from the patient. In fact, one out of six working-age adults in the United States is carrying medical debt, and 70 percent of them *had insurance* when they incurred medical debt. Many of those households carrying medical debt are middle-income people with insurance; among families that have health insurance and medical debt, as many as half have incomes greater than $40,000 (Seifert and Rukavina, 2006). At the same time, healthcare costs continue to rise, placing U.S. healthcare costs at the top of the list of industrialized nations. Despite the highest healthcare costs, outcomes such as infant mortality and life expectancy are worse in the United States than in most advanced industrial countries (Yellen, 2006).

Failing the Grade in Education

According to a Blue Ribbon Commission on Higher Education, empanelled by the National Conference of State Legislators, America is failing the grade in education. This National Commission made the following observations:

- The American higher education system is no longer the best in the world. Although the United States has some of the best institutions, it does a poor job, overall, in its mass education production.
- Nationally, for every 100 ninth-graders who enter high school, only 18 finish college within six years.
- Increasingly, lower-income students are being priced out of college. More students are assuming sizable student loans.
- Other countries are outranking the United States and significantly improving their higher education performance.
- Americans are not prepared for the dramatically changing demographic shifts in our populations. Latinos, African Americans, and recent immigrants are the fastest-growing, but lowest-participating, populations in the U.S. higher education system.

The United States is increasingly lagging in educational attainment along several measures. Among OECD nations, the United States has one of the highest college dropout rates, with only 50 percent of those entering a university achieving graduation, compared to the OECD average of 70 percent (OECD, 2006). Today, almost one in three Americans in their mid-twenties is a college dropout who plans to return to college to get his or her degree; this number has increased from one in five in the late 1960s.

Among thirty-one OECD nations, the United States was ranked 15th in reading literacy, 19th in mathematical literacy, and 14th in scientific literacy. Countries such as Finland, Korea, Japan, the United Kingdom, Canada, Norway, and France were ahead of the United States in each category. Although college enrollment rates in the United States rose over the 1980s and early 1990s, they appear to have flattened out in the recent period: enrollment rates among recent high school graduates hovered around 65 percent between 1996 and 2004 (National Center for Education Statistics, 2005). At a time when educational attainment is growing in importance for securing meaningful employment, about 50 percent of African American students in the United States are dropping out of high school before the four years are out. Yet most future jobs in the economy are going to require a postsecondary education.

According to the National Assessment of Educational Progress (NAEP), also known as "the nation's report card," a great many American students are graduating high school with "below basic" academic skills: in the 2000 science assessment, nearly half of twelfth-graders were ranked "below basic." According to Craig Barrett, chair of Intel Corporation, the U.S. standard of living will depend on the quality of the workforce, and this quality is deteriorating due to the failures of the American education system (*USA Today*, 2001). Thus, the American standard of living, as we know it, is under threat.

A Closer Focus on Science and Engineering

Harvard University economist Richard Freeman (2005) has highlighted some compelling statistics on the growing science gap between the United States and other nations. He notes that in the 1970s the United States led the world in math, science, and engineering. But by 2001 the European Union (EU) produced 40 percent more science and engineering PhDs than the United States, and by 2010 it will produce nearly twice as many PhDs as the United States. By 2010, China is expected to overtake the United States in the number of science and engineering PhDs. However, the United States remains the dominant nation in the production of patents and scientific research (Samuelson, 2005). Freeman points out that the rapid growth of PhDs in the sciences and engineering in other nations need not be a threat to the United States, but if America fails to invest adequately in science and engineering training, then the U.S. is likely to face very difficult economic adjustments.

Tom Friedman (2006) points out that the share of scientific papers written by Americans has fallen 10 percent since 1992. And while America still dominates the world in the attainment of industrial patents, its share has fallen from 60 percent in 1980 to 52 percent in 2003; during this period, Asian countries (such as Japan and Korea) significantly increased their share. He also points out that only three decades ago the United States ranked third in the world in the number of 18- to 24-year-olds who received science degrees; today, its rank has slipped to seventeenth. Between the mid-1980s and 1998 the number of engineering undergraduates in the United States declined by about 12 percent. These declines have occurred at a time when science and engineering skills are vitally needed (Friedman, 2006). Friedman notes that the United States faces increasing competition from Asian countries in the fields of science and engineering. Science and engineering degrees now represent 60 percent of all bachelor's degrees earned in China, and 41 percent in Taiwan, in contrast with 31 percent in the United States. In 2001, while the United States graduated about 60,000 engineers, China graduated 220,000.

The author of the OECD report *Education at a Glance* (OECD, 2006), Andreas Schleicher, warns that "tomorrow's high-skilled jobs in innovation and R&D will be relocated in Asia unless the EU and U.S. make significant progress [in education]" (*Financial Times*, 2006). This is, in fact, already happening. In December 2006, Cisco Systems announced the next stage of its globalization strategy with the selection of India as the site for its globalization center. In October 2005 the company had announced a $1.1 billion investment in India and its plan to triple its workforce in India over the next three to five years. Cisco chose India as the location from which to expand its globalization vision *because of India's highly skilled workforce.* In addition, India's focus on *building broadband infrastructure and fostering a first-class educational system* was also cited as a reason for this strategic location decision (Cisco, 2006a, b). And in June 2006, IBM held its annual investors' day in Bangalore, India. This annual function is usually held in New York, though it was once held in Boston. IBM announced a new $6 billion investment in India over the next three years. The message seems clear: the center of technological gravity is shifting away from the United States and toward countries whose workers possess the skills, and which have the infrastructural support, relevant for the new global economy.

Concern over a perceived falling behind in science, mathematics, and engineering was reflected in Senate testimony by Bill Gates, who in early 2007 recommended that America double the number of science, technology, and mathematics graduates in the country by 2015, and enhance the quality of high school education (by recruiting 10,000 new science and mathematics teachers annually and strengthening existing teachers' skills). He also recommended increasing enrollment in postsecondary math and science programs by providing 25,000 new undergraduate scholarships and 5,000 new graduate fellowships each year (Gates, 2007).

The Growing Importance of Affluence

Extreme wealth inequality creates a distortion in political priorities such that policies get put in place which protect the assets of the wealthy and neglect the concerns of the masses. In this political climate it is the middle classes that have lost the most ground in recent decades. In fact, in lieu of public policies to promote economic vitality for the broad middle of American families, being born into wealth is increasingly important to ensuring economic security. Research by Gary Solon (2002) shows that the correlation between parents' income and children's income in the United States is higher today than it was in the 1980s.

An examination of college enrollment begins to explain this reality. In 1976, 39 percent of students in America's elite universities came from families in the richest quartile (or top 25 percent) of the population. By 1995 the richest group had improved its share to 50 percent (*The Economist*, 2005). Only 3 percent of students at the top colleges come from the bottom quartile of the population. The rising cost of education has taken Ivy League universities out of the reach of most middle-class and poor families. The median income of families who have children studying at Harvard University is $150,000 (*The Economist*, 2005). As a result of increased fees at state colleges, students from poor backgrounds are becoming rarer even in nonelite colleges. Currently, a student from the top income quartile is six times more likely to get a college degree than one from the bottom quartile (*The Economist*, 2005). Increases in college tuitions have far outpaced family income, and grant aid has not increased proportionally; in fact, recently there have been cuts in federal student aid. Hence, college is becoming increasingly out of reach not only for low- and moderate-income families, but also for some middle-class families. At the same time, those lucky enough to get a college education find themselves burdened with college debt which is rising. In 2000, 64 percent of students who graduated college had an average debt of about $17,000.

Revisiting Public Policy for All Americans

This chapter reviews a substantial body of data that suggests there is growing economic instability anxiety among an increasing number of middle-income households. At the same time, we are aware that there is a voluminous amount of data on almost every issue to which we point, and many scholars and policy makers might choose to debate individual statistics presented. Doing so, however, would miss the point of this writing. No single statistic or data point is intended to be dispositive of a crisis impacting America's middle class. Rather, we seek only to suggest there is growing evidence that the nation is facing many challenges that do not seem to be receiving the level of public interest and attention they deserve—and that the negative trends are impacting the poor and minorities, as well as America's middle class. Honest and engaged debate over these issues and their implications for America's future is warranted.

Tom Friedman, in his book *The World Is Flat*, describing the latest phase of globalization as the "flat world," writes that "the ideal country in a flat world is one with no natural resources, because . . . [such countries] tend to dig inside themselves" (2006: 344). He contends that such countries tap the energy, entrepreneurship, creativity, and intelligence of their own people (Friedman, 2006). He recommends this strategy for America to enhance its global competitive position in the years ahead. Improving educational performance for all Americans would be an important first step. But improving educational outcomes for minority households is directly linked to reducing segregation among minority households. More than a century of experience in the United States has shown that separate but equal does not and cannot produce equal opportunities or equitable outcomes.

But enhancing the competitive landscape of America must look beyond improving the educational performance of children in public schools. The cost of higher education is increasingly beyond the reach of the typical family and needs to be addressed. Likewise, the high costs of housing, health insurance, transportation, and other necessities, which are greatly influenced by public policy, also contribute to an increasingly uncompetitive infrastructure for American workers and, therefore, demand attention from policy makers. These challenges are surmountable. But they are not self-correcting.

Only through sound and thoughtful public policy that honestly examines the complex threats facing the nation in the years ahead, and takes deliberate action to address those challenges, will we ensure the stability of America's middle class and Americans' way of life. And only through actions that eliminate the additional, artificial, and counterproductive barriers presented by residential segregation will we achieve our greatest potential as a nation and society.

References

Aron-Dine, Aviva and Isaac Shapiro (2007) "Share of National Income Going to Wages and Salaries Remains at Record Low: Share of Income Going to Corporate Profits at Highest Level Since 1950," Policy Paper (revised January 16, 2007), Center on Budget and Policy Priorities, Washington, DC.

Bernstein, Jared and Sylvia Allegretto (2006) "Assessing the Middle-Class Squeeze." Washington, DC: Fannie Mae Foundation.

Bradbury, Katharine and Jane Katz (2002) "Are Lifetime Incomes Growing More Unequal? Looking at New Evidence on Family Income Mobility," *Regional Review* (Federal Reserve Bank of Boston), Q4, pp. 3–5. Available at http://www.bos.frb.org/economic/nerr/rr2002/issues.pdf (accessed December 28, 2006).

Buchmueller, Thomas and Robert G. Valletta (2006) "Health Insurance Costs and Declining Coverage," *Federal Reserve Bank of San Francisco Economic Letter* 2006-25, September 29.

Cisco (2006a) "Cisco Selects India as Site for the Cisco Globalization Center." Available at http://newsroom.cisco.com/dlls/global/asiapac/news/2006/pr_12-06c.html (accessed December 12, 2006)

Cisco (2006b) "Cisco Provides Update on US $1.1 Billion Investment in India: Company Expects to Triple Its Workforce in India over Next Three to Five Years." Available at http://newsroom.cisco.com/dlls/global/asiapac/news/2006/pr_12-06b.htm (accessed December 12, 2006).

Collins, Chuck, Amy Gluckman, Meizhu Lui, Betsy Leondar-Wright, Amy Offner, and Adria Scharf (2004) *The Wealth Inequality Reader*. Cambridge, MA: Economic Affairs Bureau.

Dobbs, Lou (2006) *War on the Middle Class: How the Government, Big Business, and Special Interest Groups Are Waging War on the American Dream and How to Fight Back.* New York: Viking Press.

Economic Policy Institute (2006) "Share of Aggregate Family Income Received by Quintile and Top 5 percent of Families, 1947–2004." Available at www.epi.org/datazone/06/inc_share.pdf (accessed December 27, 2006).

Economist, The (2005) "Middle of the Class," *The Economist*, July 14.

Economist, The (2006) "The Rich, the Poor and the Growing Gap between Them," *The Economist*, June 17, pp. 28–30.

Faux, Jeff (2007) "Globalization That Works for Working Americans." EPI Briefing Paper 179, Economic Policy Institute, Washington, DC, January 11.

Financial Times (2006) "Ask the Expert: Global Education," *Financial Times*, October 17, 2006.

Available at http://www.ft.com/cms/s/e2d7f070-5d2c-11db-9d15-0000779e2340.html (accessed December 30, 2006).

Freeman, Richard, B. (2005) "Does Globalization of the Scientific/Engineering Workforce Threaten U.S. Economic Leadership?" National Bureau of Economic Research (NBER) Working Paper W11457, July.

Friedman, Thomas L. (2006) *The World Is Flat: A Brief History of the Twenty-first Century*. New York: Farrar, Straus and Giroux.

Gallup Poll (2003) "Gallup Poll Social Series: Economy and Personal Finance," question 17.

Gates, Bill (2007) Transcript of Oral Testimony by Bill Gates, Chair, Microsoft Corporation, before the United States Senate Committee on Health, Education, Labor, and Pensions, "Strengthening American Competitiveness for the 21st Century," Washington, DC, March 7. Available at http://www.microsoft.com/Presspass/exec/billg/speeches/2007/03-07Senate.mspx (accessed July 14, 2007).

Greenhouse, Steven (2006) "Three Polls Find Workers Sensing Deep Pessimism," *New York Times*, August 31.

Hacker, Jacob, S. (2006) *The Great Risk Shift*. New York: Oxford University Press.

Kapur, Ajay, Niall Macleod, and Narendra Singh (2006) *Revisiting Plutonomy*. Citigroup Global Markets—Citigroup Research. Available at http://www.billcara.com/arhcives/Citi%20Mar%205%202006%20Plutonomy%202.pdf (accessed December 30, 2006).

Leonhardt, David (2006) "Anxiety Rises as Paychecks Trail Inflation," *New York Times*, August 2.

National Center for Education Statistics (2005) Available at http://nces.ed.gov/programs/digest/d05/tables/dt05_181.asp (accessed April 7, 2007).

OECD (2006) *Education at a Glance, 2006*. Report available at http://www.oecd.org/dataoecd/51/20/37392850.pdf (accessed December 30, 2006).

Piketty, Thomas and Emmanuel Saez (2006) "The Evolution of Top Incomes: A Historical and International Perspective," *American Economic Review* 96(2), pp. 200–205.

Piketty, Thomas and Emmanuel Saez (2007) "How Progressive Is the U.S. Federal Tax System? A Historical and International Perspective," *Journal of Economic Perspectives* 21(1), pp. 3–24.

Samuelson, Robert (2005) "It's Not a Science Gap (Yet)," *Washington Post*, August 10, 2005, p. A17.

Scott, Janny and David Leonhardt (2005) "Shadowy Lines That Still Divide," *New York Times*, May 15.

Seifert, Robert W. and Mark Rukavina (2006) "Bankruptcy Is the Tip of a Medical-Debt Iceberg," *Health Affairs*, March/April, 25(2): w89–w92. Available at http://content.healthaffairs.org/cgi/reprint/25/2/w89 (accessed April 7, 2007).

Solon, Gary (2002) "Cross-Country Differences in Intergenerational Earnings Mobility," *Journal of Economic Perspectives* 16(3), pp. 59–66.

USA Today (2001) "U.S. System Helps Educate World, yet Fails at Home." (Interview with Craig Barrett, chair and president, Intel Corp.), November 8. Available at http://www.usatoday.com/news/opinion/2001-11-08-ncguest1.htm (accessed February 25, 2007).

Yeager, Holly (2006) "Americans Suffer Big Fall in Optimism Ratings," *Financial Times*, September 15.

Yellen, Janet L. (2006) "Economic Inequality in the United States," Speech by the President and Chief Executive of the Federal Reserve Bank of San Francisco, November 6. Available at http://www.frbsf.org/news/speeches/2006/1106.html (accessed December 1, 2006).

Notes on Contributors

Dolores Acevedo-Garcia (dacevedo@hsph.harvard.edu) is Associate Professor at the Harvard School of Public Health. Her research focuses on the effect of social determinants (e.g., residential segregation, immigrant adaptation) on health disparities along racial and ethnic lines and the role of social policies (e.g., housing policies, immigrant policies) in reducing those disparities. She is Project Director for DiversityData, an interactive website on socioeconomic indicators in U.S. metropolitan areas. She is on the Social Science Advisory Board of the Poverty and Race Research Action Council. She is Co-President of the Board of Directors of the Fair Housing Center of Greater Boston.

Dean Baker (baker@cepr.net) is codirector of the Center for Economic and Policy Research in Washington, DC. He previously worked as a senior economist at the Economic Policy Institute and as an assistant professor at Bucknell University. He has done research in a wide range of areas including Social Security, the trade-offs between inflation and unemployment, the stock market bubble, and the housing market. He has written numerous books and articles, including *The United States Since 1980* (Cambridge University Press, March 2007); *The Conservative Nanny State: How the Wealthy Use the Government to Stay Rich and Get Richer* (Center for Economic and Policy Research, 2006); and *Social Security: The Phony Crisis* (with Mark Weisbrot; University of Chicago Press, 1999). His book *Getting Prices Right: The Battle over the Consumer Price Index* (M.E. Sharpe, 1997) was the winner of a Choice Book Award as one of the outstanding academic books of the year.

Heather Boushey (hboushey@cepr.net) is coauthor of *The State of Working America 2002/2003* (Cornell University Press, 2003) and *Hardships in America: The Real Story of Working Families* (Economic Policy Institute, 2001). She studies current trends in the U.S. labor market and how social policies help or harm workers and their families. She is a research affiliate with the National Poverty Center at the Gerald R. Ford School of Public Policy, on the editorial review boards of *WorkingUSA* and the *Journal of Poverty*, and on the Voice professional women advisory committee. She received her BA from Hampshire College and her PhD in economics from the New School for Social Research.

James H. Carr (jcarr@NCRC.org) is Chief Operating Officer for the National Community Reinvestment Coalition and a visiting professor at Columbia University in New York and George Washington University in Washington, DC. Jim has also served as Senior Vice President for Financial Innovation, Planning and Research for the Fannie Mae Foundation and Assistant Director for Tax Policy with the U.S. Senate Budget Committee. Jim has served on research advisory boards at Harvard University, the University of California at Berkeley and the University of Pennsylvania, and is an Advisory Committee member of the Federal Reserve Bank of San Francisco Center for Community Development Investments. Jim is former editor of the scholarly journals *Housing Policy Debate* and *Journal of Housing Research*, and editorial board member of *The Urban Age*. Jim is a 2003 Aspen Institute Scholar and has been published in *Vital Speeches of the Day*. Jim is particularly recognized for his leadership in the development of innovative financial instruments and strategies to promote affordable lending, inner-city development, and asset development for lower-income households.

Ingrid Gould Ellen (ingrid.ellen@nyu.edu) is Associate Professor of Urban Planning and Public Policy at New York University's Wagner School and codirector of NYU's Furman Center for Real Estate and Urban Policy. Her research centers on neighborhoods, affordable housing, and racial segregation. She is author of *Sharing America's Neighborhoods: The Prospects for Stable Racial Integration* (Harvard University Press, 2000) and numerous journal articles. Before coming to NYU, Professor Ellen held visiting positions at the Urban Institute and the Brookings Institution. She attended Harvard University, where she received a bachelor's degree in applied mathematics, an MPP, and a PhD in public policy.

Kathleen C. Engel (Kathleen.engel@law.csuohio.edu) is Associate Professor of Law at Cleveland-Marshall College of Law at Cleveland State University. She received her AB from Smith College and her JD from the University of Texas School of Law. Professor Engel previously practiced civil rights law at Burnham & Hines in Boston. She has written extensively on predatory lending, home mortgage markets, and housing discrimination.

Rachel Garshick Kleit (kleit@u.washington.edu) is Associate Professor at the Daniel J. Evans School of Public Affairs and Adjunct Associate Professor of Urban Design and Planning at the University of Washington. She is a national expert on the social impacts of housing on the lives of the poor, and her work has focused on the relationship between housing location, neighborhood composition, social networks, and access to opportunity. She has written on the social network impacts of housing programs that mix incomes, the HOPE VI program, housing self-sufficiency programs, housing choice processes for low-income people, and on the role of the public housing authorities in the future of affordable housing. She holds an MA in Urban and Environmental Policy from Tufts University and a PhD in City and Regional Planning from the University of North Carolina at Chapel Hill.

Nandinee K. Kutty (nndkutty@aol.com) is an independent consultant in the field of urban, housing and community development policy. She obtained a PhD in economics from the Maxwell School, Syracuse University. She was a faculty member in the Department of Policy Analysis and Management at Cornell University from 1993 to 2000. There she taught courses on urban policy, policy evaluation techniques, and microeconomics. She has worked on developing the American Housing Survey and conducted research using this survey as a consultant to the U.S. Bureau of the Census. She worked on mortgage market regulatory issues as an economist for the U.S. Department of Housing and Urban Development. Dr. Kutty conducted policy research as a senior economist for the consulting firms Abt Associates, Inc. and Westat, Inc. Dr. Kutty has published her research papers in leading peer-reviewed journals such as the *Journal of Urban Economics, Urban Studies,* the *Journal of Housing Research, Housing Policy Debate, Applied Economics, Housing Studies,* and the *Journal of the American Real Estate and Urban Economics Association.* She has written several policy briefs and has coauthored policy research reports submitted to U.S. federal agencies.

Douglas S. Massey (dmassey@princeton.edu) is the Henry G. Bryant Professor of Sociology and Public Affairs at Princeton University. He has written extensively on the causes and consequences of segregation in the United States and is coauthor of *American Apartheid: Segregation and the*

Making of the Underclass, published in 1993 by Harvard University Press, winner of the 1995 distinguished publication award of the American Sociological Association. He is a member of the National Academy of Sciences, the American Academy of Arts and Sciences, and the American Philosophical Society, and currently serves as President of the American Academy of Political and Social Science. He is Past-President of the American Sociological Association and the Population Association of America.

Patricia A. McCoy (patricia.mccoy@law.uconn.edu) is a nationally recognized authority on consumer finance law and subprime lending. She is the George J. and Helen M. England Professor of Law at the University of Connecticut, in Hartford, Connecticut. Before entering academe she was a partner at the law firm of Mayer, Brown, Rowe & Maw in Washington, DC, where she specialized in complex securities, banking, and commercial constitutional litigation. In 2002–2003 she was a Visiting Scholar at the MIT Economics Department. Her research examines market failures and consumer protection in the banking, securities, insurance, and pension industries. She has two books to her credit: *Banking Law Manual: Federal Regulation of Financial Holding Companies, Banks and Thrifts* (2nd edn 2000 and cum. supp.) and *Financial Modernization after Gramm-Leach-Bliley* (2002).

Deborah L. McKoy (debmckoy@berkeley.edu) is the Executive Director and founder of the UC Berkeley Center for Cities and Schools and serves as a Lecturer in the Department of City Planning and Graduate School of Education. She has worked at the intersection of urban policy and education for fifteen years at national and international levels. Her diverse professional experiences include the NYC Legislative Speaker's Office, the United Nations' Education for All initiative, the NYC Housing Authority and NYC community development corporations. Deborah's work and research looks at the intersection of educational reform, community development and public policy. She has a Master's degree in Public Policy and Administration from Columbia University and a PhD in Educational Policy from the University of California at Berkeley.

Theresa L. Osypuk (t.osypuk@neu.edu) is an Assistant Professor at Northeastern University in the Bouve College of Health Sciences. She is a social epidemiologist researching racial/ethnic, nativity, and socioeconomic health disparities, their causes, and their geographic patterns across the United States. Dr. Osypuk's research examines why, when, and for whom place matters for health and health disparities, particularly in relation to housing markets and neighborhoods, as well as how social policies may mitigate racial/ethnic health inequality. She received her doctorate from Harvard University in 2005 and was a Robert Wood Johnson Health and Society Scholar at the University of Michigan from 2005 to 2007.

Gregory D. Squires (squires@gwu.edu) is Professor of Sociology and Public Policy and Public Administration at George Washington University. Currently he is a member of the Board of Directors of the Woodstock Institute, the Advisory Board of the John Marshall Law School Fair Housing Legal Support Center in Chicago, Illinois, and the Social Science Advisory Board of the Poverty & Race Research Action Council in Washington, DC. He has served as a consultant for civil rights organizations around the country and as a member of the Federal Reserve Board's Consumer Advisory Council. He has written for several academic journals including *Housing Policy Debate, Urban Studies, Social Science Quarterly, Urban Affairs Review,* and the *Journal of Urban Affairs.* In addition, he has written more than 100 op-eds and magazine articles for several publications including the *New York Times,* the *Washington Post,* the *Chicago Tribune,* and the *Chicago Defender.*

Margery Austin Turner (maturner@ui.urban.org) directs the Urban Institute's Metropolitan Housing and Communities policy center. A nationally recognized expert on urban policy and neighborhood issues, Ms. Turner analyzes issues of residential location, racial and ethnic discrimination and its contribution to neighborhood segregation and inequality, and the role of housing policies in promoting residential mobility and location choice. Ms. Turner served as Deputy Assistant Secretary for Research at the Department of Housing and Urban Development from 1993 through 1996, focusing HUD's research agenda on the problems of racial discrimination, concentrated poverty, and economic opportunity in America's metropolitan areas. She has coauthored two national housing discrimination studies, which use paired testing to determine the incidence of discrimination against minority homeseekers. She has also extended the paired testing methodology to measure discrimination in employment and to mortgage lending. Ms. Turner has directed research on racial and ethnic steering, neighborhood outcomes for families who receive federal housing assistance, and emerging patterns of neighborhood diversity in city and suburban neighborhoods.

Jeffrey M. Vincent (jvincent@berkeley.edu) is Deputy Director and cofounder of the Center for Cities and Schools at the University of California at Berkeley. He holds a PhD in City and Regional Planning from the University of California at Berkeley and has worked in city planning and community development-related positions for nearly ten years, in addition to working for five years as a teacher at a Montessori farm school. His research looks at the intersection of land-use planning, school facility planning, and community development. He is also a researcher for the BEST (Building Educational Success Together) collaborative, a national community of practice working toward a vision where all children learn in school buildings that are safe and educationally adequate and that serve as community anchors in vibrant, healthy neighborhoods.

Index